The Covenant and the Dar es Salaam

The Betrayal and The Renewal of Islam's World Order

Munawar Sabir

Order this book online at www.trafford.com
or email orders@trafford.com

Most Trafford titles are also available at major online book retailers.

Print information available on the last page.

ISBN: 978-1-6987-0928-4 (sc)
ISBN: 978-1-6987-0930-7 (hc)
ISBN: 978-1-6987-0929-1 (e)

Library of Congress Control Number: 2021917704

Trafford rev. 08/27/2021

 www.trafford.com
North America & international
toll-free: 844-688-6899 (USA & Canada)
fax: 812 355 4082

But Allah does call

To the Abode of Peace: Dar es Salaam

He does guide whom He pleases

To a way that is straight.

—Yunus 10:25, Koran

Contents

Acknowledgments

This book is the second of the four-part series that opens a debate and discussion for present-day believers. The concepts and precepts presented in these books are entirely based on the verses of the Koran in relation to the place of the believer in the contemporary world. This work addresses the Muslim and non-Muslim youth and those who wish to learn about the spirit of Islam unshackled by the traditions of the mullahs and scholars of the Umayyad and Abbasid periods of Islamic history.

Many years ago, I became conscious of recurring references in the Koran to a covenant between Allah and His believers. I began a long journey in the quest of this covenant, and for over thirty years, I made mental and written observations on the subject that have resulted in this series. Some parts of the series are in print while others, inshallah, will be published shortly.

Knowledge is a mountain of humankind's wisdom piled over thousands of years. Men and women receive knowledge and wisdom through the grace and mercy of Allah, adding up their insights and understanding to this mountain of wisdom. The mountain thus continues to rise and soar. I strode this mountain and drank from its streams the wisdom of thousands of sages to quench my thirst for their knowledge.

Twenty-five years ago, I came across the book *The Covenant in the Qur'an* written by Abd al Karim Biazer that redirected my search to the source itself—the Koran. It was in the Koran that I found the answers to my search. And the search had resulted in this work. I discovered that the remedy to the ills of modern-day Islam lies in the pages of the Holy Book.

Over the years, I have found wisdom in thousands of sages, some of whom I have mentioned and others not. They have all knowingly and unknowingly contributed to my miniscule understanding of the signs of Allah and of the divine wisdom. I wish to thank them all. May Allah bless all men and women of understanding who do beautiful works in the path of Allah and His creation.

I am touched and honored by the generous and encouraging message written by the great Muslim scholar and statesman of our time Dr. Mahathir bin Mohamad. May Allah bless him for his incredible leadership of the *ummah.*

I used the English translations of the Holy Koran of Abdullah Yusuf Ali, Hashim Amir Ali, Marmaduke Pickthall, and N. J. Dawood. I found *A Concordance of the Qur'an* by Hanna E. Kassis most useful in deciphering the Arabic text of the Koran.

In my search of the covenant of Allah, I found the monumental work of Sachiko Murata and William Chittick, *The Vision of Islam,* tremendously helpful. It should be an essential reading for everyone seeking the knowledge of the fundamentals of Islam.

I wish to acknowledge the love, understanding, and patience of my wife, Eva, and my daughters—Shamma, Sarah, Roxanna, and Laila— when for many hours, months, and years I was holed up in my study.

Finally, I wish to thank Hala Elgammal and Shamma Sabir for their helpful suggestions in the formatting and editing of this text.

Munawar Sabir

No. 1, Jalan P8H
Precinct 8
62250 Putrajaya, Wilayah Persekutuan
www.perdana.org.my
Tel.: 603 885 8900
Fax: 603 8889 1166

PERDANA
LEADERSHIP
FOUNDATION
YAYASAN
KEPIMPINAN
PERDANA
(604642-U)

MESSAGE

I would like to commend this thesis of Dr. Munawar Sabir on the covenant of Islam (i.e., the agreement or undertaking by Muslims to fulfill their duties in return for the many blessings Allah promises the believers). Dr. Munawar has chosen seventy-five verses of the Koran, thirty-seven of which begin with "O! Ye who believe" to illustrate the covenants that a Muslim enters into. I find Dr. Munawar's arguments very well grounded and persuasive. It is yet another attempt to clear the confusion in the minds of Muslims over the present state of Islam and the *ummah*. We cannot say that the oppression and humiliation of the Muslims is preordained by Allah. We are taught and we know that all that is good that happens to us is from Allah and that all that is bad is from ourselves. If we are in the parlous state that we are now, it must be because of us—because we are not following the teachings of Islam, or as Dr. Munawar puts it, we are not keeping to our covenants.

Historically, we know that when the ignorant Arab tribes embraced Islam, they were almost immediately successful, being able to set up a great civilization that lasted 1,300 years, to give themselves as Muslims a place in the world arena, and to gain respect from all quarters for themselves and for Islam. If today Muslims are looked down on and oppressed, it must be because of us, our failure to regard and practice Islam as a way of life, as *ad-deen*. We must therefore relook at the Koran and its teachings to see where we have gone wrong and, having done this, to make the necessary corrections in our understanding and practice of Islam.

I hope, in doing this, we will not end up in the creation of yet another Muslim sect that will only divide and weaken us. The one religion of Islam has become hundreds of different religions, each claiming to be the true Islam because of the different interpretations of the teachings of the Koran and the Hadith. We do not need yet another interpretation and another sect. But we cannot deny that there is a need to return to the fundamental teachings of the Koran so that we can overcome the confusion that has resulted in the breakup of the Muslim *ummah* and in Muslims killing Muslims.

I pray and hope that this thesis by Dr. Munawar will not divide us again but will lead to a greater understanding of the teachings of Islam and a reunification of the Muslim *ummah*. Let us downplay our differences and seek common grounds so that we can at least say that all Muslims are brothers. Inshallah, with the restoration of our brotherhood, we can once again be able to protect ourselves in this world and gain merit for the next world.

Dr. Mahathir bin Mohamad

Introduction

The act of creation links man to the Creator, and through the Creator, man is linked to everything that has ever been created. There is one absolute Being from which all stems; the universe of galaxies and all living things in the universe are all connected to one another and cannot be separated from that absolute Being. Allah creates His beings and then nurtures them. The body of man is fashioned to imbibe the good things on the earth. Allah gives man cells for absorption, nucleus for reproduction, and many other bits and pieces—hormones, enzymes, mitochondria, neurons, axons, osteocytes, hair follicles, renal tubules, heart valves, chondrocytes, pituitary gland, adrenal glands, and millions of other organs—so that man may flourish in comfort on the earth. And to keep the human engine in action and running, Allah keeps the atoms, electrons, neutrons, protons, and billions of other particles in motion. Allah replicates billions of cells in the human body to heal and repair the old, tired, and worn-out tissues.

Allah has bestowed humans with a mind and free will. Although man is connected to Allah in the physical sense through the act of creation and nurture, man's spiritual and intellectual communion with Allah is limited to the extent of man's experience and freewill. The mind has the ability to perceive ideas and knowledge from the divine and from the signs of Allah. The whisper of the divine, the rustle of the wind, the light of God, the fragrance of God's creation, and the sensation of the divine touch all inspire the human mind with the endless stream of ideas and knowledge. Man has been granted the ability to process his thoughts and gain knowledge with free will.

Had the blessed *nabi* Muhammad, in the year 610 of the Common Era, opened an office across from the Kaaba and from there distributed printed and bound copies of the Koran to the pilgrims coming from all across Arabia, he would have made no impact on the psyche of that population. The people did not possess the ability to grasp the concepts and precepts of knowledge of the unity of Allah, *taqwa* of Allah, and the criterion to distinguish between good and evil (*husna* and *Fahasha*) at that time.

The precept of tawhid: The Koran laid the foundation of the idea of one universal God, and from this fount arose all that is known and all that will ever be known. It laid this foundation for the believers in the first twelve years of Blessed Muhammad's prophecy, and it took another ten years to establish the precepts of truth, justice, covenant, equality, good, and evil. The Koran laid out these principles in clarity for all times to come.

In the sixth century, Arabia—at the time of the birth of the blessed *nabi*—was steeped in ignorance, superstition, spirit worship, and idol worship. There was no belief or concept of one universal God. In the Mediterranean Basin, the one God was a tribal deity of the Jews, and the God of Christians was accessible to man through the creed of Trinity, in which God had incarnated into the human Jesus and Jesus into the divine God.

By the first century BCE, the cult of Mithra had reached the Roman Empire from India and Persia after enduring some persecution. Roman emperors had adopted the religion, and the Mithra cult became popular among the Roman legionaries and the elite. The worship of Mithra was at first recognized by Emperor Aurelian. Diocletian and

Constantine were also worshippers of the sun god, which the Romans came to know as the cult of Sol Invictus, "the Invincible Sun."

Two hundred and eighty-five years before the blessed Muhammad proclaimed the oneness of the God of the universe, a historic event took place in Nicaea, in present-day Turkey. Emperor Constantine of the Romans was the high priest of Mithraism, the Sol Invictus. In June 325 BCE, a council of 318 Christian priests met in Nicaea, the city named after the temple of god of victory, under the direction of Emperor Constantine and amalgamated the cult of Mithra with the Judaic Christianity of Jesus. The priests of Christ and the high priest of Sol Invictus declared Jesus as the Son of God and God the Savior. Constantine, at that time, maintained his ties to the cult of Mithra, and he retained the title of *pontifex maximus*, the high priest. Constantine's coins of the realm bore the inscription *Sol invicto comiti* (committed to the invincible sun). Constantine, as the emperor, officially proclaimed the blend of Judaic Christianity with the cult of Mithra as Christianity.

This historical event came to be known as the First Council of Nicaea in 325 CE. It put the stamp of approval on the merger of Christian teachings and the pagan world of Mithra. In this merger, the Semitic belief of Jesus maintained the Judaic view of God: "We believe in one God the Father all powerful, maker of all things both seen and unseen." And the pagans who believed in Mithra maintained their personal pagan human god: "And in one Lord Jesus Christ, the Son of God, the only-begotten, begotten from the Father, that is from the substance *(Gr. ousia, Lat. Substantia)* of the Father, God from God, light from light, true God from true God, begotten *(Gr. gennethenta, Lat. Natum)* not made *(Gr. poethenta, Lat. Factum)*, consubstantial *(Gr. homoousion, Lat. unius substantiae [quod Graeci dicunt homousion])* with the Father[1]."

---

[1] The Christian profession of faith.

The first ecumenical council, Constantine's Council of Nicaea in 325 CE, ordered the production of a Christian scripture, the New Testament, from what historians recognized as the editing of thousands of Christian manuscripts and letters for Constantine's subjects in the Holy Roman Empire. The manuscripts and gospels that did not meet with the council's views were carefully gathered and set on fire throughout the empire by order of the emperor.

In this new religion, Jesus inherited the traits of Mithra, the Sol Invictus. Mithra was born of a virgin during the winter solstice on December 25 in the Julian calendar. Being a solar deity, Mithra was worshipped on Sundays; after Mithra had merged with Helios, he was depicted with a halo, aura, or glory around his head, and the Jesus iconography assumed the same halo of the sun.

A council of 318 mortal men met in Nicaea in June 325 CE to make Jesus, the only begotten Son of God, as God the Creator. In 381 CE, 150 mortal men met in Constantinople and passed a resolution creating a Holy Spirit or the Holy Ghost. In the year 431 CE, 200 men met in Ephesus to make Virgin Mary the Mother of God.

In June 325 BCE in Nicaea, with the birth of the new Roman Euro-Christianity came the demise of Jesus's Judaic teachings and the end of the Mithraic cult. The bonfire of all Christian documents not approved by Constantine and his collaborators, followed by the fourteen-hundred-year-long persecution and inquisition of those who disagreed with the church, destroyed all that was left of what Jesus had come to preach.

The debate and controversy on Jesus's status as Godhead was ongoing when the blessed *nabi* Muhammad arrived to declare that the God of Adam, Noah, Abraham, Moses, Jesus, and thousands of other prophets was the one God, the Creator of the universe, and that God is connected to everything that has ever existed through the act of creation.

- He is Allah; there is no Deity but He, The Sovereign, The Pure, and The Hallowed, Serene and Perfect, He is Allah, the Creator, the Sculptor, the Adorner of color and form. To Him belong the Most Beautiful Names: whatever so is in the heavens and on earth, Praise and Glorify Him; and He is the Almighty and All Wise. (Al-Hashr 59:18–24, Koran)

- ALLAH! There is no god but He, the Ever Living, the One Who sustains and protects all that exists. No slumber can seize Him nor sleep. His are all things in the heavens and on earth. Who is there to intercede in His presence except as He permits? He knows what happens to His creatures in this world and in the hereafter. Nor do they know the scope of His knowledge except as He wills. His Throne extends over the heavens and the earth, and He feels no fatigue in guarding and protecting them. He is the Most High, Most Great. (Al-Baqarah 2:255, Koran)

In contrast to the pre-Islamic concepts of God, the blessed *nabi* taught that Allah is the God of the universe and that He is the Creator and God of all that has been, all that is, and all that will be. Today we believe that the universal God is the center of belief of the three monotheistic religions—Judaism, Christianity, and Islam—which is true only with the caveat that although God is the Creator and Nurturer of the whole universe, the Jews believe that Yahweh is the exclusive God of Jews; and to the Christians, God the Savior only tends to those who follow Christ, and Jesus Christ is God.

Knowledge is defined as "the perception of agreement and disagreement between our ideas and the reality of the world." The immediate object of our mind is to perceive ideas. The mind, in all its thoughts and reasoning, has no other object but to contemplate its own ideas.

Knowledge, it seems therefore, is nothing more than perception of and consensus with any of our own ideas. Where this perception is, there is knowledge; and when there is no such perception, we come short of knowledge. All our knowledge is based on the ideas our mind produces. Clarity of our ideas produces clearness of our knowledge, which in turn depends on the way our mind perceives and harmonizes or diverges with any of our ideas. When the mind perceives this agreement or disagreement with two ideas immediately without the intervention of any other, we call it *intuitive knowledge*, in which case the mind perceives truth as the eye sees light. It is upon this *intuition* that all *certainty* and evidence of other knowledge depends.

The next degree of knowledge is where the mind cannot perceive agreement or disagreement in our ideas immediately and therefore has to depend on the intervention of other ideas for such perception. This process is called *reasoning*. In this case, the mind has no intuitive knowledge and has to depend on intervening ideas to shore up agreement between any other two ideas. These intervening ideas are called *proofs*. A quickness of mind to find such proofs is called *sagacity*, and the process of finding proofs is called *demonstration*. Although *demonstrative knowledge is certain*, it lacks the clarity of intuitive knowledge. To arrive at the certainty of demonstrative knowledge, the mind will require a sequence of steps to confirm intuitive knowledge with the next intermediate idea as proof, without which there will be no new knowledge. It is evident that with every step of reasoning to acquire knowledge, the mind perceives *intuitive certainty*, and no further steps are required to confirm ideas, to achieve certainty. The *intuitive perception* and conformity of intermediate ideas in each sequence of steps in the demonstration must be carried out precisely in the mind.

From all of the above, it is evident that our knowledge not only lags behind the reality of things but also is to the extent of our own ideas. The ideas that require concurrence and connection through intermediate ideas to confirm their validity through reason form the largest field of knowledge that has expanded the most during the last fourteen hundred years.

O mankind! if you have a doubt about the Resurrection, consider that We created you out of dust, then out of sperm, then out of a leech-like clot, then out of a morsel of flesh, partly formed and partly unformed, in order that We may manifest Our Power to you; and We cause whom We will to rest in the wombs for an appointed term, then do We bring you out as babes, then foster you that you may reach your age of full strength; and some of you are called to die, and some are sent back to the feeblest old age, so that they know nothing after having known much. And further, you see the earth barren and lifeless, but when We pour down rain on it, it is stirred to life, it swells, and it puts forth every kind of beautiful growth in pairs.

This is so, because Allah is the Reality: it is He Who gives life to the dead, and it is He Who has power over all things.

And verily the Hour will come: there can be no doubt about it, or about (the fact) that Allah will raise up all who are in the graves.

Yet there is among men such a one as disputes about Allah, without knowledge, without guidance, and without a Book of Enlightenment. (Al-Hajj 22:5–8, Koran)

Allah, Knower of the hidden and the manifest, the Rahman, the Rahim, the Sovereign, the Pure, and the Hallowed, Serene and Perfect, the Custodian of Faith, the Protector, the Irresistible, the Creator, the Sculptor, the Adorner of color and form, the Almighty and All Wise. (Al-Hashr 59:18–24, Koran)

Faith is never blind. Although belief in the unseen is important, there comes a point when the spiritual consciousness of the devout man goes beyond the level of simple faith to penetrate veils of the hidden, leading to knowledge of the true nature of things. The Koran speaks of this progression from *faith* to *knowledge* as an inward metamorphosis in which belief (*iman*) is transformed into certainty (*yaqin*). This certainty is expressed in the Koran in terms of the three types of knowledge of Allah.

The fundamental knowledge is the knowledge of certainty (*ilm al-yaqin*, Koran 102:5). This type of certitude refers to knowledge that results from the human capacity for logical reasoning and the appraisal of what the Koran calls "clear evidences' (*bayyinat*) of Allah's presence in the world.

Over time and under the influence of contemplation and spiritual practice, the knowledge of certitude may be transformed into a higher form of knowledge of Allah, which the Koran calls the "eye of certitude" (*ain al-yaqin*, Koran 102:7). This term refers to the knowledge that is acquired by spiritual intelligence that believers in the East locate metaphorically in the heart. In this context, the heart and the mind are the seat of intuitive, logical, and deductive knowledge.

Once opened spiritually, the heart receives knowledge as a type of divine light or illumination (*nur*) that leads the believer toward the remembrance of Allah. Just as with the knowledge of certainty and with the eye of certainty, the believer sees Allah's existence through His presence in this world. With the eye of certainty, what lead the believer to the knowledge of Allah are not the arguments to be understood by the rational intellect but by theophanic appearances (*bayyinat*) that strip away the veil of worldly phenomenon to reveal the divine reality underneath.

The third and most advanced type of knowledge builds on the transcendent nature of knowledge itself. The highest level of consciousness is called the "truth of certainty" (*haqq al-yaqin*). It is also known as *ilm ladduni* (knowledge "by presence").

The Koran seeks to establish a common foundation for belief that is based on such shared knowledge, perceptions, and experiences. Repeatedly, the Koran reminds the reader to think about the truths that lie behind the familiar or mundane things of the world, such as signs of Allah in nature. The Koran, therefore, appeals to both reason and experience in determining the criterion for distinguishing between truth and falsehood.

The faith of Islam is based on certain knowledge that encourages contemplation and realization of the vastness of Allah's wisdom and of the minuteness and limitations of human capabilities. The certainty of divine reality allows the human spirit to expand outward to take in the physical world and upward to realize his ultimate transcendence of the world through his link with the Absolute and then inward to reconcile all that with his intellectual and emotional self. With this expansion outward, upward, and inward, the consciousness becomes three dimensional. Nevertheless, it is also a restriction because with the knowledge of God comes a concomitant awareness of the limits and responsibilities imposed on man as a created being. Unlike a secular humanist, a true Muslim in submission to Allah cannot delude himself by claiming that he is the sole author of his destiny as he knows that a person's fate is routinely controlled by factors beyond his control.

Allah the Divine is open to the most miniscule of the beings. From this little particle (the *nuqta*), the connection to Allah, the Cherisher and the Nourisher of the universe, extends into the vastest of expanse. Within this communion of the Divine with the creation passes the

Spirit of Allah into His creatures. Man lays his heart and mind open to Allah in submission to receive Allah's Spirit and guidance. In the space and the emptiness of the universe, there flow currents and whispers of wind and energy. These winds of silence, light, and sound carry the divine whisper, and in this sound is Allah's message. This message descends into the believer's receptive heart in peace, silence, and tranquility. When the angels and the Spirit descend with Allah's guidance, the eyes perceive the most beautiful divine light, the ears hear the softest tinkle of the bell, the nose smells the fragrance of a thousand gardens, and the skin feels the most tranquil of the gentle breeze. When this happens, the soul has seen nirvana. The believer is in communion with Allah. This is the knowledge of Allah.

Allah sent thousands of prophets to mankind to teach man precepts and principles to His straight path of unity, truth, and goodness. Over thousands of years, these precepts and principles spread around the world through civilizations till mankind, as a whole, began to comprehend the knowledge of one universal God, the Creator of every particle and every being in the whole universe. Man listened and occasionally regressed into his inherent paganism, greed, selfishness, and egotism. Allah bestowed on man a vicegerency on the earth, a mind, free will, and a covenant. Allah then announced that there were to be no more prophets. The era of prophecy had ended. Man, in stages, had received the knowledge required to live in submission to Allah's will in peace and harmony on the earth in accordance with the divine laws, which were sent down as a guidance to every human community for a life of truth justice, goodness, and peace. Such knowledge consisted of the following:

Unity: There is one absolute Being from which all stems; the universe of galaxies and all the living things in the universe are all connected to one another and cannot be separated from that absolute Being. Everything alive—humans, animals, plants, and microorganisms—is created by the absolute Being, all nurtured with the same organic matter, all breathing the same air; and in turn, their physical self disintegrates to the same elements, which then return to the earth and the universe. In this cycle of creation and disintegration, the only permanence is of the Real, the Absolute. All else is an illusion and a mirage. One moment you are here, and in the next, you are gone. Nothing is left behind—no riches, no honor, no ego, and no pride. What is left, however, is an account of your deeds, upon which one day you will be judged.

Mind: Man is bestowed with a mind and free will. The mind has the ability to perceive ideas and knowledge from the Divine and from the signs of Allah. The whisper of the Divine, the rustle of the wind, the light of God, the fragrance of God's creation, and the sensation of the divine touch all inspire the human mind with an endless stream of ideas and knowledge. Man has been granted the ability to process his thoughts and given knowledge with a free will.

The verse of the light encompasses the totality of the knowledge and guidance that God sent to man through His prophets. The pagan in man confused God's message and instead began to worship the messenger. With the end of the era of the prophets, man has to open his heart to the light of Allah and learn to recognize the goodness of God within himself in his own heart.

Allah is the Light of the heavens and the earth. The parable of His Light
is as if there were a Niche and within it a Lamp: the Lamp enclosed
in Glass; the glass as it were a brilliant star: lit from a blessed Tree, an
Olive, neither of the East nor of the West, whose Oil is well-nigh
luminous, though fire scarce touched it: Light upon Light! Allah doth
guide whom He will to His Light: Allah doth set forth Parables for
men: and Allah doth know all things. (Lit is such a light) in houses,
which Allah hath permitted to be raised to honor; for the celebration,

in them, of His name: in them is He glorified in the mornings and
in the evenings, (again and again). (An-Nur 24:35–36, Koran)

His light illuminates the hearts of those who love Him, place their
trust in Him, and open their hearts in submission to Him. When
hearts are open to Allah in submission, the divine light, Spirit, and
wisdom of Allah glow in the niche of their hearts. The glow and the
luminescence of the Spirit and wisdom shines with the brilliance of a
star lit from the light of divine wisdom, the tree of knowledge—the
knowledge of Allah's signs. For those who believe, Allah is within.
The believer is aglow with Allah's radiance—light upon light. The
dwellings where Allah's name is praised and glorified in the mornings
and evenings are aglow with His light.

Allah has granted knowledge and the wisdom of *furqan* and *taqwa* to
the believers who have opened their hearts and minds to Him. Man
has been granted the freedom of choice in doing what is wholesome
and beautiful or what is corrupt and ugly. It is only man, among the
creation, who has been given the knowledge to distinguish right
activity, right thought, and right intention from their opposites. This
knowledge reminds man of the scales of Allah's justice; the two
hands of Allah, His mercy and His wrath, are reflected in the human
domain, where people have been appointed Allah's vicegerents. Deeds
of goodness and wholesomeness are associated with mercy, paradise,
and what is beautiful. Evil and corruption is rewarded with wrath, hell,
and what is ugly.

Munawar Sabir

The Blue Mosque at night, Istanbul.

The famous Blue Koran.

Part One

The Covenant of Allah

Chapter One

The Covenant of Allah: The Covenant of the Koran

Verily those who pledge their allegiance unto you, (O Muhammad) pledge it unto none but Allah; the Hand of Allah is over their hands. Thereafter whosoever breaks his Covenant does so to the harm of his own soul, and whosoever fulfils his Covenant with Allah, Allah will grant him an immense Reward. (Al-Fath 48:10, Koran)

There is an implicit assumption in the Koran that there exists an agreement between Allah and His creation portrayed as a mutual understanding in which Allah proposes a system of regulations for the guidance of man. This guidance is presented in the form of commandments to be accepted and implemented by man. Allah then makes promise of what He will do in the event that man willingly abides by these commands and regulates his life according to them. The concept of promise is clearly conditional on human obedience. The covenant of the Koran symbolizes the relationship between Allah and man; man becomes His steward, vicegerent, or custodian on the earth through submission and obedience to His will (*islam*) as expressed in His commands and is able to take advantage of Allah's promises and favors.

Allah addresses those who believe in Him directly in seventy-five verses of the Koran, giving them guidance, advice, and a promise of rewards in this world and the hereafter. Those who do not believe in Him, the infidels (the *kafirun*) are promised a place in hell forever. A similar penalty is promised to those who submit to Allah according to their word but not their deeds; such people are the hypocrites or the *Munafiqeen*. The concept of the covenant also symbolizes the relationship between man and Allah's creatures and the rest

3

of His creation. They all share one God, one set of guidance and commandments, the same submission and obedience to Him, and the same set of expectations in accordance to His promises. They all can, therefore, trust one another since they all have similar obligations and expectations. In view of the Koran, humans, communities, nations, and civilizations will continue in harmony and peace so long as they continue to fulfill Allah's covenant.

The Koran uses three terms for the word *covenant*:

- *'Ahd* is the more frequently used term than the other two. It means "commitment obligation, responsibility, pledge, promise, oath, contract, compact, covenant, pact, and treaty agreement." It also means "an era or epoch."
- *Mithaq* means "to put faith in"; it is a tie of relationship between two parties.
- *Isr* means "a firm covenant, compact, or contract that if not fulfilled constitutes punishment."
- The covenant in the Koran contains several articles not unlike a modern legal agreement:
a) Names of the two parties of the covenant, the first one being Allah
b) Reminder of Allah's favors
c) List of commandments or conditions of the covenant
d) Promises and rewards
e) Warnings of disobedience
f) Affirmation and witness
g) Oaths by Allah's signs and favors
h) Signs of the covenant
i) Lessons from the past
j) In the covenant of Allah with the believers, for instance, in Sura Al-Ma'idah, the format of the pact is illustrated clearly:

a)

In the name of Allah, Most gracious Most Merciful. O, who believe! Fulfill your obligations (Al-Ma'idah 5:1, Koran)

b)

And call in remembrance the favor of Allah unto you, and His Covenant, which He ratified with you. (Al-Ma'idah 5:7, Koran)

c)

Forbidden to you are: carrion, blood, the flesh of swine, and that on which has been invoked the name of other than Allah: that which has been killed by strangling, or by a violent blow, or by a headlong fall, or by being gored to death: that which has partly eaten by a wild animal; unless you are able to slaughter it (in due form); that which is sacrificed on stone alters; forbidden is also the division of meat by raffling with arrows: that is impiety.

This day those who reject faith have given up all hope of your religion: yet fear them not but fear Me. This day I have, perfected your religion for you, completed my favors upon you, and have chosen Islam as your religion. (Al-Ma'idah 5:3, Koran)

d)

To those who believe and do beautiful deeds, for them there is forgiveness and a great reward. (Al-Ma'idah 5:8, Koran)

e)

Those who reject faith and deny Our Signs will be companions of hell-fire.

f)

And remember Allah's favor to you and His covenant with which He bound you when you said, "we hear and obey", And fear Allah. Verily Allah is all knower of the secrets of your hearts. (Al-Ma'idah 5:7, Koran)

g)

This day have I perfected your religion for you, completed my favors upon you, and have chose Islam as your religion. (Al-Ma'idah 5:3, Koran)

h)

Allah took a Covenant from the Children of Israel and We appointed twelve leaders from among them. And Allah said "I am with you if you establish salaat, practice regular charity, believe in my Rasools honor and assist them, and loan to Allah a beautiful loan, Verily I will wipe out from you your evils, and admit you to Gardens with rivers flowing beneath; But if any of you after this disbelieved he has truly wandered from the path of rectitude.

i)

Therefore, because of breach of their Covenant, We cursed them and made their hearts grow hard. They perverted words from their meaning and abandoned a good part of the message that was sent them. Thou will not cease to discover treachery from them barring a few. But bear with them and pardon them. Verily Allah loves those who are wholesome.

Moreover, from those who call themselves Christians, We took their Covenant, but they have abandoned a good part of the Message that was sent to them. Therefore, We have stirred up enmity and hatred among them until the Day of Resurrection, when Allah will inform them of their handiwork.

O People of the Book! There has come to you Our Rasool, revealing to you much that you used to hide in the Scripture and passing over much. Indeed, there has come to you from Allah a light and a plain Book:

Wherewith Allah guides all who seek His good pleasure to ways of peace and safety, and leads them out of darkness, by His Will, unto the light, guides them to a Path that is Straight. (Al-Ma'idah 5:12-16, Koran)

The Commandments

The commandments of Allah addressed to the believers (men and women) are the fundamentals of the *din* of Islam. These commandments make up the covenant or the compact between Allah and His believers. The fulfillment of the covenant becomes obligatory to man when the fire of love for Allah is kindled in his heart, and he submits to His will, becoming His servant and steward on the earth.

1. Say, "Come I will recite what your Lord has prohibited you from:

   Join not anything in worship with Him:

Be good to your parents: kill not your children because of poverty, We provide sustenance for you and for them:

Come not near to shameful deeds (Fahasha) whether open or secret.

Take not life, which Allah hath made sacred, except by the way of justice or law: This He commands you, that you may learn wisdom.

And come not near the orphan's property, except to improve it, until he attains the age of full strength, and give full measure and full weight with justice. No burden We place on any soul but that which it can bear.

Whenever you give your word speak honestly even if a near relative is concerned:

And fulfill the Covenant of Allah. Thus, He commands you that you may remember.

Verily, this is My Way leading straight: follow it: follow not (other) paths for they will separate you from His path. This He commands you that you may remember. (Al-An 'am 6:151–53, Koran)

These commandments are similar to the Ten Commandments of Moses. They emphasize tawhid and respect for parents; prohibits infanticide, taking of life, lewd acts, adultery, fornication, and embezzlement of orphans' property; stress honesty in trade; and underline a person's responsibility to be just. Allah commands humans to be righteous and to fulfill their covenant with Allah.

Commandments of the Covenant of Allah
in Sura-Al Baqarah (2 Medina 92)[2]

2. O you who believe! Seek help with patience, perseverance, and prayer. Allah is with those who patiently persevere. (2:153, Koran)

3. O you who believe! Eat of good things provided to you by Allah, and show your gratitude in worship of Him. Forbidden to you are the carrion, blood, and flesh of swine, and on any other food on which any name besides that of Allah has been invoked. If forced by necessity, without willful disobedience or transgressing due limits, one is guilt less. Allah is Most Forgiving and Most Merciful. (2:172–73, Koran)

4. O you who believe!
    The law of equality is prescribed to you in cases of murder. The free for the free, the slave for the slave, the woman for the woman. However, if any remission is made by the brethren of the slain, then grant any reasonable demand, and compensate him with handsome gratitude. This is a concession and a Mercy from your Lord. After this, whoever exceeds the limits shall be in grave penalty.
    In the Law of Equality, there is a saving of life for you, O men of understanding; that you may restrain yourselves. (2:178–79, Koran)

5. O you who believe!
    Fasting is prescribed to you, for a fixed number of days in the month of Ramadan as it was prescribed to those before you, that you may practice self-restraint. If you are ill, or on a journey, the prescribed number of days of fasting should be made up afterwards. For those who cannot fast because of physical hardship, should feed the poor and needy but it is better to give more out of free will. However fasting is better. The Qur'an was revealed in the month of Ramadan, guidance to humankind for judgment between right and wrong. For every one except those ill or on a journey, this month should spend it in fasting. Allah intends to make it easy on you so that you may complete the prescribed period of fasting

---

[2] The first number is the traditional sequence number of the sura, followed by the period during which the sura was revealed. The second number denotes the chorological sequence of the sura.

and to glorify Him to express your gratitude for His Guidance. (2:183–85, Koran)

6. O you who believe!
Enter into submission to the will of Allah, enter Islam whole-heartedly, and follow not the footsteps of Satan, for he is a sworn enemy to you! (2:208, Koran)

7. O you who believe!
Void not your charity by boast, conceit, and insult, by reminders of your generosity like those who want their generosity to be noted by all men but they believe neither in Allah nor in the Last Day. Theirs is a parable like a hard barren rock, on which is a little soil; on it falls heavy rain, which leaves it just a bare stone. And Allah guides not those who reject Faith.
And the likeness of those who give generously, seeking to please Allah and to strengthen their souls, is as a garden, high and fertile where heavy rain falls on it and makes it yield a double the amount of harvest, and if it receives not heavy rain, light moisture suffices it. Allah notices whatever you do. (2:264–65, Koran)

> The parable of those who spend their substance in the way of Allah is that of a grain of corn: it grows seven ears, and each ear has a hundred grains. Allah gives plentiful return to whom He pleases, Allah cares for all, and He knows all things.
> Those who give generously in the cause of Allah, and follow not up their gifts with reminders of their generosity or with injury, for them their reward is with their Lord; on them shall be no fear, nor shall they grieve.
> Kind words and the covering of faults are better than charity followed by injury. Allah is Free of all wants and He is Most Merciful. (2:261–63, Koran)

8. O you who believe!
Spend out of bounties of Allah in charity and wholesome deeds before the Day comes when there will be neither bargaining, friendship nor intercession. Those who reject faith are the wrongdoers. Allah! There is no god but He, the Ever Living, the One Who sustains and protects all that exists. No slumber can seize Him or sleep. His are all things in the

heavens and on earth. Who is there can intercede in His presence except as He permits? He knows what happens to His creatures in this world and in the Hereafter. Nor shall they know the scope of His knowledge except as He wills. His Throne doth extend over the heavens and the earth, and He feels no fatigue in guarding and preserving them for He is the Most High, Most Great.

Let there be no compulsion in religion: Truth stands out clear from Error: whoever rejects Evil and believes in Allah hath grasped the most trust worthy handhold that never breaks.

And Allah hears and knows all things.

Allah is the Wali, protector of those who have faith. From the depths of darkness, He will lead them forth into light. Of those who reject faith their Wali (protectors) are the false deities: from light, they will lead them forth into the depths of darkness. They will be Companions of the Fire, to dwell therein (forever). (2:254–57, Koran)

> Those who spend of their goods in charity by night and by day, in secret and in public, have their reward with their Lord: on them shall be no fear, nor shall they grieve. Those who devour usury will not stand except stands the one whom the Satan by his touch has driven to madness. That is because they say: "Trade is like usury", but Allah hath permitted trade and forbidden usury. Those who after receiving direction from their Lord, desist, shall be pardoned for the past; their case is for Allah to judge; but those who repeat (the offence) are Companions of the Fire; they will abide therein (forever).
>
> Allah will deprive usury of all blessing but will give increase for deeds of charity, for He does not love ungrateful and wicked creatures. (2:274–76, Koran)

> Those who believe!
> Those who do wholesome deeds, establish regular prayers and regular charity have rewards with their Lord. On them shall be no fear, nor shall they grieve. (2:277, Koran)

9. O you who believe!
    Have taqwa of Allah, fear Allah, and give up what remains of your demand for usury, if you are indeed believers. If you do it not, take notice of war

from Allah and His Rasool: but if you turn back, you will still have your capital sums.

Deal not unjustly, and you shall not be dealt with unjustly.

If the debtor is in a difficulty, grant him time until it is easy for him to repay. But if you remit it by way of charity, that is best for you. (2:278–80, Koran)

10. O you who believe!

When you make a transaction involving future obligations, write it down in presence of witnesses, or let a scribe write it down faithfully. Let the party incurring the liability dictate truthfully in the presence of two witnesses from among your own men and if two men are not available then a man and two women, so that if one of them errs then the other one, can remind him. If a party is mentally or physically or unable to dictate, let his guardian do so faithfully. The witnesses should not refuse when called upon to give evidence. Disregard not to put your contract in writing, whether it be small or large, it is more suitable in the eyes of Allah, more suitable as evidence, and more convenient to prevent doubts in the future amongst yourselves.

But if you carry out a transaction instantaneously on the spot among yourselves, there is no blame on you if you do not reduce it to writing. But neither takes witnesses whenever you make a commercial contract; and let neither scribe nor the witnesses suffer harm. If you do such harm, it would be wickedness in you. So, fear Allah; for it is Allah that teaches you. And Allah is well acquainted with all things.

If you are on a journey, and cannot find a scribe, a pledge with possession may serve the purpose. And if one of you deposits a thing on trust with another let the trustee faithfully discharge his trust, and let him fear his Lord. Conceal not evidence; for whoever conceals it, his heart is tainted with sin. And Allah knows all that you do. (2:282–83, Koran)

Commandments of the Covenant of Allah
in Sura Ali 'Imran (3 Medina 93)

11. O you who believe!
    If you listen to a faction among the People of the Book, (Jews and Christians) they would render you apostates after you have believed! And how could you deny Faith when you learn the Signs of Allah, and amongst you lives the Rasool? Whoever holds firmly to Allah will be shown a Way that is straight. (3:100–101, Koran)

12. O you who believe!
    Be in taqwa of Allah, fear Allah as He should be feared, and die not except in a state of Islam. And hold fast, all together, by the Rope, which Allah stretches out for you, and be not divided among yourselves; and remember with gratitude Allah's favor on you; You were enemies and He joined your hearts in love, so that by His Grace, you became brethren and a community. You were on the brink of the pit of fire, and He saved you from it. Thus does Allah make His Signs clear to you that you may be guided.
    Let there arise out of you a band of people Inviting to all that is good, enjoining what is right, and forbidding what is wrong: they are the ones to attain happiness.
    Be not like those who are divided amongst themselves and fall into disputations after receiving clear signs: for them is a dreadful penalty. (3:102–5, Koran)

13. O you who believe!
    Devour not usury, doubled and multiplied; Be in taqwa of Allah (fear Allah) that you may prosper. Fear the Fire, which is prepared for those who reject Faith; And obey Allah and the Rasool; that you may obtain mercy.
    Be quick in the race for forgiveness from your Lord, and for a Garden whose measurement is that of the heavens and of the earth, prepared for the righteous.
    Those who give freely whether in prosperity, or in adversity, those who restrain anger, and pardon all humans, for Allah loves those who do beautiful deeds. (3:130–34, Koran)

14. O you who believe!

Take not into intimacy those outside your ranks: they will not fail to corrupt you. They only desire your ruin: rank hatred has already appeared from their mouths: what their hearts conceal is far worse. We have made plain to you the Signs, if you have wisdom.

Ah! You are those who love them, but they love you not, though you believe in the whole of the Book, when they meet you, they say, "We believe": but when they are alone, they bite off the very tips of their fingers at you in their rage. Say: "Perish in your rage; Allah knows well all the secrets of the heart." If all that is good befalls you, it grieves them; but if some misfortune overtakes you, they rejoice at it. But if you are constant and do right, not the least harm will their cunning do to you; for Allah compasses round about all that they do. (3:118–20, Koran)

15. O you who believe!

If you obey the Unbelievers, (kafaru) they will drive you back on your heels, and you will turn your back to your Faith to your own loss. Allah is your protector and He is the best of helpers. (3:149–50, Koran)

16. O you who believe!

Be not like the Unbelievers, who say of their brethren, who were traveling through the earth or engaged in fighting: "If they had stayed with us, they would not have died, or been slain." So, that Allah may make it a cause of regret in their hearts.

It is Allah that gives Life and Death, and Allah is seer of all that you do. And if you are slain, or die, in the Way of Allah, forgiveness and mercy from Allah are far better than all they could amass. And if you die, or are slain, it is unto Allah that you are brought together. (3:156–58, Koran)

17. O you who believe!

Persevere in patience and constancy; vie in such perseverance; strengthen each other; and be in taqwa of Allah, fear Allah that you may prosper. (3:200, Koran)

Commandments of the Covenant of Allah
in Sura An-Nisa (4 Medina 94)

18. O you who believe!
    You are forbidden to take women against their will. Nor should you treat
    them with harshness, so that you may recant on part of the dower you
    have given them, and that is only where they have been guilty of open
    lewdness. On the contrary, live with them on a footing of kindness and
    equality. If you take a dislike to them, it may be that you dislike a thing,
    through which Allah brings about a great deal of good. (4:19, Koran)

19. O you who believe!
    Squander not your wealth among yourselves in egotism and conceit:
    Let there be trade and traffic amongst you with mutual goodwill Nor
    kill or destroy yourselves: for verily Allah hath been Most Merciful to
    you. If any do that in rancor and injustice, soon shall We cast them
    into the fire: and easy it is for Allah. If you abstain from all the odious
    and the forbidden, Allah shall expel out of you all evil in you and admit
    you to a Gate of great honor.
    And crave not those things of what Allah has bestowed His gifts more
    freely on some than others, men are assigned what they earn and
    women that they earn.
    But ask Allah of His bounty. Surely, Allah is knower of everything.
    (4:29–32, Koran)

20. O you who believe!
    Approach not prayers with a mind befogged until you understand all
    that you utter, nor come up to prayers in a state of un- cleanliness,
    till you have bathed. If you are ill, or on a journey, or when you come
    from the closet or you have had sexual intercourse, and find no water,
    take for yourself clean sand or earth and rub your hands and face. Allah
    shall blot out your sins and forgive again and again. (4:43, Koran)

21. O you who believe!
    Obey Allah and obey the Rasool, and those charged amongst you with
    authority in the settlement of your affairs. If you differ in any thing
    among yourselves, refer it to Allah and His Rasool (The Qur'an and
    the Prophet's teachings). If you do believe in Allah, the last Day that is

best, and the most beautiful conduct in the final determination. (4:59, Koran)

22. O you who believe!

   Take your precautions, and either go forth in parties or go forth all together.

   There are certainly among you men who would tarry behind; if a misfortune befalls you, they say: "Allah did favor us in that we were not present among them."

   But if good fortune comes to you from Allah, they would be sure to say – as if there had never been ties of affection between you and them – "Oh! I wish I had been with them; a fine thing should I then have made of it!"

   Let those fight in the cause of Allah who sell the life of this world for the Hereafter, To him who fights in the cause of Allah – whether he is slain or gets victory – soon shall We give him a reward of great (value). And why should you not fight in the cause of Allah and of those who, being weak, are ill-treated (and oppressed)? Men, women, and children, whose cry is: "Our Lord! Rescue us from this town, whose people are oppressors; and raise for us from thee one who will protect; and raise for us from thee one who will help! (4:71–75, Koran)

23. O you who believe!

   When you go forth in the cause of Allah be careful to discriminate and say not to the one who greets you with alaikum as salaam, "Though art not a believer".

   Would you covet perishable goods of this life when there are immeasurable treasures with Allah. You were like the person who offered you salutation, before Allah conferred on you His favors. Therefore carefully investigate for Allah is well aware of all that you do. (4:94, Koran)

24. O you who believe!

   Stand firm for justice as witness to Allah, be it against yourself, your parents, or your family. Whether it be against rich or poor, Both are nearer to Allah than they are to you. Follow not your caprice lest you distort your testimony. If you prevaricate and evade justice Allah is well aware what you do. (4:135, Koran)

25. O you who believe!

   Believe in Allah, His Rasool, and the Book, which He has sent to His Rasool and the scriptures, which He sent to those before him. Any who deny Allah, His angels, His Books, His Rasools, and the Day of Judgment has gone astray. (4:136, Koran)

26. O you who believe!

   Take not infidels (Kafirun) for awliya (friends and protectors) in place of believers. Would you offer Allah a clear warrant against yourselves? (4:144, Koran)

Commandments of the Covenant of Allah in Sura Al-Ma'idah (5 Medina 95)

27. O you who believe!

   Fulfill your Covenants. (5:1, Koran)

28. O you who believe!

   Violate not the sanctity of the Symbols of Allah, or of the sacred month, or of the animals brought for sacrifice, nor the garlands that mark out such animals, nor the people coming to the Sacred House, seeking the bounty and good pleasure of their Lord. But when you are clear of the Sacred Precincts and of ihram, you may hunt, and let not the enmity of those who once debarred you from the sacred place make you guilty of bearing malice. Help one another in virtue and piety, but help not one another in sin and acrimony. Be in taqwa of Allah, fear Allah, for Allah is swift in reckoning. (5:2, Koran)

   Forbidden to you for food is carrion, blood, flesh of swine and on which name other than of Allah has been invoked, also the strangled, the felled, the mangled or the gored and that has been sacrificed on alters; forbidden is also the division of meat by raffling with arrows: that is impiety.
   This day have those who reject faith (kafaru) given up all hope of compromising your faith, fear them not, but only fear Me. This day have I perfected your religion for you, bestowed on you with My blessings, and decreed Islam as your religion. (5:3, Koran)

29. O you who believe!

16

When you arise for salaat, purify your self by washing your faces, your hands to the elbows, wipe your heads, and wash your feet to the ankles. If you are unclean, purify yourself. If you are ill or on a journey or you come from call of nature, or you have been in contact with women and you find no water then take for yourself clean sand or earth and rub there with your faces and hands. Allah does not wish that you should be burdened, but to make you clean, and to bestow His blessings on you, that you might be grateful. (5:6, Koran)

30. O you who believe!
Stand firmly for Allah as a witness of fair dealing. Let not the malice of people lead you to iniquity. Be just, that is next to worship. Be with taqwa of Allah, fear Allah. Allah is well aware with what you do. (5:8, Koran)

To those who believe and do deeds of righteousness, Allah has promised forgiveness and a great reward. (5:9, Koran)

31. O you who believe!
Remember Allah's blessings on you. When a people planned stretching out their hands against you and Allah did hold back their hands from you to protect you from your enemies. Be in taqwa of Allah, fear Allah, and place your trust in Allah. (5:11, Koran)

32. O you who believe!
Be in taqwa of Allah, fear Allah. Perform Jihad and strive your utmost in Allah's Cause, and approach Him so that you may prosper. (5:35, Koran)

33. O you who believe!
Take not the Jews and the Christians as your friends and protectors (awliya). They are friends and protectors unto each other. He who amongst you turns to them is one of them. Allah does not guide those who are unjust and evil-doers (zalimun). (5:51, Koran)

34. O you who believe!
If any among you turn back on his faith Allah will bring a people whom He loves and who love Him, and who are humble towards the believers, and stern towards unbelievers, who perform jihad and strive in the cause of Allah and fear not reproaches of any blamer. Such is the Grace of

Allah, which He bestows on whom He wills. Allah is All Sufficient for His Creatures and all Knowing. (5:54, Koran)

35. O you who believe!
Take not for friends and protectors (awliya) those who take your religion for mockery, whether from amongst people of the book or from amongst the kafireen. Be in taqwa of Allah, fear Allah if you have faith indeed. (5:57, Koran)

36. O you who believe!
Make not unlawful the good things that Allah hath made lawful to you. Commit no excess; Allah loves not people given to excess. Eat of things, which Allah has provided for you, lawful and good. Be in taqwa of Allah, fear Allah in whom you believe. (5:87–88, Koran)

37. O you who believe!
Forbidden to you are intoxicants and gambling, dedication of stones and divination by arrows. These are an abomination and Satan's handiwork; they hinder you from prayer and remembrance of Allah, and place enmity and hatred amongst you. Abstain from them so that you may prosper. (5:90–91, Koran)

Commandments of the Covenant of Allah in Sura Al-Anfal (8 Medina 113)

38. O you who believe!
When you meet the infidel's rank upon rank, in conflict never turn your backs to them. (8:15, Koran)

39. O you who believe!
Obey Allah and His Rasool, and turn not to others when you should hear him speak. Nor be like those who say: "We hear", but listen not. For the worst of creatures in the sight of Allah are those who neither listen, nor look or try to comprehend. (8:20–22, Koran)

Obey Allah and His Rasool, hear the Rasool's message. And grasp with your mind, and heart the Truth. The Truth that Allah speaks of is Tawhid, Nubuwwa and Ma'ad. Tawhid is accepting that there is no god but Allah and that He is the only One worthy of worship. As a principle of faith, Tawhid explains the Oneness of Allah and His creatures including the angels connected to Him. Prophecy is the belief in the Prophets of Allah and acceptance of their Scriptures. Ma'ad, the return is to Allah the Creator.

Do not be like those who say we hear but they listen not. The worse of creatures in Allah's sight are those who neither listen, nor look or try to comprehend and grasp the Truth. Allah took the light from them and they are left in the darkness.

40. O you who believe!
Respond to Allah and His Rasool when He calls you to that give you life. And know that Allah intervenes in the tussle between man and his heart, and it is to Allah that you shall return. Fear treachery or oppression that afflicts not only those who perpetrate it, but affects guilty and innocent alike. Know that Allah is strict in punishment. (8:24–25, Koran)

41. O you who believe!
Betray not the trust of Allah and His Rasool. Nor knowingly misappropriate things entrusted to you. (2:27, Koran)

42. O you who believe!
If you have taqwa of Allah, He will grant you a Criterion to judge between right and wrong, and remove from you all misfortunes and evil and forgive your sins. Allah is the bestower of grace in abundance. (8:29, Koran)

Fight the infidel until there is no more treachery and oppression and there prevails Justice and Faith in Allah altogether and everywhere. If they cease, then Allah is seer of what they do.
If they refuse, be sure that Allah is your Protector, the Best to protect, and the Best to help. (8:39–40, Koran)

43. O you who believe!

When you meet the enemy force, stand steadfast against them, and remember the name of Allah much, so that you may be successful. And obey Allah and His Rasool, and do not dispute with one another lest you lose courage and your strength departs and be patient. Allah is with those who patiently persevere. (8:45–46, Koran)

Commandments of the Covenant of Allah in Sura At-Tawbah (9 Medina 114)

44. O you who believe!

Take not for your protectors and friends (awliya) your kin who practice infidelity over faith. Whosoever does that will be amongst the wrong doers. (9:23, Koran)

45. O you who believe!

The Mushrikun (unbelievers) are unclean, so let them not approach the Sacred Mosque. If you fear poverty, soon Allah will enrich you, if He wills out of His bounty, for Allah is All-Knowing, All Wise. Fight those who believe not in Allah, the Last Day, nor forbid what has been forbidden by Allah and His Prophet, nor acknowledge the Religion of Truth from among the Jews and Christians until they pay jaziya in willing submission. (9:28–29, Koran)

46. O you who believe!

There are indeed many among the priests and clerics who in falsehood devour the substance of men and hinder them from the way of Allah. And there are those who bury gold and silver and spend it not in the way of Allah: announce unto them a most grievous penalty. On the Day when heat will be produced out of that wealth in the fire of Hell, and with it will be branded their foreheads, their flanks, and their backs, "This is the treasure which you buried for yourselves: taste then, the treasures which you buried!" (9:34–35, Koran)

47. O you who believe!

What ails you? When you are asked to march forwards in the Cause of Allah you cling to the earth! Do you find the life of this earth more alluring than the hereafter? But little is the enjoyment of this life as compared with the hereafter! Unless you go forwards in Allah's cause, He will punish you and put other people in your place. But Him you will not harm in the least. Allah has power over all things.

Whether you do or do not help Allah's Rasool, your leader, Allah strengthens him with His Peace and with forces that you do not see. The words of the infidels He humbled into the dirt but Allah's word is Exalted, High. Allah is Mighty, Wise. Go forth, advance! Whether equipped well or lightly, perform jihad strive your utmost and struggle with your wealth and your persons in the cause of Allah. That is best for you, if you knew. (9:38–41, Koran)

48. O you who believe!
Be in taqwa of Allah, fear Allah, and be with those who are true in word and deed. (9:119, Koran)

49. O you who believe!
Fight the unbelievers who surround you. Let them find you firm, and know Allah is always with those who have taqwa, who are Allah-wary. (9:123, Koran)

Commandment of the Covenant of Allah in Sura Al-Hajj (22 Medina 112)

50. O you who believe!
Bow down, prostrate yourself and serve your Lord, and do wholesome deeds that you may prosper. Perform Jihad; strive to your utmost in Allah's cause as striving (jihad) is His due. He has chosen you and Allah has imposed no hardship in your endeavor to His cause. You are the inheritors of the faith of your father Abraham. He has named you Muslims of the times before and now, so that Allah's Rasool may be an example to you and that you are an example to humankind.

Establish regular Salaat, give regular charity, and hold fast to Allah. He is your Mawla, protector, the best of Protectors and the best Helper. (22:77–78, Koran)

Commandments of the Covenant of Allah
in Sura An-Nur (24 Medina 110)

51. O you who believe!
Do not follow Satan's footsteps: if any will follow the footsteps of Satan, he will command to what is shameful (Fahasha) and wrong (Munkar): and were it not for the grace of Allah and His mercy on you, not one of you would have been unblemished: but Allah does purify whom He pleases: and Allah is all Hearer and all Knower.
Let not those among you who are blessed with grace and ample means hold back from helping their relatives, the poor, and those who have left their homes in Allah's cause. Let them forgive and overlook, do you not wish that Allah should forgive you? And Allah is Oft Forgiving, Most Merciful.
Those who slander decent women, thoughtless but believing, are cursed in this life and in the Hereafter: for them is a grievous Penalty. (24:21–23, Koran)

52. O you who believe!
Enter not houses other than yours until you have asked permission and invoked peace upon those in them. If you find none in the house whom you seek, enter not unless permission is granted. If you asked to leave go back, it is best for you that makes for greater purity for you. Allah knows all that you do. (24:27, Koran)

Commandments of the Covenant of Allah
in Sura Al-Ahzab (33 Medina 111)

53. O You who believe!
Remember the Grace of Allah, bestowed upon you, when there came down hordes to overpower you: We sent against them a hurricane and forces that that you did not see: but Allah sees all that you do.
Behold! They came on you from above you and from below you, your eyes became dim and the hearts gaped up to the throats, and you imagined various vain thoughts about Allah! (33:9, Koran)

54. O you who believe!

    Celebrate the Praises of Allah often and Glorify Him in the morning and at night. It is Allah and His Angels Who send their blessings upon you, that He may lead you out of the depths of darkness into light. Allah is full of mercy to the believers! On the Day, they meet Him with the salutation: Salaam, He has prepared for them a generous Reward.

    O Nabi, We have set thee as a witness, a bearer of glad tidings, as a Warner and as one who invites to Allah's Grace by His leave and as an inspiration and beam of light. Give glad tidings to the believers that they shall have from Allah bounty in abundance. And obey not the command of the Unbelievers (kafireen) and the hypocrites (munafiqeen), heed not their annoyances, and put your trust in Allah, for enough is Allah as Disposer of affairs. (33:41–48, Koran)

55. Allah and His angels bless the Prophet.

    O you who believe!

    You should also ask for Allah's blessings and peace on the Prophet. (33:56, Koran)

56. O you who believe!

    Be you not like those who tormented and insulted Moses, but Allah cleared Moses of the slander they had uttered: and he was honorable in Allah's sight.

    O you who believe!

    Fear Allah, and speak always the truth that He may direct you to righteous deeds and forgive you your sins: he that obeys Allah and His Rasool have already attained the highest achievement.

    We did indeed offer the Trust to the Heavens and the Earth and the Mountains; but they refused to undertake it, being afraid thereof: but man undertook it; he was indeed unjust and ignorant, so***that Allah will punish the Hypocrites (munafiqeen), men and women, and the Unbelievers (Mushrikun), men and women, and Allah turns in Mercy to the Believers, men and women; for Allah is Oft-Forgiving, Most Merciful. (33:69–73, Koran)

Commandments of the Covenant of Allah in
Sura Muhammad (47 Medina 107)

57. O you who believe!

   If you will aid (the cause of) Allah, He will aid you, and make your foothold firm. But those who reject Allah, for them is destruction, and Allah will render their deeds vain. That is because they hate the Revelation of Allah; so, He has made their deeds fruitless. Do they not travel through the earth, and see what was the end of those before them who did evil? Allah brought utter destruction on them, and similar fates await those who reject Allah.

   That is because Allah is the Protector of those who believe, but those who reject Allah have no protector. (47:7:11, Koran)

58. O you who believe!

   Obey Allah, obey the Rasool, and make not vain your deeds!

   Those who reject Allah (kafiru), and hinder men from the Path of Allah, then die rejecting Allah; Allah will not forgive them.

   Be not weak and ask for peace, while you are having an upper hand: for Allah is with you, and will never decrease the reward of your good deeds. The life of this world is but play and amusement: and if you believe, fear Allah, and guard against evil, He will grant you your recompense, and will not ask you (to give up) your possessions.

   If He were to ask you for all of them, and press you, you would covetously withhold, and He would bring out your entire ill wills. ****Behold, you are those invited to spend of your wealth in the Way of Allah: but among you are some that are parsimonious. But any who are miserly are so at the expense of their own souls. But Allah is free of all wants, and it is you that are needy. If you turn back (from the Path), He will substitute in your stead another people; then they would not be like you! (47:33–38, Koran)

Commandments in the Covenant of Allah in Sura Al-Hujurat (49 Medina 109)

59. You who believe!
Be not presumptuous and impudent before Allah and His Rasool, but fear Allah: for Allah is He Who hears and knows all things. (49:2, Koran)

60. O you who believe!
Raise not your voices above the voice of the Prophet, nor speak aloud to him in talk, as you may speak aloud to one another, lest your deeds become vain and you perceive it not. (49:2, Koran)

61. O you who believe!
If an impostor (fasiq) comes to you with any news, ascertain the truth, lest you harm people unsuspectingly and afterwards become full of remorse for what you have done.
And know that among you is Allah's Rasool: were he, in many matters, to follow your desires, you would certainly fall into misfortune: but Allah has bestowed on you the love of iman.
(Faith), and has made it beautiful in your hearts, and He has made abhorrent to you disbelief, wickedness, and disobedience to Allah: such indeed are those who are the righteous (rashidun). This is a grace from Allah, and a favor; and Allah is All Knowing and All Wise. If two parties among the Believers fall into a quarrel, make peace between them: but if one of them transgresses beyond bounds against the other, then fight you all against the one who transgresses until he complies with the Command of Allah; but if he complies, then make peace between them with justice, and fairness: for Allah loves those who are fair and just.888The Believers are but a single Brotherhood: so make peace and reconciliation between your two brothers; and fear Allah, that you may receive Mercy. (49:6–10, Koran)

62. O you who believe!
Let not some folk among you ridicule others: it may be that they are better than you are: nor let some women mock others: it may be that the others are better than them: nor defame or revile each other by offensive names: ill-seeming is wicked name calling for the one who has believed; and those who do not desist are indeed wrong-doers (zalimun). (49:11, Koran)

63. *O you who believe!*
Avoid suspicion, for suspicion in some cases is sin; and spy not on each other, nor speak ill of each other behind their backs. Would any of you eat the flesh of his dead brother? No, you would abhor it. Be in taqwa of Allah, fear Allah: for Allah is Forgiving, Most Merciful.
O humankind!
We created you from a single pair of a male and a female, and made you into nations and tribes, that you may know each other. Verily the most honored of you in the sight of Allah is the one with taqwa of Allah, the most righteous of you. And Allah is All Knowing, All Aware. (49:12–13, Koran)

Commandment of the Covenant of Allah in Sura Al-Hadid (57 Medina 97)

64. *O you who believe!*
Be in taqwa of Allah, Fear Allah, and believe in His Rasool, and He will bestow on you the double portion of His Mercy: He will provide for you a Light by which you shall walk straight in your path, and He will forgive you; for Allah is Most Forgiving, Most Merciful: That the People of the Book may know that they have no power whatever over the Grace of Allah that His Grace is entirely in His Hand, to bestow it on whomsoever He wills. For Allah is the Lord of Grace abounding. (57:28–29, Koran)

Commandments of the Covenant of Allah in Sura Al-Mujadila (58 Medina 98)

65. *O you who believe!*
When you hold secret counsel, do it not for iniquity and hostility, and disobedience to the Rasool; but do it for righteousness and self-restraint; and be in taqwa of Allah, to Whom you shall be brought back.
Secret counsels are only inspired by the Satan, in order that he may cause grief to the Believers; but he cannot harm them in the least, except as Allah permits; and on Allah let, the Believers put their trust. (58:9–10, Koran)

66. O you who believe!

    When you are told to make room in the assemblies, spread out and make room: ample room will Allah provide for you. And when you are told to rise up, for prayers, Jihad or other good deeds rise up: Allah will exalt in rank those of you who believe and who have been granted Knowledge. And Allah is well acquainted with all you do. (58:11, Koran)

Commandment of the Covenant of Allah in Sura Al-Hashr (59 Medina 99)

67. O you who believe!

    Be in taqwa of Allah and fear Allah, and let every soul judge as to the provision he has sent forth for the morrow. Yes, be in taqwa of Allah and fear Allah: for Allah is well acquainted with all that you do.*

    And be not like those who forgot Allah, and He made them forget their own souls! Such are the rebellious transgressors (fasiqun)!

    Not equal are the Companions of the Fire and the Companions of the Garden: it is the Companions of the Garden that will achieve felicity. Had We sent down this Qur'an on a sold rock, verily, you would have seen it tremble and cleave asunder in deference to Allah. Such are the similitudes which We give out to men that they may reflect.***He is Allah, there is no Deity but He; Knower of the hidden and manifest. He is the Rahman (the Most Gracious), the Rahim, (Most Merciful.) He is Allah, There is no Deity but He,

    The Sovereign, The Pure and The Hallowed,

    Serene and Perfect,

    The Custodian of Faith, the Protector, the Almighty,

    The Irresistible, the Supreme,

    Glory be to Allah, He is above all they associate with Him.

    He is Allah, the Creator, the Sculptor, the Adorner of color and form. To Him belong the Most Beautiful Names: whatever so is in the heavens and on earth, Praise and Glory Him; and He is the Almighty and All Wise. (59:18–24, Koran)

Commandments of the Covenant of Allah in Sura Al-Mumtahanah (60 Medina 100)

68. O you who believe!
Take not My enemies and yours as awliya (friends and protectors), offering them love and regard, even though they have rejected the Truth bestowed on you. And they have driven out the Rasool and yourselves from your homes, because you believe in Allah as your Rabb (Lord)! You have come out to strive in My Cause and to seek My favor, take them not as friends, holding in secret regard and friendship for them: for I know all that you conceal and all that you reveal. And any of you that do this has strayed from the Straight Path.
If they were to gain an upper hand over you, they would treat you as enemies, and stretch forth their hands and their tongues against you with evil; and they desire that you should reject the Truth. (60:1–2, Koran)

69. O you who believe!
Befriend not people who have incurred Allah's wrath. They are already in despair of the Hereafter, just as the Unbelievers are in despair about those in graves. (60:13, Koran)

Commandments of the Covenant of Allah in Sura As-Saf (61 Medina 101)

70. O you who believe!
Why do you promise what you do not carry out? Hateful is indeed to Allah that you say what you do not act upon. Allah loves those who fight in His cause in array of unison and solidarity. (61:2–4, Koran)

71. O you who believe!
Shall I guide you to a bargain that will save you from a painful torment? That you believe in Allah and His Rasool, and that you perform Jihad (strive to your utmost) in the way of Allah, with all that you own and in all earnestness: that will be best for you, if you but knew! He will forgive you your sins, and admit you to Gardens beneath which rivers flow, and to beautiful dwellings in Jannat of I (Gardens of Eternity): that is indeed the supreme blessing. And another favor will He bestow, which you will

cherish; help from Allah and a speedy victory. So, give the glad tidings to the believers. (61:10–13, Koran)

72. O you who believe!
    Be you helpers of Allah: as said Jesus, the son of Mary, to the Disciples, "Who will be my helpers in the work of Allah?" Said the Disciples, "We are Allah's helpers!" Then a portion of the Children of Israel believed, and a portion disbelieved: but We gave power to those who believed against their enemies, and they became the ones that prevailed. (61:14, Koran)

Commandment of the Covenant of Allah in Sura Al-Jumu'ah (62 Medina 102)

73. O you who believe!
    When the call is proclaimed to prayer on Friday, the day of assembly, hasten earnestly to the Remembrance of Allah, and leave off business and everything else: that is best for you if you but knew! And when the Prayer is finished, then may you disperse through the land, and seek of the Grace of Allah: remember and praise Allah a great deal: that you may prosper. (62:9–10, Koran)

Commandment of the Covenant of Allah in Sura Al-Munafiqun (63 Medina 103)

74. O you who believe!
    Let not your wealth or your children divert you from the remembrance of Allah. If any act thus, the loss is their own. And give freely, out of which We have bestowed on you, before death should come to each of you and he should say, "O my Lord! Why didst Thou not give me respite for a little while? I should then have given generously and be among the righteous. But to none does Allah give respite when his time has come; and Allah is well acquainted with all that you do. (63:9–11, Koran)

Commandment of the Covenant of Allah in Sura At-Taghabun (64 Medina 104)

75. O you who believe!

Truly, among your wives and your children are some that are contenders of your obligations: so beware! But if you forgive them and overlook their faults, verily Allah is Most –Forgiving, Most Merciful. Your riches and your children may be but a temptation: Whereas Allah! With Him is an immense reward. So be in taqwa of Allah and fear Allah as much as you can; listen and obey; and spend in charity for the benefit of your own souls. And those saved from their own greed are the ones that prosper. If you loan to Allah a beautiful loan, He will double it for you, and He will forgive you: for Allah is both Appreciative (Shakoor) and Magnanimous (Haleem), Knower of what is hidden and what is manifest, Exalted in Might, Full of Wisdom. (64:14–18, Koran)

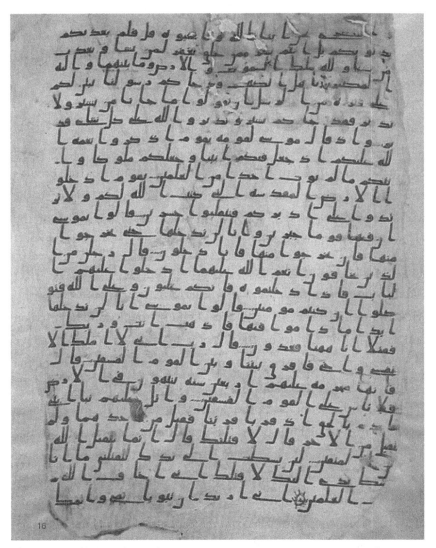

Ma'ili manuscript from first century AH. This is an example of what is thought to be one of the earliest styles of Koran copying. Dated to the first Islamic century. Located in the Tareq Rajab Museum in Kuwait.

Chapter Two

The Covenant of Allah in the Present Times: The Thirty-Seven Commandments

The verses or *ayahs* in this chapter contain thirty-seven commandments of Allah[3]. The essence of the Koran is in the seventy-five verses in which Allah addresses the believers directly with the words *O you who believe!* They form the core of his belief of the believer and the nucleus of his *din*.

The synthesis of the three dimensions of *din* (religion)—*islam* (submission), *iman* (faith), and *ihsan* (performance of good deeds)—is what links the true believer to the Divine through total submission and faith in the reality of the Creator in addition to performance of virtuous and wholesome actions of devotion and worship of the Sublime and through beautiful deeds in the service of Allah and His creation. With this practice, the polarity between faith and actions is reversed; instead of faith being the prerequisite for practice, practice defines faith. This reverse polarity is a reminder that Islam is defined not only as a set of beliefs but also as a body of actions that reveal the inner convictions of the believer. This practice-oriented picture of Islam is dependent on the commandments of Allah in the verses of the Koran, and the traditions provide explanatory statements that act as a complement to the Koran. In this relationship, the Koran's word-centered approach to Islam in which the divine word arouses knowledge of Allah in the human consciousness, in contrast the Hadith (tradition) expresses a law-centered perspective on Islam,

---

[3] For references to the *ayahs* and the suras, please see the thirty-seven commandments in chapter 1. In chapter 2, the *ayahs* from different suras have been combined according to subject matter.

in which the knowledge of spiritual realities is less important than performance of appropriate actions.

1. Belief in Allah

He is Allah, there is no Deity but He; Knower of the hidden and the manifest. He is the Rahman the Most Gracious, the Rahim, Most Merciful.

The Sovereign, The Pure and The Hallowed, Serene and Perfect,

The Custodian of Faith, the Protector, the Almighty, the Irresistible, the Supreme,

He is Allah, the Creator, the Sculptor, the Adorner of color and form. To Him belong the Most Beautiful Names, whatever so is in the heavens and on earth, Praise and Glorify Him; and He is the Almighty and All Wise.

There is no god but He, the Ever Living, the One Who sustains and protects all that exists.

His are all things in the heavens and on earth. Who is there to intercede in His presence except as He permits?

He knows what happens to His creatures in this world and in the hereafter. Nor do His creatures know the scope of His knowledge except as He wills.

His Throne extends over the heavens and the earth, and He feels no fatigue in guarding and protecting them.

He is the Most High, Most Great.

Believe in Allah, His Messenger, and the Book that He has sent to His Messenger and the Scriptures that He sent to those before him. Any who deny Allah, His angels, His Books, His Messengers, and the Day of Judgment has gone astray. (An-Nisa 4:136, Koran)

Verily, this is My Way leading straight: follow it: follow not (other)
paths for they will separate you from His path. This He commands
you that you may remember. (Al-An'am 6:151–53, Koran)

Islam: The Arabic word *islam* means "to resign oneself to or to submit
oneself." In religious terminology, it means submission or surrender
of oneself to Allah or to Allah's will. Allah is the only true reality,
and everything else in the universe is dependent on Him for its reality
and existence. Since Allah created the universe, all things in the
universe are, as a result, totally dependent on Allah and thus are totally
"submissive" to Him. Allah, being the Creator of all things, is the
Rabb, the Sustainer of the whole creation. Thus God the Creator is the
universal God.

The Koranic notion of religious belief (*iman*) as dependent on
knowledge is actualized in practice in the term *islam*. This term
signifies the idea of surrender or submission. The type of surrender
Islam requires is a deliberate, conscious, and rational act made by a
person who knows with both intellectual certainty and spiritual vision
that Allah, who is the subject of Koranic discourse, is the reality.

A *Muslim* (fem. *Muslimah*) is "one who submits" to the divine
truth and whose relationship with God is governed by *taqwa*, the
consciousness of humankind's responsibility toward its Creator.
However, consciousness of God alone is not sufficient to make a
person a Muslim. Neither is it enough to be merely born a Muslim
or to be raised in an Islamic cultural context. The concept of *taqwa*
implies that the believer has the added responsibility of acting in a way
that is in accordance with three types of knowledge: *ilm al-yaqin, ain
al-yaqin,* and *haqq al-yaqin* (knowledge of certainty, eye of certainty,
and the truth of certainty). The believer must endeavor at all times to
maintain himself in a constant state of submission to Allah. Trusting
in the divine mercy of his divine Master yet fearing Allah's wrath,

the slave of Allah walks the road of life with careful steps, making his actions deliberate so that he will not stray from the straight path that Allah has laid out for him. It is an all-encompassing and highly personal type of commitment that has little in common with academic understanding of Islam as a civilization or a cultural system.[4]

The universality of religious experience is an important premise of the Koran's argument against a profane or secular life. This universalism has never been more important than it is in the present time when the majority of the believers do not speak Arabic. Such transcendence of culture is necessary for the Koran, as the vehicle of the word of God, to overcome linguistic and cultural differences and express itself in a metalanguage that can be understood even when its original Arabic is translated into a non-Semitic language such as English, Mandarin, or Hindi. Most people, whatever their experiences and cultural background, think in similar ways and have similar wants and needs. The Koran seeks to establish a common foundation for belief that is based on such shared perceptions and experiences. Over and over again, the Koran reminds the reader to think about the truths that lie behind the familiar or mundane things of the world, such as signs of God in nature, the practical value of virtue, and the cross-cultural validity of moral principles. The Koran, therefore, appeals to both reason and experience in determining the criterion for distinguishing between truth and falsehood.

The most important theological point made by the Koran is that there is one God, Allah, universal and beyond comparison, the Creator, who creates and sustains both the material world and the world of human experience. All other forms of so-called truth are either false in their initial premises or contingently true only in limited situations. The

---

[4] Vincent Cornell, "Fruit of Tree of Knowledge," in *Oxford History of Islam*, ed. John L. Esposito (Oxford University Press).

recognition of this fact produces a profound effect on the human soul that it forever transforms the outlook of the believer.

Iman: Faith of Islam is based on certain knowledge that is both a liberation and a limitation. It is a liberation in the sense that certainty of divine reality allows the human spirit to expand inward, outward, and upward so that consciousness becomes three dimensional. Nevertheless, it is also a limitation because with the knowledge of Allah comes a concomitant awareness of the limits and responsibility imposed on a person as a created being. Unlike a secular humanist, a true Muslim believer who submits to Allah cannot delude himself by claiming that he is the sole author of his destiny as he knows that a person's fate is routinely controlled by factors beyond his control.

Ihsan: This means doing good, virtuous, and wholesome deeds. The third dimension of *din* is *ihsan*. The word *ihsan* is derived from the word *husn*, which designates the quality of being good, beautiful, virtuous, pleasing, harmonious, or wholesome. The Koran employs the word *hasana*, from the same root as *husn*, to mean a good or a beautiful deed. For example:

> Whatever beautiful touches you, it is from Allah, and whatever ugly touches you, it is from yourself. And We have sent thee as a Rasool to instruct humanity. And enough is Allah for a witness. (An-Nisa 4:79, Koran)

> If any does beautiful deeds, the reward to him is better than his deed; but if any one does evil, the doers of evil are only punished (to the extent) of their deeds. (Al-Qasas 28:84, Koran)

> And for him who has faith and does wholesome works, his recompense shall be most beautiful. (Al-Kahf 18:88, Koran)

The word *ihsan* is a verb that means "to establish or to perform what is good and beautiful." The Koran employs the word *ihsan* and its active particle *muhsin* (the one who does what is beautiful and good) in seventy verses. The Koran often designates Allah as the One who does what is beautiful, and *al-Muhsin* is one of Allah's divine names. Allah's beautiful work is the creation of the universe of galaxies, stars, sun, and moon, all in their ordained orbits, destined in their paths by Allah's mysterious forces. All are shining and luminescent with Allah's blessed light (*nur*), providing life and vigor to billions of Allah's creatures so that they may acknowledge and praise their Creator, who made this beautiful and wholesome universe.

The Koran ascribes the love of Allah in about fifteen verses. One of the emotions most closely associated with *ihsan* is *hubb*. To have *ihsan* is to do what is beautiful. According to the Koran in five verses, Allah loves those who have *ihsan* because, by doing what is beautiful, they themselves have developed beautiful character traits and are worthy of Allah's love. In every Koranic verse where Allah is said to love something, the object of this love is human beings, not the human species, whose traits and activities are beautiful.

The phrase *amilu al saalihaaat* (to do good, to perform wholesome deeds) refers to those who persist in striving to set things right, who restore harmony, peace, and balance. Other acts of good works recognized in the covenant of the Koran are to show humility, to be generous and charitable, to be truthful, to seek knowledge and wisdom, to be kind, to be peaceful, to love others, and to perform beautiful deeds.

Those who submit to Allah must believe in Allah, His blessed Messenger, and the Book that Allah has sent to His Messenger, the Qur'an and the Scriptures that He sent to those Prophets before him.
Any one who denies Allah, His angels, His Books, His Messengers, and the Day of Judgment has gone astray. Verily, this is Allah's Way leading straight, follow it, and do not follow other paths for they will separate you from Allah's path. Do not join any other being in worship with Allah.
This He commands that you may remember.

Celebrate the Praises of Allah often, and Glorify Him in the morning and in the night.
It is Allah and His Angels who send their blessings upon you, that Allah may lead you out of the depths of darkness into light. Allah is full of mercy to the believers! On the Day they meet Him with the greeting Salaam, He has for them a generous reward.
Be quick in race to forgiveness from your Lord for He has prepared for the righteous a garden whose measurement is that of the heavens and of the earth.
Allah loves those who do beautiful deeds, those who give freely in charity whether in prosperity or in adversity, and those who restrain anger and pardon all humans. (Koran, various ayahs)

Allah made a covenant with all the peoples of the book—the children of Israel, those who call themselves Christians, and then the Muslims as an essential observation of their religion. Those who chose to ignore their obligations to Allah therefore suffered from dire consequences.

Allah took a covenant from the Children of Israel and We appointed twelve leaders from among them. And Allah said "I am with you if you establish salaat, practice regular charity, believe in my messengers, honor and assist them and loan to Allah a beautiful loan, Verily I will wipe out from you your evils and admit you to Gardens with rivers flowing beneath. But if any of you after this disbelieved he has truly wandered from the path of rectitude.

Therefore, because of breach of their covenant, We were annoyed with them and made their hearts grow hard. They perverted words from their meaning an abandoned a greater part of the message that was sent them. Thou will not cease to discover treachery from them barring a few. Nevertheless, bear with them and pardon them. Verily Allah loves those who are wholesome.

Moreover, We took the Covenant from those who call themselves Christians, but they have abandoned a good part of the Message that was sent to them. Therefore, We have stirred up enmity and hatred amongst them until the Day of Resurrection, when Allah will inform them of their handiwork.

O People of the Book! There has come to you Our Messenger, revealing to you much that ye used to hide in the Scripture and passing over much. Indeed, there has come to you from Allah a light and a plain Book, in which Allah guides all those who seek His good pleasure to the path of peace. He brings them out of darkness into light by His will and guides them to a straight path." (Al-Ma'idah 5:12–16, Koran)

The verses in the above sura show the importance of the Koran:

A light and plain Book from Allah where Allah guides all those who seek His good pleasure to the path of peace. He brings them out of darkness into light by His will and guides them to a straight path.

The Koran is a guide and Allah's covenant a code of conduct for all humans to trust and believe in the Creator, the one universal God, Allah. Allah will lead all those people who believe in Him to His straight path and to the path of peace. The children of Israel disobeyed Allah, and they lost His favor. As for those who call themselves Christians, Allah took their covenant, but they abandoned the central part of the message Allah sent them, to trust and believe in the Creator, the one God of the universe. Therefore, Allah had stirred up hatred and enmity among them because of their transgressions. Having split into sects and nations, they have constantly battled among themselves for the last two thousand years over doctrine, gold, wealth, and possessions. Allah has left every human ways open to His straight path through His covenant. Allah demands of the believers to fulfill His covenant by observing its thirty-seven commandments.

Therefore, a believer is the one who has submitted of his own free will to the will and command of the one universal God (*islam*), maintains his faith (*iman*) in God by being constantly aware of Allah's presence with him (taqwa), obeys the covenant of Allah in the Koran, and performs wholesome and beautiful deeds (*ihsan*) in the service of God and His creation.

Believe in Allah:

He is Allah, there is no Deity but Him; Knower of the hidden and the manifest. He is the Rahman, the Most Gracious, the Rahim and Most Merciful.

He is Allah, there is no Deity but He; Knower of the hidden and the manifest. He is the Rahman the Most Gracious, the Rahim, Most Merciful.

He is Allah; there is no Deity but Him,

The Sovereign, the Pure and the Hallowed,

Serene and Perfect,

The Custodian of Faith, the Protector, the Almighty,

The Irresistible, the Supreme,

Glory be to Allah, He is above all they associate with Him

He is Allah, the Creator, the Sculptor, the Adorner of color and form. To Him belong the most beautiful names.

All that is in the heavens and on earth, praise and glorify Him; and He is the Almighty and All-Wise. (Al-Hashr 59:18–24, Koran)

Allah is the only true reality, and everything else in the universe is dependent on Him for its reality and existence. Since Allah created the universe, all things in the universe are therefore totally dependent on Allah and hence totally submitted to Him. The Koran uses the term *submission* (*islam*) and its derivatives more than seventy times; its definition, in the broadest sense, is that true religion is established by Allah alone and that everything in the universe praises and glorifies Him. All creatures simply by existing demonstrate the Creator's glory and perform acts that acknowledge Allah's mastery over them.

Verily I am Allah. There is no god but I, so worship Me and perform salaat in remembrance of Me. (Taha 20:14, Koran)

Shirk: Those who worship other deities and associate them with Allah have fallen into *shirk*. Other gods associated with Allah by some "Muslims" and non-Muslims are their *caprice, wealth and material possessions, and power and influence over others*. Absolute power corrupts. Religious figures, royals, and dictators in Islamic countries have lost track of their mortality and settled themselves on an elevated status—"I am divine, I am real, and others cannot have the same rights as I do"—leading them to serve their own egos in place of Allah. This leads to *shirk*, loss of tawhid. Sycophancy and blind subservience of self-serving courtiers leads these dictators into actions inimical to the community of Islam. People who claim to be kings and others who become dictators with the might of arms and take life and wealth on a whim commit acts of *shirk* by misappropriating Allah's prerogative.

Acts of worship, supplication, and remembrance (*dhikr*) have a specific ritual and devotional nature in which the worshipper orients himself to Allah and obeys His commands and prohibitions. To worship is to orient one's life and existence to Allah (*Haqq*), to beseech Allah (*Rahman* and *Rahim*) for guidance and help, and to show gratitude for the blessings already received. Such humility precludes a man's superiority over others.

Allah's guidance to mankind is through divine revelation through His prophets, who were charged with the task of communicating the word of Allah. Allah's blessed *rasul* Muhammad took precautions to prevent Allah's guidance to humanity from becoming tainted with his own or with anyone else's expressions. Scholars in Iran two and a half centuries after the *nabi's* death resurrected sayings and parables attributed to the blessed *nabi* and circulated them in the Muslim world. These collections of sayings and parables attributed to the blessed *nabi* Muhammad were in the words of the narrators. Over the next one thousand years, these Hadith began to take the divine role of Allah and His *rasul* in the minds of the common man through the teachings of Muslim ulema. Only Allah is worthy of worship. Those who worship other deities and associate them with Allah have fallen into *shirk*. Those who give a divine status to the Hadith of the third century and equate them with Allah's word have also lost their way. This is *shirk*, which leads to loss of tawhid and *furqan* (Allah's guidance).

Tawhid, the oneness and reality of Allah, demands that human beings recognize the greatness of Allah and the minuteness of the human—the reality of the Real and the unreality of the unreal, which places people in their correct relationship with Allah and allows them to understand that they are His servants and that they must act in submission (*islam*). They must therefore recognize human failings and follow divine guidance brought by the prophets and their scriptures.

Verily, this is My Way leading straight: follow it: follow not (other) paths for they will separate you from His path. This He commands you that you may remember. (Al An'am:151–53, Koran)

Join not any thing in worship with Him. (Al-An'am 6:151–53, Koran)

Believe in Allah, His Messenger and the Book that He has sent to His Rasool and the Scriptures that He sent to those before him. Any who deny Allah, His angels, His Books, His Messengers and the Day of Judgment has gone astray. (An-Nisa 4:136, Koran)

Celebrate the Praises of Allah often and Glorify Him in the morning and at night. It is Allah and His Angels Who send their blessings upon you, that He may lead you out of the depths of darkness into light. Allah is full of mercy to the believers! On the Day they meet Him with the salutation: Salaam, He has prepared for them a generous Reward. (Al-Ahzab 33:41–48, Koran)

2. The *Nabi,* the *Rasul*

> O Nabi, We have sent thee as a witness, a bearer of glad tidings, as a Warner and as one who invites to Allah's Grace by His leave and as an inspiration and beacon of light.
>
> O Nabi, We have sent thee as a witness, a bearer of glad tidings, as a Warner and as one who invites to Allah's Grace by His leave and as an inspiration and beacon of light. Give glad tidings to the believers that they shall have from Allah bounty in abundance. Moreover, obey not the command of the unbelievers (kafireen) and the hypocrites (munafiqeen), heed not their annoyances and put your trust in Allah, for enough is Allah as Disposer of affairs. (Al-Ahzab 33:41–48, Koran)
>
> Believe in Allah, His Messenger and the Book that He has sent to His Rasool and the Scriptures that He sent to those before him. Any who deny Allah, His angels, His Books, His Messengers and the Day of Judgment has gone astray. (An-Nisa 4:136, Koran)

Allah—in His mercy, grace, and love of His creation—has from the beginning of time communicated with humans and taught them all that they know of His workings, His universe, and His creation. Humans have always been resistant to accepting Allah's guidance regarding worship of Allah and man's relationship with other humans in matters of truth, justice, peace, equality, and sharing of their resources. Man's ego, selfishness, and greed always have come in the way of his salvation. Allah inspired truthful men—prophets—with *taqwa* of Allah, humility, spiritual purity, and knowledge to convey His teachings and commandments to man so that he may continue to exist in the world during his short span of life in submission of Allah and in love, peace, and harmony with his fellow humans. To follow Allah's wisdom, man must first agree to submit himself to the total, unquestioning mercy and will of Allah with the knowledge that, on an appointed day, he will meet his Maker to be questioned and judged on his conduct during his life on the earth.

Those who have faith and do wholesome deeds, them we shall admit to gardens through which rivers flow. (An-Nisa 4:57, 122, Koran)

Allah will measure out good and evil, the wholesome and the corrupt things that the humans carried out in their lifetime. Humans have enough freedom to make their own choices; if they make the choice to do beautiful and wholesome deeds (*saalihaat*) motivated by faith (*iman*) and god-wariness (*taqwa*), they please Allah and bring harmony and wholesomeness to the world, resulting in peace, justice, mercy, compassion, honor, equity, well-being, freedom, and many other gifts through Allah's grace. Others choose to do evil and work with corruption (*mufsidun*), destroying the right relationship among the creation, causing hunger, disease, oppression, pollution, and other afflictions. In the universal order, corruption is the prerogative of humans, and vicegerency gives humans the freedom to work against the Creator and His creation. When humans choose wrong and corrupt actions, they displease Allah. Allah loves those who do what is beautiful, not those who do what is ugly:

When he turns his back, he hurries about the earth to work corruption there and destroy the tillage and the stock. Allah loves not corruption.
(Al-Baqarah 2:205, Koran)

Obey Allah and His Messenger and turn not to others when you should you should hear him speak. For the worst of creatures in the sight of Allah are those who neither listen, nor look or try to comprehend. (Al-Anfal 8:20, Koran)

And how could you deny Faith when you learn the Signs of Allah and amongst you lives the Messenger? Whoever holds firmly to Allah will be shown a Way that is straight. (Ali 'Imran 3:100–101, Koran)

3. The Covenant of Allah

And fulfill the Covenant of Allah. Thus He commands you that you may remember. (Al-An 'am 6:151–53, Koran)

Believers! Fulfill your Covenant. (Al-Ma'idah 5:1, Koran)

Verily those who pledge their allegiance unto you (O Muhammad), pledge it unto none but Allah; the Hand of Allah is over their hands. Thereafter whosoever breaks his Covenant, does so to the harm of his own soul and whosoever fulfils his Covenant with Allah, Allah will grant him an immense Reward. (Al-Fath 48:10, Koran)

Islam is a way of life in the straight path to Allah. There is an implicit assumption in the Koran that there exists an agreement between Allah and His creation portrayed as a mutual understanding in which Allah proposes a system of regulations for the guidance of the humans. This guidance is presented in the form of commandments to be accepted and implemented by people. Allah then makes promise of what He will do in the event that man willingly abides by these commands and regulates his life in accordance with them. The concept of promise is clearly conditional on the human's obedience. The covenant of the Koran symbolizes the relationship between Allah and man; man becomes His steward, vicegerent, or custodian on the earth through submission and obedience to His will (*islam*) as expressed in His commands and is able to take the advantage of Allah's promises and favors.

The concept of covenant also symbolizes the relationship between humans and among Allah's creatures and the rest of His creation. They all share in one God, one set of guidance and commandments, the same submission and obedience to Him, and the same set of expectations in accordance with His promises. They all can, therefore, trust one another since they all have similar obligations and expectations. In view of the Koran, humans, communities, nations, and civilizations will continue to live in harmony and peace so long as they continue to fulfill Allah's covenant.

Economics plays a significant role in the social structure of Islam, so significant that Allah has not let the economic aspect of life to be solely determined by human intellect, experience, caprice, and lust. Allah has made it subject to revelation. Thus, Muslims prosper when they follow Allah's laws but subject themselves to scarcity when they turn to human systems. The Koran promises peace and plenty for those who obey their covenant with Him, and for those who turn away from Allah's covenant, the Koran portends a life of need, scarcity, and want.

"But whosoever turns away from My Message, verily for him is a life narrowed down and We shall raise him up blind on the Day of Judgment."

And thus do We recompense him who transgresses beyond bounds and believes not in the Signs of his Lord: and the Penalty of the Hereafter is far more grievous and more enduring.

It is not a warning to such men (to call to mind) how many generations before them We destroyed, in whose haunts they (now) move? Verily, in this are Signs for men endued with understanding. (Taha 20:124, 127–28, Koran)

In the above *ayah* of the Koran, the word *ma'eeshat* comes from the word *ma'ashiyyat*, which is the recognized meaning of the word "economics." The consequences of rejection of Allah's covenant and guidance are clearly portrayed. A life narrowed down or constricted is a miserable one, one of need, scarcity, unhappiness, poverty, hunger, disease, pestilence, and famine all at the same time or separately.

The Koran's covenant does not put off the realization of the fruits of obeying or ignoring Allah's guidance until after death, nor does it hide it in spiritual abstractness. Observance of the covenant makes life on the earth economically, physically, and spiritually rich and happy. Nonobservance of the covenant makes life on the earth economically miserable and physically and spiritually depressing. In fact, the economic, physical, and spiritual condition of a people provides a pragmatic test of the soundness of the revealed guidance.

Furthermore, the Koran declares that the people who transgress Allah's guidance and are economically deprived in this world will also be worse off in the hereafter.

> Verily for him is a life narrowed down and We shall
> raise him up blind on the Day of Judgment.

According to the Koran, the economics and the observance of the moral code of Allah's covenant goes hand in hand, and they cannot be separated from each other.

He has created the heavens and the earth for just ends: far is He above having the partners they ascribe to Him!

He has created man from a sperm-drop; and behold this same (man) becomes an open disputer!

And cattle He has created for you (men): from them you derive warmth and numerous benefits and of their (meat) you eat.

And you have a sense of pride and beauty in them as you drive them home in the evening and as you lead them forth to pasture in the morning.

And they carry your heavy loads to lands that you could not (otherwise) reach except with souls distressed: for your Lord is indeed Most Kind, Most Merciful.

And (He has created) horses, mules and donkeys, for you to ride and use for show; and He has created (other) things of which you have no knowledge.

And unto Allah leads straight the Way, but there are ways that turn aside: if Allah had willed, He could have guided all of you.

It is He Who sends down rain from the sky. From it you drink and out of it (grows) the vegetation on which you feed your cattle.

With it He produces for you corn, olives, date palms, grapes and every kind of fruit: verily in this is a Sign for those who give thought.

He has made subject to you the Night and the Day; the Sun and the Moon; and the Stars are in subjection by His Command: verily in this are Signs for men who are wise.

And the things on this earth which He has multiplied in varying colors (and qualities): verily in this a Sign for men who celebrate the praises of Allah (in gratitude).

It is He Who has made the sea subject, that you may eat thereof flesh that is fresh and tender and that you may extract there from ornaments to wear and You see the ships therein that plough the waves, that you may seek (thus) of the bounty of Allah and that you may be grateful.

And He has set up on the Earth mountains standing firm, lest it should shake with you; and rivers and roads; that you may guide yourselves;

And marks and sign-posts; and by the stars (Men) guide themselves.

Is then He Who creates like one that creates not? Will you not receive admonition?

If you would count up the favors of Allah, never would you be able to number them; for Allah is Oft-Forgiving, Most Merciful. (An-Nahl 16:3-18, Koran)

Sama in the Koran signifies the universe, and *ardh* is man's domain on the earth pertaining to his social and economic world. Allah is the Lord of the heavens and the earth and all that comes forth from them. The divine laws under which the universe functions so meticulously and smoothly should also apply to the economic life of man so that he might achieve a balanced, predictable, equitable, and just financial life. *Sama* is the source of Allah's benevolence to mankind and of His universal laws that govern human subsistence and sustenance on the earth (*ardh*), controlling man's economic life in this world. Allah's kingdom over the heavens and the earth sustains man's economic life and directly affects man's conduct and his obedience to Allah's covenant.

4. *Taqwa* of Allah

The word *taqwa* means "to be dutiful to Allah, to be wary of Allah, to be conscious of Allah, to be pious toward Allah, and to fear Allah." A person with *taqwa* always has Allah in mind with every action and word spoken, "as if Allah sees you and you see Him."

Be in taqwa of Allah and fear Allah and let every soul judge as to the provision he has sent forth for the morrow. Yes, be in taqwa of Allah and fear Allah: for Allah is well acquainted with all that you do. (Al-Hashr 59:18–24, Koran)

So be in taqwa of Allah and fear Allah as much as you can; listen and obey; and spend in charity for the benefit of your own souls. And those saved from their own greed are the ones that prosper. If ye loan to Allah a beautiful loan, He will double it for you and He will forgive you: for Allah is both Appreciative (Shakoor) and Magnanimous (Haleem), Knower of what is hidden and what is manifest, Exalted in Might, Full of Wisdom. (At-Taghabun 64:14–18, Koran)

Humankind! We created you from a single pair of a male and a female and made you into nations and tribes, that ye may know each other. Verily the most honored of you in the sight of Allah is the one with taqwa of Allah, the most righteous of you. And Allah is All Knowing, All-Aware. (Al-Hadid 57:28–29, Koran)

Be in taqwa of Allah, Fear Allah and believe in His Messenger and He will bestow on you the double portion of His Mercy: He will provide for you a Light by which ye shall walk straight in your path and He will forgive you ; for Allah is Most Forgiving, Most Merciful. That the People of the Book may know that they have no power whatever over the Grace of Allah, that His Grace is entirely in His Hand to bestow on whomsoever He wills. For Allah is the Lord of Grace abounding. (Al-Hadid 57:28–29, Koran)

Be in Taqwa of Allah and be with those who are true in word and deed.
(At-Tawbah 9:11, Koran)

Be not presumptuous and impudent before Allah and His Messenger; be in taqwa
of Allah, fear Allah: for Allah is He Who hears and knows all things.
(Al-Hujurat 49:2, Koran)

The believer protects himself by always keeping Allah in view with every action and thought, ensuring that his every action is in accord with Allah's way. Perform every act and utter every word as if you see Allah, and if you do not see Him, be aware that Allah not only sees your deeds but also knows your thoughts. To ensure that one is dutiful to Allah, conscious of His presence, and God fearing, the believer recites with every action:

In the name of Allah, Most Gracious, Most Merciful.

There is a distinction between two types of divine mercy. In the broader sense, mercy refers to Allah's gentleness and kindness to all His creation, for He brings into existence, nurtures, and protects it to its destination. In a narrower sense, Allah's mercy refers to closeness to Allah that is given to those with *taqwa* in contrast to the chastisement inflicted on those who have chosen to stay distant from Him. Their distance from Allah in itself is chastisement because to be distant from the wholeness and harmony of the Real (Truth) is to be overcome by the turmoil and chaos of the unreal (falsehood). Allah's mercy is achieved by *taqwa* of Allah, which itself demands both submission (*islam*) and faith (*iman*).

My Chastisement I mete out to whomsoever I will; but My Mercy extends to all things. That Mercy I shall ordain for those who are muttaqun, those who have taqwa and practice regular charity and those who believe in Our Signs.

Those who follow the Rasool, the Nabi of the unlettered, about whom they find mentioned in the Taurat (Torah) and the Injeel (Gospel). He bids them what is just and forbids them what is evil; he allows them as lawful what is good and pure and prohibits them from what is bad and impure; he relieves them of their heavy burdens and from the fetters that are on them. So it is those who believe in him, honor him, help him and follow the Light which is sent down with him, it is they who will prosper. (Al-A'raf 7:156–57, Koran)

5. Worship of Allah: Bow down, Prostrate Yourself, and Serve Your Lord

Establish regular Salaat, give regular charity and hold fast to Allah. He is your Mawla, Protector, the best of Protectors and the best Helper. (Al-Hajj 22:77–78, Koran)

Those who do wholesome deeds, establish regular prayers and regular charity have rewards with their Lord. On them shall be no fear, nor shall they grieve. (Al-Baqarah 2:227–80, Koran)

Seek help with patience, perseverance and prayer. Allah is with those who patiently persevere. (Al-Baqarah 2:153, Koran)

When you arise for salaat, purify yourself by washing your faces, your hands to the elbows, wipe your heads and wash your feet to the ankles. If you are unclean purify yourself. Allah does not wish that you should be burdened, but to make you clean and to bestow His blessings on you, that you may be grateful. (Al-Ma'idah 5:6, Koran)

Approach not prayers with a mind befogged until you understand all that you utter, nor come up to prayers in a state of un-cleanliness, till you have bathed. (An-Nisa 4:43, Koran)

Bow down, prostrate yourself and serve your Lord and do wholesome deeds that you may prosper. Perform Jihad; strive to your utmost in Allah's cause as striving (jihad) is His due. He has chosen you and Allah has imposed no hardship in your endeavor to His cause. You are the inheritors of the faith of your father Abraham.

He has named you Muslims of the times before and now, so that Allah's Rasool may be an example to you and that you are an example to humankind. (Al-Hajj 22:77-78, Koran)

When the call is proclaimed to prayer on Friday, the day of assembly, hasten earnestly to the Remembrance of Allah and leave off business and everything else: that is best for you if ye but knew! And when the Prayer is finished, then may ye disperse through the land and seek of the Grace of Allah: remember and praise Allah a great deal: that ye may prosper. (Al-Jumu'ah 62:9-10, Koran)

The Koran, Allah's word, is the fundamental source of the believers' spiritual well-being. Recitation of the Koran imparts peace, tranquility, and closeness to Allah and also renews the believers' vows to obey Allah's covenant. All believers memorize some parts of the Koran, particularly Sura Al-Fatihah, and certain other verses to recite the salat. The salat is the daily renewal of the Koran in the believer, a daily rejuvenation of his or her covenant with Allah and communion with Him.

The blessed *nabi* said, "*Iman is* knowledge in the heart, a voicing with the tongue and activity with the limbs." The term *heart*, often used in the Koran, refers to a specific faculty or a spiritual organ that provides the humans *intellect* and *rationality*. Therefore, *iman* in effect means confidence in the reality and truth of things and commitment to act on the basis of the truth that they know. Thus, *iman* (faith) involves words and actions on the basis of that knowledge. The Koran is Allah's speech to the believers, and it is the foundation of everything Islamic. Thus, humans connect with Allah by speaking to Him. The believer speaks to Allah through daily salat and supplication (*du'a*). The words are accompanied by action of the body and limbs, symbolizing subservience, respect, and humility. The salat consists of cyclic movements of standing in humility in the presence of Allah, bowing down to Him, going down in prostration in the Lord's presence, sitting in humility, reciting verses from the Koran, and praising Allah.

Recitation of the Koran serves to embody the Koran within the person reciting salat. Allah is the light, and His word, the Koran, is His luminosity. To embody the Koran through faith and practice is to become transformed by this divine light that permeates through the believer in his closeness to Allah. Such proximity to Allah's presence gives the worshipper a "luminous presence."

6. Fasting Is Prescribed to You in the Month of Ramadan

Fasting is prescribed to you, in the month of Ramadan as it was prescribed to those before you, that you may practice self-restraint. The Qur'an was revealed in the month of Ramadan, guidance to humankind for judgment between right and wrong. For every one except those ill or on a journey, this month should spend it in fasting. Allah intends to make it easy on you so that you may complete the prescribed period of fasting and to glorify Him to express your gratitude for His Guidance. (Al-Baqarah 2:178–79, Koran)

The month of fasting, Ramadan, is a month of self-reflection, self-discipline, prayer, and remembrance of Allah. This is a month of renewal of a believer's commitment to Allah's covenant and a vow to follow His guidance. During this month, there is heightened attention to the rules of right conduct, which helps the believer in his commitment to follow Allah's straight path during the following year. This month is a reminder to the believers of their obligation to Allah's creatures in need of sustenance, shelter, protection, peace, and other help.

7. Zakat

And the likeness of those who give generously, seeking to please Allah and to strengthen their souls, is as a garden, high and fertile where heavy rain falls on it and makes it yield a double the amount of harvest and if it receives not heavy rain, light moisture suffices it.
The parable of those who spend their substance in the way of Allah is that of a grain of corn: it grows seven ears and each ear has a hundred grains. Allah gives plentiful return to whom He pleases, Allah cares for all and He knows all things. Those who give generously in the cause of Allah and follow not up their gifts with reminders

of their generosity or with injury, for them their reward is with their Lord; on them shall be no fear, nor shall they grieve. Kind words and the covering of faults are better than charity followed by injury. Allah is Free of all wants and He is Most Merciful. (Al-Baqarah 2:261–63, Koran)

Let not those among you who are blessed with grace and ample means hold back from helping their relatives, the poor and those who have left their homes in Allah's cause. Let them forgive and overlook, do you not wish that Allah should forgive you? And Allah is Oft Forgiving, Most Merciful.
(An-Nur 24:21–23, Koran)

Spend out of bounties of Allah in charity and wholesome deeds before the Day comes when there will be neither bargaining, friendship nor intercession. Those who reject faith are the wrongdoers. (Al-Baqarah 2:254–57, Koran)

Void not your charity by boast, conceit and insult, by reminders of your generosity like those who want their generosity to be noted by all men but they believe neither in Allah nor in the Last Day. Theirs is a parable of a hard barren rock, on which there is a little soil, washed by heavy rain, which leaves it just a bare stone. And Allah guides not those who reject Faith. And the likeness of those who give generously, seeking to please Allah and to strengthen their souls, is as a garden, high and fertile where heavy rain falls on it and makes it yield a double the amount of harvest and if it receives not heavy rain, light moisture suffices it. Allah notices whatever you do.
(Al-Baqarah 2:264–65, Koran)

Alms are for the poor and the needy and those employed to administer the funds; for those whose hearts have been recently reconciled to the truth ; for those in bondage and in debt; in the cause of Allah; and for the wayfarer: thus is it ordained by Allah and Allah is full of knowledge and wisdom. (At-Tawbah 9:60, Koran)

In the above verses, the clear indication is that a human is given bounty by Allah. In return, his obligation is to distribute the surplus after his needs have been met to the needy. The Koran specifies that the zakat be distributed to the *fuqara* (the poor who ask), to *al-masakin* (the poor and the needy who do not ask), to zakat administrators, to those who spread the light of Islam to those inclined, for freedom of those in bondage, to those in debt, for the cause of Allah, and for the wayfarer who treads the path for Allah's service.

In the covenant, the believer surrenders to Allah his life and belongings in return for His guidance, a place in paradise in the hereafter, and peace with prosperity in this world. Every believer according to his or her covenant with Allah has the obligation to extend the benefits that He has provided him or her to those who did not receive the same. Such acts of generosity will be rewarded by Allah with a place in *Jannat* (place of peace and plenty) in the afterlife. Life of *Jannat* is to be attained in this world also, provided the compact with Allah is adhered to. The believer is Allah's instrument in fulfilling His promise to Adam that, among his progeny,

> none will remain without food or clothes and none will
> suffer from heat or thirst. (Koran 20:118)

In the verses below, Allah has promised those who believe and obey His covenant a reward for their acts of charity. He will double the harvest of their labors, forgive their sins, and provide them with His bounties, and they shall not grieve. Fear and grief arise from misfortunes, which cause anxiety, depression, and panic. Allah promises to safeguard the believers from misfortunes.

And to those who devour usury, Allah will deprive all blessings. Obedience of Allah's covenant provides *Jannat* in the hereafter and a life of *Jannat*, peace, and plenty in this world. It also brings balance, harmony, and stability to the economic life of the world in that it meets the necessities of each person and eliminates unnecessary suffering.

> O you who believe! Give of the good things that you have honorably earned and
> of the fruits of the earth that We have produced for you and do not even aim

at giving anything which is bad, that you would not receive yourself except with closed eyes. And know that Allah is free of all wants and worthy of all praise.

The Satan threatens you with poverty and bids you to unseemly actions. Allah promises you His forgiveness and bounties. And Allah cares for all and He knows all things.

He grants wisdom to whom He pleases; and those who are granted wisdom receive indeed a magnificent benefit, but none will grasp the Message but men of knowledge and understanding.

And whatever you spend in charity or devotion, be sure Allah knows it all. But the wrongdoers have no helpers. (Al-Baqarah 2:267–70, Koran)

The covenant of Allah has laid down principles and guidelines for the well-being of the economic life of the believers. Obedience of these principles will bring peace, harmony, spiritual enlightenment, and economic prosperity. Disobedience means misery, ruin, and Allah's wrath.

Land and sources of production do not become the personal property of individuals. *Ardh* is the source of life and means of sustenance and production of food and resources and therefore must remain available to the community, the *ummah*. Every Muslim, man and woman, who at the end of the year is in possession of about fifteen dollars or more in cash or articles of trade must give zakat at the minimum rate of 2.5 percent. Zakat is incumbent on all liquid, visible, movable, and immovable properties belonging to Muslims. Two and a half percent of all the liquid assets of a Muslim adult after deduction of reasonable amount of expenses for the maintenance of the person's family and other dependents is not an excessive amount of money. Allah constantly reminds the believers to practice regular charity. Giving to the needy with love and respect out of love of Allah is a profound act of spiritual cleaning. The more one gives in wealth and in kindness, the higher is his status with Allah.

In the united Muslim lands of the Dar es Salaam, if every adult man and woman gives minimum of *$15* in zakat, the total collected will amount to *$12 billion*. If every one of one thousand billionaires and one million millionaires in the Islamic world contributes a minimum of 2.5 percent of their liquid wealth in the way of Allah, the total collected will be in the tune of another *$50 billion*. If we approach another ten million prosperous businesspeople with liquid assets of five hundred thousand dollars to pay their minimum zakat, the sum collected from them will amount to another *$125 billion*. The total sum thus collected amounts *$187 billion*. Now we say to the same population that, in the twenty–first century, 2.5 percent is not really enough to feed and house a large population and ask for 5 percent of their liquid assets. The total collected will amount to *$379 billion*. Ten percent zakat on the same wealth will bring in *$758 billion annually*. Half this sum may then be used to feed, clothe, house, and educate the poor and needy population and the remaining half to create industries and jobs and job training for the people who have not been able to exit the cycle of poverty.

There is an estimated forty-five thousand tons of accumulated gold hoardings in the Islamic countries in the form of jewelry, gold bricks, gold bars, gold artifacts, and national treasures in museums with an estimated value of *$548 billion*. In addition, there is a hoard of precious stones worth another $100 billion. The zakat levy on the bullion and the precious stones will amount to another *$13 billion*. Even though the Islamic states have been milked dry by our elite and their colonial cohorts, the *ummah* acting in accordance with Allah's covenant shall be able to eradicate all poverty and destitution within the Dar es Salaam within *three years*. The resources will come from within the community of believers. The remedy lies within the *ummah* and amounts to $1.76 trillion over three years without ever touching any of the government revenues. So why is the *ummah* so destitute?

Were the precepts of the covenant of Allah applied to the rest of humanity, all poverty, deprivation, and disease will disappear from the world in one year. Less than ten percent of the world's population owns 80 percent of the world's wealth. This disparity has been caused by unbridled feudalism and capitalism in man's history. The total wealth of the world is estimated to be $330 trillion.

If every human gives away 2.5 to 5.0 percent of their surplus income in zakat to eradicate poverty, disease, and hunger in the global village, *$7.5 to $15.0 trillion* will become available, half of which might be used to eradicate hunger, illiteracy, unemployment, and disease annually and the remaining to build the world's infrastructure for environmentally sustainable agriculture and industrial production to sustain mankind. In no time, the world will be a stable place, with no wars, famines, epidemics, ignorance, and hunger.

The solution to the ills of humanity lies in Allah's Word:

And the likeness of those who give generously, seeking to please Allah and to strengthen their souls, is as a garden, high and fertile where heavy rain falls on it and makes it yield a double the amount of harvest and if it receives not heavy rain, light moisture suffices it.

The parable of those who spend their substance in the way of Allah is that of a grain of corn: it grows seven ears and each ear has a hundred grains. Allah gives plentiful return to whom He pleases, Allah cares for all and He knows all things. Those who give generously in the cause of Allah and follow not up their gifts with reminders of their generosity or with injury, for them their reward is with their Lord; on them shall be no fear, nor shall they grieve.

8. Hajj: Proclaim the Pilgrimage to Mankind

They will come to thee on foot and mounted on every kind of camel, lean on account of journeys through deep and distant mountain highways; whoever honors the sacred rites of Allah, for him it is good in the sight of his Lord.

And proclaim the Pilgrimage to mankind; they will come to thee on foot and mounted on every kind of camel, lean on account of journeys through deep and distant mountain highways; that they may witness the benefits provided for them and celebrate the name of Allah, through the Days Appointed, over the cattle which He has provided for them for sacrifice: then eat you thereof and feed the distressed ones in want. Then let them complete the rites prescribed for them, perform their vows and again circumambulate the Ancient House. Such is the Pilgrimage: whoever honors the sacred rites of Allah, for him it is good in the sight of his Lord. Lawful to you for food in Pilgrimage are cattle, except those mentioned to you as exceptions: but shun the abomination of idols and shun the word that is false. (Al-Hajj 22:27-30, Koran)

Violate not the sanctity of the Symbols of Allah, or of the sacred month, or of the animals brought for sacrifice, nor the garlands that mark out such animals, nor the people coming to the Sacred House, seeking the bounty and good pleasure of their Lord. Help one another in virtue and piety, but help not one another in sin and acrimony. Be in taqwa of Allah, fear Allah, for Allah is swift in reckoning. (Al-Ma'idah 5:2, Koran)

For thirteen hundred years, Muslims traveled to Mecca by foot or on horse- or camelback, taking more than a year to complete the rituals of the hajj. This slow pace helped the believer in his spiritual pursuit and his worldly quest to get acquainted with Muslims of other lands that kept the *ummah* united. The hajj since then has been seen as a grand rite of passage from this worldly life to a person's total devotion to Allah. Hajjis have been treated as models of piety and blessedness. With modern air travel, hajj has become accessible to a larger population, bringing the Islamic world closer. To the large number of children and young adults performing hajj, the rituals at the house inspire the renewal of their vows to the covenant of Allah, and they carry forward their passion to inspire others to perform the good works in the path of Allah.

9. Truth: Always Speak the Truth

O you who believe! Have taqwa of Allah, fear Allah and always speak the truth, that He may direct you to deeds of righteousness and forgive your sins: he that obeys Allah and His Rasool have already attained the highest achievement.

We did indeed offer al-Amanah, the Trust to the Heavens and the Earth and the Mountains; but they shrank from the burden, being afraid of it, but man assumed it and has proved to be a tyrant and a fool, with the result that Allah has to punish the munafiqeen, truth concealers, men and women and the mushrikeen, unbelievers, men and women and Allah turns in Mercy to the Believers, men and women; for Allah is Forgiving, Most Merciful. (Al-Ahzab 33:69–73, Koran)

To live up to the trust of Allah, the vicegerent—the human—has to distinguish between good and evil, truth and falsehood, *'adl* and *zulm*. Falsehood is the abomination that corrupts the very basis of Allah's vicegerency and His covenant with the human. The Koran discredits workers of corruption, the worst among them being the *Munafiqeen*, truth concealers, the hypocrites who claim to be doing good deeds but whose inner intentions are vile and harmful to others. Good deeds and truth are motivated by faith and *taqwa*. Corruption, dishonesty, and falsehood come about when humans—Allah's vicegerents—turn away from Allah's covenant and forget the message of the prophets:

But those who break the Covenant of Allah, after having pledged their word on it and sever that Allah has commanded to be joined together and who work corruption on earth, on them shall be the curse and theirs is the ugly abode. (Ar-Ra'd 13:25, Koran)

10. Come Not Near Shameful Deeds (*Fahasha*) Whether Open or Secret

Fahasha means indecency, iniquity, abomination, shameful deeds, or scandalous acts. Allah's covenant forbids the believers from shameful deeds such as adultery, fornication, sodomy, deception, treason, lying, cheating, stealing, and murder whether in open or in secret. People who commit such deeds are not immune from other abominations against their community and humankind. A believer's life and soul are akin to a dew pond of crystal clear water from which a fountain gushes forth, pure and refreshing; in the same manner, the beautiful deeds of the believers quench the thirst of humanity and bring peace and satisfaction. Acts of indecency and shame sully the dew pond with water so foul that the believers and humanity fall prey to plague, pestilence, and diseases of the body and spirit and lose Allah's grace.

When people and the rulers of Muslim lands indulge in shameful deeds (*Fahasha*), they do indeed follow Satan's footsteps and lose *furqan*, the criterion to distinguish right from wrong. Shameful actions open the gates to the world of iniquity, where there are no inhibitions nor shame. One licentious act leads to another till all thoughts of Allah are lost in a haze of debauchery and decadence. Intoxication leads to loss of inhibitions, licentiousness, and indecent acts against oneself and others. Inequity trespasses boundaries of self-control until there are trespasses against oneself, other people, the community, the state, and above all the commandments of Allah.

When Allah's gifts and grace are deemed inadequate, there begins a struggle for the acquisition of wealth. Wealth condones *Fahasha* and facilitates the activities of lewdness, debauchery, and indecency. Under every pile of wealth lies the sweat and blood of its victims. Wealth is the engine of *Fahasha*, and wealth and power are begotten through foul means. The covenant of Allah forbids shameful deeds, dishonesty, and deceit. To sustain the incumbent royals and dictators' riches and power, the conscientious and those who fight for decency and truth are taken into custody, tortured, and imprisoned. Some simply disappear, never to be heard of again. The *Fahasha* and the powerful are not accountable to Allah, and they thrive in the company of Satan. Their acts of shame and profanity are perpetrated in the open and obvious to those who surround them in the circles of power.

Enter into submission to the will of Allah, enter Islam whole-heartedly and follow not the footsteps of Satan, for he is a sworn enemy to you!
(Al-Baqarah 2:208, Koran)

Do not follow Satan's footsteps: if any will follow the footsteps of Satan, he will command to what is shameful (Fahasha) and wrong (Munkar): and were it not for the grace of Allah and His mercy on you, not one of you would have been unblemished: but Allah does purify whom He pleases: and Allah is all Hearer and all Knower. (An-Nur 24:21–23, Koran)

Come not near to shameful deeds (fornication, adultery and shameful activities) whether open or secret. (Al-An'am 151–53, Koran)

11. Unity of the *Ummah*

And hold fast, all together, by the Rope, which Allah stretches out for you and be not divided among yourselves; and remember with gratitude Allah's favor on you; you were enemies and He joined your hearts in love, so that by His Grace, you became brethren and a community. You were on the brink of the pit of fire and He saved you from it. Thus does Allah make His Signs clear to you that you may be guided.

Let there arise out of you a band of people inviting to all that is good, enjoining what is right and forbidding that is wrong. They are the ones to attain happiness.

Be not like those who are divided amongst themselves and fall into disputations after receiving clear signs: for them is a dreadful penalty.
(Ali 'Imran 3:103–5, Koran)

Persevere in patience and constancy; vie in such perseverance; strengthen each other; and be in taqwa of Allah, fear Allah that you may prosper. (Ali 'Imran 3:200, Koran)

This is a grace from Allah and a favor; and Allah is All Knowing and All Wise. If two parties among the Believers fall into a quarrel, make peace between them: but if one of them transgresses beyond bounds against the other, then fight you all against the one who transgresses until he complies with the Command of Allah; but if he complies, then make peace between them with justice and fairness: for Allah loves those who are fair and just. The Believers are but a single Brotherhood: so make peace and reconciliation between your two brothers; and fear Allah, that you may receive Mercy. (Al-Hujurat 49:6–10, Koran)

Just as the bond to Allah is indivisible, all the Believers shall stand behind the commitment of the least of them. All the Believers are bonded one to another to the exclusion of other men. (The Covenant of Muhammad)

All Muslims are one brotherhood, one *ummah*, all servants of one Allah, the First and the Last, fulfilling His covenant, witnessed over by Allah's messenger—an *ummah* that is witness over other nations. After the peace conference at Versailles Palace, the French and the British met quietly in San Remo in Italy to carve up the former possessions of the Ottoman Empire. France was given Syria and Lebanon, Persia became a British protectorate, and Mesopotamia and Palestine came under British possession.

The map of modern Middle East was conceived by a young Englishman drunk with power and alcohol. Winston Churchill traveled to Cairo in March 1921. He and Thomas Edward Lawrence had reviewed the aspirants of the Arabian thrones at the Ship restaurant in London over dinner and, afterward, brandy and liqueurs. The two likeliest candidates were Sharif Hussein's sons Faisal and Abdullah. On March 21, 1921, the Cairo Conference opened with thirty-eight participants, out of whom thirty-six were British. Churchill wrote afterward a description of this meeting: "Lawrence suggested that Feisal be crowned head of Iraq, not only because of his personal knowledge and friendship of the individual, but also on the ground that in order to counteract the claims of rival candidates and in order to pull together the scattered elements of a backward and half civilized country it was essential that the first ruler should be an active and inspiring personality."[5]

His motion with Churchill's approval carried without dissent. Abdullah, in Lawrence's view, was "lazy and by no means dominating"; but though unfit to rule Iraq, he would be permitted to rule over Transjordan under the watchful eye of a British high commissioner. Churchill announced his intention to appoint Abdullah in Palestine. Years later, Churchill would say, "Emir Abdullah is in Transjordania where I put him one Sunday afternoon in Jerusalem."

Zionism's hopes were honored. Sir Herbert Samuel—a Jew, Winston Churchill's cabinet colleague—was appointed high commissioner in Palestine and instructed to foster a Jewish homeland in Palestine. An Englishwoman who attended the conference remembered, "Winston going around the hotel followed by an Arab carrying a pail and a bottle of wine. When things got boring at the conference everyone would cheer when Winston came in.

On March 23, 1921, Winston Churchill, Sir Herbert Samuel, and Lawrence left Cairo Station by rail for Jerusalem. Between them, they drew the boundaries of the British-mandated territory. What was once one land for hundreds of years became Syria, Lebanon, Palestine, Iraq, Kuwait, and Hejaz. Hejaz was soon occupied with the British encouragement by Ibn Sa'ud. Israel was carved out of Palestine. Little desert domains of desert Bedouins, after treaties with Britain, became the Trucial States with further hinterland added to their territories for the exploitation and exploration of oil by the British. The Arabian

---

[5] William Manchester, *The Last Lion* (Bantam Double Day Publishing Group Ltd.), 700.

Peninsula was further carved into Oman, Muscat, and the South and North Yemen.

The borders between the Muslim communities and the kingdoms of Islam are Western innovation for division, exploitation, and control of Muslim lands, the Dar es Salaam. Such a division has been carried out and maintained by the West with the connivance of the self-imposed rulers of Islam against the commandments of Allah's covenant.

12. Perseverance and Patience

O ye who believe! persevere in patience and constancy; vie in such perseverance; strengthen each other; and fear Allah; that ye may prosper.

Ṣabr, ṣābir, ṣabbār, and *ṣābara* denote the qualities of patience, steadfastness, self-restraint, forbearance, endurance, and perseverance. One of Allah's ninety-nine names is *al-Ṣabur,* the Patient. It is one who does not precipitate an act before its time but decides matters according to a specific plan and brings them to fruition in a predefined manner, neither procrastinating nor hastening the matters before their time but disposing each matter in its appropriate time according to its needs and requirements and doing all that without being subjected to a force opposing Allah's will. *Ṣabr, ṣābir, ṣabbār,* and *ṣābara* are mentioned in the Koran sixty-nine times. Allah reassures the believers:

O Believers, be patient and vie you with patience. (3:200)

Pray for succor to Allah and be patient. (7:128)

Be thou patient, Allah will not leave to waste the wage of good-doers. (11:115)

Be thou patient; Surely Allah's promise is true. (30:60)

Bear patiently whatever may befall you. (31:17)

So be thou patient with a sweet patience. (70:5)

And be patient unto your Lord. (74:7)

O Believers, seek you help in patience and prayer. (21:153)

But come sweet patience. (12:18, 83)

Surely Allah is with the is with the patient. (2:153, 249)

Allah loves the patient. (3:146)

For a man and a woman to be patient (*ṣabr*), it requires endurance and discipline to affirm a rational resolve in opposing the impulses of passion or anger. It involves balancing two opposing desires. The believer has to overcome the impulse leading to rashness and haste and at the same time lean toward the delay of the act. To be patient, one has to resolve the conflict between acts of anger and rashness, on one hand, and procrastination and delay, on the other.

Lack of *ṣabr*, self-restraint, patience, and self-discipline has overwhelmed the Muslim world at the beginning of the twenty-first century. The Muslim world has been rudderless and leaderless over one hundred years and poorly led during the previous one thousand years. The result is 1.5 billion people following their own instincts for the sake of mere survival. *Ṣabr* teaches self-restraint in the matters of need and giving precedence to others over oneself in matters of need. Islam teaches that the elderly, the sick, the needy, the women, and the children take precedence in matters of care, shelter, and food and that spirituality takes precedence over one's daily needs. Consideration of the well-being of the kin, the neighbor, and the fellowman requires a thought before fulfilling one's own requirements. The state of *ṣabr* in the Muslim world is obvious when one looks at the lines at bus and rail stations. People are trampled at the holy sites. Old men, women, and the disabled are pushed and trampled during the holiest act of circumambulation around the Kaaba, at Safa and Marwah, and during the ritual stoning of the devil. The same is true in the shopping centers, down the streets, and inside the classrooms.

The extreme desire for immediate gratification of desires and ambitions leads to small and major crimes. Lying, theft, and robbery are common acts involved in the impulse of possession of the unreachable. Military revolutions, palace coups, conspiracies, and conquests bring power to the hands of the unjust and ambitious without a capacity for hard work, honesty, and *ṣabr* (patience).

Persevere in patience and constancy; vie in such perseverance; strengthen each other; and be in taqwa of Allah, fear Allah that you may prosper. (Ali 'Imran 3:200, Koran)

13. Theft, Deception, Fraud, Honesty, and Justice

Betray not the trust of Allah and His messenger. Nor knowingly misappropriate wealth entrusted to you, whether on behalf of an orphan or another party. Be honest in handling property, goods, credit, confidences, and secrets of your fellow men and display integrity and honesty in using your skills and talents. Whenever you give your word, speak truthfully and justly, even if a near relative is concerned.

Similarly, the *amri minkum*—those entrusted with the administration of the affairs of the believers—should not betray the trust of Allah, the *rasul*, and the believers and knowingly misappropriate the wealth of the Muslims. The populations of the Islamic lands are akin to the orphans whose land and heritage has been forcibly sequestered by conquest, soon to be redeemed, and those who seized it will, on the appointed day, be asked to account for every grain of stolen sand and gold. The Arabian Peninsula and other Muslim lands have been the plundering fields of the royal families and their kin for one hundred years, in partnership with the *circle of evil*. The rulers of the Arabian Peninsula and their royal relatives regularly skim the cream off the top one-third of the wealth of the *ummah* for their personal benefit. The dictators, the royals, and their circle of sycophants and cheerleaders in all Muslim nation-states have siphoned off the cream of their national wealth. Suharto, Benazir Bhutto, Nawaz Sharif, Reza Shah of Iran, Saddam Hussein, Anwar Sadat, Hosni Mubarak, kings of the Arabian Peninsula, their families, and the inner circle of their regimes have plundered trillions of dollars from their nation's treasuries over their prolonged reign.

The greatest pillage and plunder in history took place systematically when the descendants of ten barefoot, camel-herding Bedouins took control of the Arabian Peninsula with the help of British money and arms. In the second half of the twentieth century, over a short period of forty-five years, they heisted $4.5 trillion. In the Arabian Peninsula, in the kingdoms of Oman, Kuwait, the United Arab Emirates, Qatar, Bahrain, and Saudi Arabia, there are now six kings and over five hundred billionaires and thousands of millionaires among this narrow circle of ten clans. Over this short period, these tent dwellers who had never been inside the four walls of a dwelling now owned hundreds of palaces in Arabia, Europe, and America.

Yet this plunder is ongoing. The total amount of petty cash taken out by the ever-increasing progeny of these Bedouin sheikhs in allowances, salaries, commissions, and expenses is so immense that their take of twenty-five billion dollars annually is more than the total combined annual budget of the nation-states of Pakistan, Afghanistan, Iran, Syria, and Jordan, with a population of 250 million people. The cost of security of these "royals" (90,000 troops), personal jets, helicopters, yachts, travel, and private air terminals in Jeddah, Riyadh, Dubai, and Doha is an additional ten billion dollars. This is going on when most Arabs and Muslims live in conditions of utter poverty and deprivation.

Two fundamental terms used in the Koran are *haqq* (right and honest means of income) and *batil* (wrongful and dishonest way of making money). The ways of making money approved by the Koran are halal, and those forbidden are haram.

Muslims the world over follow the verses about fasting in Surah Al-Baqarah 2:183–87 but very conveniently ignore the following verse (188):

And do not devour each others wealth dishonestly, nor use it as bait for the judges, with intent that ye may devour dishonestly and knowingly a little of (other) people's wealth.

O you who believe! Fasting is prescribed to you as it was prescribed to those before you, that ye may (learn) self-restraint,

(Fasting) for a fixed number of days; but if any of you is ill, or on a journey, the prescribed number (should be made up) from days later. For those who can do it (with hardship), is a ransom, the feeding of one that is indigent but he that will give more, of his own free will, it is better for him. And it is better for you that ye fast, if ye only knew.

Ramadan is the (month) in which was sent down the Qur'an, as a guide to mankind, also Clear (Signs) for guidance and judgment (between right and wrong). So every one of you who is present (at his home) during that month should spend it in fasting, but if any one is ill, or on a journey, the prescribed period (should be made up) by days later. Allah intends every facility for you; He does not want to put you to difficulties. (He wants you) to complete the prescribed period and to glorify Him in that He has guided you; and perchance ye shall be grateful.

When My servants ask thee concerning Me, I am indeed close (to them): I listen to the prayer of every suppliant when he calls on Me: let them also, with a will, listen to My call and believe in Me: that they may walk in the right way.

Permitted to you, on the night of the fasts, is the approach to your wives. They are your garments and ye are their garments. Allah knows what you used to do secretly among yourselves; but He turned to you and forgave you; so now associate with them and seek what Allah hath ordained for you and eat and drink until the white thread of dawn appear to you distinct from its black thread; then complete your fast till the night appears; but do not associate with your wives while ye are in retreat in the mosques. Those are limits (set by) Allah: approach not nigh thereto. Thus doth Allah make clear His Signs to men: that they may learn self-restraint.

And do not devour each others wealth dishonestly, nor use it as bait for the judges, with intent that ye may devour dishonestly and knowingly a little of (other) people's wealth. (Al Baqarah 2:183–88, Koran)

There are several dishonest financial practices—cheating, bribery, stealing, embezzlement, hoarding, and swindling—but one mentioned specifically by the Koran is often overlooked. That is the one practiced by the aristocrats, clergy, clerics, and claimants of spiritual leadership all across the world:

> O you who believe! There are indeed many among the leaders,
> priests and clerics, who in falsehood devour the substance of men
> and hinder (them) from the Way of Allah. And there are those who
> bury gold and silver and spend it not in the Way of Allah: announce
> unto them a most grievous penalty. (At-Tawbah 9:34, Koran)

Like the politicians and dictators, these priests and spiritual leaders deceive the unlettered masses with false doctrines and fallacies to keep them entrapped in their web to safeguard their own power over people and their wealth.

14. Obey Allah and His *Rasul* and Those Charged with Authority among You

Obey Allah and obey the Messenger and those charged amongst you with authority in the settlement of your affairs. If you differ in any thing among yourselves, refer it to Allah and His Rasool (The Qur'an and the Prophet's teachings). If you do believe in Allah and the last Day that is best and the most beautiful conduct in the final determination. (An-Nisa 4:43, Koran)

The Koran teaches that all affairs of individuals and the Muslim community is to be conducted through mutual consultation (*ijma*) and decisions arrived through consensus. Furthermore, the Koran proclaims consultation as the principle of governance and the method that must be applied in the administration of public affairs. The sovereignty of Islamic state belongs exclusively to Allah, whose will and command binds the community and state. The dignified designation in the Koran of the community as vicegerent of Allah on the earth makes the Muslim community, the *ummah*, a repository of the "executive sovereignty" of the Islamic state. The community as a whole, after consultation and consensus, charges people from among themselves with authority to manage its affairs (*ulil amri minkum*). Those charged with authority act in their capacity as the representative (*wakil*) of the people and are bound by the Koranic mandate to consult the community in public affairs, and consensus is the binding source of the law. The community, by consultation and in consensus, has the authority to depose any person charged with authority, including the head of state, in the event of gross violation of Allah's law.

Those who hearken to their Lord and establish regular prayer; who (conduct) their affairs by mutual Consultation; who spend out of what We bestow on them for Sustenance; And those who, when an oppressive wrong is inflicted on them do not flinch and courageously defend themselves. (Ash-Shura 42:38–39, Koran)

Islam pursues its social objectives by reforming the person. The ritual ablution before prayer, the five daily prayers, the fasting during the month of Ramadan, and the obligatory giving of charity all encourage punctuality, self-discipline, and concern for the well-being of others. An individual is seen not just a member of the community and subservient to its will but also as a morally autonomous agent who plays a distinctive role in shaping the community's sense of direction and purpose. The Koran has attached to the individuals the duty of obedience to the government and the right of the individual to simultaneously dispute with rulers over government affairs. The individual obeys the ruler on the condition that the ruler obeys the covenant of the Koran and Allah's commandments, which are obligatory to all Muslims regardless of their status in the social hierarchy. This is reflected in the declaration of the blessed *nabi*: "There is no obedience in transgression; obedience is only in the righteousness."

The citizen is entitled to disobey an oppressive command that is contrary to the covenant of the Koran. The blessed *nabi*, Allah's emissary, brought Allah's word to the world and disseminated it to the populations of the continents. Therefore, it is essential to obey the commandments that Blessed Muhammad brought from Allah for mankind.

O you who believe! Obey Allah and obey the Messenger and those charged with authority among you. If ye differ in anything among yourselves, refer it to Allah and His Messenger, if ye do believe in Allah and the Last Day: that is best and most suitable for final determination. (An-Nisa 4:59, Koran)

15. Freedom of Religion: Let There Be No Compulsion in Religion

Let there be no compulsion in religion: Truth stands out clear from Error: whoever rejects Evil and believes in Allah hath grasped the most trustworthy handhold that never breaks. And Allah hears and knows all things. (Al-Baqarah 2:254-57, Koran)

The Koranic notion of religious belief (*iman*) as dependent on knowledge is actualized in practice in the term *islam*. *Islam* signifies the idea of surrender or submission. Islam is a religion of self-surrender: Islam is the conscious and rational submission of dependent and limited human will to the absolute and omnipotent will of Allah.

The type of surrender Islam requires is a deliberate, conscious, and rational act made by a person who knows with both intellectual certainty and spiritual vision that Allah, who is the subject of Koranic discourse, is the only reality.

The knower of God is a Muslim (fem. *Muslimah*), "one who submits" to the divine truth and whose relationship with God is governed by *taqwa*, the consciousness of humankind's responsibility toward its Creator. However, consciousness of God alone is not sufficient to make a person a Muslim. Neither is it enough to be merely born a Muslim or to be raised in an Islamic cultural context. The concept of *taqwa* implies that the believer has the added responsibility of acting in a way that is in accordance with the three types of knowledge, *ilm al-yaqin*, *ain al-yaqin*, and *haqq al yaqin* (knowledge of certainty, eye of certainty, and truth of certainty). The believer must endeavor at all times to maintain himself or herself in a constant state of submission to Allah. By doing so, the believer attains the honored title of "slave of Allah" (*abd Allah*, feminine: *amat Allah*), for he recognizes that all power and all agency belongs to God alone. Thus, the believer surrenders to the will of Allah. No one can compel anyone to undergo submission without his will and understanding.

16. *Awliya*: Allah Is the *Waliy*, Protector of Those Who Have Faith

Oh you who believe! Allah is the Waliy and the protector of the Believers. Allah commands Believers not to take people outside their ranks in closeness and confidence; who in their loathing for them wish them destruction.

Allah, in the covenant, reminds the believers repeatedly:

Not to take the Kafirun (infidels), Jews and Christians as their awliya, (friends and protectors) in place of Believers. They are friends and protectors unto each other. He who amongst Believers turns to them is one of them. Allah does not guide those who are unjust and evil doers (zalimun). He that from amongst the Believers turns to them is from amongst the Kafirun, Mushrikun and the zalimun.

Take not for Awliya, friends and protectors, from amongst your kin who are Kafirun.

Allah also admonishes believers:

Not to take My enemies and yours as Awliya (friends and protectors), offering them love and regard, even though they have rejected the Truth bestowed on you. You have come out to strive in My Cause and to seek My favor, take them not as friends, holding in secret regard and friendship for them, for I know full well all that you conceal and all that you reveal. And any of you that do this, has strayed from the Straight Path.

Befriend not people who have incurred Allah's wrath.

There is a recurring cycle in Islamic history of destruction and humiliation of Islam by the manipulations of the circle of evil. The story starts sometimes with a scheming Jew who spins a web, meticulously planning to amass the world's wealth, and uses the power and the organization of the strongest Christian monarch by tempting him with acquisition of a world empire and its fabulous wealth. Then meticulous planning starts; the execution of such an expedition may take several years in which intelligence services, diplomats, and armed services play a role, while only the top select echelon is aware of all the moves on the chessboard. A willing victim, a weak Muslim—a *Munafiq*—with propensity toward greed and lust for power and usually endowed with overwhelming vanity and conceit is picked up, trained, and slowly eased into a position of power to be used at the opportune moment.

Ottoman Empire: The plan to destabilize the Ottoman Empire was hatched by the Jewish Rothschild cousins in Berlin, Paris, and London. Each branch of the family collaborated with their favorite governments in those cities. The German chancellor von Bethmann Hollweg, a Jew and a Rothschild cousin, won the day, and the kaiser began to make overtures to the Young Turks and assisted their revolution against the sultan. Enver Pasha was the Turkish *Munafiq* who joined the circle of evil, the *Yahudi, Salibi,* and *Munafiq* coalition. Talat, Cemal, and Enver *presided* over the dissolution of the Ottoman Empire, subjugating the Middle East to the West for the next one hundred years.

State of Israel: The history of the creation of the State of Israel tells us that Theodor Herzl and Chaim Weizmann were the founding fathers of Israel. The hidden hand that helped create the Jewish state is seldom mentioned. The actual creators of Israel were a group of English and Jewish conspirators in the British cabinet. David Lloyd George appointed Alfred Milner, a Jew, to his war cabinet in 1916 as secretary of war. After becoming the secretary of war, he brought in Leo Amery, another Jew, albeit a secret one, as secretary of the war cabinet. Milner had close contacts with the Rothschilds; in 1912, he had helped Natty Rothschild unify the divided Jewish community of London under one spiritual head, Chief Rabbi Joseph Herman Hertz.[6]

Another Jew, a cabinet minister, Herbert Samuel, convinced the cabinet in 1915—when Palestine was still a Turkish possession—that Palestine should become a British protectorate, "into which the scattered Jews in time swarm back from all quarters of the globe, in due course obtain home rule and form a Jewish Commonwealth like that of Canada and Australia." Lord Walter Rothschild, as the leader of the British Jews, twisted the ears of the prime minister Lloyd George and his foreign secretary for a declaration about Palestine. Lloyd George had previously served as the legal counsel for the British Zionist Federation. Balfour suggested that "they submit a declaration for the cabinet to consider." The declaration was written by Milner and

---

[6] Niall Ferguson, *The House of Rothschild* (Penguin Books), 259.

revised several times. The final version was drafted by Leo Amery, which read,

His Majesty's Government view with favor the establishment in Palestine a national home for the Jewish people and will use their best endeavors to facilitate the achievement of this object, it being clearly understood that nothing shall be done which may prejudice the civil and religious rights of existing non-Jewish communities in Palestine, or the rights and political status enjoyed in any other country.

This declaration was approved by the British cabinet and was addressed to Lord Walter Rothschild and signed by the foreign secretary Balfour. The Balfour Declaration—as this Jewish Magna Carta came to be known, the document that gave the illegitimate birth to the state of Israel—was written by Lord Alfred Milner, a Jew, revised and finalized by Leo Amery, another Jew, at the behest of and addressed to Lord Walter Rothschild, the leader of the Jews in London, for the purpose of the creation of a Jewish state in the name of the British government on a land that did not belong to either the Jews or the British. In fact, this was an agreement among a group of conspiring *Yahudi-Salibi* conspirators belonging to a secret organization that had a long history of fraud and extortion to grab the world's wealth.

In this case, the plotters made a full circle in their relationship. Lord George Joachim Goschen, a German Jew, patronized Alfred Milner, another German Jew, and brought him into the English establishment and introduced him to the Rothschilds. Milner, in turn, brought Leo Amery, a secret Jew, into the war cabinet; and together, they wrote the Balfour Declaration for the Lord Rothschild. To complete the circle, George Goschen's daughter Phyllis Evelyn Goschen married Francis Cecil Balfour, Foreign Secretary Balfour's son, on August 31, 1920.

Herbert Samuel was appointed overseer of Palestine to guide and control King Abdullah of Jordan to facilitate the Jewish migration to Palestine. Arthur Hirtzel, a Jew, was appointed as head of the British India Office, which also controlled the British governance of Iraq and Arabia. Hirtzel, at that time, expressed the need for Ibn Sa'ud to establish himself in Mecca. Rufus Isaacs, Lord Reading, another Jew, was appointed as the British viceroy of India. Isaacs directed the British policy in Iraq, Palestine, and Arabia. He used 'Abd al-'Aziz to remove Sharif Hussein's son Ali from Hejaz. He had a free hand in Arabia and Iraq. He used British Indian troops to quell uprisings in Iraq. Isaacs also facilitated the massacres and repression in At Ta'if, Bureida, and Huda by providing 'Abd al-'Aziz with money, artillery, rifles, ammunition, training, and transport.

From this time onward, Zionists were considered an ally of the British government, and every help and assistance was forthcoming from each government department. Space was provided for the Zionists in Mark Sykes's office with liaison to each government department. The British government provided financial, communication, and travel facilities to those working in the Zionist office. Mark Sykes, who had negotiated the Sykes-Picot Agreement giving Syria to the French, was now working for the Zionists, offering them a part of the same territory.

Partition of the Land of Islam in the Middle East: To complete the circle of evil, Sharif Hussein and his sons—hungry for power, fame, and gold—were the willing recruits of the British to destabilize the Ottoman Empire and carve out a Jewish state in Palestine. Hussein led a revolt against his caliph, sultan, country, and coreligionists under the protection of an alien, *kafir*, colonial, expansionist power under the full knowledge that parts of the Islamic state—including Syria, Lebanon, Palestine, and Iraq—would pass from Islamic rule to an economic and colonial serfdom of a non-Muslim, *kafir* power. While the British set out to expedite the war against the Turks, they also began to lay the groundwork for an indirect postwar British political control of Arabia.

June 1916 was a historical moment when, for the first time in the history of Islam since the Battle of Badr in the first year of hijra, combined forces of the *kafireen* and *Munafiqeen* and British and Hussein's armies attacked the city of the *nabi* of Islam, though unsuccessfully; this attack introduced the combined evil dominion of the *Mutaffifeen*, *kafireen*, and *Munafiqeen* over the heartlands of Islam for the century to come.

For his treachery, Sharif Hussein received his first reward in gold sovereigns in March 1916, a shipment amounting to £53,000, three months before he announced his revolt. Commencing on August 8, 1916, the official allowance was set at £125,000 a month, a sum that was frequently exceeded on Hussein's demand; for example, in November 1916, £375,000 in gold sovereigns was dispatched to Hussein by the British for hajj expenses. The payments were broken down into five categories representing the four armies under the command of Hussein's sons and an allotment for the upkeep of the mosque at Kaaba and for hajj facilities as well as for the operation of Hussein's government in Mecca and Jeddah. Forty thousand pounds was allotted to Faisal, £30,000 to Abdullah, £20,000 each for Ali and Zeid, and £15,000 for expenses at Mecca and Jeddah.

The year 1916 must have been the lowest point in the history of Islam, when it was surrounded by powerful enemies around the world; and inside, it was being destroyed by self-serving traitors at the very heart of the faith, the Kaaba. For the first time in the history of Islam, the very upkeep of the holy mosque of Mecca and the Kaaba and hajj expenses were being paid for by the *kafireen*, at the behest of the *Munafiqeen*, under the claim of their lineage from the holy prophet. While claiming the bloodline, they forgot the teachings of the Koran and the example of the prophet.

'Abd al-'Aziz was picked as a willing tool by British scouts in around 1902 and was kept on a short leash with small handouts to keep him available and above starvation level. 'Abd al-'Aziz set out to conquer Arabia with the financial and military assistance of the British. Sir Percy Cox, a British resident in the Persian Gulf, wrote, "With Ibn-Saud in Hasa (the Gulf Coast of Arabia) our position is very much strengthened." Percy Cox openly encouraged Ibn Sa'ud to attack the remaining territory of the Ibn Rashids to divert them from reinforcing Turkish troops against the British. Ibn Sa'ud had constant British financial aid, arms, and advisers, initially William Shakespeare and Percy Cox and later Harry St. John Philby.

After they helped him master eastern Arabia in 1917, the British found another use for Ibn Sa'ud. In 1924, Hussein declared himself caliph of Islam without the consent of the British. Ibn Sa'ud, with British encouragement, started his thrust to Hejaz; although the British ostensibly cut off the arms supplies to both sides, they continued to supply small but crucial amounts of money and arms to Ibn Sa'ud and his merciless Ikhwan. Some of the military equipment used by Ibn Sa'ud was expensive and could only have been obtained from the British and used with the help of British instructors. At the time, statements by British officials did point to the British hand in Ibn Sa'ud's attack on Mecca. Arthur Hirtzel—a Jew, head of the British India Office at that time—expressed the need for Ibn Sa'ud to establish himself in Mecca. The British viceroy of India at that time, another Jew, Rufus Isaacs, Lord Reading, directed the British policy in Arabia. He used 'Abd al-'Aziz to remove Sharif Hussein's son Ali from Hejaz.

Ibn Sa'ud afforded Britain the comfort of keeping the Arabs and Muslims divided and protected its commercial and political interests, which opposed a unified Muslim state. Sharif Hussein and his sons Faisal and Abdullah continued to be clients and servants of the British. For a few thousand pounds and personal glory, they and their descendants, Faisal, Abdullah, Hussein, and Abdullah sold the honor of Islam for the next one hundred years. 'Abd al-'Aziz's sons inherited their father's debauchery and treason against Islam for their personal gain.

Treason runs deep in the veins of the descendants of Sharif Hussein and 'Abd al-'Aziz. They are *Munafiqeen* who have taken their *awliya* from among the *kafireen*. According to the covenant, they are of the *kafireen*. This circle of evil, the coalition of the *Yahudi, Salibi,* and *Munafiqeen* triumphed over Islam for over one hundred years. The Jewish money in London, New York, Berlin, and Paris collaborated with the ' Christian powers of Europe and America and the *Munafiqeen*—Enver Pasha, Cemal Pasha, Talat Pasha, Sharif Hussein and sons, and Ibn Sa'ud and sons—to defeat the Islamic Empire and fragment it into scores of impoverished mini-client-states for political and economic exploitation by the *Yahudi, Salibi, Munafiq* coalition.

Egypt and the Slavery in Palestine: Anwar Sadat and the Egyptian Army won partial victory over the Jewish state of Israel in 1973. The victory made Sadat a hero in the eyes of many Arabs—if not equal to, then almost comparable to the great Arab hero Gamal Abdel Nasser. Puffed up by success and sycophancy from the likes of Henry Kissinger, Sadat forgot his own roots and began to take advice and comfort from Kissinger and Israeli lobbyists in Washington. Against the advice of his closest advisers and the leaders of other Arab countries, Sadat offered himself as a servant and a tool of the circle of evil, the *Yahudi-Salibi* confederation. He made a trip to Israel and addressed the Knesset, the Israeli Parliament. Under American tutelage and patronage, he abandoned his Arab allies, negotiated, and signed a peace treaty with many secret appendices with Israel at the expense of the Palestinians, Syrians, and Muslims in general.

As a consequence, all Palestine and the Golan Heights are under Israeli occupation. The Arabs are disunited and in disarray. Sadat sold the Egyptian sovereignty, the Islamic nation, and the holy Islamic places in Jerusalem for three billion dollars a year. Sadat took Jews and Christians as *awliya* and willfully disobeyed the covenant that every Muslim has pledged to obey. He also disobeyed the provisions of the covenant of Yathrib and the blessed *nabi's* teaching:

Just as the bond to Allah is indivisible, all the believers shall stand behind the commitment of the least of them. All believers are bonded one to another to the exclusion of other men. This Pax Islamica is one and indivisible. No believer shall enter a separate peace without all other believers whenever there is fighting in the cause of God, but will do so only on the basis of equality and justice to all others. In every expedition for the cause of God we undertake, all parties to the covenant shall fight shoulder to shoulder as one man. All believers shall avenge the blood of one another when any one falls fighting in the cause of God.

Once again, the *Yahudi-Salibi* ingenuity used a *Munafiq* to grow the seeds of discord in the Islamic world.

The Ruin of Iraq: Saddam Hussein replaced al-Bakr as president of Iraq in July 1979. The bloodbath that followed eliminated all potential opposition to him. Saddam was now the master of Iraq with no one around him daring to question his actions. Two actions that he initiated led the Islamic community to disastrous disunity and debt. He attacked fellow Muslims, Iran in 1980 and Kuwait in 1990.

The Iran-Iraq War turned out to be a battle between two egomaniac personalities with a Messiah complex, neither of them willing to call a truce to the hostilities. The result was emaciation and bleeding of both countries to near bankruptcy. The Iraqi troops launched a full-scale invasion of Iran on September 22, 1980. France supplied high-tech weapons to Iraq, and the Soviet Union was Iraq's largest weapon supplier. Israel provided arms to Iran, hoping to bleed both the nations by prolonging the war. At least ten nations sold arms to both the warring nations to profit from the conflict. The United States followed a more duplicitous policy toward both warring parties to prolong the war and cause maximum damage to both.

The Iran-Iraq War was not between good and evil. Islam forbids fighting among the Muslims, murder, and taking of life unless it is in the cause of justice. Saddam Hussein launched a murderous war to regain a few square miles of territory that his country had relinquished freely in the 1975 border negotiations. There were one and a half million Muslim casualties in this senseless fraternal war. The war ended in a ceasefire that essentially left prewar borders unchanged. The Covenant of Allah not only forbids such an internecine war but also provides a mechanism for dispute resolution.

Instead of condemning the aggressor, the Arab states sided with Saddam Hussein, providing him with funds for further bloodletting. Saddam Hussein used banned chemical weapons against fellow Muslims, Iranians, and Kurds. The eight-year-long war exhausted both countries. Primary responsibility for the prolonged bloodletting must rest with the governments of the two countries, the ruthless military regime of Saddam Hussein and the ruthless clerical regime of Ayatollah Khomeini in Iran. Whatever his religious convictions were, Khomeini had no qualms about sending his followers, including young boys, to their deaths for his own greater glory. This callous disregard for human life was no less characteristic of Saddam Hussein. Saudi Arabia gave $25.7 billion and Kuwait $10 billion to Iraq to fuel the war and the killings. Saddam also owed the Soviets, the USA, and Europe $40 billion for the purchase of arms. The cost of war to the Iranians was even greater. The world community sold arms for eight and a half years and watched the bloodletting. The USA sold arms and information to both sides to prolong the war strategically and to profit and gain influence and bases in Gulf countries. Ayatollah Khomeini, in particular, was a hypocrite in dealing with Israel in secret when his public pronouncements were venomously anti-Israel.

Iran, Iraq, and all the Arab states of the Persian Gulf took the Western countries, the Soviet Union, and Israel as their *awliya*, in contradiction to the commandments of the covenant. The ayatollah and his clerics should have known and understood their obligations to Allah and to their people as spelled out in Allah's covenant. The uncontrolled Arab-Iranian hostility left a deep, festering wound in the body of the nation of Islam. The West made gains by setting up permanent bases in Saudi Arabia, Oman, the United Arab Emirates, Bahrain, Qatar, and Kuwait. This is the land that Muhammad, the blessed *rasul* of Allah, freed from infidels, only to be handed over to infidels by the *Munafiqeen*.

After the Kuwait war, at the invitation of King Fahd, the USA has continued to maintain large operational army and air force bases and command and control facilities that enable them to monitor air and sea traffic and civilian and military communications in the Middle East. Bahrain became the headquarters of a US naval fleet. The Middle East, at the beginning of the twenty-first century, is under the absolute military and economic control of the USA and NATO. The circle of evil—the *Yahudi*, *Salibi*, and *Munafiqeen*—continue to dominate the lives of Muslims.

17. Jihad

Fight the infidel until there is no more treachery and oppression and there prevails Justice and Faith in Allah altogether and everywhere. If they cease, then Allah is seer of what they do. If they refuse, be sure that Allah is your Protector, the Best to protect and the Best to help. And why should you not fight in the cause of Allah and for those men, women and children, who are weak, abused and oppressed, those who beseech their Lord to deliver protectors and helpers.

The Koranic use of the term *jihad* means "struggle." The Koran commonly uses the verb along with the expression *in the path of Allah*. The path of Allah, of course, is the path of right conduct that Allah has set down in the Koran. Jihad is simply the complement to *islam*, the surrender to the will of Allah. The surrender takes place in Allah's will, and it is Allah's will that people struggle in His path. Hence, submission and surrender to Allah's will demands struggle in His path. Submission to Allah's command requires the believers to struggle against all negative tendencies in their self. Salat, zakat, fasting, and hajj are all struggles in the path of Allah. The greatest obstacles that people face in submitting themselves to Allah are their laziness, lack of imagination, and currents of contemporary opinion. These weaknesses and events carry them along without resisting. It takes an enormous struggle to submit to an authority that breaks one's likes and dislikes of current trends and pressures of society to conform to the crowd.

The jihad, which is normally a daily struggle within oneself against temptations and evil, will sometimes take an outward form against the enemies of Islam. Such a war is permitted strictly in the path of Allah in today's contemporary world to enforce truth, justice, and freedom.

And why should you not fight in the cause of Allah and for those men, women and children, who are weak, abused and oppressed, those who beseech their Lord to deliver them from their oppressors and those who ask Allah to send for them protectors and helpers. (An-Nisa 4:71–75, Koran)

The oft-repeated phrase in the Koran to proclaim jihad is to fight *fitnah*, tyranny, and oppression. Yet most of the wars in the Muslim world were civil wars, with Muslims killing Muslims for the sake of territory, wealth, and power.

Life is a chain of emotions, intentions, and actions. Before each deed, man stops to intend an action. Each intention is the product of an emotion that acts on man's self, the *nafs*. The *nafs* may intend to act on its animal instincts of craving and lust, or in situations where the human *self* is sufficiently refined with the *taqwa* of Allah, man will follow the path of Allah as commanded by the covenant. The self is in continuous battle whether to follow its base cravings or to perform wholesome deeds. Such ongoing fluctuation of intent between the base and the honorable is stressful. Such stress leads to anxiety, anger, and depression, which in the end will cause an emotional turmoil and breakdown. When man intends to do his deeds with the knowledge that Allah is with him, that Allah is aware of his intent, and that Allah guides him to the right objective and action, there is peace and satisfaction.

When the believer is in *taqwa* of Allah, His *nur* cleans his *nafs* and aids him to obey the covenant of Allah. Jihad is this struggle that prepares the believer to follow and obey Allah's commandments without questioning. Jihad is the struggle of the individual on his way from the path of ignorance to the path of Allah. Man hears Allah's call though the noise and the commotion of the world and, through the eye of his soul, lets the *nur* of Allah into the niche of his heart. Allah's call is to obedience, goodness, and selflessness. Man bows down his head on the earth in submission and in humility to his Lord. The Lord guides, and the believer follows; the believer has faith in his Allah, and Allah holds his hand. Allah shows His believer the way to goodness, and the believer performs wholesome deeds. The *nur* of Allah glows in the believer's heart, and the believer accepts Allah in his heart.

This communion between the believer and Allah becomes exclusive. Submission establishes a link between the believer and Allah. Allah commands, and the believer follows. The believer asks, and Allah gives. The believer loves Allah, and Allah loves him in return. The believer asks for the straight path, and Allah shows him the way. The believer praises Allah, and Allah showers His mercy and grace upon him. The believer remembers Allah, and Allah responds to those who praise Him.

The *nafs*, unlike the Freudian ego, is capable of both good and bad. The *nuqta* of the *nafs*, when magnified a million times, becomes visible as a shiny disk, a mirror. The inherent nature (*fitra*) of the *nafs* is to shine like a mirror with Allah's *nur*. When man walks the path of Allah in *taqwa* of Him with the knowledge that Allah is with him, watching him and guiding him, Allah's *nur* shines on the *nafs*, keeping it pure and safe. However, when man's desires, cravings, and ego overpower his love and obedience for Allah, the shiny mirror of his *nafs* becomes obscured by the dirt and smoke of his desires, and he loses sight of the *nur* of Allah and trips into error and decadence.

The effort required to keep focus on Allah's *nur* and the *taqwa* of Him is the inner jihad. And this jihad is the obedience to Allah's commandments when He calls on His believers with the words *O you who Believe* and commands them to do acts of faith and goodness in *seventy-five* verses of the Koran. Obedience to every such command is jihad.

Jihad, foremost, is the struggle to fulfill the commandments of Allah in the covenant. The *taqwa* of Allah shines His light (*nur*) into core of man, in the self (*nafs*), that clears the smoke of evil and temptation from the *nafs*, allowing man to follow God. Once the believer has purified himself with Allah's *nur*, he has prepared himself for the external jihad. When the believer has purified his own *nafs* and soul with submission to Allah (*islam*) and faith (*iman*) in the only reality, the Lord, and by performance of wholesome deeds in the name of

Allah, he is ready for the outer struggle for his *din* to fight the *fitnah* of tyranny and oppression.

The blessed *nabi* of Allah wrote the following covenant in the first year of hijra in Medina. This is the essential constitution of the whole *ummah*. This is a covenant given by Muhammad to the believers.

1. They constitute one *ummah* to the exclusion of all other men.
2. The believers shall leave none of their members in destitution without giving him in kindness and liberty what he needs.
3. No believer shall slay a believer in retaliation for an unbeliever, nor shall he assist an unbeliever against a believer.
4. All believers shall rise as one against anyone who seeks to commit injustice, aggression, or crime or spread mutual enmity among the Muslims, even if such a person is their kin.
5. Just as the bond to Allah is indivisible, all the believers shall stand behind the commitment of the least of them. All believers are bonded to one another to the exclusion of other men.
6. This Pax Islamica is one and indivisible. No believer shall enter a separate peace without all other believers whenever there is fighting in the cause of God except on the basis of equality and justice to all others. In every expedition for the cause of God we undertake, all parties to the covenant shall fight shoulder to shoulder as one man. All believers shall avenge the blood of one another when any one falls fighting in the way of Allah.
7. The pious believers follow the best and the most upright guidance. Whoever is convicted of killing a believer deliberatively but without righteous cause shall be liable to the relatives of the killed. Until the latter are satisfied, the killer shall be subject to retaliation by each and every believer.

Allah speaks to the believers thus about the struggle in His way:

Fight in the cause of Allah those who fight you, but do not
transgress limits; for Allah loves not transgressors.

And slay them wherever you catch them and turn them out from where they
have turned you out; for Fitnah, tumult and oppression are worse than slaughter;
but fight them not at the Sacred Mosque, unless they fight you there first ; but
if they fight you, slay them. Such is the reward of those who suppress faith.

But if they cease, Allah is Oft-Forgiving, Most Merciful.

And fight them on until there is no more Fitnah, tumult or oppression and
there prevail justice and faith in Allah; but if they cease, let there be no hostility
except to those who practice oppression. (Al-Baqarah 2:190–93, Koran)

"And why should you not fight in the cause of Allah and for those
men, women and children, who are weak, abused and oppressed, those
who beseech their Lord to deliver them from their oppressors and
those who ask Allah to send for them protectors and helpers."

Those who believe fight in the cause of Allah and those who reject
Faith fight in the cause of Evil: so fight you against the friends of Satan:
feeble indeed is the cunning of Satan. (An-Nisa 4:75–76, Koran)

And slacken not in following up the enemy; if you are suffering hardships, they
are suffering similar hardships; but you have hope from Allah, while they have
none. And Allah is full of Knowledge and Wisdom. (An-Nisa 4:104, Koran)

If Allah helps you none can overcome you: if He forsakes you,
who is there, after that, that can??? help you? In Allah, then,
let Believers put their trust. (Ali 'Imran 3:160, Koran)

We did indeed send, before you Rasools to their respective peoples, with Clear
Signs: To those who transgressed, We meted out Retribution: and as a right those
who earned from us, We helped those who believed. (Ar-Rum 30:47, Koran)

Here is a declaration to the human, a guidance and advice
to those who live in awareness, Taqwa of Allah!

So lose not hope nor shall you despair, for you shall
achieve supremacy, if your are true in Faith.

If you have suffered a setback, verily a setback has been there for the
other party too. We make such days of adversity go around amongst the
humans so that Allah may distinguish those who believe and choose His
witnesses from amongst them. And Allah loves not the evil doers.

Allah's objective is to distinguish the True Believers from
those who reject Faith. (Ali 'Imran 3:138–41, Koran)

Wars and slaughter are abhorrent to Allah. Allah says:

If anyone slew a person, unless it is in retribution for murder or for spreading
mischief, fasaad in the land it would be as if he slew the whole people.
And if any one saved a life, it would be as if he saved the life of the whole
people. Take not life, which Allah has made sacred, except by the way of
justice or law. This He commands you, that you may learn wisdom.

And then Allah declares to the believers that *fitnah*, treachery, and
oppression are worse than slaughter and taking of life. *Fitnah*, treason,
and oppression are so vile and repugnant to Allah that He commands
the believers to fight those who assail them and inflict oppression:

And slay them wherever you catch them and turn them out from where they
have turned you out; for Fitnah, tyranny and oppression are worse than slaughter;
And fight them on until there is no more Fitnah, tumult or oppression and
there prevail justice and faith in Allah; but if they cease, let there be no hostility
except to those who practice'. oppression. (Al-Baqarah 2:190–93, Koran)

Allah's command to fight *fitnah*, however, is conditional:

If the oppressors cease, let there be no further hostility except
to those who practice oppression. Do not transgress limits. Allah
does not love transgressors. (Al-Baqarah 2:190–93, Koran)

When the Believers fight against Fitnah and oppression, they
fight in the cause of Allah. Those who reject faith in Allah, they
fight in the cause of evil. (An-Nisa 4:75–76, Koran)

Fitnah: Allah has granted each believer a right to freedom; right to
practice his and her *din* in accordance with his and her beliefs since,
in Islam, there is no compulsion in matters of religion; right to life,
which includes mental, physical, and emotional well-being; right
safeguard to one's property; right to intellectual endeavors, acquisition
of knowledge, and education; right to make a living; and right to
free speech and action to enjoin good and forbid evil. In enjoying his
freedoms, the individual ensures that his activities do not impinge
on the similar rights of others. Oppression and tyranny—which
deprives an individual believer, a community of believers, or their
nation (the *ummah*) of their God-given right to such a freedom—is
fitnah as described in the Koran. The perpetrators of such tyranny and
oppression cannot belong to the fellowship of Allah, the fellowship of
His covenant, nor the fellowship of the blessed *Nabiien* of Allah.

In the above *ayahs*, Allah commands the believers to fight such infidels
until there is no more *fitnah*, treachery, and oppression and there
prevails justice and faith in Allah everywhere. He orders them to slay
them wherever they catch them and turn them out from where they
have turned them out, for *fitnah*, tumult, and oppression are worse
than slaughter. Allah has forbidden the taking of life. "Take not life,
which Allah has made sacred, except by the way of justice or law."
Fitnah, tyranny, and oppression are so vile and repugnant that Allah
commands the believers to fight those who assail them and inflict
oppression. "Go forth, advance! Whether equipped well or lightly,
perform *jihad* strive your utmost and struggle with your wealth and
your persons in the cause of Allah." Allah loves those who fight in
His cause in unison and solidarity. *Fitnah*, treachery, and oppression
not only afflict those who perpetrate it but also affect everyone, guilty

and innocent alike. Allah's command to fight *fitnah* is conditional, however: if the oppressors cease, let there be no further hostility except to those who practice *fitnah*. Do not transgress limits. Allah does not love transgressors.

In the twenty-first century, weakness, poverty, disunity, and fragmentation of the *ummah* arise from its lack of appreciation of the immense store of understanding and knowledge that is in the Koran. Muslims look at the word of Allah but do not see it. They listen to the word but do not hear it. Allah's *nur*, His light, is with them, but they do not let it enter their hearts. The mirror of their *nafs* is covered with the smoke of their greed and craving of worldly wealth. They cannot see Allah's *nur* through the smoky darkness in their heart. *Fitnah*, treachery, and oppression are by-products of darkened hearts, causing blindness to the *nur* of Allah. Without His *nur*, there cannot be *taqwa* of Allah; and in the absence of the consciousness of the reality of Allah, the darkened soul is open to the evil haunts of Satan.

Muslim societies have been plagued by *fitnah* and oppression since the death of the blessed *nabi*. In Muslim countries, *fitnah* is the result of the combination of internal and external forces. Although the perpetrators of *fitnah* often proclaim Allah as their Savior, their actions always belie their faith in Him.

Most believers, men and women, are not aware that Allah has granted each believer rights and freedom. Most do not know that when the blessed Muhammad died, every believer inherited the Koran, Allah's covenant, His *din*, and the Dar es Salaam. Every believer became the successor, inheritor, and the custodian of the blessed *nabi's* legacy till the end of time. Consequently, in the twenty-first century, majority of believers are unaware of their rights granted by Allah. They are unaware that Allah commands them to fight the fitnah of tyranny and oppression perpetrated by their self-appointed rulers, kings, military dictators, and infidel *awliya*, their Euro-Christian patrons.

Internal *Fitnah*: Hundreds of years of rule of sultans and later of the Western colonial masters produced three unique sources of internal *fitnah* that rule the roost in the Muslim societies of our day.

Priesthood. There is no priesthood in Islam; the believer has a highly personal and exclusive relationship with Allah. Such relationship does not permit the intervention of another human being between Allah and His believer. When the blessed Muhammad was taken up by Allah, every believer inherited the Koran, Allah's covenant, and His *din*. Every believer became the successor, inheritor, and custodian of the prophet's legacy till the end of time. The priests and clerics of Islam assumed the legacy of the pagan priesthood and began to speak on behalf of Allah. Through distortion and misrepresentation of the word of Allah and the pronouncements of His *nabi*, over the last fourteen hundred years, the priests and imams of Islam have created divisions and schisms to generate hundreds of self-righteous sects and subsects among the Muslims. Each sect is the enemy of the other. Every group has the dagger in the back of the other. This gradually smoldering *fitnah* of the priesthood is slowly consuming the body of the *ummah*.

Mercenary Armies of Islam. The blessed nabi said,

> *All believers shall rise as one man against anyone who seeks to commit injustice, aggression, crime, or spread mutual enmity amongst the Muslims. All believers are bonded one to another to the exclusion of other men. The believers shall leave none of their members in destitution without giving him in kindness that he needs by the way of his liberty.*

However, this fight for unity, equality, and justice did not occur in the lands of Islam; the army of God and the army of Islam did not arise to fight in the cause of Allah to defend against *fitnah*, tyranny, and oppression and to seek retribution against injustice. The absolute loyalty of the army of Islam is to God, the Koran, and the *ummah*. The army of Islam defends the believers, their faith, their land, their wealth, and their honor and fights only against *fitnah* for truth and justice. In case of injury to the believers, their faith, their land, their wealth, and their honor, the believers are obliged to exact retribution. No believer shall side with an unbeliever against a believer. Whosoever is convicted of killing a believer without a righteous cause shall be liable to the relatives of the killed. The killers shall be subject to retaliation by each believer until the relatives of the victim are satisfied with the retribution.

Had the Muslim communities stood united as one to avenge the blood of every fallen Muslim and rejected a separate peace with the pagans without all the Muslims participating in it, there would have been no *fitnah* and massacres in Algeria, Palestine, India, Afghanistan, Iraq, Bosnia, Chechnya, Kosovo, and Darfur. This unity demands revenge, retribution, and reprisal for every act of murder and injury in Dayr Yasin, Sabra, Shatila, Srebrenica, Jenin, Sarajevo, Falluja, Kosovo, Chechnya, Gujarat, Kashmir, Iraq, Guantanamo Bay, and Abu Ghraib. Had the Muslims stood up for one another and fought those who perpetrated *fitnah*, they would not have been groveling in the dustheap of humanity today.

Contrary to the stipulations of the covenant of Allah, the present six-million-man mercenary armies of Muslim states serve to bolster illegal regimes of *Munafiqeen*, the traitors to the cause of Islam. Instead of relieving the believers from *fitnah* and oppression, they cause them. They are the source of dichotomy and division in Islam; they are the defenders of the foreign hegemony over Islam. The armies of the sultans of the previous centuries and the rulers of modern times are the perpetrators of *fitnah*, and they are the enemies of Islam. They are the defenders of the borders created by the Western colonial powers that divide Islam today. They are the *fitnah*.

Rulers of Islam. Islam is a religion of voluntary submission of a human to the will of Allah after a considered conviction that He is the only reality and that everything else springs out of that reality. Allah has given every man the freedom of choice to submit or not to His will. There is no compulsion in matters of the *din*. Yet there are humans who by force of arms compel other humans to submit to their will. They demand obedience through imprisonment, torture, and murder. Every Muslim state in this day is a police state. Every Muslim ruler abuses his authority to plunder and debase the lands of Islam. Every Muslim state today is the source of *fitnah* that is eating into the heart and the soul of Islam.

The External *Fitnah* of the Circle of Evil: Two hundred years ago, the circle of evil began its control of the world's wealth through conspiracy, subterfuge, and secrecy by undermining the stability of countries through war, strife, and discord and by weakening governments through creation of confusion in financial markets. The Western armies and intelligence services are the foot soldiers of the circle of evil, and the rulers of both the East and the West are their pawns and puppets to be manipulated at will to control the power and wealth of the world. The circle of evil is the external *fitnah* whose intent is to destroy Islam. It has always been its intention to corrupt, divide, and control the wealth of the Islamic land through the manipulation of its rulers, who were initially placed in positions of power by the circle with the help of the Western armies, intelligence, and diplomacy.

The weakness of the mercenary armies of the modern Islamic states clearly arises from the nonfulfillment of Allah's injunctions in the covenant. Faith in Allah's promise and power, unity of the *ummah*, justice, and the struggle to end *fitnah* and tyranny are essential actions ordained in the covenant. When a believer reneges on his covenant with Allah, he only does it to the detriment to his own soul. However, such an action on the part of the community and its appointed leaders leads to the undermining, enslavement, and impoverishment of the whole Islamic community for many generations.

The foundation of the regimes of the imperial families of the Arabian Peninsula, Jordan, Brunei, and Morocco and the imperial occupation governments of Hosni Mubarak of Egypt and the generals of Pakistan are supported by the external *fitnah*—the British, US, and NATO armed forces, intelligence, and diplomatic services—in opposition to the aspirations of their own people. In return, these regimes provide services to the circle of evil to subvert, undermine, and weaken the neighboring Islamic and Arab countries of Iran, Afghanistan, Iraq, Syria, Libya, Algeria, Sudan, and Mauritania. The *ummah* is saddled with the curse and the *fitnah* of the priesthood, the mercenary armies of Muslim states, their corrupt rulers, and the foreign masters of their rulers.

Imagine a country with the largest land base, with coasts rimmed by thousands of miles of blue oceans, and with a vast number of rivers flowing from hundreds of snowcapped mountains through its deserts, grasslands, fertile valleys, and plains into rich deltas, lakes, and oceans bursting with marine life and other resources—a land blessed by Allah with resources never equaled in history, peopled with a devout, hardworking population with the knowledge of how to utilize such resources in the service of Allah and His creatures. Again, see in your mind's eye an army, the largest in history of mankind, keeping this land, its borders and resources, its oceans and skies, and its people and wealth secure from marauders who have traditionally raided other lands for their resources. These defense forces compose of an army of six million men in about 300 infantry and mechanized divisions equipped with 30,000 tanks and armored vehicles, an air force of 3,580 aircraft of varying models, and a naval force equipped with 230 coastal and oceangoing ships equipped with armaments bought from the West and Russia. There are also 60 submarines in the armada. These armed forces are also equipped with short- and medium-range missiles tipped with about sixty nuclear bombs. The country has a budding arms-manufacturing industry producing low- and medium-technology arms. The annual budget of the combined forces is eighty-five billion dollars, of which thirty billion dollars annually goes to Western countries to purchase their discarded and obsolete weaponry. The West then uses these funds to refurbish its own arsenal with the latest, high-tech weapons.

You might have guessed that we are talking about the combined might of the Islamic world at the onset of the twenty-first century. This army has never won any battle of significance since the war for the Gallipoli Peninsula about a century ago. These armed forces have not defended in any significant manner the Islamic world since the disintegration of the Ottoman Empire. The wars of independence of Islamic lands from the colonial rule in India, Iran, Iraq, Syria, Egypt, Morocco, and Algeria were fought by the masses with civil disobedience and guerrilla warfare. The state-organized armies of Islam have failed to safeguard the freedom of the people of Palestine, Iraq, Kashmir, Sinkiang, Iraq, Kosovo, Bosnia, Mindanao, Chechnya, and Russia.

What went wrong? The Muslim army of the twentieth and the twenty-first centuries has its guns pointed toward its own people, whereas the external borders of Islam are guarded and patrolled by the naval fleets of America and Europe. The Muslim state armies should be fighting the treachery and oppression by enemies of Allah and Islam—the *kafaru, mushrikun, Munafiqeen,* and *zalimun,* who have usurped and plundered resources of the believers for the last two hundred years. Instead, the Muslim armies and security services are themselves the source of oppression and treachery to the *momineen,* resisting tyranny of the circle of evil of the *Munafiqun* and the *Mutaffifeen.* The clear examples are the armed and security forces of Reza Shah Pahlavi, the mullahs of Iran, Saddam Hussein of Iraq, the Taliban, the Pakistani governments, the Saudi family, Suharto, Syria, Anwar Sadat, Hosni Mubarak, Gaddhafi, the Algerian military, and Morocco's royalty.

This is a clear testimony that the believers of the covenant of Allah and those who control the so-called armies of Islam have not surrendered to the will of Allah and do not strive in His path. The obligations assigned to the individual believer in the covenant of Allah are the same for the community of Islam and for the leaders whom the believers appoint to look after and to protect their individual and communal interests. The covenant is specific in pointing out the responsibilities of the individual, the community, and its appointed leaders.

Jihad is the internal struggle of the believer to cleanse oneself of the temptations of the evil that surrounds him or her. It is also a constant external struggle to rid the community of the treachery and oppression by the enemy of the covenant and *din.* The enemy may be obvious, visible, and easily overpowered. The web of intrigues and conspiracies of the *kafaru, mushrikun, Munafiqeen,* and *zalimun* is hard to detect and overcome. The deception may come from familiar people working from within the community for the circle of evil whose motive is to tempt you away from Allah's path and also take control of your land and wealth, enslaving you in the process. The following four principles should guide the believers in their striving for Allah's cause.

1. Faith in Allah's Covenant and Promise.

Join not anything in worship with Him. Allah is the *Waliy* (Friend and Defender) of the believers who obey His covenant. Allah promises His strength and power (*al-qawiyy al-Aziz*) to aid the believer and promises victory in his striving for Allah's *din*. Therefore, the believer shall maintain his faith in Allah's promise always. Trust in Allah's promise endows the believer with the greatest strength from Allah's might in his determination to struggle and fight for Allah's cause. All strength belongs to Allah. All physical, worldly, political, and cosmic strength is nothing before the infinite strength of Allah.

> Allah is the All-powerful the Almighty, Al-qawiyy al-Aziz. (Hud 11:66, Koran)

> There is no Power except in Allah. (Al-Kahf 18:39, Koran)

> Verily it is I and My Messengers who will be victorious Verily Allah is All-powerful, All-mighty. (Al-Mujadila 58:21, Koran)

2. Unity.

The believers constitute one *ummah* to the exclusion of all other men. Just as the bond with Allah is indivisible, all believers shall stand in commitment with the least of them. All believers shall rise as one against anyone who seeks to commit injustice, aggression, or crime or spread mutual enmity among the Muslims. The believers shall leave none of their members in destitution without giving him in kindness and liberty what he needs. The pious believers follow the best and the most upright guidance of Allah's covenant.

3. Jihad.

All believers shall rise as one against anyone who seeks to commit injustice, aggression, or crime or spread mutual enmity among the

Muslims. This Pax Islamica is one and indivisible. No believer shall enter a separate peace without all other believers whenever there is fighting in the cause of Allah but will do so only on the basis of equality and justice to all others. In every expedition for the cause of Allah, all parties to the covenant shall fight shoulder to shoulder as one man. All believers shall avenge the blood of one another when anyone falls while fighting for the cause of Allah.

4. Murder.

No believer shall slay a believer in retaliation for an unbeliever, nor shall he assist an unbeliever against a believer. Whoever is convicted of killing a believer deliberately but without righteous cause shall be liable to the relatives of the killed. Until the latter are satisfied, the killer shall be subject to retaliation by each and every believer.

5. Justice.

Justice ('adl) is a divine attribute defined as "putting in the right place." The opposite of 'adl is zulm, which in Koranic terms means "wrongdoing." Wrongdoing is a human attribute defined as "putting things in the wrong place." Zulm (wrongdoing) is one of the common terms used in the Koran to refer to the negative acts employed by human beings. Wrongdoing is the opposite of justice, putting everything in its right place, and every act of humans as prescribed by Allah. Wrongdoing is to put things where they do not belong. Hence, wrongdoing is injustice, for example, associating others with Allah; others do not belong in the place for the divine. It is to place false words in place of the truth and to put someone else's property in place of your own. Other examples are taking a life against the divine commandments, replacing people's liberty with oppression, waging war instead of peace, and usurping people's right to govern themselves. The Koran repeatedly stigmatizes men of wrongdoing.

The Koran, when it points out who is harmed by injustice and wrongdoing, always mentions the word *nafs* (self). People cannot harm Allah. By being unjust or by putting things in the wrong place, people harm themselves. They distort their own natures, and they lead themselves astray. Who can one wrong? It is impossible to wrong or do injustice against Allah since all things are His creatures and do His work. Hence, wrongdoing and injustice is an activity against people and Allah's creation. Allah had prescribed His covenant to the humans for the good of human beings. People, tribes, and nations are being helped since Allah leads them into accord, harmony, and justice, which in turn create peace in the world. Allah has laid out all the basic principles for justice in His covenant for the humans to live in harmony. Those who refuse to follow His commandments are therefore ungrateful and hence *kafirs*. Thus, they are wrongdoers (*zalimun*) and only harm themselves. Therefore, there can be no jihad unless it is for justice and against wrongdoing.

There is a clear reason for the glaring weakness of the state-run armies of the Muslim nation-states. The Muslim states are governed by self-appointed kings, dictators, and politicians who are divorced from their *din* and their people. They belong to and serve the interests of the circle of evil.

Make careful preparations and take precautions. Then go forth in groups or all together to the endeavor.

There amongst you is he who will linger behind, if misfortune befalls you he will say, "Allah did favor him as he was not with you." When good fortune comes to you from Allah, he would wish that he had been with you.

Those who swap the life of this world for the hereafter let them fight in the cause of Allah. Whosoever fights in the cause of Allah, whether he is slain or he is victorious, there is a great award for him from Allah.

And why should you not fight in the cause of Allah and for those men, women and children, who are weak, abused and oppressed, those who beseech their Lord to deliver them from their oppressors and those who ask Allah to send for them protectors and helpers. (An-Nisa 4:71-75, Koran)

Remember Allah's blessings on you. When a people planned stretching out their hands against you and Allah did hold back their hands from you to protect you from your enemies. Be in taqwa of Allah, fear Allah and place your trust in Allah. (Al-Ma'idah 5:11, Koran)

Be in taqwa of Allah, fear Allah. Perform Jihad and strive your utmost in Allah's Cause and approach Him so that you may prosper. (Al-Ma'idah 3:35, Koran)

If any among you turn back on his faith Allah will bring a people whom He loves and who love Him and who are humble towards the believers and stern towards unbelievers, who perform jihad and strive in the cause of Allah and fear not reproaches of any blamer. Such is the Grace of Allah that He bestows on whom He wills. Allah is All-Sufficient for His Creatures and all Knowing.
(Al-Ma'idah 5:54, Koran)

When you meet the infidels rank upon rank, in conflict never turn your backs to them. (Al-Anfal 8:15, Koran)

Respond to Allah and His Rasool when He calls you to that gives you life. And know that Allah intervenes in the tussle between man and his heart and it is to Allah that you shall return. Fear treachery or oppression that afflicts not only those who perpetrate it, but affects guilty and innocent alike. Know that Allah is strict in punishment. (Al-Anfal 8:24-25, Koran)

Fight the infidel until there is no more treachery and oppression and there prevails Justice and Faith in Allah altogether and everywhere. If they cease, then Allah is seer of what they do. If they refuse, be sure that Allah is your Protector, the Best to protect and the Best to help. (Al-Anfal 8:39-40, Koran)

When you meet the enemy force, stand steadfast against them and remember the name of Allah much, so that you may be successful. And obey Allah and His Messenger and do not dispute with one another lest you lose courage and your strength departs and be patient. Allah is with those who patiently persevere. (Al-Anfal 8:45–46, Koran)

Whether you do or do not help Allah's Messenger, your leader, Allah strengthens him with His Peace and with forces that you do not see. The words of the infidels He humbled into the dirt but Allah's word is Exalted, High. Allah is Mighty, Wise. Go forth, advance! Whether equipped well or lightly, perform jihad strive your utmost and struggle with your wealth and your persons in the cause of Allah. That is best for you, if you knew. (At-Tawbah 9:38–41, Koran)

Fight the unbelievers who surround you. Let them find you firm and know Allah is always with those who have taqwa, who are Allah-wary. (At-Tawbah 9:123, Koran)

Remember the Grace of Allah, bestowed upon you, when there came down hordes to overpower you: We sent against them a hurricane and forces that that you did not see: but Allah sees all that ye do.

Behold! They came on you from above you and from below you, your eyes became dim and the hearts gaped up to the throats and you imagined various vain thoughts about Allah! (Al-Ahzab 33:9, Koran)

If ye will aid (the cause of) Allah, He will aid you and make your foothold firm. But those who reject Allah, for them is destruction and Allah will render their deeds vain. That is because they hate the Revelation of Allah; so He has made their deeds fruitless. Do they not travel through the earth and see what was the end of those before their times, who did evil? Allah brought utter destruction on them and similar fates await those who reject Allah. That is because Allah is the Protector of those who believe, but those who reject Allah have no protector. (Muhammad 47:7–11, Koran)

Be not weak and ask for peace, while you are having an upper hand: for Allah is with you and will never decrease the reward of your good deeds.

The life of this world is but play and amusement: and if ye believe, fear Allah and guard against evil, He will grant you your recompense and will not ask you (to give up) your possessions.

Behold, you are those invited to spend of your wealth in the Way of Allah: but among you are some that are parsimonious. But any who are miserly are so at the expense of their own souls. But Allah is free of all wants and it is ye that are needy. If ye turn back (from the Path), He will substitute in your stead another people; then they would not be like you! (Muhammad 47:33–38, Koran)

When ye are told to make room in the assemblies, spread out and make room: ample room will Allah provide for you. And when ye are told to rise up, for prayers, Jihad or other good deeds rise up: Allah will exalt in rank those of you who believe and who have been granted Knowledge. And Allah is well acquainted with all you do. (Al-Mujadila 58:11, Koran)

Why do you promise what you do not carry out? Hateful is indeed to Allah that you say what you do not act upon. Allah loves those who fight in His cause in array of unison and solidarity. (As-Saf 61:2–4, Koran)

Shall I guide you to a bargain that will save you from a painful torment? That you believe in Allah and His Messenger and that you perform Jihad (strive to your utmost) in the way of Allah, with all that you own and in all earnestness: that will be best for you, if you but knew! He will forgive you your sins and admit you to Gardens beneath which rivers flow and to beautiful dwellings in Jannat of adn (Gardens of Eternity): that is indeed the supreme blessing. And another favor will He bestow, which you will cherish; help from Allah and a speedy victory. So give the glad tidings to the believers. (As-Saf 61:10–13, Koran)

18. Forgiveness: Be Quick in the Race for Forgiveness from Your Lord, Restrain Anger, and Pardon All Humans

O you who believe! Be quick in the race for forgiveness from your Lord. Those who give freely whether in prosperity, or in adversity, those who restrain anger and pardon all humans, for Allah loves those who do beautiful deeds. Fear the Fire, which is prepared for those who reject Faith; And obey Allah and the Messenger; that ye may obtain mercy. Be quick in the race for forgiveness from your Lord and for a Garden whose measurement is that of the heavens and of the earth, prepared for the righteous.

Those who give freely whether in prosperity, or in adversity, those who restrain anger and pardon all humans, for Allah loves those who do beautiful deeds. (Ali 'Imran 3:130–34, Koran)

Among Allah's names are *ar-Rahman* (the Beneficent), *ar-Rahim* (the Merciful), and *al-Ghafoor* (the Forgiving). His mercy overtakes His punishment and anger.

Say: "O my Servants who have transgressed against their souls! Despair not of the Mercy of Allah: for Allah forgives all sins: for He is Oft-Forgiving, Most Merciful."

Every human action in daily life reaches back into the divine reality that everything in the universe is governed by tawhid, yet Allah has granted humans a freedom of choice, which can upset the balance in the creation, the balance of justice, and the balance of atmospheric elements and lead to environmental pollution, destruction of animal species, and destruction of populations, cities, and agriculture through human actions. The covenant tells people why they should be Allah's servants and explains which path they should follow to become His vicegerents. It makes it clear that human activity is deeply rooted in the Real, and this has everlasting repercussions in this world and in the hereafter.

The wholesome (*salihun*) are the ones who live in harmony with the Real (*Haqq*) and establish wholesomeness (*saalihaat*) through their words and deeds throughout the world. In contrast, the corrupt (*mufsidun*) destroy the proper balance and relationship with Allah and His creation. *Fasid* means "corrupt, evil, wrong."

Allah measures out good and evil, the wholesome and the corrupt. Humans have enough freedom to make their own choices; if they make the choice to do beautiful and wholesome deeds (*saalihaat*) motivated by faith (*iman* and god-wariness (*taqwa*), they please Allah and bring harmony and wholesomeness to the world, resulting in peace, justice, mercy, compassion, honor, equity, well-being, freedom, and many other gifts through Allah's grace. Others choose to do evil and work with corruption (*mufsidun*), destroying the right relationship among the creation, causing hunger, disease, oppression, pollution, and other afflictions. In the universal order, corruption is the prerogative of humans, and vicegerency gives humans the freedom to work against the Creator and His creation. Only misapplied trust can explain how moral evil can appear in the world. When humans choose wrong and corrupt actions, they displease Allah. Allah loves those who do what is beautiful, not those who do what is ugly:

When he turns his back, he hurries about the earth to work corruption there and destroy the tillage and the stock. Allah loves not corruption.
(Al-Baqarah 2:205, Koran)

Allah loves doing what is beautiful, and because of His love for those who do the beautiful, He brings them near to Himself, and His nearness is called Allah's mercy:

Work not corruption in this world after it has made wholesome and call upon Allah in fear and hope. Surely the mercy of Allah is near to those who do what is beautiful. (Al-A'raf 7:56, Koran)

The covenant of the Koran presents us the scope of the freedom of choice that humans have in doing what is wholesome and beautiful or what is corrupt or ugly. The human's role among the creation distinguishes right activity, right thought, and right intention from their opposites. It reminds us of how the scales of Allah's justice, the two hands of Allah—His mercy and His wrath—are reflected in the human domain, where people have been appointed Allah's vicegerents. Deeds of goodness and wholesomeness are associated with mercy, paradise, and the beautiful. Evil and corruption is rewarded with wrath, hell, and the ugly.

To err is human. Allah is most forgiving to those who have erred and repented. Above all, Allah's mercy knows no bounds. The Koran and the teaching of the blessed *nabi* guide those who seek the path of Allah. Allah says:

O my Servants who have transgressed against their souls! Despair not of the Mercy of Allah: for Allah forgives all sins: for He is Oft-Forgiving, Most Merciful.

Turn ye to your Lord (in repentance) and bow to His (Will), before the Penalty comes on you: after that ye shall not be helped. (Az-Zumar 39:53, Koran)

Allah, in His mercy, has laid down guidelines for punishment of the transgressors. For transgressors and sinners, there is Allah's wrath in this world and the next. If they repent, however, Allah forgives them. The Koran constantly emphasizes repentance and reform of a person and Allah's mercy and grace. Allah's mercy knows no bounds. Justice (*'adl*) is a divine attribute defined as "putting every object in the right place." When the transgressor repents, mends his ways, and does not repeat the wrongdoing, evil has been replaced with good. Allah bestows His mercy.

The community's obligation is to pardon and help educate and reform an individual. Allah advises every human to restrain from anger and resentment. Anger is a smoldering volcano quietly burning the human from the inside, robbing his tranquility and peace. Forgiving others restores peace and brings nearness to Allah. For the unrepentant transgressor, the penalty is prescribed in the Koran. Never is the gate to Allah's mercy closed. The key to this gate is repentance and a walk in Allah's path.

19. Murder

> If anyone slew a person, unless it be for punishment for murder or for spreading mischief in the land, it would be as if he slew the whole people: and if any one saved a life, it would be as if he saved the life of all the people.

Life is sacred. Allah forbids the taking of life unless it is by the way of justice (jihad against tyranny and oppression) or when ordained by the law of equality or punishment for murder, where the Koran recommends clemency. As the covenant forbids the believers and the community of Islam to take a life and murder, the same injunction applies to the ruler or the *amri minkum* appointed by the believers. War against Muslims and others for acquisition of territory and wealth is forbidden, and anyone waging such a war blatantly disobeys Allah's covenant and is not of the believers. Persecution, punishment, imprisonment, and murder of the citizens of the Islamic state who strive for the cause of Allah is a heinous crime. Rulers and their bureaucracy responsible for such crimes are unfit to discharge their responsibility and liable for punishment for their crime according to the law of the Koran.

If anyone slew a person - unless it be for murder or for spreading mischief in the land - it would be as if he slew the whole people: and if any one saved a life, it would be as if he saved the life of the whole people. (Al-Ma'idah 5:32, Koran)

Take not life, which Allah hath made sacred, except by the way of justice or law: This He commands you, that you may learn wisdom. (Al-An'am:151–53, Koran)

20. Usury and Hoarding of Wealth

> Devour not usury, doubled and multiplied; Be in *taqwa* of Allah (fear Allah) that ye may prosper.

Forbidden is the practice of usury to the Muslims. Also forbidden is making money from money. Money in its present form is only a medium of exchange, a way of defining the value of an item, but in itself has no value and therefore should not give rise to more money by earning interest through deposit in a bank or loaning it to someone else. The human endeavor, initiative, and risk involved in a productive venture are much more important than the money used to finance it. Money deposited in a bank or hoarded is potential capital rather than capital. Money becomes capital only when it is invested in a venture. Accordingly, money loaned to a business is regarded as a debt and is not capital; and as such, it is not entitled to any return, such as interest.

Muslims are encouraged to spend (purchase necessities or spend in the way of Allah) or invest their money and are discouraged from keeping their money idle. Hoarding money is unacceptable. Allah's commandments in His covenant with the believers in the following three *ayahs* exhort Muslims to (a) spend in charity after their needs are met, (b) devour not in usury, and (c) hoard not gold and silver.

They ask thee how much they are to spend (in charity); say: "What is beyond your needs." Thus doth Allah make clear to you His Signs: in order that ye may consider. (Al-Baqarah 2:222, Koran)

Allah will deprive usury of all blessing but will give increase for deeds of charity; for He loves not creatures ungrateful and wicked. (Al-Baqarah 2:275–76, Koran)

And there are those who hoard gold and silver and spend it not in the Way of Allah: announce unto them a most grievous penalty. (Al-A'raf 9:34, Koran)

Gharar (uncertainty, risk, or speculation) is forbidden. Any transaction entered into should be free from uncertainty, risk, and speculation. The parties cannot predetermine a granted profit, and this does not allow an undertaking from the borrower or the customer to repay the borrowed principal, plus an amount to consider inflation. Therefore, options and futures are regarded as un-Islamic; so are foreign exchange transactions because rates are determined by interest differentials.

An Islamic government is forbidden to lend or borrow money from institutions such as international banks, the World Bank, or the International Monetary Fund on interest as both usury and interest are expressly forbidden. Banking based on fiat money is also forbidden. The value of money is diluted by the creation of new money out of nothing; the property rights of savers and those who have been promised future payments, such as pensioners, are violated. This is stealing. The trappings of the money and banking system have been compared to that of a cult; only those who profit from it understand its inner workings. They work hard to keep it that way. The central banks print notes adorned with signatures, seals, and pictures of a president or that of a queen; counterfeiters are severely punished; governments pay their expenses with them; and populations are forced to accept them. They are printed like newspapers in such vast quantity, representing an equal worth to all the treasures of this world, all the resources above and under the ground, all assets of populations, and their work and labor to fabricate every item that has ever been manufactured. And yet these notes cost nothing to make. In truth, this has been the greatest hoax, the worst crime against humanity, a swindle of proportions never seen by humanity before.

As we have found, the Koran forbids usury, gambling, speculation, and hoarding of gold and silver. The Koran does advocate trade; spending on good things in life, kith, and kin; and giving wealth for the cause of Allah. The modern economic system is entirely alien to the teachings of the Koran and full of pitfalls and trappings laid down by Satan. The Dar es Salaam has slid downhill, submerged into the quicksand of make-believe economy. Every successful businessman and trader is forced to operate in the pagan, sinful system of economy. Here is the solution for a successful economic system as laid down in the covenant of the Koran:

1. Elimination of usury and interest in Dar es Salaam.

2. Elimination of fiat money and of banking based on money created out of nothing with a printing press. There will be no more creation and lending of capital nine times that of the bank deposits. It is dishonest and forbidden because it is based on institutionalized theft, supported by the state and international institutions.

3. Creation of a single currency for the united Islamic state, such as gold dinars and silver dirhams based on the measures established by Umar ibn al-Khattab, the second caliph. A currency bureau, an arm of the state of Dar es Salaam, will supervise the minting and circulation of the currency.

4. Drastic changes to Dar es Salaam's trading relations with the rest of the world. All goods utilized within the state—whether industrial, agricultural, manufactured, or raw—will be produced within the country so that the *ummah* is self-sufficient and independent of foreign trading systems. The goods for export—oil, minerals, raw and manufactured goods—shall be sold against gold and gold-based currency as well as barter. Paper and printed money will not be acceptable. Pricing for international trade will use an index of equal value to human labor internationally.

Those that spend of their goods in charity by night and by day, in secret and in public, have their reward with their Lord: on them shall be no fear, nor shall they grieve.

Those who devour usury will not stand except stands the one whom the Satan by his touch has driven to madness. That is because they say: "Trade is like usury," but Allah hath permitted trade and forbidden usury. Those who after receiving direction from their Lord, desist, shall be pardoned for the past; their case is for Allah to judge; but those who repeat (the offence) are Companions of the Fire; they will abide therein (forever).

Allah will deprive usury of all blessing but will give increase for deeds of charity; for He does not love ungrateful and wicked creatures. (Al-Baqarah 2:274–76, Koran)

Those who believe and perform wholesome deeds, establish regular prayers and regular charity have rewards with their Lord. On them shall be no fear, nor shall they grieve.

Fear Allah and give up what remains of your demand for usury, if you are indeed believers. If you do it not, take notice of war from Allah and His Messenger: but if you turn back, you will still have your capital sums.

Deal not unjustly and ye shall not be dealt with unjustly.

If the debtor is in a difficulty, grant him time until it is easy for him to repay. But if ye remit it by way of charity, that is best for you. (Al-Baqarah 2:277–80, Koran)

Devour not usury, doubled and multiplied; Be in taqwa of Allah (fear Allah) that ye may prosper.

Fear the Fire, which is prepared for those who reject Faith; and obey Allah and the Messenger; that ye may obtain mercy.

Be quick in the race for forgiveness from your Lord and for a Garden whose measurement is that of the heavens and of the earth, prepared for the righteous.

Those who give freely whether in prosperity, or in adversity; those who restrain anger and pardon all humans; for Allah loves those who do beautiful deeds (Al-muhsinun). (Ali 'Imran 3:130–34, Koran)

There are indeed many among the priests and clerics who in falsehood devour the substance of men and hinder them from the way of Allah. And there are those who bury gold and silver and spend it not in the way of Allah: announce unto them a most grievous penalty.

On the Day when heat will be produced out of that wealth in the fire of Hell and with it will be branded their foreheads, their flanks and their backs, "This is the treasure which you buried for yourselves: taste then, the treasures which you buried!" (At-Tawbah 9:34–35, Koran)

21. Be Good to Your Parents; Allah Forbids Infanticide and Abortion

The Koran repeatedly commands the believers to do what is beautiful to be brought under the sway of Allah's gentle, merciful, and beautiful names. Human qualities gain their reality from the most beautiful divine qualities. When humans turn to Allah, their beautiful qualities become indistinguishable from Allah's own.

To Allah belongs all that is in the heavens and on earth; so that He rewards those who do ugly, according for what they have done and He rewards those who do beautiful with the most beautiful. (An-Najm 53:31, Koran)

The first beautiful act that believers perform after tawhid is to do what is beautiful and do good to their parents, those who brought them into existence. It is parents who provide means that Allah employs in creating people, nurturing, educating, and making them beautiful and God fearing. Allah takes credit for His creation, which is the requirement of tawhid. Allah expects his creatures to act appropriately toward His intermediaries of creation. Only in this manner can humans expect other creatures, including their own children, to act beautifully toward them.

Respect and care for the parents is the fundamental act in the Islamic society to maintain the cohesion of the family structure. The family is the underlying unit of the community that forms the support group for children, adults, the elderly, the relatives, the neighborhood, the kin, and the communal structure around the mosque and schools.

Infanticide and its modern version, abortion, and the taking of life of both humans and animals are forbidden by the Koran. Allah has made life sacred. And avoid *Fahasha*, the shameful deeds that set the human down a slippery slope of the ugly and evil.

Worship none but Allah; treat with kindness your parents and kindred and orphans and those in need; speak fair to the people; be steadfast in prayer; And practice regular charity. (Al-Baqarah 2:82, Koran)

Say: "Come, I will rehearse what Allah hath (really) prohibited you from": join not anything as equal with Him; be good to your parents; kill not your children on a plea of want - We provide sustenance for you and for them - come not nigh to shameful deeds, whether open or secret; take not life, which Allah hath made sacred, except by way of justice and law: thus doth He command you, that ye may learn wisdom. (Al-An' am 6:151, Koran)

Take not with Allah another object of worship; or thou wilt sit in disgrace and destitution Thy Lord hath decreed that ye worship none but Him and that ye be kind to parents. Whether one or both of them attain old age in thy life, say not to them a word of contempt, nor repel them, but address them in terms of honor. And out of kindness, lower to them the wing of humility and say: "My Lord! Bestow on them thy Mercy even as they cherished me in childhood."
(Al-Isra 17:22, 24, Koran)

We have enjoined on man kindness to his parents: in pain did his mother bear him and in pain did she give him birth. The carrying of the (child) to his weaning is (a period of) thirty months. At length, when he reaches the age of full strength and attains forty years, he says: "O my Lord! grant me that I may be grateful for Thy favor which Thou hast bestowed upon me and upon both my parents and that I may work righteousness such as Thou may approve; and be gracious to me in my issue. Truly have I turned to Thee and truly do I bow (to Thee) in Islam."
(Al-Ahqaf 46:15, Koran)

22. Women and Equality

> You are forbidden to take women against their will. Nor should you treat them with harshness, on the contrary treat them with them on a footing of equality kindness and honor.

Fifty percent of the population of the believers, the women, has been excluded from the mainstream Islam by the mullahs, jurist-scholars, and the Hadith scholars against the commandments of the Koran. Women were regarded as inferior beings in most pre-Islamic cultures, including among the Arabs, Persians, Greeks, and Romans as well as the Hindus. Their status was not any higher among the Turkish and the Mongol tribes of Central Asia. In Judaism, women were forbidden from the inner sanctuary of the temple; and in the early Pauline Christianity, their position was relegated to the entrance of or outside the church at prayer time.

Islam brought dignity and grace to the status of women—the mothers, wives, and daughters. Women had their rights established and their social status elevated as equal to that of men. They attended prayer services at the Prophet's Mosque; they held regular and frequent discourse with the *nabi* of Allah on religious, women's, and family issues. They participated in battles alongside their men. Women worked outside their homes. The first person to convert to Islam, Khadijah, was a successful international trader and owned an import and export business, dealing goods from India, Persia, Africa, Yemen, and the Byzantine Empire. She employed several men to assist her in her business. Other women memorized the Koran and taught other Muslims. A'ishah gave regular talks and discourses on religious matters. Other women led the ritual prayers and *dhikr-e-Allah* gatherings.

The ulema and other followers of the *Hadith collections* over the last one thousand years have totally excluded women from congregation prayers, businesses, public and social affairs, and most importantly education. The Muslim communities have betrayed Allah and His *rasul* concerning their obligations to the women—their mothers, wives, sisters, and daughters. Allah's covenant provides equality to every individual within the community, both men and women. Allah has elevated the rank and dignity of the children of Adam, both men and women, with special favors above that of most of his creation, including the angels. The dignity and favors promised by Allah include six special values: faith, life, intellect (education), property, lineage, and freedom of speech and action.

Equality of Men and Women: The Koran addresses men and women who submit to Allah, who believe, who are devout, who speak the truth, who are righteous, who are humble, who are charitable, who fast and deny themselves, who guard their chastity, and who remember Allah and promises them a great reward and forgiveness for their transgressions. In this address, Allah treats men and women equitably with the promise of a similar reward for their good acts. In Allah's eyes, all men and women who do good deeds carry an equal favor with Him.

Allah admonishes believing men and women to lower their gaze and guard their chastity. Allah is well acquainted with what men did. Allah also admonishes women to dress modestly and not display their adornments outside their immediate family environment. Allah commands believers, men and women, to turn *all together* toward Allah so that they may prosper. This can happen only when the believers, men and women, turn to Allah collectively as a community in a mosque as was customary during the lifetime of the *nabi* of Allah.

According to the Koran, men and women are autonomous and answerable to Allah for their own deeds and actions, and only they as individuals are rewarded or punished for their deeds. In a community, men as a group or the state has no authority from the Koran to enforce any restrictions on the freedom of righteous and believing women. To every man and woman, Allah has bestowed rights to *faith, life, intellect, property, education, and freedom of action and speech*. The authority of a ruler who denies these basic freedoms to men or to women is openly disputable. A person obeys the ruler on the condition that the ruler obeys the Koran and Allah's covenant.

For men and women who surrender unto Allah,

For men and women who believe,

For men and women who are devout

For men and women who speak the truth,

For men and women who persevere in righteousness,

For men and women who are humble,

For men and women who are charitable,

For men and women who fast and deny them selves

For men and women who guard their chastity,

For men and women who remember Allah much,

For them Allah has forgiveness and a great reward.

Say to the

Believing men that they should lower their gaze and guard their modesty:

That will make for greater purity for them:

And Allah is acquainted with all that they do.

And say to the

Believing women that they should lower their gaze and guard their modesty;

That they should not display their adornments except what is ordinarily obvious,

That they should draw a veil over

Their bosom and not display their adornments

(Except to the immediate family)

And that they should not strike their feet

In order to draw attention

To their hidden adornments.

and O ye Believers!

Turn ye all together Toward Allah that ye may prosper.

The believer's men and women are protectors one of another;

They enjoin what is just and forbid what is evil;

They observe regular prayers, practice regular charity obey Allah and His messenger.

On them will Allah pour His mercy, for Allah is exalted in power, wise.

Oh ye who believe! Guard your souls,

If ye follow [right] guidance,

No hurt can come to you from those who stray;

The goal of you all is to Allah,

It is He who will show you the truth of all that ye do.

The Koran, as in the sura above, addresses men and women equally, subjecting them together to similar obligations of submission to Allah, regular prayer, giving in charity, modesty in dress and behavior, righteousness, humility, chastity, worship, truthfulness, remembrance of Allah, and being kind and just. Allah blessed mankind (*insan*), both men and women, with dignity, justice, and equality. He promised them the same rewards and gave them the same obligations. *Be steadfast in prayer and practice regular charity* is an ongoing and repetitive theme in the Koran. Allah calls those who believe, both men and women, to hasten to the congregation prayer on Friday, the day of assembly.

O ye who believe! (Men and women) When the call is proclaimed to prayer on Friday (the Day of Assembly), hasten earnestly to the Remembrance of Allah and leave off business (and traffic): that is best for you if ye but knew! and when the Prayer is finished, then may ye disperse through the land and seek of the Bounty of Allah: and celebrate the Praises of Allah often (and without stint): that ye may prosper. (Al-Mumtahanah 62:9–10, Koran)

Women attended obligatory prayers, *jum'ah* prayers, and Eid prayers in the Prophet's Mosque. Whenever the apostle of Allah finished his prayers with *Taslim*, the women would get up first, and he would stay in his place for a while before getting up. The purpose of staying was that the women might leave before the men who had finished their prayer.

Soon after the *nabi* died, there occurred an enormous expansion of the Islamic domain. Women, for a while, enjoyed their newly won freedom and dignity given by Islam and proclaimed by the blessed *nabi*

Muhammad. Soon afterward, the Arabs reached an unprecedented level of prosperity and began to accumulate large harems of wives, concubines, and female slaves and servants. These women were increasingly confined to their quarters and not allowed to go out unchaperoned. Subsequently, the architecture of the Middle East dwellings changed to suit the new circumstances. The courtyard of the house had high walls, and the only entrance was where the master of the house sat. The master of the harem was so jealous of the chastity of his women that he only employed eunuchs as his servants and guards at his house. The institution of eunuchs was a peculiar Middle Eastern practice related to the institution of the harems of the elite.

The trampling of women's rights was and is a betrayal of the blessed *nabi* Muhammad's emancipation of women. As more Arabs, Romans, Persians, Hindus, Turks, and Mongols embraced Islam, they brought with them their peculiar bias against women and female infants. The Islamic emancipation of women was ignored; women were confined within their houses, covered head to foot in cloth, denied spiritual growth, and denied access to education and to places of worship. Shamefully, the scholars and the ulema encouraged this state of affairs. Women were gradually discouraged from praying in the mosque and were excluded from congregational worship. Thus, the Muslims for centuries have betrayed the *nabi* of Allah and disobeyed Allah's covenant.

Pre-Islamic Arab and other cultures regarded women as their chattel and possession. Abduction and rape of opponents' women was a favored pastime of those victorious in battle to humiliate the vanquished. Thus, the birth of a female child was regarded as a matter of shame, which led to the practice of infanticide. This practice was forbidden earlier on during the prophet's mission. However, the primordial masculine instinct resurfaced in the new Muslim. His subconscious shame and embarrassment of the female in his household was sublimated into gentler and more socially acceptable alternative. As the Koran points out, he chose to retain the female child on sufferance and contempt rather than bury her in the dust. And the Koran says, *"What an evil choice they decide on!"* The shame and cultural burden in some of the Muslim societies is so intense that the female infant is buried in the coffin of yashmak (burka) in the confines of her brick house. She is not killed off physically but intellectually and spiritually by withholding the intellectual and spiritual sustenance that Allah had provided for her.

Indeed Lost are those who slay their children, foolishly and without knowledge and have forbidden that which Allah has provided for them and inventing lies against Allah. They have indeed gone astray and heeded no guidance.
(Al-An' am 6:140, Koran)

When news is brought to one of them, of the birth of a female child, his face darkens and he is filled with inward grief! With shame does he hide himself from his people, because of the bad news he has had! Shall he retain it on sufferance and contempt, or bury it in the dust? Ah! What an evil choice they decide on?
(An-Nahl 16:58–59, Koran)

Women have their freedoms, bestowed by the covenant of Allah. Women can achieve their God-given equality and respect only when they stand up to men to demand equality and respect in all the spheres of life in Muslim societies. This will occur only when women have an intellectual awakening to understand and assert their rights. The dignity and favors promised by Allah include six special values: faith, life, intellect (education), property, lineage, and freedom of speech and action.

Until Muslim men do not eliminate their *fitnah* against 50 percent of believers—their mothers, wives, sisters, and daughters—they will continue to be mired in the pit of ignorance, poverty, and *Fahasha*. To arise out of the pit of decadence, they will have to swallow their ego and pride and learn to respect and honor their women.

To every man and to every woman Allah has bestowed Equal rights to Freedom, Faith, Life, Intellect, Property, Education and Freedom of Speech and Action, enjoining what is right and forbidding what is wrong.

You are forbidden to take women against their will. Nor should you treat them with harshness, so that you may renounce of the dower you have given them and that is only permitted where they have been guilty of open lewdness. On the contrary live with them on a footing of kindness and honor. If ye take a dislike to them it may be that you dislike a thing, through which Allah brings about a great deal of good. (An-Nisa 4:19, Koran)

Truly, among your wives and your children are some that are contenders to your obligations so beware! If ye forgive them and overlook their faults, verily Allah is Most -Forgiving, Most Merciful. Your riches and your children may be but a temptation: Whereas Allah! With Him is an immense reward.

So be in taqwa of Allah and fear Allah as much as you can; listen and obey; and spend in charity for the benefit of your own souls. And those saved from their own greed are the ones that prosper. If ye loan to Allah a beautiful loan, He will double it for you and He will forgive you: for Allah is both Appreciative (Shakoor) and Magnanimous (Haleem), Knower of what is hidden and what is manifest, Exalted in Might, Full of Wisdom. (At-Taghabun 64:14-18, Koran)

Those who slander decent women, thoughtless but believing, are cursed in this life and in the Hereafter: for them is a grievous Penalty. (An-Nur 24:21-23, Koran)

23. Wealth

Crave not those things of what Allah has bestowed His gifts more freely on some than others, men are assigned what they earn and women that they earn.

Allah created the earth and then bestowed on man His favors to extract sustenance from it. He also created the sun, moon, and stars to create a just equilibrium and harmony in the universe. The sun provides energy for the growth, sustenance, and well-being of humans, plants, and animals. Gradually, man began to extract more than his personal needs from the earth; and the boom of economics, trade, and commerce started, creating cycles of imbalance, disharmony, wars, poverty, and injustice throughout the globe. Not only did this disharmony caused by greed blemish humans but animal life also suffered by the disappearance of whole species. Pollution and contamination of the environment resulted from the race trying to accumulate and hoard the world's wealth in a few hands. Man disobeyed Allah's universal laws and covenant.

In return for all of Allah's favors, Allah commands the following:

- Justice (*al-'adl*). Justice, fairness, honesty, integrity, and evenhanded dealings are a prerequisite of every Muslim's conduct when dealing with others whether socially or in a business transaction.
- Doing what is good and what is beautiful (*ihsan*). This attribute includes every positive quality such as goodness, beauty, and harmony. Human beings have an obligation to do what is wholesome and beautiful in their relationship with Allah and His creatures.
- Providing for those near to you (*qurba*) and kith and kin. Help them with wealth, kindness, compassion, humanity, and sympathy.

Allah forbids *Fahasha*—all evil deeds, lies, false testimony, fornication, selfishness, ingratitude, greed, and false belief. One must fulfill the covenant of Allah, and whosoever does beautiful and righteous deeds will be given a new life and rewarded with greater wages by Allah.

Allah commands justice, the doing of good and liberality to kith and kin and He forbids all shameful deeds and injustice and rebellion: He instructs you, that ye may receive admonition.

Fulfill the Covenant of Allah when ye have entered into it and break not your covenants after ye have confirmed them: indeed ye have made Allah your surety; for Allah knows all that you do. (Koran 16:90–91)

Whoever works righteousness, man or woman and has Faith, verily, to him will We give a new Life, a life that is good and pure and We will bestow on such their reward according to the best of their actions. (Koran 16:97)

Tawhid, the main pillar of Islam, signifies that man's economic life depends wholly on Allah's laws of the universe and that their relationship to those who believe is through the obedience to the covenant of Allah. Allah maintains in the Koran that there is no creature on the earth whose sustenance is not provided by Allah.

No creature crawls on earth that Allah does not nourish. He knows its essential nature and its varying forms; every detail has its place in the obvious plan. (Koran 11:6)

How Are the People in Need Provided for Their Sustenance and Needs of Daily Lives?

All wealth belongs to Allah, who bestows it on some people more than others. This wealth is given in trust, whereby the possessor is obliged to give the surplus for Allah's cause, to his kin, to the widows and orphans, and to the needy first in his community and then in the other communities around him. Wealth is to be shared so that not a single individual of the *ummah*, or indeed in the world should go hungry or without education and shelter.

It is not righteousness that ye turn your faces towards East or West; but it is righteousness to believe in Allah and the Last Day and the Angels and the Book and the Messengers; to spend of your substance, out of love for Him, for your kin, for orphans, for the needy, for the wayfarer, for those who ask and for the ransom of slaves; to be steadfast in prayer and practice regular charity, to fulfill the contracts which you have made; and to be firm and patient, in pain (or suffering) and adversity and throughout all periods of panic. Such are the people of truth, the God-fearing. (Al-Baqarah 2:177, Koran)

And when they are told, "Spend you of (the bounties) with which Allah has provided you," The Unbelievers say to those who believe: "Shall we then feed those whom, if Allah had so willed, He would have fed, Himself? Ye are in nothing but manifest error. (Koran 36:47)

Alms are for the poor and the needy and those employed to administer the funds; for those whose hearts have been (recently) reconciled (to the truth); for those in bondage and in debt; in the cause of Allah; and for the wayfarer: (thus is it) ordained by Allah and Allah is full of knowledge and wisdom.
(At-Tawbah 9:60, Koran)

In the above two verses, the clear indication is that man is given bounty by Allah. In return, his obligation is to distribute the surplus after his needs have been met to the needy. The Koran specifies that the charities be disbursed to the *fuqara* (the poor who ask), to *al masakin* (the poor and the needy who do not ask), to zakat administrators, to those who spread the light of Islam to those inclined, for the freedom of those in bondage, to those in debt, for the cause of Allah, and for the wayfarer who treads the path in Allah's service.

In the covenant between the individual believer and Allah, the individual surrenders to Allah his life and belongings in return for His guidance, a place in paradise in the hereafter, and peace with prosperity in this world. Every believer according to his or her covenant with Allah has the obligation to extend the benefits that

Allah has provided them to those who did not receive the same benefits. Such acts of generosity will be rewarded by Allah with a place in *Jannat* (place of peace and plenty) in the afterlife. Life of *Jannat* is to be attained in this world also, provided the compact with Allah is adhered to. The believer is Allah's instrument who will fulfill His promise to Adam that

> none will remain without food or clothes and none will
> suffer from heat or thirst. (Koran 20:118)

In the verses below, Allah has promised those who believe and obey His Covenant that, as the reward for their acts of charity, He will double the harvest of their labors, forgive their sins, and provide them of His bounties; nor shall they have fear or grieve. Fear and grief arise from misfortunes, which cause anxiety and depression. Allah's promise, therefore, is to safeguard the believers from misfortunes. And to those devouring usury, Allah will deprive them of all blessings. Obeying of Allah's covenant provides *Jannat* in the hereafter and in this world. It also brings balance, harmony, and stability to the economic life of the world in that it meets the necessities of each person and eliminates unnecessary suffering.

> O you who believe! Do no render in vain your charity by reminders of your generosity or by injury, like him who spends his wealth to be seen of men, but he does not believe in Allah nor in the Last Day. His likeness is the likeness of a smooth rock on which is a little soil; on it falls heavy rain, which leaves it bare. They will not be able to do any thing with what they have earned. And Allah does not guide the disbelieving people.

> And the he likeness of those who spend their substance, seeking to please Allah and to strengthen their souls, is as a garden, high and fertile; heavy rain falls on it but makes it yield a double increase of harvest and if it receives not heavy rain, light moisture suffices it. And Allah is seer of what you do. (Al-Baqarah 2:264–65, Koran)

O ye who believe! Give of the good things that ye have (honorably) earned and of the fruits of the earth that We have produced for you and do not even aim at getting anything which is bad, in order that out of it ye may give away something, when ye yourselves would not receive it except with closed eyes. And know that Allah is free of all wants and worthy of all praise.

The Evil One threatens you with poverty and bids you to conduct unseemly. Allah promises you His forgiveness and bounties. And Allah cares for all and He knows all things.

He grants wisdom to whom He pleases; and he to whom wisdom is granted receives indeed a benefit overflowing; but none will grasp the Message but men of understanding.

And whatever ye spend in charity or devotion, be sure Allah knows it all. But the wrongdoers have no helpers. (Al-Baqarah 2:267–70, Koran)

Those who (in charity) spend of their goods by night and by day, in secret and in public, have their reward with their Lord: on them shall be no fear, nor shall they grieve.

Those who devour usury will not stand except as stands one whom the Satan by his touch hath driven to madness. That is because they say: "Trade is like usury," but Allah hath permitted trade and forbidden usury. Those who after receiving direction from their Lord, desist, shall be pardoned for the past; their case is for Allah (to judge); but those who repeat (the offence) are Companions of the Fire; they will abide therein (forever.)

Allah will deprive usury of all blessing but will give increase for deeds of charity; for He loves not creatures ungrateful and wicked. (Al-Baqarah 2:274–76, Koran)

Economic Principles of the Covenant of Allah

The covenant of Allah in the Koran has laid down principles and guidelines for the well-being of the economic life of the believers. Obeying the principles will bring peace, harmony, spiritual enlightenment, and economic prosperity. Disobeying means misery, ruin, and Allah's wrath.

First Principle: Land and sources of production are not the personal property of individuals. *Ardh* is the source of life and means of sustenance and production of food and resources and therefore must remain available to the community, the *ummah*.

Allah created *ardh* and *sama* and has power over everything in and between them. To Allah belong the heaven and the earth and what is in between them. *Sama* in the Koran signifies the universe and *ardh* man's domain on the earth pertaining to his social and economic world. Allah is the Lord of the heavens and the earth. The divine laws under which the universe functions so meticulously and smoothly should also apply to the economic life of man so that he might achieve a balanced, predictable, equitable, and just financial life. *Sama* is the source of Allah's benevolence to mankind and of His universal laws that govern the human subsistence and sustenance on the earth (*ardh*), controlling man's economic life. Allah's kingdom over the heavens and the earth sustains man's economic life and directly affects man's conduct and his obedience to Allah's covenant.

Ayahs in Sura An-Nahl are explicit. Allah created the heavens and the earth for just ends—to bring peace, harmony, equilibrium, and justice to the universe. He is Allah, the One, Lord of creation. He sends water from the heavens for the sustenance of life on the earth—humans, plants, and animals. Allah sends sunshine to the earth to provide warmth and light to sustain human, plant, and animal life. Allah created the moon and the stars to create equilibrium in the universe, with every object in its intended place revolving in its fixed orbit in perfect harmony and balance. Allah has the secrets and mysteries of the heavens and the earth, the so-called sciences, and the knowledge of particles, elements, cells, mitochondria, chromosomes, gravity, and black holes, only an infinitesimal portion of which he revealed to man.

In other *ayahs* of Sura An-Nahl, Allah clearly mentions all the comforts He has provided man for the sustenance of life and for his economic well-being. Allah created cattle for humans for warmth, food, and transport and horses, mules, and donkeys for riding and to show. With the moisture from the skies, He produces for man corn, olives, date palms, grapes, and every type of fruit. Allah made good things for humans in different colors and quantities so that man can celebrate and praise Allah in gratitude. Allah made the sea subject to humans so that they may eat fresh and tender seafood, obtain beautiful ornaments from the ocean, sail their ships, and plow the oceans around the world. From the cattle, Allah produces milk, pure and wholesome to drink; and from the fruit of the date palm and vine, you get food and drink. And from the bees, there is honey of varying colors that heals ailments.

Historically, land was there for man and the beasts to roam around freely and spread through the world. Later, tribes and communities laid claims on pieces of land they needed for their needs with some extra surrounding area for their security. At the beginning of the Islamic era, productive land and water resources were owned by tribes for the use of their clan members. After the message of the Koran was established, the clans, tribes, former kingdoms, and nations amalgamated to form the community of Islam, the *ummah*, which in principle owned the title to the land and resources with theoretical tenancy. The owner ship of land by the *ummah* began to change with the downfall of the Abbasid caliphate.

From 1040 to 1200, with the collapse of the central authority, there were many regional power struggles that allowed for the breakdown of the eastern Iranian frontiers against nomadic invasions. Central

Asian nomads searching for pasturage in the tenth, eleventh, and the twelfth centuries spilled over into the region north of the Aral Sea and into Transoxania and Afghanistan. From contact with settled peoples, trade, and the activities of the missionaries, these Turkish peoples began to convert to Islam. Their chieftains became acquainted in the ways of agriculture, trade, city administration, and imperial conception of rule and order. Most of the useful land in the Islamic states was taken over by the Turkish chiefs and soldiers for their own use and for the advancement of their own political power.

The Seljuk decline opened the way for the third phase in the history of the region from 1150 to 1350. This was a period of further nomadic invasion from inner Asia, culminating in the devastating Mongol invasions and the establishment of Mongol regimes over most of the Middle East. With every change of the ruling class, the land and resources shifted from the peasantry to the tribal chiefs and the soldiery. To the west, the slave military forces in Egypt and Syria consolidated the Mamluk regime, with land being distributed among the new elite.

The final phase was the Timurid period, 1400–1500. The Mongol period was succeeded by new times of troubles and conquest by Timur, also known as Tamerlane. This era of repeated nomadic invasions brought demographic changes in the ethnic and religious identity of populations. A new Turkic-speaking population migrated into Transoxania, the Hindu Kush mountain range, Iran, the Caucasus, Anatolia, and Mesopotamia. Turkish settlement led to the Islamization of northeastern Iran, Armenia, and Anatolia both by settlement of newcomers and by the conversion of existing populations.

To consolidate their power, control of provinces was delegated to the family members and the nomadic chieftains. *Iqta* lands were assigned to the military leaders. The result was usurpation of power at both the provincial and local levels, with the formation of microregimes funded by the resources of the land and heavy taxation of the peasants.

The Ottoman cavalry were recruited from among Turkish warriors. They were not garrisoned as a regular army, but they were provided with land grants and timars (Arabic equivalent of *iqtas*) throughout the empire. The timar holders provided local security and served in Ottoman campaigns. The timar system was based on an old-fashioned feudal pattern. The Ottomans also used the resources of the land to maintain their control over the empire and toward their new conquests. The timar holders exploited the peasants and the subject population.

The subject population belonged to a lesser order of existence. All commoners, Muslim and non-Muslim, were considered the *reava* (flocks) to be shorn in the interests of the political elite. The Ottomans operated on the principle that the subjects should serve the interests of the state; the economy was organized to ensure the flow of tax revenues, goods in kind, and the services needed by the government and the elites. The populace was systematically taxed by maintaining a record of the population, households, property, and livestock.

All the lands in the empire were owned by the ruler; some lands (*tapulu*) were on perpetual lease to the peasants who had the right to assign that right to their male descendants, and *mukatalu* lands were leased to a tax collector in return for a fixed payment for a lease. In the fifteenth century, the Ottomans had conceded to Turkish military rulers and Muslim religious rulers the ownership right to the land. In the course of the next century and a half, the sultans dispossessed the local notables and reassigned the tax rights to the timar holders appointed by the sultan. Ottoman policies were inimical to accumulation of private property. Large private fortunes were regularly confiscated by the state. The Ottoman economic policy on taxation and trade was based on fiscalism that was aimed at accumulation of as much bullion as possible in the state treasury, which was primarily used for the expenditure of running the Topkapi court and the ongoing wars in the West.

The ownership of land in the Islamic world is not owned or distributed according to the covenant of the Koran, causing the present unequal distribution of wealth, poverty, deprivation, and degradation of a large part of the Islamic society. Land, therefore, belongs to Allah, who bestowed it to man and woman, His regents on the earth. The covenant expects man to take care of the land for all of Allah's creatures—men and beasts—as well as conserve its resources for future generations. Whatever is left over after his own needs are met goes to the necessities of the rest of humanity, starting with his *qurba* (near and dear) and then his community, followed by the surrounding communities. The land does not belong to the states, governments, tribal chiefs, military, aristocracy, timars, or *iqta*. Land cannot be owned by individuals or families nor inherited.

Men and women live in small communities. These form a fellowship and a brotherhood that looks after its own who are in need, and such a need may be of sustenance, clothing, shelter, knowledge, well-being, spirituality, understanding, protection, justice, or simple reassurance. And such assistance is extended to the surrounding communities till it reaches the far-flung communities of the *ummah*. Each basic community owns the land in its surrounds, tilled and administered by the community as a whole for its well-being in justice and harmony according to the covenant of Allah. The Islamic economic system is based on capitalism in the production of wealth and communism in its expenditure, with the difference being that individuals are free and able to make wealth but are responsible for the needs of kith and kin and their neighbor. The state has little role in the welfare system. The land owned by the community may be assigned to individuals or may be tilled communally for the mutual benefit of the whole community, producing food and paying for schools, hospitals, roadways, municipal services, and so. on. The community is meant to be self-sufficient economically and responsible for each and every individual's welfare, health, schooling, and old-age pensions.

Second Principle: All surplus money and resources should not remain with individuals. How much is enough for one's needs? A hundred? A thousand? A hundred thousand? A million? A billion? How much is enough? After accumulation of a certain amount of money, any further hoarding becomes an act of obscenity and evil. All surplus money and resources shall be used for the benefit and uplift of the community and humanity.

They ask thee how much they are to spend (in charity); say: "What is beyond your needs". Thus doth Allah make clear to you His Signs: in order that ye may consider. (Al-Baqarah 2:222, Koran)

Third Principle: Wealth and commodities should not be hoarded. Surplus wealth is to be spent for the needs of the community as prescribed by Allah.

O you who believe! There are indeed many among the priests and anchorites, who in falsehood devour the substance of men and hinder (them) from the Way of Allah. And there are those who bury gold and silver and spend it not in the Way of Allah: announce unto them a most grievous penalty. (At-Tawbah 9:34, Koran)

Fourth Principle: Wealth shall be spread throughout the community, the *ummah*, and shall not be impounded, stolen, and looted by conquerors, tribes, rulers, classes, and the *Mutaffifeen* (dealers in fraud) as practiced in un-Koranic societies, Muslim and Non-Muslim.

What Allah has bestowed on His Rasool from the people of the townships, belongs to Allah, to His Rasool and to the near of kin and orphans, the poor and the homeless, in order that it may not (merely) make a circuit between the wealthy among you. So, take what the Rasool assigns to you and deny yourselves that which he withholds from you. And fear Allah, for Allah is strict in Punishment. (Al-Hashr 59:7, Koran)

Fifth Principle: No one shall subsist on the earnings of another, and except for those who are incapacitated, everyone shall work. Everyone—man and woman—shall also contribute their labor and sweat toward community well-being.

The Koran calls the people who stint *Mutaffifeen*, those who get the full measure from others but stint when measuring for others. They lead an easy life from the earnings of others. The Koran mentions three such groups. One group consists of people who "take with an even balance and give less than what is due."

Woe to those that deal in fraud, those who, from others exact full measure,

But when measuring or weighing for others, give less than due.

Do they not think that they will be called to account, on a Mighty Day,

A Day when (all) mankind will stand before the Lord of the Worlds? (Mutaffifeen 83:1-6, Koran)

Another group comprises those who inherit money, land, and property, and they use that wealth to accumulate more and more without ever giving back to the needy. The third group gobbles up the earnings of others:

O ye who believe! There are indeed many among the priests and clerics, who in falsehood devour the substance of men and hinder (them) from the Way of Allah. And there are those who bury gold and silver and spend it not in the Way of Allah: announce unto them a most grievous penalty. (Al-A'raf 9:34, Koran)

Squander not your wealth among yourselves in egotism and conceit: Let there be trade and traffic amongst you with mutual goodwill nor kill or destroy yourselves: for verily Allah hath been Most Merciful to you. If any do that in rancor and injustice, soon shall We cast them into the fire: and easy it is for Allah. If you abstain from all the odious and the forbidden, Allah shall expel out of you all evil in you and admit you to a Gate of great honor.

And crave not those things of what Allah has bestowed His gifts more freely on some than others, men are assigned what they earn and women that they earn. But ask Allah of His bounty. Surely Allah is knower of everything.

O you who believe! Let not your riches or your children divert you from the remembrance of Allah. If any act thus, the loss is their own.

And spend something (in charity) out of the substance which We have bestowed on you, before Death should come to any of you and he should say, "O my Lord! Why didst Thou not give me respite for a little while? I should then have given (largely) in charity and I should have been one of the doers of good." (Al-Munafiqun 63:9–11, Koran)

24. Justice and Truth

Stand firmly for Allah as a witness of fair dealing. Let not the malice of people lead you to iniquity. Be just, that is next to worship. Be with taqwa of Allah, fear Allah.

O you who believe! Fear Allah and speak always the truth that He may direct you to righteous deeds and forgive you your sins: he that obeys Allah and His Rasool have already attained the highest achievement. (Al-Ahzab 33:69–73, Koran)

Stand firm for justice as witness to Allah be it against yourself, your parents, or your family, whether it is against rich or poor, both are nearer to Allah than they are to you. Follow not your caprice lest you distort your testimony. If you prevaricate and evade justice Allah is well aware what you do.
(An-Nisa 4:135, Koran)

O you who believe! Stand firmly for Allah as a witness of fair dealing. Let not the malice of people lead you to iniquity. Be just, that is next to worship. Be with taqwa of Allah, fear Allah. Allah is well aware with what you do. (Al-Ma'idah 5:8, Koran)

Betray not the trust of Allah and His Messenger. Nor knowingly misappropriate things entrusted to you. (Al-Anfal 8:27, Koran)

If you have taqwa of Allah and fear Allah, He will grant you a Criterion to judge between right and wrong and remove from you all misfortunes and evil and forgive your sins. Allah is the bestower of grace in abundance. (Al-Anfal 8:29, Koran)

Be in taqwa of Allah, fear Allah and be with those who are true in word and deed. (At-Tawbah 9:119, Koran)

Deal not unjustly and ye shall not be dealt with unjustly.
(Al-Baqarah 2:277–80, Koran)

Whenever you give your word speak honestly even if a near relative is concerned.
(Al-An'am 6:151–52, Koran)

And come not near the orphan's property, except to improve it, until he attains the age of full strength. (Al-An'am 6:151–52, Koran)

And give full measure and full weight with justice. No burden We place on any soul but that which it can bear. (Al-An'am 6:151–52, Koran)

If an impostor (fasiq) comes to you with any news, ascertain the truth, lest you harm people unsuspectingly and afterwards become full of remorse for what you have done. And know that amongst you is Allah's Messenger: were he in many matters to follow your desires, you would certainly fall into misfortune: but Allah has bestowed on you the love of iman (faith) and has made it beautiful in your hearts and he has made abhorrent to you disbelief, wickedness and disobedience to Allah: such indeed are those who are righteous (rashidun).
(Al-Hujurat 49:6–10, Koran)

Justice (*'adl*) is a divine attribute defined as "putting all things in the right place." The opposite of *'adl* is *zulm*, which in Koranic terms means "wrongdoing." *Wrongdoing* is a human attribute defined as "putting things in the wrong place." *Zulm* is one of the common terms used in the Koran to refer to the negative acts employed by human beings.

Wrongdoing is the opposite of justice, and justice is to put everything in its right place and every act of the humans to be performed as prescribed by Allah. Hence, wrongdoing is to put things where they do not belong. *Zulm* (injustice) is to, for example, associate others with Allah. Others do not belong in the place for the divine; it is to place false words in place of the truth and to put someone else's property in place of your own. Other examples are taking a life against the divine commandments, replacing people's liberty with oppression, waging war instead of peace, and usurping people's right to govern themselves.

The Koran repeatedly stigmatizes humans of wrongdoing. When it points out who is harmed by injustice, wrongdoing, or *zulm*, the Koran always mentions the word *nafs* or self. People cannot harm Allah. By being unjust or doing wrong or by putting things in the wrong place, people harm themselves. They distort their own natures, and they lead themselves astray. Whom can one wrong? It is impossible to wrong or do injustice against Allah since all things are His creatures and do His work. Hence, wrongdoing and injustice is an activity against people and Allah's creation.

Allah has prescribed His covenant to humans for the good of human beings. People, tribes, and nations are being helped since Allah leads them into accord, harmony, and justice, which in turn create peace in the world. Allah has laid out all the basic principles for justice in His covenant for humans to live in harmony. Those who refuse to follow His commandments are therefore ungrateful and hence *kafirs*. Thus, they are wrongdoers (*zalimun*) and only harm themselves. Of the 250 verses where the Koran mentions *zulm* or *zalimun*, it mentions the object of wrongdoing in only 25 verses. In one verse, the object of wrongdoing are people:

> The blame is only against those who oppress men with wrongdoing and insolently transgress beyond bounds through the land defying right and justice: for such there will be a Penalty grievous (Ash-Shura 42:42, Koran)

In a second verse, the object of wrong and injustice is the signs of Allah:

136

The weighing that day will be true. He whose scales are heavy,
are the prosperous. Those whose scale are light, they have lost
themselves for wronging Our Signs. (Al-A'raf 7:8–9, Koran)

Allah reveals His signs in nature and in scriptures so that the people
may be guided. By disobeying these signs, they wrong only themselves.

In the remaining 23 verses in which the object of wrongdoing is
mentioned, the wrongdoers are said to wrong only themselves.

And We gave you the shade of clouds and sent down to you Manna
and quails, saying: "Eat of the good things We have provided for
you:" (but they rebelled); to Us they did no harm, but they wronged
their own souls. (Al-Baqarah 2:57, Al-A'raf 7:160, Koran)

Verily Allah will not deal unjustly with humans in anything: it is
the human who wrongs his own soul. (Yunus 10:44, Koran)

And We wronged them not, but they wronged themselves. (Hud 11:101, Koran)

If anyone does evil or wrongs his own soul but afterwards
seeks Allah's forgiveness, he will find Allah Oft-Forgiving,
Most Merciful. (An-Nisa 4:110, Koran)

The Koran admonishes:

Deal not unjustly and you shall not be dealt with
unjustly. (Al-Baqarah 2:278, Koran)

25. Knowledge

O you who believe! Allah will exalt in rank those of you who believe and who have
been granted Knowledge. Proclaim! And thy Lord is Most Bountiful, He Who
taught (the use of) the Pen, Taught man that which he knew not. O my Lord!
Enrich me in knowledge.
When ye are told to make room in the assemblies, spread out and make room:
ample room will Allah provide for you. And when ye are told to rise up, for prayers,
Jihad or other good deeds rise up: Allah will exalt in rank those of you who believe

and who have been granted Knowledge. And Allah is well acquainted with all you do. (Al-Mujadila 58:11, Koran)

> Proclaim! In the name of thy Lord and Cherisher, Who created,
> Created man, out of a (mere) clot of congealed blood: Proclaim!
> And thy Lord is Most Bountiful, He Who taught (the use of) the
> Pen, Taught man that which he knew not. (Iqra 96:1–5, Koran)

> And he who brings the Truth and believes therein, such are
> the men who do right. (Az-Zumar 39:33, Koran)

> High above all is Allah, the King and the Truth! Be not in haste with
> the Qur'an before its revelation to thee is completed, but say, "O
> my Lord! Enrich me in knowledge." (Taha 20:114, Koran)

Is one who worships devoutly during the hours of the night prostrating himself or standing (in adoration), who takes heed of the Hereafter and who places his hope in the Mercy of his Lord, (like one who does not)? Say: "Are those equal, those who know and those who do not know? It is those who are endued with understanding that receive admonition. (Az-Zumar 39:9, Koran)

Knowledge of God: Humans have always looked at God in two ways:

Emotionally. It is a personal and humanized god that is tribal. This god has favorite children whom he protects and rewards over and above others. He is readily accessible in a temple, shrine, mausoleum, or mosque and has priests in attendance as intermediaries. The priest class formulates dogma, creed, and rituals to appease the god. This god is unpredictable, loving, or demanding, subject to anger and joy in accord with the deeds and sacrifices of his devotees. He has a specially trained class of helpers who acts as cheerleaders and who performs crowd control for him. These helpers include the popes, bishops, priests, ayatollahs, rabbis, imams, ulema, pundits, and various classes of religious police. Proximity to their god provides this class's power over other men and women. This source of power naturally leads to competition and often wars between the devotees. Wars fought in the name of this god leads to injustice and usurpation of the rights of others.

The priest class, scholars, and writers introduced and interjected ideas that made their god dependent on creed and dogma invented by them. Writers of the Old and New Testaments fashioned Yahweh and Jesus according to their own caprice. Muslim scholars produced Hadith and interpreted Sharia that made Allah and Muhammad subject to their own fancy and caprice. Such collective manipulations, at first, divided humans and then splintered communities into factions. Marriages of Henry VII fragmented the Christian Europe, and nonsuccession of Ali split the Muslim world. These mechanizations of men interrupted the message of the God of Abraham that Moses, Jesus, and Muhammad had come to teach. In the fundamental emotional nature of humans, there is an essence of paganism under the surface that wells over in times of stress, grief, and failing belief. The signs of disbelief, mistrust, and *shirk* lies in the faith in astrology, horoscope, saint worship, amulets, and worship of gods of wealth, power, and politics.

Intellectually, humans wholeheartedly accept the concept of God as the Creator of everything that is. He wills, and it is. He is beyond human comprehension, and His divine systems do not conform to human concepts, creed, and dogma. Allah, God the Creator, created the galaxies, worlds, stars, sun, moon, little atoms, protons, neutrons, and tiny particles that show the complexity of His genius. Allah, the Lord of creation, sends water from the heavens for the sustenance of life on the earth. Allah directs sunshine to the earth to provide warmth and light to sustain, human, plant, and animal life. Allah formed the sun, moon, and stars to create equilibrium in the universe, every object in its intended place, revolving in its fixed orbit in perfect harmony and balance. Allah created the secrets and the mysteries of the heavens and the earth, the so-called sciences, and the knowledge of particles, elements, cells, mitochondria, chromosomes, gravity, and black holes, only a minute portion of which he revealed to man. Allah clearly provided humans a mind to wonder at His infinitesimal wisdom. Yet man is conceited and arrogant to believe that God is driven by man-created creed, testament, dogma, Sunna, and Sharia.

Allah does not require a shrine, a temple, a tent, or a talisman to live in. His presence is everywhere. He is present in the smallest particle (*nuqta*) and in the greatest expanse. He is accessible to each and every object He has created. Every object obeys Allah's will except for man. Man has been given free will. The covenant of the Koran presents us with the scope of the freedom of choice that humans have in doing what is wholesome and beautiful or what is corrupt and ugly and in the human role among the creation that distinguishes right activity, right thought, and right intention from their opposites. It reminds us of how the scales of Allah's justice—the two hands of Allah, His mercy and His wrath—are reflected in the human domain, where people have been appointed Allah's vicegerents. Deeds of goodness and wholesomeness are associated with mercy, paradise, and the beautiful. Evil and corruption is rewarded with wrath, hell, and the ugly.

Allah the Divine is open to the most miniscule of beings. From this little particle, the *nuqta*, the connection to Allah, the Cherisher and the Nourisher of the universe, extends into the vastest of expanse. Within this communion of the Divine with the creation passes the Spirit of Allah into His creatures. Man lays his heart and mind open to Allah in submission to receive His Spirit and guidance.

In the space and emptiness of the universe, there flow currents and whispers of wind and energy. These winds of silence, light, and sound carry the divine whisper, and in this sound is Allah's message. This message descends into the believer's receptive heart in peace, silence, and tranquility. When the angels and the Spirit descend with Allah's guidance, the eyes perceive the most beautiful divine light, the ears hear the softest tinkle of the bell, the nose smells the fragrance of a thousand gardens, and the skin feels the most tranquil of the gentle breeze. When this happens, the soul has seen nirvana. The believer is in communion with Allah. This is the knowledge of Allah.

Allah sent thousands of prophets to mankind to teach man precepts and principles to His straight path of unity, truth, and goodness. Over thousands of years, these precepts and principles spread around the world through civilizations till mankind, as a whole, began to comprehend the message of one universal God, the Creator of every particle and every being in the whole universe. Man listened and occasionally regressed into his inherent paganism, greed, selfishness, and egotism. Allah bestowed on man a vicegerency on the earth, a mind, a free will, and a covenant. Allah then announced that there would be no more prophets; the era of prophecy had ended. Man, in stages, had received the knowledge required to live in submission to Allah's will in peace and harmony on the earth in accordance with the divine laws, which were sent down as a guidance to every human community to a life of truth justice, goodness, and peace. Such knowledge consisted of the following:

Unity: There is one absolute Being from which all stems; the universe of galaxies and all the living things in it are all connected to one another and cannot be separated from that absolute Being. Everything alive—humans, animals, plants, and microorganisms—is created by the absolute Being, all nurtured with the same organic matter, all breathing the same air; and in turn, their physical self disintegrates to the same elements that then return to the earth and the universe. In this cycle of creation and disintegration, the only permanence is of the Real, the Absolute. All else is an illusion and a mirage. One moment you are here, and in the next, you are gone. Nothing is left behind—no riches, no honor, no ego, and no pride. What is left, however, is an account of your deeds, on which one day you will be judged.

Mind: Man is bestowed with a mind and free will. The mind has the ability to perceive ideas and knowledge from the Divine and from the signs of Allah. The whisper of the Divine, the rustle of the wind, the light of God, the fragrance of God's creation, and the sensation of the Divine touch all inspire the human mind with an endless stream of ideas and knowledge. Man has been granted the ability to process his thoughts and the knowledge with free will.

The verse of the light encompasses the totality of the message and guidance that God sent to man through His prophets. The pagan in man confused God's message and instead began to worship the *rasul*. With the end of the era of the prophets, man has to open his heart to the light of Allah and learn to recognize the goodness of God within himself, in his own heart.

> Allah is the Light of the heavens and the earth. The parable of His Light is as if there were a Niche and within it a Lamp: the Lamp enclosed in Glass; the glass as it were a brilliant star: lit from a blessed Tree, an Olive, neither of the East nor of the West, whose Oil is well-nigh luminous, though fire scarce touched it: Light upon Light! Allah doth guide whom He will to His Light: Allah doth set forth Parables for men: and Allah doth know all things. (Lit is such a light) in houses, which Allah hath permitted to be raised to honor; for the celebration, in them, of His name: in them is He glorified in the mornings and in the evenings, (again and again). (An-Nur 24:35–36, Koran)

For mankind, parable of divine light is the fundamental belief in one universal God for the whole humankind. Allah is the light of heavens and the earth. Allah's love, mercy, and grace nurture His creation. The divine light illuminates the depths of the hearts of those who bow down in submission to, love for, and trust in Allah. Aglow is the lamp in their heart with the divine light that shines with the brightness of a star—a star lit from the light of divine wisdom, the tree of knowledge, the knowledge of Allah's signs. For those who believe, Allah is within. The believer is aglow with Allah's radiance—light upon light. The dwellings where Allah's name is praised and glorified in the mornings and evenings are luminous with Allah's light.

The fundamental knowledge is the "knowledge of certainty" (*ilm al-yaqin*, Koran 102:5). This type of certitude refers to knowledge that results from the human capacity for logic and reasoning and the appraisal of what the Koran calls "clear evidence" (*bayyinat*) of Allah's presence in the world. This knowledge also comes through the study of Koran, the teachings of the prophets, and the signs of Allah. The signs of Allah encompass the whole knowledge of the creation; man's scientific and philosophical disciplines include only a miniscule fragment of this knowledge. The knowledge of certainty is rational and discursive, a point that the Koran acknowledges when it admonishes human beings to

> Say: "Travel through the earth and see how Allah did originate creation; so will Allah produce a later creation: for Allah has power over all things. (Al-'Ankabut 29:20, Koran)

> It is He Who gives life and death and to Him (is due) the alternation of Night and Day: will ye not then understand? (Al-Mu'minun 23:80, Koran)

Over time and under the influence of contemplation and spiritual practice, the knowledge of certitude may be transformed into a higher form of knowledge of Allah, which the Koran calls the "eye of certitude" (*ain al-yaqin*, Koran 102:7). This term refers to the knowledge that is acquired by spiritual intelligence that believers in the East locate metaphorically in the heart. Before attaining this type of knowledge, the heart of the believer must first be "opened to Islam."

> Is one whose heart Allah has opened to Islam, so that he has received enlightenment from Allah. Woe to those whose hearts are hardened against celebrating the praises of Allah! They are manifestly wandering (in error)! (Az-Zumar 39:22, Koran)

143

Once opened, the heart receives knowledge as a type of divine light or illumination (*nur*) that leads the believer toward the remembrance of Allah. Just as with the knowledge of certainty, with the eye of certainty, the believer sees Allah's existence through His presence in this world. With the eye of certainty, what lead the believer to the knowledge of Allah are not the arguments to be understood by the rational intellect but by theophanic appearances (*bayyinat*) that strip away the veil of worldly phenomenon to reveal the divine reality underneath.

From the spiritual perspective, the one who perceives reality through the knowledge of Allah is a true "intellectual." Unlike the scholar, who develops his or her skills through years of formal study, the spiritual intellectual does not need book learning to understand the divine light. A spiritual intellectual can be anyone, scholarly or otherwise, whose knowledge extends both outward to take in the physical world and upward to realize his or her ultimate transcendence of the world through his or her link with the absolute. Without such a vertical dimension of spirit, the scholar's knowledge, whatever its extent may be in academic terms, is of little worth.

The third and most advanced type of knowledge builds on transcendent nature of knowledge itself. The highest level of consciousness is called the "truth of certitude" (*haqq al-yaqin*).

> But truly (Revelation) is a cause of sorrow for the Unbelievers.
> But verily it is Truth of assured certainty. So, glorify the name
> of thy Lord Most High. (Al-Haqqah 69:50–52, Koran)

It is also known as *ilm ladduni* (knowledge "by presence"). This form of knowledge partakes directly of the divine reality and leaps off directly across the synapses of human mind to transcend both cognitive reasoning and intellectual vision at the same time. The "truth of certainty" refers to a state of consciousness in which a person knows the Real through direct participation in it without resorting to logical proofs. This type of knowledge characterizes God's prophets and messengers, whose consciousness of the truth is both immediate and participatory as what it is based on comes from direct inspiration.

According to both the word of Allah as expressed in the Koran and the tradition of the blessed *nabi* Muhammad, faith in Islam has as much to do with theoretical and empirical knowledge as it does with simple belief. This multidimensional conception of knowledge comprehends a reality that lies hidden within the unique world yet can be revealed by the human mind and the vision of the spiritual intellect through the signs of Allah that are present in the world itself. In the Koran, Allah calls humanity:

So I do call to witness what you see

And what you see not,

(This is) a Message sent down from the Lord of the Worlds.

But verily it is Truth of assured certainty. (Al-Haqqah 69:38–39, 43, 51)

The lure of abundance beguiles you, Until you reach the graves. But in the end you will know. Soon you shall know! Nay, were you to know with the knowledge of certainty. That you shall surely see the flaming fire. You shall see it with the eye of certainty. Then, you will be questioned on that Day about the pleasures you indulged in. (At-Takathur 102:1–8)

26. Inviting to All That Is Good and Right and Forbidding What Is Wrong

Let there arise out of you a band of people inviting to all that is good, enjoining what is right and forbidding what is wrong: they are the ones to attain happiness. (Ali 'Imran 3:103–5, Koran)

The Koranic principle of enjoining what is good and forbidding what is evil is supportive of the moral autonomy of the person, man and woman. This principle authorizes a person to act according to his or her best judgment in situations in which his or her intervention will advance a good purpose. The following saying of the blessed *nabi* also supports individual action by a believer:

If any one of you sees an evil, let him change it by his hand and if he is unable to do that, let him change by his words and if he is still unable to do that let him denounce it in his heart, but this is the weakest form of belief.

This principle assigns to the individual an active role in the community in which he or she lives. *The Koran annunciated the principle of free speech fourteen hundred years ago.* Believing men and women are reminded that they are the best of people, a witness over other nations. Such a responsibility carries with it a moral burden of an exemplary conduct of one who submits to the divine truth and whose relationship with Allah is governed is by *taqwa*, the consciousness of humankind's responsibility toward its Creator. The believer has the responsibility of acting in accordance with the three types of knowledge—the knowledge of certitude (*ilm al-yaqin*), the eye of certitude (*ain al-yaqin*), and the truth of certitude (*haqq al-yaqin*). With that knowledge and faith, the believer is well equipped to approach others to enjoin what is right and forbid what is wrong. This moral autonomy of the individual, when bound together with the will of the community, formulates the doctrine of infallibility of the collective will of the *ummah*, which is the doctrinal basis of consensus.

27. Do Not Say to Another Muslim, "You Are Not a Believer"

When you go forth in the cause of Allah be careful to discriminate and say not to the one who greets you with alaikum o salaam, "Though art not a believer". Would you covet perishable goods of this life when there are immeasurable treasures with Allah? You were like the person who offered you salutation, before Allah conferred on you His favors. There fore carefully investigate for Allah is well aware of all that you do. (An-Nisa 4:94, Koran)

Every believer's journey into Islam cannot be the same and uniform. A lot depends on the cultural background, education, and intellectual biases of the person. The first principle of faith is tawhid, the assertion that God is one, that there is only a single worthy object of worship, Allah. All other objects of worship are false. To serve anything else is to fall into error, misguidance, and sin of *shirk*. The Koranic notion of religious belief (*iman*) as dependent on knowledge is actualized in practice in the term *islam*. The term *islam* signifies the idea of surrender or submission. Islam is a religion of self-surrender; it is the conscious and rational submission of a dependent and limited human will to the absolute and omnipotent will of Allah. The type of surrender Islam requires is a deliberate, conscious, and rational act made by a person who knows with both intellectual certainty and spiritual vision that Allah, who is the subject of Koranic discourse, is reality itself. The knower of God is a Muslim (fem. *Muslimah*), "one who submits" to the divine truth and whose relationship with God is governed by *taqwa*, the consciousness of humankind's responsibility toward its Creator.

However, consciousness of God alone is not sufficient to make a person a Muslim. Neither is it enough to be merely born a Muslim or to be raised in an Islamic cultural context. The believer must endeavor at all times to maintain himself or herself in a constant state of submission to Allah. By doing so, the believer attains the honored title of "slave of Allah" (*abd Allah*, feminine: *amat Allah*), for he recognizes that all power and agency belongs to God alone. After submission to the will of Allah, observation of the five pillars opens the way for the believer to understand *ihsan* and perform good deeds for humanity:

Those who believe, do deeds of righteousness and establish regular prayers and regular charity, will have their reward with their Lord: on them shall be no fear, nor shall they grieve. (Al-Baqarah 2:277, Koran)

Every individual is at a different stage of their life's journey. Only Allah is the judge and the knower of the hidden and the manifest. Only He knows what is in a person's heart.

28. Suspicion and Lack of Trust

Avoid suspicion, for suspicion in some cases is sin; and spy not on each other, nor speak ill of each other behind their backs.

Avoid suspicion, for suspicion in some cases is sin; and spy not on each other, nor speak ill of each other behind their backs. Would any of you eat the flesh of his dead brother? No, you would abhor it. Be in taqwa of Allah, fear Allah: for Allah is Forgiving, Most Merciful. (Al-Hujurat 49:12–13, Koran)

Allah gave humans the trust of vicegerency over the earth with the stipulation that they acknowledge Him as their Lord and worship and thank Him for His benevolence. As part of that trust, people are free to make their choices about their actions. Allah does not force them to make the correct choices without taking the trust away from them, and if He took the trust away, they no longer are humans.

With the abuse of vicegerency came selfish acquisition of wealth, land, and women. Acquisition of wealth breeds greed, covetousness, and hoarding of wealth. The prospect of loss of such acquisitions produces insecurity and constant watchfulness. Such paranoia in humans has had a forceful impact on the society of man that leads to assumptions, suspicions, and suppositions that result in quarrels among people and wars between nations, thus a breakdown of the world order. Suspicion among nations has produced expensive and intricate security and intelligence systems that use spying equipment on the ground, in the air, and in space to obtain information on other nations. People and police spy on other people; cities are full of cameras tracking the movement of citizens. Big Brother watches everyone. Mistrust and suspicion prevails over the world, suggesting sickness in society. The same insecurity in people's psyche gives rise to resentment, jealousy, anger, and mistrust, leading to feuds and social disruption.

29. Do Not Ridicule Other Believers or Revile Each Other with Wicked Names

Let not some folk among you ridicule others: it may be that they are better than you are: nor let some women mock others: it may be that the others are better than them: nor defame or revile each other by offensive names: ill-seeming is wicked name calling for the one who has believed; and those who do not desist are indeed wrong-doers. (Al-Hujurat 49:11, Koran)

The covenant of Allah forbids suspicion, spying on each other, backbiting, and ridiculing other believers. The heart is like a shining mirror. Troublesome deeds are like smoke that will cover the mirror; you will not be able to see yourself, and you will be veiled from the reality of Allah. To understand the reality of Allah, you have to uncover ignorance and darkness so as to see the light and the reality. Some traits of this darkness are arrogance, ego, pride, envy, vengeance, lying, gossiping, backbiting, and other unwholesome characteristics. To be rid of these evils and odious traits, one has to clean and shine the mirror of the heart. This cleansing of the heart is done by acquiring knowledge and acting upon it to fight against one's ego by ridding oneself of multiplicity of being through unity. When the heart becomes alive with the light and *nur* of unity, the eye of the clean heart will see the reality of Allah's attributes.

30. Secret Counsels and Pacts

Secret counsels are only inspired by the Satan, in order
that he may cause grief to the Believers

When you hold secret counsel, do it not for iniquity and hostility and
disobedience to the Messenger; but do it for righteousness and self-
restraint; and fear Allah, to Whom ye shall be brought back.

Secret counsels are only inspired by the Satan, in order that he may cause grief
to the Believers; but he cannot harm them in the least, except as Allah permits;
and on Allah let the Believers put their trust. (Al-Mujadila 58:9–10, Koran)

No believer, individual, community, or ruler shall make a compact on behalf of the *ummah* or part of it in secret with the unbelievers. Islam regards secret pacts with enemies and hostile actions against one's own people as treason. When the *nabi* was in Medina, there were some people who professed Islam but at the same time conspired with the enemy, the *kafirun*, against fellow Muslims. The Koran has the following description of the fate of the *Munafiqeen*.

Of the people there are some who say: "We believe in Allah
and the Last Day;" but they do not really believe.

Fain would they deceive Allah and those who believe, but
they only deceive themselves and realize it not!

In their hearts is a disease; and Allah has increased their disease: and
grievous is the penalty they incur, because they are false to themselves.

When it is said to them: "Make not mischief on the earth,"
they say: "Why, we only want to make peace!"

Of a surety, they are the ones who make mischief, but
they realize (it) not. (Al-Baqarah 2:8–12, Koran)

Allah will throw back their mockery on them and give them rope in
their trespasses; so they will wander like blind ones to and fro.

These are they who have bartered guidance for error: but their
traffic is profitless and they have lost true direction.

Their similitude is that of a man who kindled a fire; when it lighted
all around him, Allah took away their light and left them in utter
darkness. So they could not see. Deaf, dumb and blind, they will
not return to the path. (Al-Baqarah 2:15–18, Koran)

In our age, we have people who think that they can get the best of both worlds by compromising their nations and Islam's interests with the enemy. King Abdullah of Transjordan secretly met with Zionist leaders from 1922 onward, merely a year after the creation of Transjordan. These meetings continued during the Palestinian disturbances in 1932 and 1936. The amity between the two conspiring sides was so total that, in a meeting, Abdullah and the Jewish envoy discussed ways of eliminating the mufti of Jerusalem, the leader of Palestinians, and the enemy of both sides[7]. He secretly conspired with Chaim Weizmann for the partition of Palestine in 1947.

Abdullah's grandson Hussein started his secret contacts with Israeli leaders in 1957, and by 1963, meetings with the leaders became a regular occurrence. In 1963, Hussein made a secret visit to Tel Aviv[8]. In the period preceding 1967, Hussein performed several treasonable acts that were openly anti-Arab. In response to the creation of PLO,

[7] Avi Shlaim, *The Politics of Partition*, 203.

[8] Dan Raviv and Yossi Melman, *Every Spy a Prince*, 213.

which wanted to replace him as the Palestinian representative, Hussein's intelligence service provided the names and location of the Palestinian fighters infiltrating and battling the Israelis[9]. Hussein did not stop here. His intelligence service also provided the Israelis information about other Arab countries[10]. From 1970 onward, there were several secret meetings between Hussein and the Israeli defense minister Moshe Dayan and with Israeli prime minister Golda Meir[11]. This extensive period of secret Jordanian-Israeli cooperation produced the most treasonable act of Hussein's life, informing Israel of the impending Egyptian-Syrian attack on October 1973[12].

The rulers of Islam who work against their own faith and their own people have a disease in their hearts. They make mischief on the earth against their own faith and nation in secret collusion with the enemies in return for personal gain, power, and wealth. Allah promises a grievous penalty for them because they are false to themselves and do not realize it. Every Muslim today is enslaved by an infidel international diplomatic and financial system run through a network of secretive and deceitful treaties and clauses. Every Muslim carries the burden of four monkeys that direct his daily life. The monkeys of secret international finance, diplomacy, crime, and intelligence syndicates sit on the back of every Muslim through the connivance and ignorance of Muslim rulers, mercenary armies, and religious leaders.

31. Intoxicants and Gambling

Forbidden to you are intoxicants and gambling, dedication of stones and divination by arrows. These are an abomination and Satan's handiwork; they hinder you from

---

[9] Ian Black and Benny Morris, *Israel's Secret Wars*, 238.

[10] Raviv and Melman, *Every Spy*, 214.

[11] *Secret Channels*, Mohamed Heikal, 310.

[12] Morris and Black, *Israel's Secret Wars*, 265.

prayer and remembrance of Allah and place enmity and hatred amongst you. Abstain from them so that you may prosper. (Al-Ma'idah 5:90–91, Koran)

Today the world is bedeviled with evils that consume people and deprive them of self-control and motivation to lead a life of purpose and usefulness for themselves, their families, and their fellow humans. The urge for immediate gratification and relief from the stresses of daily life sends people scurrying to alcohol and drugs. In the Western world, a tenth of the adult population is addicted to alcohol or drugs, and another half are habitual users of intoxicants. One in every three families carries the burden of an addicted dear one. In the Muslim world, although alcohol is the lesser substance of abuse, marijuana, cocaine, hashish, and khat use is rampant. Tobacco, a substance of extreme addiction but of mild intoxicant properties, is the weed of popular use. A fifth of the world's workforce is underproductive and disabled physically and intellectually because of intoxication and addiction.

The covenant of the Koran fourteen hundred years ago forbade humans from the use of intoxicants in an effort to save mankind from self-destruction. Gambling in all forms—including lotteries, slot machines, betting, card playing, and entertainment in casinos—is forbidden. The covenant says,

These are an abomination and Satan's handiwork; they hinder you from prayer and remembrance of Allah and place enmity and hatred amongst you. Abstain from them so that you may prosper. (Al-Ma'idah 5:90–91, Koran)

32. Forbidden to You Are the Carrion, Blood, and Flesh of Swine and Any Other Food on Which Any Name Besides That of Allah Has Been Invoked

Eat of good things provided to you by Allah and show your gratitude in worship of Him. Forbidden to you are the carrion, blood and flesh of swine and on any other food on which any name besides that of Allah has been invoked. If forced by necessity, without willful disobedience or transgressing due limits, one is guilt less. Allah is Most Forgiving and Most Merciful. (Al-Baqarah 2:172–73, Koran)

Allah, in His mercy, has permitted the believers to eat of all good things provided by Him. Expressly forbidden is to eat unclean food, which constitutes four things: carrion, blood, flesh of swine, and animals slaughtered in the name of any other than Allah.

During the last millennium, science has discovered harmful parasites and bacteria in the flesh of diseased animals, swine, and the blood of animals. Before the establishment of veterinarian and pathological sciences, the Koran had made a clear distinction between food that was clean and good and what was bad and harmful for humans.

33. Make Not Unlawful the Good Things That Allah Hath Made Lawful to You

Make not unlawful the good things, which Allah hath made lawful to you. Commit no excess; Allah loves not people given to excess. Eat of things that Allah has provided for you, lawful and good. Be in taqwa of Allah, fear Allah in whom you believe. (Al-Ma'idah 5:87–88, Koran)

Allah has, in very explicit words, laid out in His covenant the acts forbidden to the believers:

1. *Shirk*: Join not anything as equal with Him. (Worship Allah and do not associate others with Him.)

2. Mistreatment of parents: Be good to your parents.

3. Infanticide and abortion: Kill not your children on a plea of want. We provide sustenance for you and for them.

4. *Fahasha*: Come not near shameful deeds, whether open or in secret.

5. Taking of life: Take not life, which Allah hath made sacred, except by way of justice and law.

6. Stealing: Come not near to the orphan's property, except to improve it, until he attains the age of full strength. The term *orphan* may also include other helpless citizens who may be subject to oppression.

7. Cheating: And give measure and weight with justice; (do not cheat) no burden do we place on any soul but that which it can bear.

8. Lying and falsification: Whenever you speak, speak the truth, even if a near relative is concerned.

9. Violation of Allah's Covenant: Fulfill the covenant of Allah: "Thus, does He command you that ye may remember. Verily, this is My Way leading straight: follow it; follow not other paths: they will scatter you about from His Path; thus, doth He command you, that ye may be righteous" (Al-An'am 6:151–53, Koran).

10. Intoxicants.

11. Gambling.

12. Dedication of stones.

13. Divination by arrows: "These are an abomination and Satan's handiwork; they hinder you from prayer and remembrance of Allah and place enmity and hatred amongst you. Abstain from them so that you may prosper" (Al-Ma'idah 5:90–91, Koran).

14. Carrion.

15. Blood.

16. Flesh of swine.

17. "Any other food on which any name besides that of Allah has been invoked" (Al-Baqarah 2:172–73, Koran).

18. Usury (*riba*): "Devour not usury double and multiplied: Be in taqwa of Allah, that you may prosper" (Ali 'Imran 3:130, Koran).

19. Disrespect toward women: "It is not lawful for you to take women against their will, nor should you treat them with harshness. On the contrary treat then with honor and kindness" (An-Nisa 4:19, Koran).

20. Any actions that infringe on the unity of the ummah and the nation of Islam: "And hold fast, all together, by the Rope which Allah stretches out for you and be not divided among yourselves. You were enemies and He joined your hearts in love, so that by His Grace, you became brethren and a community. Thus, does Allah makes His Signs clear to you that you may be guided. Be not like those who are divided amongst themselves and fall into disputations after receiving clear signs; for them is a dreadful penalty."

These twenty actions have been forbidden (haram) by the covenant of Allah. At the same time, Allah commands:

Make not unlawful the good things, which Allah hath made lawful to you. Commit no excess; Allah loves not people given to excess. Eat of things that Allah has provided for you, lawful and good. Be in taqwa of Allah, fear Allah in whom you believe. (Al-Ma'idah 5:57, Koran)

Islamic scholar-jurists frequently quote various Hadith and proclaim many aspects of the daily life of pious and observant believers as haram. Such actions include listening to music, women's education, women's role in congregational prayers, and other mundane activities such as kite flying, tourism, pursuit of Western education, and use of modern technology. Those are the personal views of the mullahs and do not have the divine sanction of the covenant between Allah and His believers.

Music: Music is part of the human soul. Every child, when happy, springs up to a melody and dance to the rhythm. When the blessed *nabi* received the revelation from Allah, at times, it appeared in the form of a tinkle or the chimes of a bell, and the words of the revelation blossomed in Blessed Muhammad's mind. The Koran, when recited in rhythmic Arabic, produces a heavenly song of Allah's revelation. Singing Allah's *dhikr* with or without instrument or music has a powerful and profound effect on the listener's soul, which reflects divine beauty. Listening to mere wind chimes makes one aware of the divine origin of the sounds of the wind, the rustle of trees, and the sound of running water in rivers, falls, and oceans. Allah gave the human the ability to produce the most beautiful sounds in His remembrance, to celebrate life and happiness, and to enjoy Allah's other provisions to mankind.

Observation of Allah's covenant bestows peace and tranquility to the soul and hence happiness and contentment on the believer. Islam is not a religion of gloom, sorrow, and melancholia but that of celebration of Allah's blessings and of doing beautiful deeds. To show contentment, peace, harmony, happiness, and proper balance of things in life is to express *shukr*, gratitude to Allah for His mercy and grace. The human is asked to use all his senses—sight, hearing, smell, taste, and touch— to recognize Allah's truth and signs. They signify the perception of Allah's *nur* (light), resonance of the sound of Allah's harmonious music in nature, the fragrance of Allah's garden, the flavor of Allah's bounty, and the feel of Allah's creation around us. Allah does not forbid against His divine gift of harmony and song; on the contrary, He urged the recitation of the Koran in slow, rhythmic tones and the celebration and praising of Allah often, glorifying Him in the morning and at night. It is Allah and His angels who also send their blessings on the believers so "He may lead the Believers you out of the depths of darkness into light." Celebration of Allah's praises and glorifying Him means to rejoice, to be happy, and to be joyous. The word *celebrate*, therefore, has the connotation of a happy occasion, which includes song and music.

Confinement of believing and devout women: Believers is not a mandate of Allah's covenant nor is covering women from head to toe.

Acquisition of knowledge: Education is Allah's gift to humanity and is incumbent on every believer, man or woman. Scholars of Islam ignore the Koranic admonition

Make not unlawful the good things, which Allah hath made lawful to you. Commit no excess; Allah loves not people given to excess.

34. Contracts and Agreements

When you make a transaction involving future obligations, write it down in presence of witnesses.

When you make a transaction involving future obligations, write it down in presence of witnesses, or let a scribe write it down faithfully. Let the party incurring the liability dictate truthfully in the presence of two witnesses from among your own men and if two men are not available then a man and two women, so that if one of them errs then the other one, can remind him. Disregard not to put your contract in writing, whether it be small or large, it is more suitable in the eyes of Allah, more suitable as evidence and more convenient to prevent doubts in the future amongst yourselves. (Al-Baqarah 2:282–83, Koran)

Fourteen hundred years ago, the Koran laid out the basis of the modern legal system of written and witnessed agreements. Muslim jurists have used this *ayah* to curtail the rights of women as witnesses in the modern court system, where they consider the testimony of two women equivalent to the testimony of one man. The mullahs imply that women have an inferior memory and intellectual capacity. Although the Koran is silent on the reason for the need for two women witnesses, it is obvious that women carry the burden and the responsibilities of nurturing and taking care of their infants and families. Women are Allah's instruments of creation and the nurturer of mankind. The act of creation and nurture has precedence over worldly affairs of commerce. Women cannot neglect their divine obligation of creation to attend to the communal affairs as witnesses in the transactions of this world. The need for a second woman witness becomes necessary when one of them becomes preoccupied with her obligations of procreation and upbringing of a family.

There is abundant of scientific evidence that the intellectual capacity of both men and women is unique in their development. This uniqueness complements the intellect and memory of men and women in the functioning of mankind. This uniqueness is a gift of Allah to humankind.

The human memory is affected by the inbuilt nature and development of the brain and its environment. Adolescent brain development is different in boys and girls. Male's aged six to seventeen years display more prominent age-related reduction in gray matter (the part of the brain that allows us to think) and increases in white matter (which transfers information between distant regions) than females. These changes in brain composition are linked to developmental processes in which nerve cell connections are "pruned" in gray matter and made more efficient (myelinated) in white matter. The more dramatic changes seen in males may be related to the different effects of estrogen and testosterone on the brain[13]. Women have smaller brains than men and have smaller bodies; women have more gray matter, and men have more white matter. This finding may help explain why

---

[13] De Bellis, MD, et al., "Sex Differences."

women are typically better than men at verbal tasks, while men are typically better than women at spatial tasks, as well as why the sexes perform equally well on intelligence tests in spite of males having larger brains[14].

Several studies have evaluated sex differences in the histology of the cerebral cortex. One study in humans detected higher neuronal density in the female cortex compared with males[15]. In contrast, other studies have shown that the number of neurons in the cerebral cortex is greater in males than in females. Studies by Rabinowicz et al. demonstrated that males have 15 percent more cortical neurons and 13 percent greater neuronal density than females[16]. Similarly, Pakkenberg et al. showed a 16 percent higher neuronal number in males, but sex differences in neuronal density were not present[17]. Although women have fewer neocortical neurons, certain anatomical and histological characteristics of female brains may allow for more extensive dendritic arborization and more neuronal connections among nerve cells[18]. Certain diseases that cause neuronal loss in the cerebral cortex may be more detrimental to women due to their lower number of cortical neurons compared with men[19].

The cerebellum, an area of the brain important for posture and balance, and the pons, a brain structure linked to the cerebellum that helps control consciousness, are larger in men than in women[20]. As the brain ages, the amount of tissue mass declines, and the amount of fluid increases. This effect is less severe in women than in men, suggesting

---

[14] Gur et al., "Sex Differences."

[15] Haug, "Brain Sizes."

[16] Rabinowicz et al., "Gender Differences."

[17] Pakkenberg and Gundersen, "Neocortical Neuron Number."

[18] de Courten-Myers, "Human Cerebral Cortex."

[19] Rabinowicz et al., "Structure of the Cerebral Cortex."

[20] Raz et al., "Age and Sex Differences."

that women are somewhat less vulnerable to age-related changes in mental abilities[21-22]. However, women are more prone to dementia than men perhaps because of the potentially greater susceptibility to loss of neurons and neuronal connections.

Language Differences. Although men and women have been shown to process some language tasks similarly, in other aspects of language processing, there are significant sex differences[23]. Imaging studies of the living brain show that in women neurons on both sides of the brain are activated when they are listening, while in men neurons on only one side of the brain are activated. Men and women appear to process single words similarly, but in the interpretation of whole sentences, women use both sides of the brain, while men use one side[24]. Boys have a higher incidence than girls of developmental language disorders, such as developmental dyslexia. Despite these differences during childhood, it is not clear whether adult women have better verbal skills than men.[21]

Spatial Information Differences. Men and women process spatial information differently[25]. When negotiating a virtual reality maze, both men and women use the right hippocampus to figure out how to exit. However, men also use the left hippocampus for this task, while women do not. Women also use the right prefrontal cortex, while men do not[26]. In an imaging study, men were found to activate a distributed system of different brain regions on both sides of the brain while performing a spatial task. Women, however, activated these regions on only the right side of the brain. Women appear to rely on

---

[21] Gur et al., "Gender Differences."

[22] Witelson, "Sex Differences."

[23] Ibid.

[24] Kansaku and Kitazawa, "Imaging Studies."

[25] Ragland et al., "Sex Differences."

[26] Gron et al., "Brain Activation."

landmarks to navigate their environments, whereas men tend to use compass directions[27].

Memory Differences. Some functions of memory appear to be different in males and females[28]. Higher rates of blood flow in certain portions of the brain are associated with increased memory of verbal tasks in women but not in men [29]. Compared with men, women have been shown to be better at remembering faces[30]. A key part of the brain involved in processing emotionally influenced memories acts differently in men and women.

The amygdala, an almond-shaped structure found on both sides of the brain, behaves very differently in males and females while the subjects are at rest. In men, the right amygdala is more active and shows more connections with other regions of the brain. Conversely, in women, the left amygdala is more connected with other regions of the brain. In addition, the regions of the brain with which the amygdala communicates while a subject is at rest are different in men and women. These findings suggest that the brain is wired differently in men and women. In men, the right-hemisphere amygdala showed more connectivity with brain regions such as the visual cortex and the striatum. In contrast, the left amygdala in women was more connected to regions such as the insular cortex and the hypothalamus.

Many brain areas communicating with the amygdala in men are engaged with and responding to the external environment. For example, the visual cortex is responsible for vision, while the striatum coordinates motor actions. Conversely, many regions connected to the left-hemisphere amygdala in women control aspects of

---

[27] Saucier et al., "Are Sex Differences in Navigation?"

[28] Duff and Hampson, "Sex Difference."

[29] Ragland et al., "Sex Differences."

[30] Gur et al., "Computerized Neurocognitive Scanning."

the environment within the body. Both the insular cortex and the hypothalamus, for example, receive strong input from the sensors inside the body.

Throughout evolution, women have had to deal with a number of internal stressors, such as childbirth, that men have not had to experience. The brain seems to have evolved to be in tune with those different stressors. One of the brain areas communicating with the amygdala in women is implicated in disorders such as depression and irritable bowel syndrome, which predominantly affect women.

The sexes use different sides of their brains to process and store long-term memories. Another study in 2002 demonstrated how a particular drug, propranolol, can block memory differently in men and women. Differences between men and women in cognitive pattern are now well established. On average, men outperform women on a variety of spatial tasks, with the largest difference occurring on tests of spatial rotation and manipulation, where an object must be identified in an altered orientation, or after certain imaginary manipulations such as folding. Men also excel at tests of mathematical reasoning, with the differences between sexes especially marked at the higher end of the distribution. Women, in contrast, are generally better able to recall the spatial layout of an array of objects, to scan perceptual arrays quickly to find matching objects, and to recall verbal material, whether word lists or meaningful paragraphs.

Some of these differences are found early in development and last throughout the life span. The sex differences in verbal memory, spatial orientation, and mathematical reasoning have been found across cultures. These differences are due to our long evolutionary history as hunter-gatherers, in which the division of labor between men and women was quite marked. Men more often traveled farther from the home base during hunting and scavenging, whereas women gathered food nearer home. In parallel with nonhuman studies, this would tend to show different navigational strategies, with men, for example, relying more on geometric cues and women more on landmark cues.

Summary: At present, when men and women have begun to perform similar tasks, each sex has certain specialization that, on the whole, complements the other sex's abilities. None is better, and none is inferior to the other. Mullahs will continue with their age-old prejudices to maintain women's lower status. Allah, in His infinitesimal wisdom, has bestowed on men and women unique strengths that complement each other for the benefit of humanity.

We digressed from the main topic of the written agreements because of an ongoing controversy in certain legal, scholastic Muslim circles about women's capacity as witnesses in the modern court system. This controversy about women's witnessing needed to be addressed in an informed and scientific manner. It is hoped that the above discussion will go a long way to contradict those mullahs who claim to be privy to Allah's intentions.

35. Respect Other People's Privacy

Enter not houses other than yours until you have asked permission and invoked peace upon those in them. If you find none in the house whom you seek enter not unless permission is granted. If you asked to leave go back, it is best for you that makes for greater purity for you. Allah knows all that you do.
(An-Nur 24:27, Koran)

The four walls of every person's home are his circle of privacy, within the confines of which he has freedom from intrusion by outsiders, be it the neighbor or the state. The residents of the home are protected from physical intrusion or intrusion with electronic devices. This dwelling is the basic autonomous unit of the Islamic state that amalgamates with other such units to form a community. The communities, with some complexity, join other communities to form the state. What is important is that the residents of each dwelling have their seclusion protected by the mandate of the covenant of the Koran. Importantly, each of the adult residents has a voice in the administration of the common affairs of the community. Each family is an independent, autonomous, basic unit of the *ummah*.

36. This Day I Have Perfected Your Religion for You

This Day I have perfected your religion for you. We have made the (Qur'an) easy in your own tongue, that with it you may give glad tidings to the righteous and warnings to people given to contention. Therein is proclaimed every wise decree, by command from Our Presence, for We are ever sending revelations, as a Mercy from your Lord. We have explained in detail in this Qur'an, for the benefit of mankind, every kind of similitude.

This day have those who reject faith (kafaru) given up all hope of compromising your faith, fear them not but only fear Me. This day have I perfected your religion for you, bestowed on you with My blessings and decreed Islam as your religion. (Al-Ma'idah 5:3, Koran)

Ha Mim. By the Book that makes matters lucid; We revealed it during the blessed night, verily We are always warning against Evil. Therein is proclaimed every wise decree, by command from Our Presence, for We are ever sending revelations, as a Mercy from your Lord: for He is the hearer and knower. The Lord of the heavens and the earth and all that is in between them, if you have an assured faith. There is no god but He: it is He who gives life and death, the Lord and Cherisher, your Lord and Lord of your forefathers. (Ad-Dukhan 44:1-8, Koran)

So have We made the (Qur'an) easy in your own tongue, that with it you may give glad tidings to the righteous and warnings to people given to contention. But how many (countless) generations before them have We destroyed? Canst thou find a single one of them (now) or hear (so much as) a whisper of them?
(Taha 19:97, Koran)

We have explained in detail in this Qur'an, for the benefit of mankind, every kind of similitude: but man is, in most things, contentious. And what is there to keep

back men from believing, now that guidance has come to them, nor from praying for forgiveness from their Lord, but that (they ask that) the ways of the ancients be repeated with them, or the Wrath be brought to them face to face?
(Al-Kahf 18:54–55, Koran)

The blessed *nabi* of Allah, Muhammad, proclaimed to the world on the mount of Arafat Allah's *wahiy* (message) on the last Friday, the ninth day, of *Zul-hajj* in the tenth year of hijra (631 CE).

This day have I perfected your religion for you.

This day have those who reject faith (kafaru) given up all hope of compromising your faith, fear them not but only fear Me. This day have I perfected your religion for you, bestowed on you with My blessings and decreed Islam as your religion.
(Al-Ma'idah 5:3, Koran)

On that day, the *din* of Islam was complete, and all man-made innovations after that were just novelties; anyone indulging in such innovations was making a sport of his religion. Those believers who fulfill the commandments of the Koran, Allah's covenant, are the *muttaqeen*. From that day on, men and women who obey and keep their covenant with Allah are the believers (*muttaqeen*) of Allah and the Koran, the word that Allah revealed to the blessed *nabi*, Muhammad. The Believers who follow the Qur'an and fulfill the Covenant of Allah, for their din Allah only suffices them. They are not Shia or Sunni nor any other sect.

The Koran establishes a universal order based on the divinely ordained values of life. Were every human to fulfill the covenant of the Koran, the world shall be at peace forever, and justice will prevail. By following the Hadith collections of the third-century hijra, *Muslims* have relegated their faith from a divinely ordained order to a human set of values, misleading themselves and deviating others from Allah's path. According to the Koran, *iman* is not just belief but also, in fact, knowledge. *Iman* is the conviction that is based on reason and knowledge. The Koran does not recognize belief that involves blind acceptance. Islam does include acceptance of certain things that cannot be explained by perception through human senses. Our reason and thinking will compel us to recognize the existence of such things. *Iman*, according to the Koran, signifies conviction based on full mental acceptance and intellectual satisfaction. *Iman* gives a person inner contentment, a feeling of *amn* (same common root). Thus, *iman* means to believe in something and to testify to its truthfulness, to have confidence in that belief, and to bow down in obedience.

There are five fundamental facts stated in the Koran that a believer must accept: *iman* in Allah, the law of *mukafat* and the afterlife, angels (*malaika*), the revelations, and the messengers. Belief in Allah means not only to profess obedience to Him and His Covenant but also to show it in one's actions and to be always in *taqwa* of Allah. Belief in the law of *mukafat* means to have conviction that every action of the human has an inescapable consequence of reward or retribution. Angels are not the winged creatures depicted in children's literature. They are heavenly forces that carry out laws of Allah governing the universe. They bow to Allah since they follow his orders. They also bow to the humans because we are able to study, understand, and manipulate the laws of nature for the benefit of mankind. Belief in revelations and messengers implies that human intellect alone cannot safely reach the final destination without the divine guidance in the form of *wahiy*, revelation delivered by the messengers to mankind. This guidance is to whole humankind sent through many messengers. The Muslim tradition began with *Ibrahim*, our father (Abraham of the Bible). The believers have a belief system and a course of action to witness over and spread the message to mankind that began with *Ibrahim* and was completed with *Muhammad*. Whereas the message of *wahiy* is divine and universal for all human races, the message of Hadith collections of the third century are human and therefore subject to error and cannot be equated with the Koran.

37. Those Who Believe and Perform Beautiful Deeds Are Companions of the Garden, Where They Shall Abide Forever

After his submission to the will and mercy of Allah, the believer is obliged to obey and fulfill the covenant he has made with Allah as part of the compact of submission and has to perform wholesome and good deeds.

The covenant of the Koran is a total belief system of an individual based upon total submersion of one's personality with Allah with total awareness and *taqwa* of Him at all times through observance of the thirty-seven commandments of Allah's covenant. This communion is not only with Allah but also, through Him, with other humans and Allah's creation, both alive and inanimate. The phrase *amilu al saalihaat* (to do good, to perform wholesome deeds) refers to those who persist in striving to set things right, who restore harmony, peace, and balance. Other acts of good works recognized in the covenant of the Koran are to show compassion, to be merciful and forgive others, to be just, to protect the weak, to defend the oppressed, to be generous and charitable, to be truthful, to seek knowledge and wisdom, to be kind, to be peaceful, to love others, and to perform beautiful deeds.

On those who believe and do good, will [Allah] Most Gracious bestow love.

There are fifty such verses in the Koran that remind the believers of the rewards of righteous deeds. The following are some of the *ayahs* in the Koran mentioning the righteous deeds.

Munawar Sabir

Alladhina aaminu wa 'amilu al saalihaat.[31]

But those who believe and work righteousness. They are Companions of the Garden: therein shall they abide (forever). (Al-Baqarah 2:82, Koran)

Those who believe, do deeds of righteousness and establish regular prayers and regular charity, will have their reward with their Lord: on them shall be no fear, nor shall they grieve. (Al-Baqarah 2:277, Koran)

As to those who believe and work righteousness, Allah will pay them in full their reward; but Allah loves not those who do wrong (zalimeen).
(Ali 'Imran 3:57, Koran)

But those who believe and do deeds of righteousness, We shall soon admit to Gardens, with rivers flowing beneath, their eternal home and therein shall they have companions pure and holy: We shall admit them to shades, cool and ever deepening. (An-Nisa 4:57, Koran)

But those who believe and do deeds of righteousness, We shall soon admit them to Gardens - with rivers flowing beneath - to dwell therein forever. Allah's promise is the truth and whose word can be truer than Allah's? (An-Nisa 4:122, Koran)

If any do deeds of righteousness, be they male or female and
have faith, they will enter Heaven and not the least injustice
will be done to them. (An-Nisa 4:124, Koran)

But to those who believe and do deeds of righteousness, He will give their
due rewards and more, out of His bounty: but those who are disdainful
and arrogant, He will not punish with a grievous penalty; nor will they find,
besides Allah, any to protect or help them. (An-Nisa 4:173, Koran)

To those who believe and do deeds of righteousness hath Allah
promised forgiveness and a great reward. (Al-Ma'idah 5:9, Koran)

---

[31] Koran 2:25; 2:82, 277; 4:57, 122; 5:5; 7:42; 10:9; 11:23; 13:29; 14:23; 18:2, 88, 107; 19:60, 96; 20:75, 82, 112; 21:94; 22:14; 23:50, 56; 24:55; 25:70–71; 26:67; 28:80; 29:7, 9, 58; 30:15, 45; 31:8; 32:19; 34:4, 37; 38:24; 41:8; 42:22–23, 26; 45:21, 30; 47:2, 12; 48:29; 64:9; 65:11; 84:25; 85:11; 95:6; 98:7; 103:3.

On those who believe and do deeds of righteousness there is no blame
for what they ate (in the past), when they guard themselves from evil
and believe and do deeds of righteousness - (or) again, guard themselves
from evil and believe,(or) again, guard themselves from evil and do
good. For Allah loves those who do good. (Al-Ma'idah 5:93, Koran)

But those who believe and work righteousness - no burden do We
place on any soul, but that which it can bear - they will be Companions
of the Garden, therein to dwell (for ever). (Al-A'raf 7:42, Koran)

To Him will be your return, of all of you. The promise of Allah is true
and sure. It is He Who began the Creation and its cycle, that He may
reward with justice those who believe and work righteousness; but
those who reject Him will have draughts of boiling fluids and a Penalty
grievous, because they did reject Him. (Yunus 10:4, Koran)

Those who believe and work righteousness, their Lord will guide them because of
their Faith: beneath them will flow rivers in Gardens of Bliss. (Yunus 10:9, Koran)

But those who believe and work righteousness and humble
themselves before their Lord, they will be Companions of the
Garden, to dwell therein forever! (Hud 11:23, Koran)

For those who believe and work righteousness is every blessedness
and a beautiful place of (final) return. (Ar-Ra'd 13:29, Koran)

Islam is concerned with everyday activities of the believer,
differentiating right from wrong and guiding the individual along the
correct path. It defines *sin* as "breaking the commandments of Allah"
and *good works* as "following Allah's instructions and the prophet's
teachings."

Iman adds a dimension to the understanding of human activity in that
every human action in daily life reaches back into the divine reality
that everything in the universe is governed by tawhid, yet Allah has
granted humans a freedom of choice, which can upset the balance in
the creation, the balance of justice, and the balance of atmospheric

elements and of environmental pollution and lead to the destruction of animal species, populations, cities, and agriculture through human actions. It tells people why they should be Allah's servants and explains which path they should follow to become His vicegerents. It makes clear that human activity is deeply rooted in the Real, and this has everlasting repercussions in this world and in the hereafter.

Ihsan adds to *islam* and *iman* a focus on people's intention to perform good and wholesome deeds on the basis of awareness of Allah's presence in all things. According to the Koran, doing wholesome deeds, along with faith, will yield paradise.

Whoso does wholesome deeds, be it male or female and has faith, shall enter the garden, therein provided for without reckoning. (Ghafir 40:40, Koran)

Those who have faith and do wholesome deeds, them we shall admit to gardens through which rivers flow. (An-Nisa 4:57, 122, Koran)

Another fifty verses in the Koran mention that people who perform beautiful deeds and have faith shall inherit the garden. The Koran uses the word *saalihaat* for beautiful and wholesome deeds and the word *salihun* for wholesome people. The root word for both *saalihaat* and *salihun* means "to be beautiful, sound, wholesome, right, proper, and good." Another word used in the Koran about thirty times is *islah*, which means "establishing wholesomeness." In modern times, the word *islah* has been used to mean "reform." The word *sulh* is used in the Koran once to mean "peace and harmony in family relationships." In modern times, the word *sulh* has come to mean "peace in the political sense." While the Koran calls the wholesome people as *salihun*, it employs the opposite, *fasid*, for the corrupt, ruined, evil, and wrong. The wholesome are the ones who live in harmony with the Real (*Haqq*) and establish wholesomeness through their words and deeds throughout the world. In contrast, the corrupt (*mufsidun*) destroy the proper balance and relationship with Allah and His creation. *Fasid* means "corrupt, evil, and wrong."

Allah measures out good and evil, the wholesome and the corrupt. Humans have enough freedom to make their own choices; if they make the choice to do beautiful and wholesome deeds (*saalihaat*) motivated by faith (*iman*) and god-wariness (*taqwa*), they please Allah and bring harmony and wholesomeness to the world, resulting in peace, justice, mercy, compassion, honor, equity, well-being, freedom, and many other gifts through Allah's grace. Others choose to do evil and work with corruption (*mufsidun*), destroying the right relationship among the creation, causing hunger, disease, oppression, pollution, and other afflictions. In the universal order, corruption is the prerogative of humans, and vicegerency gives humans the freedom to work against the Creator and His creation. Only misapplied trust can explain how moral evil can appear in the world. Modern technology; scientific advancement; nuclear, chemical, and biological weapons of mass destruction; genetic engineering of plants, animals, and humans; and exploitation of nonrenewable resources of the earth have made destruction of the human race and all life on the planet a distinct and imminent possibility.

> Corruption has appeared on the land and in the sea because what peoples hands have earned, so that He may let them taste some of their deeds, in order that they may turn back from their evils. (Ar-Rum 30:41, Koran)

When humans choose wrong and corrupt actions
they displease Allah. Allah loves those who do what
is beautiful, not those who do what is ugly:

> When he turns his back, he hurries about the earth to work corruption there and destroy the tillage and the stock. Allah loves not corruption. (Al-Baqarah 2:205, Koran)

Allah loves doing what is beautiful, and because of His love for those who do the beautiful, He brings them near Him, and His nearness is called Allah's mercy:

> Work not corruption in this world after it has made wholesome and call upon Allah in fear and hope. Surely the mercy of Allah is near to those who do what is beautiful. (Al-A'raf 7:56, Koran)

The covenant of the Koran presents us the scope of the freedom of choice that humans have in doing what is wholesome and beautiful or what is corrupt or ugly. The human's role among the creation distinguishes right activity, right thought, and right intention from their opposites. It reminds us of how the scales of Allah's justice, the two hands of Allah—His mercy and His wrath—are reflected in the human domain, where people have been appointed Allah's vicegerents. Deeds of goodness and wholesomeness are associated with mercy, paradise, and the beautiful. Evil and corruption is rewarded with wrath, hell, and the ugly.

Part Two

The Betrayal of the Covenant of Allah: The Downfall of Islam's World Order

Chapter Three

The Abdication of the Covenant and the Dar es Salaam to Fragmentation

But Allah doth call

To the Abode of Peace:

He doth guide whom He pleases

To a way that is straight.

—Koran 10:25

Allah calls to the Dar es Salaam and guides to His straight whom He pleases. The blessed *nabi* of Allah began to call humanity to Allah's straight path in Mecca and then, at Allah's command, on June 28, 622, in Yathrib, which later came to be known as Al-Madinah al-Munawwarah. This auspicious day was to become the first day of the year, a new century, a new millennium, a new era, and a new calendar. This was also the beginning of a new world empire, an *Islamic world order*.

The Covenant of Medina, described as the first constitution of the Dar es Salaam, read:

- In the name of Allah the Compassionate and the Merciful.

- This is a covenant given by Muhammad to the believers.

- They constitute one Ummah to the exclusion of all other men.

- The believers shall leave none of their members in destitution without giving him in kindness that he needs by the way of his liberty.

177

- No believer shall take as an ally a freedman of another Muslim without the consent of his previous master. All believers shall rise as one man against anyone who seeks to commit injustice, aggression, crime, or spread mutual enmity amongst the Muslims even if such a person is their kin.

- No believer shall slay a believer in retaliation for an unbeliever, nor shall he assist an unbeliever against a believer.

- Just as the bond to Allah is indivisible, all the believers shall stand behind the commitment of the least of them. All believers are bonded one to another to the exclusion of other men.

- This Pax Islamica is one and indivisible. No believer shall enter a separate peace without all other believers whenever there is fighting in the cause of God, but will do so only on the basis of equality and justice to all others. In every expedition for the cause of God we undertake, all parties to the covenant shall fight shoulder to shoulder as one man. All believers shall avenge the blood of one another when any one falls fighting in the cause of God.

- The pious believers follow the best and the most upright guidance.

- Whoever is convicted of killing a believer deliberatively but without righteous cause shall be liable to the relatives of the killed. Until the latter are satisfied, the killer shall be subject to retaliation by each believer.

- Any Jew who follows us is entitled to our assistance and the same rights as any one of us, without injustice and partisanship. As the Jews fight on the side the believers, they shall spend their wealth on equal par with the believers. The Jews are an Ummah along side the believers. The Jews have their religion and the Muslims theirs. Both enjoy the security of their populace and clients except the unjust and the criminal amongst them. The unjust and the criminal destroy only himself and his family.

- None of the Jewish tribes may go to war without the permission of Muhammad, though none may be prevented from taking revenge for a wound inflicted upon them. Whosoever murders anyone will have murdered him self and the members of his family, unless it be the case of the man suffering a wrong, for God will accept his actions. The Jews shall bear their public expenses and so will the Muslims. Each shall assist the other against any violator of this covenant. Their relationship shall be one of mutual advice and consultation and mutual assistance and charity rather than harm and aggression. Assistance is due to the party suffering an injustice not to one perpetrating it. Yathrab shall constitute a sanctuary to the parties of this covenant. Whatever the difference or dispute between the parties to this covenant remains unsolved shall be referred to God and to Muhammad. The Jews are entitled to the same rights as this covenant has granted to other parties together with the goodness and charity of the latter.

- Allah is the guarantor of the truth and goodwill of this covenant. Allah grants his protection to whosoever acts in piety, charity goodness.

The Covenant of Medina is a political document that the *nabi* Muhammad wrote fourteen hundred years ago. It contains nearly fifty articles, some of them repetitive. In this covenant between the Muslims emigrating from Mecca, eight Arab and nine Jewish clans of Medina formed a federation that became the basis of the Islamic state until the fall of the Umayyad dynasty in the year AD 750. This covenant established a community; freedom of faith and opinion; the inviolability of the city, human life, and property; and forbiddance of crime and establishment of a judicial system.

Within ten years of writing this covenant, to the time of the blessed *nabi's* death in June 632, from this small *ummah* of Yathrib, the whole of Arabia had converted to the *din* of Islam. In another eighty years, Islam had spread to the Atlantic in the West and to the confines of China in the East.

Succession to *Nabi* Muhammad's temporal authority became a problem from the very beginning. The period of the first four rightly guided caliphs is regarded by the Muslims as the ideal period of Islamic history, when Islam was practiced perfectly. This is far from obvious when one looks at the contemporary records. For one thing, three of the four caliphs were assassinated. Abu Bakr was *elected in consensus* after *Nabi* Muhammad's death. Umar succeeded Abu Bakr. It was during Umar's rule that most of the expansion into Syria, Iraq, and Egypt gained momentum. Umar established the administrative system of the new provinces. He also organized the treasury. Umar was assassinated while praying in a mosque in Medina. He was succeeded by Uthman from the clan of Umayyad, who continued the expansion of the empire. Opposition to some of his policies led to his assassination in 656. Ali ibn Abi Talib, *Nabi* Muhammad's cousin and son-in-law, was elected caliph; but Mu'awiyah, son of Abu Sufyan of the clan of Abd Shams, who happened to be the governor of Syria at the time, refused to recognize him as the caliph. Five years of civil war resulted between Mu'awiyah, based in Damascus, and Ali ibn Abi Talib of Beni Hashim, based in Kufah. During the prophet's lifetime, descendants of Abd Shams had been bitter enemies of Islam and the prophet's family, the descendants of Hashim. Fighting among Muslims, bloodshed, and killing of Muslims are forbidden.

In 661, Ali was assassinated, and Mu'awiyah became the caliph by force of arms and established the Umayyad dynasty, which ruled the Muslim world for ninety years, from 661 to 750. All the first four caliphs had been elected by consultation and consensus. Husayn, son of Ali, and the grandson of the blessed *nabi* of Allah, was brutally killed by the Umayyad at Karbala in Iraq on October 10, 680. The feud between the Umayyad and Beni Hashim split the Muslim world down to our times. Those who supported the claims of Ali ibn Abi Talib and his descendants to the caliphate became known as the Shia and constituted a sect spiritually divided from their fellow Muslims.

In the Umayyad period, the basic principle of the covenant of Allah that the executive sovereignty of the state rested with the *ummah* was abandoned, and the succession to the caliphate became hereditary. Thus began the rot in the Muslim community. The ruler took an increasingly autocratic and aristocratic stance. The royal court and governance became gradually modeled on the Greek and Byzantine style.

In AD 750, the descendants of Abbas—the blessed prophet's uncle— rose in revolt and overthrew the Umayyad, the descendants of Abu Sufyan, with much bloodshed and killing of Muslims by Muslims. This was an open betrayal of Allah's covenant. Thereafter, the Abbasid dynasty ruled the Muslim empire until 861. Abandoning Damascus, the Umayyad capital, the Abbasids built Baghdad as their capital.

The empire had been conquered by the Arabs, commanded by the Umayyad. After 750, there were no more conquests; the empire was on the defensive and began to shrink. The Abbasids had succeeded in overthrowing the Umayyad with the support of the Muslims of Persia. During the Umayyad period, the Arabs had been the rulers of the empire. Thereafter, the empire became an international Muslim state.

The earlier Abbasid caliphs were strong monarchs; the best known was Harun al-Rashid. By the time his son al-Ma'mun came to the throne, difficulties were increasing. To deal with these, al-Ma'mun set up the so-called inquisition (*mihnah*). The judges and people in authority had to state publicly that they believed that the Koran was created and rejected the view that it was an uncreated word of Allah. This was not a piece of theological hairsplitting but an important sociopolitical and legal question.

Soon after *Nabi* Muhammad's death, some people had the belief that the caliph was or should be a divinely inspired person whose decisions should be binding on Muslims. In other words, they wanted an autocracy; this was also the viewpoint of the caliph al-Ma'mun. If the Koran, though it was Allah's word, was created, then a leader inspired by Allah could presumably change it. Al Ma'mun wanted to have the prerogative to change the Koran.

The opposite point of view was that of scholar-jurists, who had become an important class in Islamic lands. Quite a large population of the empire could not speak or read Arabic and required the services of ulema to understand the complex issues in the Koran. The scholars insisted that the Koran was the uncreated word of Allah and therefore unchangeable and that they alone were the authorized interpreters of the Koran, and only they could pronounce how it was to be applied to contemporary situations. That implied that it was they and not the caliph who had the final word. The policy of inquisition was finally discontinued in around 850 because it failed to reconcile the rival interests.

Every believer inherited the legacy of the Koran, the covenant of Allah, the *din*, and the Dar es Salaam. When the blessed *nabi* passed away, every believer inherited the Koran and the *din*. This custodianship of the Koran, the covenant, the *din*, and the Dar es

Salaam rests with every believer individually till the last day. In the Dar es Salaam, individual believers collectively bestow this custodianship to a worthy person of their choice for a defined period with conditions attached; in return, that individual is to exercise authority to manage the affairs of the Islamic state. While this authority can be bestowed on a person, it can also be withdrawn if that individual fails to exercise his charge to the satisfaction of the believers.

In the latter part of ninth century, the power of the Abbasids began to decline. They were not strong enough to assert their authority over Spain. The Fatimid dynasty occupied Tunisia and then went on to conquer Egypt. The Abbasids were unable to control their governors who began to insist that sons or relatives should succeed them, and they were forced to acquiesce. In 936, an army general took over what remained of the Abbasid power. The Abbasid caliphs, though without real power, retained a nominal headship of the Islamic community until 1258, when the non-Muslim Mongol army sacked Baghdad and killed or expelled the Abbasids. From the ninth century onward, Islamic history tended to become a history of dynasties so numerous that it would be wearisome to mention them all.

In the central Islamic lands, there was the rise and spread of the Ottoman Turks. By the fourteenth century, the Ottomans had moved to the northwest of Anatolia and created a formidable military machine. They were able to cross over into Europe in 1357 and then subdue much of the Balkans.

In the early sixteenth century, the Ottomans were at the peak of their strength. They conquered Syria, Egypt, Tunisia, Algeria, Iraq, and much of Arabia, and they had a naval fleet in the Indian Ocean. In Europe, the Ottomans occupied Hungary for over a century. Gradually, the Ottoman Empire declined, and European powers gained strength. From the eighteenth century onward, the Ottomans were forced to withdraw from their European conquests until the post–First World War settlement of 1919, when only European Turkey was left. Ottomans lost all their Asian provinces to the British and the French. North African provinces had already been lost to the French and the Spanish.

After the fall of Baghdad to the Mongols in 1258, the Abbasid caliphate came to an end, but a member of the Abbasid family escaped to Egypt and claimed he was caliph, though it was only in Egypt that he was recognized. In the nineteenth century, the Ottoman sultans claimed that the caliphate had been transferred to them by the last of these Egyptian Abbasids, and this claim gained some recognition. The caliphate was formally abolished by the new Turkish secular republic and has not since then been reestablished. After the defeat of the Ottoman Empire in the First World War, most of the Islamic lands fell into the domain of the European colonial powers.

What brought ignominy to the Islamic world with eventual domination by Christian powers needs to be studied closely. With the breakup of the Abbasid Empire, provinces and even districts came under the rule of new military elites. Nomadic people invaded and broke through frontier defense sand migrated en masse into the Middle East. Agriculture and trading economies were greatly damaged, and the economy declined.

Sultanate Era: AD 950–1500

The breakup of a united Islamic state occurred in four phases.

AD 950–1050: With the decay of the Abbasid central authority, local elites took control of the empire's former provinces. In Egypt and Syria, the Fatimid—a Shia rival of the Abbasids—came to power with their own claims to the caliphate; and in Mesopotamia, tribal forces seized control. Military adventurers from Daylam seized control of western Iran, much of Iraq, and Baghdad that were the axial lands of the Abbasid caliphate. Eastern Iran and Transoxania were ruled by the Samanids, who were supplanted by the Ghaznavids, a regime based on slave military forces, which for the first time selected their own sultan.

AD 1040–1200: The second phase lasted from 1040 to 1200; with the collapse of the central authority, there were many regional power struggles that allowed for the breakdown of the eastern Iranian frontiers against nomadic invasions. Central Asian nomads searching for pasturage in the tenth, eleventh, and twelfth centuries spilled over into the region north of the Aral Sea and into Transoxania and Afghanistan. From contact with settled peoples, trade, and the activities of the missionaries, these Turkish peoples began to convert to Islam. Their chieftains became acquainted in the ways of agriculture, trade, city administration, and imperial conception of rule and order. By the end of the tenth century, the Turkish Qarluq people established their regime in Transoxania, while the Oghuz peoples under the leadership of the Seljuk family went on to conquer much of the former Abbasid Empire.

The Seljuks took control of Khorasan in 1040 and Baghdad in 1055. Further migration to the west led to the formation of Seljuk states in Mesopotamia, Syria, and Egypt. Turkish people also moved into lands that had not been under the control of the caliphate, which brought the Islamic dominion to Armenia, Georgia, and Anatolia. The Seljuk conquests lent a temporary and superficial political unity to the Islamic world. The conflicts of the nomadic people seeking independence and the ruling families seeking to subordinate the tribal forces, the rivalries among the ruling families for fiefdoms and territories, and the widespread distribution of *iqtas*—lands instead of salaries—led to the decentralization, fragmentation, and dispersal of political power.

Seljuk-related regimes broke down into numerous independent states and territorial fragments.

AD 1150–1350: The Seljuk decline opened a way for a third phase in the history of the region from 1150 to 1350. This was a period of further nomadic invasion from Inner Asia, culminating in the devastating Mongol invasions and the establishment of Mongol regimes over most of the Middle East. To the west, the slave military forces in Egypt and Syria consolidated the Mamluk regime.

AD 1400–1500: The final phase was the Timurid period, 1400–1500. The Mongol period was succeeded by new times of trouble and the conquest by Timur, also known as Tamerlane. This era of repeated nomadic invasions brought demographic changes in the ethnic and religious identity of populations. A new Turkic-speaking population the Hindu Kush mountain range, Iran, the Caucasus, Anatolia, and Mesopotamia. Turkish settlement led to the Islamization of northeastern Iran, Armenia, and Anatolia both by settlement of newcomers and by the conversion of existing populations. Turkish migration increased at the expense of agriculture. Turkish tribal formations also became a lasting part of the political process. Under the leadership of warrior chieftains and holy men, the migrations shifted the balance of power in favor of tribes at the expense of centralized states.

Political and Social Order

From the Umayyad period to the present, governance of the Muslim peoples became established on un-Koranic principles that chose to betray the principles of the covenant of Allah. The concept of the sovereignty of Allah over heaven and earth and of the vicegerency of the *ummah* with the accompanying executive sovereignty and autonomy was rejected.

The downfall of the Islamic state came with a life of luxury, loss of faith, and disregard of Allah's covenant by the people who chose to seize Muslim countries and their governments. They professed to abide by the covenant of Allah in words but not with their deeds. The rulers imposed themselves on the believers and began the plunder of the land and wealth of the people through oppression, treachery, deceit, injustice, and murder with the help and manipulation of the ecclesiastical hierarchy and establishment of the mosque. It was a long period of *fitnah*. With the misappropriated wealth of their subjects came the decline of moral values, use of alcohol, gambling, shameful deeds, cheating and fratricide, and killing of their fathers, brothers, and their own children in the quest for the throne.

The wealth required for luxurious living was at first plundered from their own subjects and then from the neighboring principalities. When these riches were exhausted, the rulers turned to Western and Illuminati Jewish bankers for loans with exorbitant interest rates. Familiarity with the Western financial system brought further indebtedness, followed by secret alliances with the Western powers against fellow Muslim states, causing disunity among the Muslims, and finally capitulation, humiliation, and total political and economic subjugation. All this occurred because Islam's land was usurped, taken over, and ruled through force of arms by people who pretended to be believers but in effect were *Munafiqeen, Mutaffifeen,* and common thieves. There was no consultation with the *ummah* and no consensual decision-making. The rulers disobeyed Allah's covenant.

The believers lost their freedom; in Islam, every man, woman, and child has a God-given right to liberty; right to practice their faith in accordance with their beliefs as there is no compulsion in matters of religion; right to life, which means intellectual, physical, and emotional well-being; right to safeguard one's property; right to intellectual endeavors, acquisition of knowledge, and education; right to earn a living; and right to free speech and action to enjoin good and forbid evil. The *ummah* was robbed of its dignity. The dignity of an individual brings with it six God-given values—faith, life, freedom, intellect, property, and lineage—that must be protected by the law as a matter of priority. This moral autonomy of the individual, when bound together with the will of the community, formulates the doctrine of infallibility of the collective will of the community (*ummah*), which is the doctrinal basis of consensus.

The believers were no longer the *ummah* with the God-given right to appoint someone among themselves to run their affairs through consultation and consensus; instead, they became slaves and subjects of people bearing arms. The believers abdicated their executive sovereignty over the Dar es Salaam, permitting tyrants—their rulers—to have free rein to disaster. Muslims and their rulers failed to observe Allah's covenant and indulged in what was forbidden. Dictators, kings, and military tyrants continue to this day to plunder, terrorize, and control the *ummah*, openly defying Allah's covenant.

Monarchy

The legacy of Islamic caliphate and the heritage of Byzantine and Persian concepts of imperial monarchy were blended with Turkish concepts of political chieftaincy, law, and world conquest. While regimes came and went and while conquerors succeeded one another, the system of governing came to be fixed in the same mode from east to west. The caliphate, though deprived of administrative power, retained its symbolic importance as the emblem of Muslim world order as a bearer of ultimate guarantees for religious belief, justice, and political order. For centuries, all provincial governors and warlords looked to the caliphs for their right to rule. After the extinction of the Abbasid line in 1258, in Egypt, the Mamluks crowned the survivor of the Abbasid family as their caliph. Great warlord sultans considered themselves caliphs, and the Safavids regarded themselves as the descendants and embodiments of Shiite imams. The Ottoman claimed implicitly and explicitly to embody the caliphate in their persons.

The conquerors and the warlords cultivated a parallel non-Muslim concept of authority. They gave themselves such titles of shah, malik, sultan, and all-supreme rulers. They recalled historical tribal genealogies to guarantee their descent from famous past rulers.

Two types of governments developed after the fall of the Abbasids. Qarakhanids, Seljuks, and Mongols were nomadic chieftaincies transformed into monarchies. The nomadic chief ruled by virtue of his conquests or decent from conquerors. He was supported by a coalition of aristocratic tribal lineages who were entitled to share in the spoils of victory. Nomadic states divided their territories into domains of the leading members of the ruling family. These states were built on the support of tribal populations that extended the reach of the ruling circle beyond that of the ruling family coalition. The Turkish chieftains commonly built up a governing apparatus that made them independent of their own nomadic supporters. They created court complexes of family retainers, servants, noble companions, military officers, and high-ranking administrators that constituted the political elite of their regime. The sultans built up a slave military corps to serve as praetorian guards to serve in battle against foreign enemies as well as their own nomadic supporters. The slaves were supposed to be the most loyal subjects.

The second type of regime was the purely military slave elite. The slave officers themselves overthrew dynastic rulers and built governments solely of slaves, from ordinary soldiers to the head of the state. Examples are that of the Mamluks of Egypt and the Ghaznavids of Afghanistan.

These regimes faced two political problems. The first problem was the inherent tendency toward decentralization of power. Control of provinces was delegated to the family members and the nomadic chieftains. *Iqtas* were assigned to the military leaders. The weakness of the bureaucratic apparatus prevented control over these assignments. The result was usurpation of power at both the provincial and local levels with the formation of microregimes within the nominal territories of the state.

The second problem was the relationship of the sultans and the central government to the nomadic forces. The nomads conquered the new territories, but soon they came into conflict with their own chieftains. The royal families wanted to protect the conquered and the settled populations and their productive taxable economies, while the nomadic interest lay in obtaining booty, lands for pasturage, and freedom from government control.

The Islamic Communities in the Post-Abbasid Period

The political upheavals of this intermediate era caused a profound transformation of social organization of the Middle Eastern populations. The population was exposed to tremendous danger to their lives and property and suffered extraordinary economic hardships caused by marauding armies. There were rapid changes of political overlords, decline in older landowning and bureaucratic elites, and imposition of new foreign rulers. With every new marauding army, there was a period of massacres, looting, destruction, and confiscation of property. Agricultural lands were assigned to the new military elite, causing further instability in the region. In response, the people throughout the region drew together in defensive movements and created a new communal structure. This new order was based on

Islam. This was, in fact, the first defensive movement of the Muslim peoples to take control of their lives.

The Abbasid Empire, in many ways, delayed the diffusion of Islam to the mass of Middle Eastern populations. Although the empire was the official sponsor and protector of Islam, the new religion remained a religion of the minority. The Abbasid Empire accepted the existing Christian, Jewish, and Zoroastrian communities and the authority of their religious institutions.

With the breakup of the Abbasid Empire, the old social elites were swept away. Churches could no longer protect their members, landowning families were dispossessed, and the administration crumbled. The result was a vacuum of leadership into which was drawn the only surviving elite element—Muslim scholars, teachers, preachers, and holy men. The *Karramiya*—a religious movement that combined theological principles, Sufi practices, and social mission— established networks of khankahs (Sufi hospices) that eventually became the basis of community organizations and conversion to Islam. Town quarters became organized under the auspices of Islamic schools of law, Shia communities, or Sufi or other religious leadership. By the twelfth century, the majority of the Middle Eastern populations were identified with Islam. Communal leaders were Muslim ulema and Sufis. Christians, Jews, and Zoroastrians had become minorities everywhere. The newly Islamized populations of newly converted Christians, Jews, and Zoroastrians of differing backgrounds coalesced to form new community organizations, which form today's *ummah*.

As early as AD 660, Muslims had begun to divide into two camps: the Sunnis or the supporters of the existing Umayyad and later Abbasid caliphates and the Shiites, who opposed the established regimes and insisted that only the descendants of Ali had the right to the leadership of Muslims. In the tenth century, the Shiites—then deprived of living imams—codified their tradition in the books of Hadith, law, and theology and elaborated a ritual calendar focused on the veneration of tombs of Ali at Najaf and his son Husayn at Karbala.

Among the Sunnis, a variety of small communities took form as people gathered around readers of the Koran, reciters of Hadith, scholars of law, and theologians and mystics to whom they looked for inspiration and guidance. The legal schools evolved from the informal discussion of scholars, students, and judges into quasi-administrative bodies producing codes of law, staffing the judiciary, carrying on legal instruction, and providing informal leadership and instruction for the common people.

Among the Sunnis, a variety of small communities took form as people gathered around readers of the Koran, reciters of Hadith, scholars of law, and theologians and mystics to whom they looked for inspiration and guidance. The legal schools evolved from the informal discussion of scholars, students, and judges into quasi-administrative bodies producing codes of law, staffing the judiciary, carrying on legal instruction, and providing informal leadership and instruction for the common people.

The ulema (scholars) also assumed a larger role in the communities by organizing groups, lodges, and sectarian associations under their leadership. The ulema also represented the urban populations to the conquerors; provided local administration and justice; and arranged for local security, public works, taxation, charities, and other services. With the expansion of the madrassas and religious education, the Koran became the focus of recitation and personal piety, while the Hadith became the focal point for the study of the Sharia and the science of jurisprudence. While there was little dissension in the discussion of the intricacies of the Koran, the scholar-jurists became locked in arguments on the merits of various Hadith. For the elucidation of the truth of the Koran, the logic and convoluted debates became moored to the elusive Hadith.

At the same time, a new form of Islamic communal organization under Sufi auspices came into being. Sufis, for centuries, had gathered under charismatic, holy men in khankahs for meetings, worship, and instruction. In the twelfth century, Sufi organizations under the influence of the legal schools and state support became more formal. Soon Sufis became organized into brotherhoods. The transmission of *dhikr*, the meditational method of concentrating the soul on the veneration of Allah, became the defining quality of fellowship. As Sufi organizations became more organized, they took on important roles in the towns and villages. In towns and villages throughout the Islamic lands, lay Muslims came to the Sufis for supplementary worship, spiritual consolation, healing, and charity. The Sufi brotherhoods also adopted the role of mediators of problems between the peoples and the governments and between factional and tribal rivals. Alongside the legal schools, Sufi communities emerged as a basic organizing social force among the Muslims.

The State and Religion

For the Muslims, the blessed *nabi* himself embodied both religious and political authority. He revealed Allah's will and law for the people. He was the ruler of the community and, as such, also collected taxes, waged wars, and arbitrated disputes. The early caliphs also claimed religious authority to make pronouncements on religious laws and beliefs and claimed political prerogatives of emperors. In the evolution of the caliphate, the new rulers, as the conquerors and emperors, increasingly became political leaders with only symbolic religious authority. The caliphs maintained only nominal religious authority. By the time of collapse of the Abbasid Empire, the authority to promulgate or discover law, to make judgments on religious belief, and to instruct ordinary Muslims devolved on the ulema and the holy men.

The Turkish invasions and the establishment of nomadic or slave military regimes made acute the question of religious or state authority functions. Nomads and slaves were foreigners in origin and culture, warriors imposed on civilian populations; their allegiance to Islam was often suspect, while the town and village elites were Muslim religious leaders. Turkish nomadic and slave military authorities were eager to establish internal order, to facilitate taxation, and to minimize resistance from their subject populations. They needed legitimating and recognition, which only the holders of religious purity could supply. They invited cultivated scholars, holy men, poets, philosophers, historians, teachers, intellectuals, and artists to adorn and glorify their courts. The illiterate and uncouth nomadic rulers craved to enter into the fraternities of cultured Middle Eastern people.

The military elites thus sought the support of the religious elite by underwriting their activities. They provided endowments of mosques and khankahs and stipends for teachers, holy men, and students. Seljuk rulers endowed madrassas in every major city of their empires. They endowed Sufi khankahs to foster holy men who served as missionaries of Islam. In return, the religious leaders accepted Seljuk states, recognized their legitimacy, justified them to the subjects, and taught the necessity of obedience.

The Muslim society became, in practice, governed by state elites who patronized Islam and religious leaders who, in turn, legitimized alien states. *The collaboration of elites of state and religion and the cooperative relationship between these two institutions would be, for many centuries, the Middle Eastern Muslim solution to the problem of state and religion. It bypassed the covenant of Allah and the common person, the vicegerent of God.*

Not all Middle Eastern peoples accepted the governing collaboration of the elites of state (kings) and religion (priest class). Many people looked back to the image of the prophet as the embodiment of both religious and political authorities. And many a community ruled according to the laws laid out in the Koran. To unite disparate small communities and to organize and justify resistance to state control, such groups looked to holy Sufi men for a unified *religious-political* leadership in opposition to established states.

The Safvid Empire

The Turkish and Mongol migrations had profoundly changed the character of the Middle East from the Oxus River and northern Iran to eastern Anatolia. The Turkish presence radically changed both the economy and society. Large districts were converted from agriculture to pasturage. Turkish territories were parceled out among tribal chieftains who gathered their families, clients, bands of freebooters, and others into a single political entity. These tribes or *uymaq* used their power to bring lesser chieftains into line and to subdue and govern local towns and villages. They became the de facto government in much of northern Iran.

In reaction, religious leaders emerged to shelter the local populations from the excesses of the nomadic tribal rulers. Sufi preachers promised to invoke occult and mysterious powers that would protect their followers. Other leaders taught the doctrine of *qutb*, a saintly pillar of the world that would protect oppressed peoples. Still others taught that a savior would appear to redeem the good people from the upheavals of the times.

One of these Sufi leaders was a Persian mystic, Sheikh Safi al-Din (1252–1334), who founded the Safavid Sufi brotherhood. He provided schools and residences and cultivated a hierarchy of students, disciples, lieutenants, and missionaries. The Safavid devotees, by the end of the fifteenth century, had come to believe that the head of the order—their Sufi master, their shah or king—was the reincarnation of Ali and the hidden imam whom they awaited as Allah's Messiah. This clearly was the influence of the pre-Islamic culture of Persia. In the turbulent fifteenth century, after the breakup of Timurid Empire, the Safavids turned to more political militant activities. Bound together by religious belief, the Safavids waged war against Turkish principalities as well as against Christian populations of Georgia and eastern Anatolia and conquered Iran in a rapid set of victories between 1500 and 1510.

Soon after the conquest, the first Safavid ruler—Shah Isma'il—and his successors began to replace their Sufi followers with the apparatus of central control. They built up a loyal cadre of slaves apart from their tribal and religious followers. The rulers attempted to develop a cultural policy that would support their new regime not just as a Sufi religious movement but also as the successor of the historic Iranian monarchy. They encouraged cultural and literary activities glorifying and celebrating the ancient Iranian monarchy and the Safavids as the heirs of that tradition. The first period expressed the need for political legitimating. In the seventeenth century, a more mature regime desired artistic depiction of beauty and love—an expression of the taste of aristocratic soldiers, officials, and courtiers for luxury and good life.

The new Shiite establishment was built up over the course of a century. The new cadres were organized into an administration controlled by the state. An official called the *sadr* was appointed the intermediary between the shahs and the ulema. Eventually, this functionary was given the responsibility for appointment of judges and teachers and for administration of endowments. The Safavids further extended their control over the religion by endowing the principal Shiite shrines, founding the teaching colleges, and providing grants of income from land estates for the leading ulema families. Ulema landed aristocracy were created as a buttress of the regime. *The Safavids brought the ulema from the position of clients to that of the servants of the state.* The Safavids also suppressed all rival forms of religion in Iran, destroying Iranian religious pluralism by persecution of Sunni, alternate Shiite, and Sufi rivals. The pilgrimage to Mecca was de-emphasized and replaced by visitation to Shiite shrines.

Relationship between the state and religion gradually became strained. The religious leaders gradually began to question the notion that the Safavid shahs were the representatives of the hidden imam. The Shiite scholars instead claimed that they themselves were the highest religious authority and true representatives of the imam.

In the late seventeenth century, the Safavid Empire fell apart. The *uymaq*—Afghans, Afshars, Kajar, Zands, and others rose and partitioned the country among them. The Safavids were a direct continuation of the political system of the Mongols and the Timurids. The Safavid state remained a court regime in which the power was widely dispersed among competing tribal forces.

While the earlier states of the Umayyads and the Abbasids were the patrons of the Islamic activity, the Safavids took this further. They claimed to be the living representatives of the divine command. They created highly centralized and controlled religious elite as the backbone of their regime.

The Ottoman Empire

The Ottoman Empire had its origins in the trends of the earlier centuries—the Turkish migrations and the post-Abbasid reconstruction of the state and society. The legacy of Persian monarchy and Byzantine, Roman, Seljuk Anatolian, Mongol, and Timurid precedents interacting with Turkish culture synthesized to evolve into a highly imperial Ottoman Empire.

The Seljuk invasions had brought Oghuz peoples into Georgia, Armenia, and Byzantine Anatolia. Accompanying the conquering armies were small bands of nomadic peoples under the leadership of beys (warrior chiefs) and Sufi holy men (*babas*). The Sufi holy men not only provided military leadership but also created an infrastructure of settled life among the nomadic warriors. They established residences; brought lands under cultivation; built hospices, mills, and schools; and mediated disputes among their followers. In the wake of the conquering bands came the Seljuk nobility, which set up a centralized administrative structure on the model of those that had been created by Seljuk family elites in Iran and Iraq. The Seljuk built up slave military forces, administrative cadres, and an Islamic religious infrastructure. Judges were appointed, colleges were built, and professorships were endowed.

As a result of the activities of the state and the migratory Sufi influences, there was transformation of Anatolia into a Muslim society. Under the Seljuk rule (1071–1243), much of the Greek, Armenian, Georgian, and Syrian populations were progressively converted to Islam. Sufis played an important role in these conversions. Sufis established residences as centers for social service and assistance to local population. They also created a devotional, charitable, educational, and communal environment that led to the Islamic conversion of Anatolia.

The Seljuk Turkish system of expansion and occupation led to chronic tensions between central states and peripheral principalities and nomadic warrior chiefs. The state tried to consolidate and assert its authority, while the nomads and the warrior chiefs sought to maintain their autonomy. This prompted many of them to expand into western

Anatolia into the Byzantine territory as the local chieftains sought to enhance their power, seek glory for Islam, and maintain their independence from the Seljuk state.

The Ottoman (Osman, Othman) Empire had its beginnings in such a band of frontier warriors operating in the thirteenth century in western Anatolia. Ertugrul was the founder of a dynasty that, over the course of two centuries, first conquered Bursa in western Anatolia in 1326; crossed the straits of Gallipoli in 1345; conquered Bulgaria, Macedonia, and much of Greece; and defeated the Serbian Empire at the Battle of Kosovo in 1389. The Ottomans then turned eastward and absorbed the Muslim-controlled Anatolia. In 1453, the Ottomans seized Constantinople, bringing to an end the eleven-hundred-old Byzantine Empire and established themselves as successors to the Roman Empire.

Mehmed the Conqueror (1451–1481) saw himself as successor to Roman emperors and Arab caliphs. The conquest of the Balkans opened the way for a two-century struggle against the powers of Europe. In central Europe, the Ottomans pushed beyond the Danube River and absorbed Romania in 1529. Belgrade was taken in 1520, and Hungary came under Ottoman rule in 1529. Vienna was unsuccessfully besieged the same year.

In the Mediterranean, the Ottomans waged war and captured Algiers in 1529 and Tunis in 1574. Mehmed and his successors extended Ottoman domains eastward to the borders of Iran-absorbed Arab provinces, North Africa, and the holy places of Arabia. Ottoman expansion, beginning in Anatolia, continued for three centuries until the Ottomans brought southern and eastern Europe as far as Vienna; the north steppes off the Black Sea, including the Ukraine, Anatolia, and the borders of the Safavid Empire; and the Arab countries Egypt,

Yemen, and North Africa as the borders of Morocco under their control.

The Ottoman state was built on the same institutional basis as its Middle Eastern predecessors. The nerve center of the Ottoman Empire was at the Topkapi Serai overlooking the Golden Horn of Istanbul. The palace or the court center was divided into two. The inner section was made of the residences of the sultan, his harem, his extended family, the treasury, and a school for pages and officers. In the rest of the court complex resided his favorite companions, his highest-ranking officers, administrators, and religious functionaries. The outer section of the court was the administrative zone, which included state offices and the offices and residences of palace functionaries.

In the Ottoman society and politics, the women of the royal family were particularly important. In the traditional Turkish cultural understanding, power were vested not only in the reigning prince but also collectively in his family. Women therefore played an important role in the ceremonials of the regime, negotiations, and intrigue at the court. They also participated in the selection of officers and in formulating important policies.

The city of Istanbul could be regarded as an extension of the royal palace. Successful sultans built in Istanbul great mosques, school complexes, and facilities such as hospitals, libraries, bazaars, residences, public baths, and soup kitchens.

The backbone of the Ottoman sultanate was the military. To ensure their power, the sultans earlier on in their reign began to build slave forces as an alternative to the traditional free Turkish warriors. In any previous Middle Eastern regimes, the slave soldiers originally came from the Caucasus or from Central Asia. The Ottomans instead ensured a steady supply of slave soldiers from the Christian populations of the Balkans by instituting a tax in manpower, the *devsirme*. This was the first systematic recruitment of slaves from within the domain itself.

Whereas most Middle Eastern slave forces were trained to be elite cavalry, the Ottomans trained their most important units as infantry and provided them with firearms and used phalanx tactics to combine musket firepower with artillery. The cavalry were recruited from among Turkish warriors. They were not garrisoned as a regular army; they were provided with land grants (timars, Arabic equivalent iqtas) throughout the empire. The timar holders provided local security and served in Ottoman campaigns. The timar system was based on old-fashioned feudal pattern. The slave system was used to build a powerful bureaucratic apparatus to bolster the Ottoman power. The Ottomans converted their young slaves to Islam and educated them in palace schools to be pages in the royal households, officers in the army, and government officials. The slaves were personally devoted to the sultan.

The Ottoman regime was not built on the support of the populace or on any ethnic homogeneity. The supporting pillars of the regime were the slaves and the clients of the rulers from differing backgrounds who were trained and educated at the palace schools and who provided an unquestioning loyalty to the regime.

The Ottoman sultans created the position of *shaykh al-Islam* or chief mufti (an expert in Islamic law) to increase religious legitimacy of the state in response to criticism of the regime's secularization. Originally, the man occupying this position served as a personal religious adviser to the sultan. The earlier muftis had no administrative duties. In the middle of the sixteenth century, the chief mufti was recognized as the head of the ulema. The power of appointing other ulema was then bestowed on the chief mufti. The Ottomans strove to centralize the domain of religion. They patronized the ulema and the Sufis; they built mosques and madrassas and organized judicial administration. However, they not only patronized the religious elite but also incorporated them into a hierarchical bureaucracy that made them functionaries of the state.

As the ulema and the Sufis became functionaries of the state, they could no longer protect the people from the abuses of political power. As paid servants of the state and defenders of Ottoman legitimacy, the ulema ceased to represent the mass of Muslim believers, and they could not effectively resist corruption in the government. The ulema, as a class, became dependent on government largess and therefore a powerful interest group within the state. They were able to acquire considerable properties through *waqf* (endowments), and they were not threatened with confiscation of the property after death. A small group of families dominated the religious establishment; from 1703 to 1839, eleven families accounted for twenty-nine of fifty-eight *shaykh al-Islam.*

The authority of the Ottoman sultans was derived from several traditions of Middle Eastern and Eastern Roman cultures. The Ottomans primarily derived their legitimacy from their tribal roots of

- royal family supremacy,
- sovereignty by conquest,
- divinely given mission to conquer the world.

This patrimonial concept based the right to rule on aristocratic lineage, combined with the privileges of the conqueror, having its origin in the Turkish Central Asian pre-Islamic tribal nomadic past. In the earlier phase of the Ottoman rule, there was an open and brutal struggle for power among the sons of the deceased ruler. The winner of the struggle was considered to have been selected by God to be the ruler.

The whole of the conquered domains was considered to be the personal property of the sultan. The state was his household. The soldiers, courtiers, and administrators were his slaves. The subjects were his flocks. The territory of the empire was his to be distributed among his family and his favored retainers.

Islamic Tradition: From the Islamic tradition, the sultans claimed to be the defenders of Islam and therefore successors to the caliphate as temporal successors to the *nabi* of Islam. Suleyman I (1520–1566) took the title *khalife-i-ru-yi zemin* (caliph of the world). The caliphs were viewed in terms as the defenders of faith, a ghazi and a warrior who waged war to expand the domain of Islam. He protected Muslims against Christian enemies.

The Cosmopolitan Culture: The sultan's authority was further based on the cosmopolitan culture, comprising Arab, Persian, Turkish, Byzantine, and European elements. From the Middle Eastern tradition came the concept of *universal glory*.

Eastern Roman Tradition: From the Eastern Roman tradition was borrowed the notion that the Ottoman sultan was emperor and heir to the Roman Empire, which made him take the title of *padishah*, the supreme king. The Ottoman sultan was portrayed in mystical terms as the viceroys of God on the earth who were meant to bring order to the affairs of humans. During festivals and royal ceremonies, the language of divine selection and personal charisma was invoked to glorify the sultan as a divine being.

The Elite of the Palace: The Ottoman *elite* were a heterogeneous, cosmopolitan class recruited from diverse origins, which included Turkish, Arab, and Balkan Muslims. The Ottoman Empire was not a regime of Muslims over non-Muslims. These elite also included Jewish bankers and merchants, Phanariot Greek merchants, and European renegades. The elite were a caste elevated above the common people by their wealth, court and political connections, and personal devotion to the sultan.

The Subject Population: The subject population belonged to a lesser order of existence. All commoners, Muslim and non-Muslim, were considered the *reava* (the flocks), to be shorn in the interests of the political elite. Both Muslim and non-Muslim communities were organized into small religious communities that were permitted considerable internal autonomy, regulated by religious laws and values. This small community organization, called the millet system, served to administer educational, judicial, familial, and charitable affairs under the authority of the religious, clerical, and priestly leaders. These leaders were part of a religious hierarchy of state functionaries responsible to the sultan and the Ottoman authorities. These religious leaders assisted the state in collecting the taxes and enforcing social discipline. The Ottomans operated on the principle that the subjects (*reava*) should serve the interests of the state; the economy was organized to ensure the flow of tax revenues, goods in kind, and the services needed by the government and the elites. The populace was systematically taxed, and a systematic record of the population, households, property, and livestock was maintained.

All the lands in the empire were owned by the ruler; some lands (*tapulu*) were on perpetual lease to the peasants who had the right to assign that right to their male descendants, and *mukatalu* lands were leased to a tax collector in return for a fixed payment for a lease. In the fifteenth century, the Ottomans had conceded to Turkish military rulers and Muslim religious rulers the ownership right to the land. In the course of the next century and a half, the sultans dispossessed the local notables and reassigned the tax rights to the timar holders appointed by the sultan. Ottoman policies were inimical to accumulation of private property. Large private fortunes were regularly confiscated by the state.

The Ottoman economic policy on taxation and trade was based on fiscalism that was aimed at accumulation of as much bullion as possible in the state treasury. The Ottomans did not see trade policy or scientific and technological development as means of creating wealth. Rather, they sought wealth from conquered and annexed territories.

As it happened with all the great empires, the rot in moral standards set in, and that brought the decline and fall of the Ottoman Empire.

- The Ottoman state power was built on the fusion of Byzantine, Muslim, and Seljuk Turkish and Mongol precedents of government. Absolute power rested with the sultan, who ruled his vast domains with the assistance of Turkish chieftains, slave army, slave bureaucracy, and religious functionaries. The population played no role in the governance, whether advisory or administrative.

- With the decline of the central state, the slave elites got full control of the government. Slave soldiers demanded and were allowed to establish families to work in the civilian economy and to remain on the state payroll without ever providing military service. The religious functionaries, who were entrenched in the system, began to serve their own interests rather than those of the sultan or of the people. Provincial officials began to usurp local resources, control local economies, convert tax farms into various types of private properties, and build up local military support. Officials at all levels established large households resembling the sultan's household, which included a large harem and accommodation for a large number of retainers. This served as a basis for patronage network for a large number of men. Prominent chieftains and tax farmers made themselves independent and built a political base in the countryside. Throughout the empire, the local notables—beys, pashas, and 'ayns—were taking power in their own hands.

- Silver brought back from the newly discovered American mines undermined the price stability in the whole of the Mediterranean, and it unleashed an intense competition in the Ottoman Empire for control of resources. Raw materials became costlier, but selling prices declined. There were deep disturbances in the economy of Anatolia, the heartland of the empire. European competition was winning away at the control of international trade. *In the Ottoman Empire until the end of the sixteenth century and for most of the seventeenth century, there was a self-controlled trading system not dependent on the world economy. In the eighteenth century, European economic superiority was assured, and the Ottoman Empire became a dependent part of a European-dominated world economy.*

- Ottoman security and prosperity was undermined by the seventeenth century because of a deteriorating economy. There was a rising population, a large increase in the number of unemployed, demobilized and unsalaried soldiers, undisciplined students, and bands of armed peasants roaming and ravaging the countryside. There were frequent armed clashes among the provincial administrators, irregular soldiers, and government forces. To reinforce central authority, the government stationed permanent garrisons, which then became identified with local economic interest groups who exploited their position for their own benefit.

What Brought the Downfall of the Mighty Islamic Empires?

The covenant of Allah is the code of conduct to be fulfilled by the believers. People who covet power and wealth through murder and conquest do not have the commitment to equality of man, honesty, justice, and the law according to the covenant of Allah. The Umayyads, Abbasids, and Turko-Mongol-Seljuk tribal formations robbed, stole, and plundered the wealth and heritage of the new believers of Islam and took political control of Islam through the destruction of the caliphate (khilafat). Their aim and that of their modern successors was to take control of the lands of Islam and then hang on to power and wealth of Islamic lands, to the detriment of the *din* and the well-being and prosperity of the believers. The rulers from the time of the Umayyads to the present have betrayed the covenant of the Koran.

No one can rule over Islam yet fulfill the covenant of Allah because the executive sovereignty of the land and the affairs of Islam rests with the individual believer. The believer has to bestow this authority on his *wakil* for him to exercise his mandate to administer the affairs of the believer and his community.

The sultans introduced the concept of the privileged position of the ruler acquired by conquest through which all land and wealth became the personal possession of the monarch. All the conquered domains were considered to be the personal property of the sultan. The state was his household. The soldiers, courtiers, and administrators were his slaves. The subjects were his flocks. The territory of the empire was his to be distributed among his family and his favored retainers. The greed for power has been present in man since the beginning of human history. Twenty-three verses in the Koran mention traits in humans that Allah does not love—*Munafiqeen* (truth concealers), *kafirun* (the wrongdoers), *zalimun* (workers of corruption), *mufsidun* (the transgressors), and *ta'adda* (the immoderate, the proud, and the boastful). These are the covetous people who have, in Islamic history, gone on to usurp power, land, and wealth from the *ummah* and have destroyed its unity. The Koran's covenant clearly forbids the misappropriation of the public trust of Allah and the *rasul*, which in this case is the caliphate and the wealth of the *ummah*:

> O you who believe! Betray not the trust of Allah and the Messenger, nor misappropriate knowingly things entrusted to you. (Al-Anfal 2:27, Koran)

Although the Muslim rulers appeared in the guise of adherents to Islam, their conduct belied their true inner nature. In fact, they were all, in varying degrees, the *Munafiqeen*, *kafirun*, *zalimun*, *mufsidun*, and *ta'adda*.

The blessed *nabi* and his early successors established a system of governance based on the covenant of the Koran. As with any new institution, the caliphate had some difficulties in the first forty years relating to the succession of the caliph. However, the principles of the governance, human rights, property rights, gender equality, finance and commerce, war and peace, and social interaction were all carried out as well laid out in the covenant of Allah.

The problems began with the Umayyads. Even in the early years, the sultans began to digress from the covenant of Allah, and the first victim was the caliphate. The palace replaced the mosque as the place of assembly and consultation. The caliph took over the role of an Eastern Roman emperor, and his impoverished family within the palace assumed the role of a royal clan. A transformation of the caliphate took place from the time of Umar, the man in simple garb who shared his camel with his companion when he traveled to Jerusalem to accept its surrender from the Romans to bejeweled sultans who claimed to be shadows of God on the earth.

The Islamic society is an *ummah* of autonomous believers who fulfill the covenant of Allah. In this arrangement, every individual man, woman and child has God-given rights. To reiterate to each believer (man and woman), Allah has bestowed a right to freedom and equality. No one is superior to the other except in righteousness and virtue.

- Every Muslim community is the basic Islamic state. It is autonomous and free to conduct its own affairs. *Sixty thousand* such autonomous states voluntarily join together under the protection of Allah to form the *ummah wast* and the Dar es Salaam.
- In the affairs of Allah, in the communities of Islam, there are no sultans and kings nor any dictators.
- In the affairs of Allah, there are no priests, nor are there any ulema or self-proclaimed spokespersons of Allah.
- In the affairs of Allah, the believers share their wealth and their sweat.
- In Islam, there are no mercenary armies. Every believer is a *mujahid* and a ghazi. Every believer should have military training, knowledge of military tactics, and military technology. Every believer is the defender of his community and country.
- Every believer is free.

The Five Curses That Caused the Downfall of Islam

This state of equilibrium and stability provided to the believers by the covenant of Allah was disrupted when the Umayyads, the Abbasids, and the Turko-Mongol conquerors imposed their five curses on the Muslims.

1. The *Fitnah* of the Rulers of Islam: Islam is a religion of voluntary submission of a human spirit to the will of Allah after a considered conviction that Allah is the only reality and that everything else springs out of that reality. Allah has given every human the freedom of choice to submit or not to His will. There is no compulsion in matters of the *din*. And yet there are humans who, by force of arms, compel other humans to submit to their will. They demand obedience through imprisonment, torture, and murder. Every Muslim state in this day is a police state. Every Muslim ruler abuses his authority to plunder and debase the lands of Islam.

There is a clear reason for the glaring weakness of the state-run armies of the Muslim nation-states. The Muslim states are governed by self-appointed kings, dictators, and politicians who are divorced from their *din* and their people—the believers. They belong to and serve the interests of the circle of evil. In this process, the Muslim kings/dictators/politicians disobey every commandment of Allah.

Two hundred years ago, the circle of evil began its control of the world's wealth through conspiracy, subterfuge, and secrecy by undermining the stability of countries through war, strife, and discord and by weakening governments through creation of confusion in financial markets. The Western armies and intelligence services are the foot soldiers of the circle of evil, and the rulers of both the East and the West are their pawns and puppets to be manipulated at will to control the power and wealth of the world. The circle of evil is the external *fitnah* whose intent is to destroy Islam. The intent of the circle of evil has always been to corrupt, divide, and control the wealth of the Islamic land through the manipulation of its rulers, who were initially placed in positions of power by the circle with the help of the Western armies, intelligence, and diplomacy.

The weakness of the nation-state mercenary armies of the modern Islamic states clearly arises from the nonfulfillment of Allah's injunctions in the covenant. Faith in Allah's promise and His power, unity of the *ummah*, justice, and struggle to end oppression and tyranny are essential actions ordained in the covenant. When an individual believer reneges in the fulfillment of his covenant with Allah, he only does it to the detriment to his own soul. However, such an action on the part of the community and its appointed leaders leads to the undermining, enslavement, and impoverishment of the whole Islamic community for many generations.

The foundation of the regimes of the imperial families of the Arabian Peninsula, Jordan, Brunei, and Morocco and the imperial government of Hosni Mubarak of Egypt and the generals of Pakistan is supported by the *external fitnah*—the British, US, and NATO armed forces, intelligence, and diplomatic services—in opposition to the aspirations of their own people. In return, these regimes provide services to the circle of Evil to subvert, undermine, and weaken the neighboring Islamic and Arab countries of Iran, Afghanistan, Iraq, Syria, Libya, Algeria, Sudan, and Mauritania.

2. The Curse of the Priesthood: There is no priesthood in Islam; the believer has a highly personal and exclusive relationship with Allah. Such relationship does not permit the intervention of another human being. When the blessed Muhammad was taken up by Allah, every believer inherited the Koran, Allah's covenant, and His *din*. Every believer became the successor, inheritor, and the custodian of the prophet's legacy until the end of time. The priests and clerics of Islam assumed the legacy of the pagan priesthood and began to speak on behalf of Allah. Through distortion and misrepresentation of the word of Allah and the pronouncements of His *nabi*, over the last fourteen hundred years, the priests and imams of Islam have created divisions and schisms in Islam to generate hundreds of self-righteous sects and subsects among the Muslims. Each sect is the enemy of the other; every group has the dagger in the back of the other. This gradually smoldering *fitnah* of the priesthood is slowly consuming the body of the *ummah*.

Islam is a relationship between Allah and His believers. The *din* of Allah is an all-encompassing and highly personal type of relationship in which Allah's *nur* or light resides in the believer's heart. The believer is conscious of Allah's closeness and mercy. The believer obeys trusts and loves Allah, and Allah in return loves those who love Him and perform beautiful deeds.

Allah has granted knowledge and the wisdom of *furqan* and *taqwa* to the believers who have opened their hearts and minds to Him. Man has been granted the freedom of choice in doing what is wholesome and beautiful or what is corrupt or ugly. This knowledge reminds the human of the scales of Allah's justice; the two hands of Allah, His mercy and His wrath, are reflected in the human domain, where people have been appointed Allah's vicegerents. Deeds of goodness and wholesomeness are associated with Allah's mercy, paradise, and what is beautiful. Evil and corruption is rewarded with Allah's wrath, hell, and what is ugly.

Everything in the universe is connected to Allah through its creation, birth, sustenance, existence, demise, and death. Every particle and atom spins at the command of Allah's majesty; it has done so for billions of years and will continue to do so at Allah's command. They continue to spin in the cells of the living when they are alive and when the cells are devoid of life at Allah's command. Nothing ever happens without Allah's will and knowledge. No human, howsoever proud or strong, is independent of Him. The newborn is thus physically connected to Allah through His mercy. The particles and atoms in his cells spin at Allah's mercy in life and in death. Through Allah's mercy, his cells grow and multiply with sustenance from Allah.

Every man and woman in this journey is born alone and innocent. The individual leads his short life in this world, and when he dies, he leaves this world alone. In death, his cells disintegrate, yet the particles and atoms continue to spin at Allah's command forever. His life was a miracle and a mirage. Now the human was here, and in an instant, he was gone and all alone. The only reality is Allah. Every substance and relationship the human accumulated is left behind—parents, friends, wealth, children, priests, kings, human laws, honors, comforts, and so on. They all accompanied the human to the edge of his life and then parted to wait for their own demise one day.

In this journey, the human is presented with Allah's covenant as his guide, *taqwa* of Allah as his shield against evil, and *furqan*, the criterion to distinguish between the right and evil, as Allah's compass to the straight path of righteousness. If the human accepts these, he becomes a believer and among the righteous. The way to righteousness is in Allah's guidance and in His covenant in the Koran. Righteousness lies in the inspiration from the Koran through its recitation at leisure, at dawn, during the day, and under the glow of the lamp at night. Every little bit of devotion makes the *nur* of Allah glow in the heart till the believer is connected to Him and begins to follow His path. In this path, the believer does what is righteous and what is beautiful. Beautiful actions please Allah.

This communion between the believer and Allah is exclusive. Submission establishes the link between the believer and Allah. The believer asks, and Allah gives. The believer loves Allah, and Allah loves him in return. The believer asks for the straight path, and Allah shows him the way. The believer praises Allah, and Allah showers His mercy and grace on him. The believer remembers Allah, and Allah responds to those who praise Him, thank Him, and ask Him.

The believer on his chosen journey on the path of Allah is well equipped. He has Allah's protection, guidance, and direction. Does the believer need dogmas and laws based on human systems? Aren't Allah's word and the covenant sufficient as guidance? Allah is the absolute truth (*haqq*). All worldly, human, and priestly systems are not based on *haqq*. Allah is the only *Haqq*. What is not *haqq* is *batil*, the untruth. Those who let go of Allah's hand and clutch at the human priestly dogma and creed have fallen astray in Satan's footsteps

The most important theological point made by the Koran is that there is one God, Allah, universal and beyond comparison, who creates and sustains both the material world and the world of human experience. Allah is *Haqq*, the absolute truth. All other forms of so-called truth are either false in their initial premises or contingently true only in limited situations. The recognition of this fact is of paramount importance to all believers. That Allah is *Haqq* is undeniable. *Haqq* does not fall into the domain of human fancy nor human ideas, but it stands for beliefs that manifest in concrete form. These beliefs must be in harmony with changing needs of time and with Allah's laws of the universe. No belief relating to this world can be called *haqq* unless its truth is established by positive demonstration of Allah's reality. This truth is permanent and unchanging.

There is no priesthood in Islam. *Haqq* does not need priests. Yet there are people among the believers who talk like priests, dress like priests, and preach like priests. They are indeed the priests. They preach dogma and creed to the believers in the name of Allah and His blessed *nabi*. Yet what they preach distances the believers from Allah, the Koran, and the blessed prophet. The priests spread hatred among the believers and discord in the *ummah*. They concern themselves with obscure Hadith and man-made Sharia and *fiqh* that do not constitute the *din* of Allah. Their teachings and fatwas often contradict the Koran and the spirit of the blessed *nabi's* teaching.

If miraculously one day all the mullahs, self-proclaimed ulema, ayatollahs, imams, and Wahhabi preachers were to disappear from the face of this earth, from that day on, there will be no Shia, no Sunni, nor any other sect in the world. Every Muslim will be a believer of Allah. The mullahs, self-proclaimed ulema, ayatollahs, imams, and Wahhabi preachers sustain one another through their own inbred dogma and creed. In turn, the mullahs and priests sustain their sects through their man-made belief systems. It is a cycle in which the priests continue to perpetuate their creeds generation after generation with "quote and reference" to their earlier imams and priests, repeating distortions, misquotations, and misrepresentations. The believers cannot hear the gentle message of Allah over all the noise and commotion created by the mullahs and religious scholars in the world of Islam. In the same token, if there were no rabbis, Christian priests, ministers, clerics, preachers, pastors, bishops, popes, pundits, and mullahs, there will be no Judaism, Christianity, Hinduism, nor sectarian Islam. All those who believe in one God will then be servants of the same Allah, the religion of Abraham, Moses, Jesus, and Muhammad.

Yet priests have been with us since the times when man attained civilization. The priesthood of the Sumerian civilization left a powerful legacy on the generations to follow. Within a short time, the priestly culture spread to all human civilizations, to the Indus valley, Babylon, Egypt, Greece and Rome. Priesthood independently sprung up in the Americas.

Humans crave a belief in the supernatural. They seek comfort and security in the thought of supernatural protection from gods. Priesthood is ever present and ready to exploit this need. Sumerians and all other civilizations were served by many gods—gods of war, fertility goddesses, sun god, moon god, gods of rain, gods of death, and so on. Priests were at hand to provide the protection at a cost, an offering to gods. The cult of gods did not operate in isolation. Though communities had their own particular guardian gods, they did share other gods with other towns and villages. Devotees traveled to far, distant places to pay homage to their gods. There was considerable exchange and sharing of patronage, protection, and blessing of gods among varying communities. Priesthood became the original corporations and propaganda machine for their gods.

Such publicity also took advantage of the sense of weaknesses and vulnerabilities of the people. The greater the insecurity among the population, the more the devotees of particular gods were, the greater the wealth and influence of the priests. There were festivals of all sorts involving seasons, planting of seed, harvest, fertility, human sacrifice, fire, light, and many others. The priests began to control commerce, levy tithe, lend money on interest, organize professional armies, and provide temple prostitutes, alcohol, and protection against calamities. What mattered in the end was the power and wealth. Priesthood became a network of guilds connected through secret societies that began to control the affairs of the world for all times to come.

3. The Curse of the Mercenary Armies of Islam: The blessed nabi said, "All believers shall rise as one man against anyone who seeks to commit injustice, aggression, crime, or spread mutual enmity amongst the Muslims. All believers are bonded one to another to the exclusion of other men. The believers shall leave none of their members in **destitution without giving him in kindness that he needs by the way of his liberty**" (The Covenant of Muhammad). However, this fight for unity, equality, and justice did not occur in the lands of Islam; the army of God and of Islam did not arise to fight in the cause of Allah to defend against *fitnah*, tyranny, and oppression and to seek retribution against injustice. The absolute loyalty of the army of Islam is to God, the Koran, and the *ummah*. The army of Islam defends the believers, their faith, their land, their wealth, and their honor and fights only against *fitnah* for truth and justice. In case of injury to the believers, their faith, their land, their wealth, and their honor, the

216

believers are obliged to exact retribution. No believer shall side with an unbeliever against a believer. Whosoever is convicted of killing a believer without a righteous cause shall be liable to the relatives of the killed. The killers shall be subject to retaliation by each believer until the relatives of the victim are satisfied with the retribution.

Had the Muslim communities stood united as one to avenge the blood of every fallen Muslim and rejected a separate peace with the pagans without all the Muslims participating in it, there would have been no *fitnah* and massacres in Algeria, Palestine, India, Afghanistan, Iraq, Bosnia, Chechnya, Kosovo, and Darfur. This unity demands revenge, retribution, and reprisal for every act of murder and injury in Dayr Yasin, Sabra, Shatila, Srebrenica, Janin, Sarajevo, Fallujah, Kosovo, Chechnya, Gujarat, Kashmir, Iraq, Guantanamo Bay, and Abu Ghraib. Had the Muslims stood up for one another and fought those who perpetrated the *fitnah*, they would not have been groveling in the dustheap of humanity today.

Contrary to the stipulations of the covenant of Allah, the present six-million-man mercenary armies of Muslim states serve to bolster illegal regimes of *Munafiqeen, the* traitors to the cause of Islam. Instead of relieving the believers of *fitnah* and oppression, they cause them. They are the source of dichotomy and division in Islam; they are the defenders of the foreign hegemony over Islam. The armies of the sultans of the previous centuries and the rulers of modern times are the perpetrators of *fitnah* and the enemies of Islam. They are the defenders of the borders created by the Western colonial powers that divide Islam today. They are the *fitnah*.

4. The Curse of the Elite: In the great drivel of court and palace life developed a class of parasites, the so-called upper classes and the aristocracy. They are admitted and initiated to this circle through invitation and personal connections. And this circle has perpetuated itself through a class system of inbreeding, special education, mannerism, corruption, *Fahasha*, and monopoly in governing posts. The mediocrity of this class has turned Muslim states into the laughing stock of the whole world. This class of greed, *Fahasha*, and utter depravity is the curse and the ball and chain around the neck of each believer. While this curse lasts, the Muslim society continues to decay in ignorance, illiteracy, and poverty because this class of obscenity in the Arabian Peninsula and in every Muslim state will not allow equality, justice, and progress in the life of the average citizen.

5. The Curse of Usury: When the corrupt sultans, their hierarchical priesthood, the mercenary armies, and the elite had sucked the remaining lifeblood out of the subject populace, they were unable to maintain their life of debauchery and decadence. Desperate for more treasure, the Ottomans, Safavids, and Moguls embarked on foreign adventures of loot and plunder. Sometimes they brought back trains of treasure and bullion. At other times, their troops limped back in humiliation and defeat. As it has been etched in the stone of history, reparation and debt had to be paid. Thus came into the Muslim lands the fifth curse—the curse of the European and Jewish moneylenders and usury.

The *ummah* is saddled with the curse and the *fitnah* of the priesthood, the mercenary armies of Muslim states, their corrupt rulers, and the parasitic elite of the state. While these sources of *fitnah* continue to rule over Islam, the Muslim society will continue to decay in ignorance, illiteracy, and poverty because this curse will not permit equality, justice, and progress in the Muslim society. Greed for wealth and luxury introduced the all-encompassing evil of false wealth and usury.

The covenant of Allah bestowed unity, equality, justice, and protection to all believers. Yet during a large part of the Islamic history, ruling classes of conquerors created a hierarchical elite and a privileged class of bureaucrats who were parasites on the subject population of the *ummah* for hundreds of years. The *ummah* was kept from managing its own affairs, kept in a position of subservience, and maintained in that position to be milked of their resources in the interest of the elite and privileged.

The Umayyads, Abbasids, Safavids, and the Turko-Mongol-Seljuk tribal formations usurped the Islamic state and used the name of Islam to rule over the believing and devout Muslims through the intermediary representation of the priests, imams, and *ulema*, who in effect were the paid functionaries of the un-Koranic ruling elite. While the rulers practiced their Arab, Turko-Mongol-Seljuk pre-Islamic tribal traditions, the *ulema*, in the same vein, regressed into the courtly priesthood of the earlier pagan religions, exercising their power over the subjects of the empire.

The Shah Mosque in Isfahan

Chapter Four

The Nineteenth Century: The Betrayal of the Covenant

The groundwork of what occurred in the Islamic heartland in the twentieth century had already been laid out in the early and midnineteenth century. In Europe, the wars of the French Revolution produced military power based on an improvement of weapon organization and fighting techniques. A sign of weakening Ottoman power was the brief French occupation of Egypt in 1798. Of more lasting importance was the Russian advance into the Ottoman domains in Europe and in the Caucasus, where Georgia and Azerbaijan were absorbed. The British increased their influence in the Persian Gulf and signed treaties with rulers of small ports, some of which today constitute the United Arab Emirates. In India, the British expanded into Baluchistan and Sind and increased pressure on the Kajar of Iran.

After 1830, the introduction of the steamship and the telegraph brought Middle Eastern cities closer to Europe and America. After the wars of the French Revolution, the European merchant ships began to bring manufactured goods of a new kind to eastern Mediterranean ports. For the goods brought from northern Europe, cotton textiles and iron products, Middle Eastern countries were able to pay only by producing raw materials for factories in Europe, in particular high-grade cotton, which Egypt began to produce in large quantities after 1830.

The indigenous governments responded to the European threats and pressures with their own reform. The Ottoman government began to create a new army on the European model; it brought in new legal statutes based on those in Western Europe, incorporating in them the idea of citizenship, equality between citizens of different religions, and existence of an Ottoman nation. Such changes strengthened the power of the central government, though within considerable limitations. France occupied the westernmost Ottoman province of Algeria from 1830 to 1847. Serbia fought to become autonomous, and Greece became an independent kingdom after a revolt in 1833 by the intervention of European powers.

In the regions lying within the empire, some provincial rulers were able to secure autonomous power. In modern times, the quest for personal power and treason against the unity of the *ummah* started in Tunisia and Egypt. In Tunis, a local ruling dynasty that had ruled under the Ottoman sovereignty since the eighteenth century assumed control with the collaboration of European merchants. In Egypt, an Albanian soldier of fortune, Muhammad Ali, was able to make himself governor with the help of new military elite from Anatolia and the Balkans. He created a new army and a more effective administration. He created conditions under which the European merchants could work more freely in Egypt. Muhammad Ali had great ambitions for himself and tried to detach Egypt from the Ottoman Empire. He and his descendants through their folly, greed, and extravagance introduced European economic and military domination into the Middle East, which began the Western dominance of the Muslim lands. When the Egyptian forces invaded Syria and came within the sight of Istanbul, the great powers—Britain, France, Russia, Austria, and Prussia—allied themselves to the Ottoman government to drive the Egyptian forces out of Syria. A British fleet bombarded Beirut in September 1840; an Anglo-Turkish force landed, taking Acre in November; and the British fleet anchored off Alexandria in the same month. The Egyptian Army was forced to retreat to Egypt, and Muhammad Ali was forced to accede to the British demands.

According to the treaty of 1841, Muhammad Ali was stripped of all conquered territory except for Sudan and was granted hereditary governorship of Egypt. In 1838, Muhammad Ali was compelled to accept the Anglo-Ottoman convention, which established free trade in Egypt, which meant that Muhammad Ali was forced to abandon his monopolies and establish new tariffs that were favorable to European imports. Thus, Egypt was unable to control the flood of cheap manufactured imports that decimated local industries and impoverished the local population as it had done to the Indians.

Under the pretext of the danger to the British communications posed by the Egyptian adventure into Arabia, the British government in India established the first British colony in the Middle East in Aden, and the British then occupied Cyprus, an Ottoman domain. In the Ottoman Empire, merchants who engaged in trade with Europe grew richer and more powerful. In Ottoman cities and in Egypt, they were European or local Christians and Jews; in Iran, they were Muslims. On the other hand, merchants who engaged in the older type of trades by land routes lost some of their position as did craftsmen whose products were replaced by the new kinds of imports from Europe.

In the countryside, the domination of landowners grew as the government extended its control. In Egypt, Muhammad Ali expropriated most of the land to himself and became the chief landowner. In the Ottoman provinces, a land law of 1858 led to the formation of large estates by merchants, urban notables, and tribal chieftains.

With the new methods of communication, railways, telegraphs, and steamships, it was possible for the Ottoman government to establish direct administration at the expense of local chieftains. With the opening of the Suez Canal in 1869 and the building of the Hejaz Railway at the beginning of the twentieth century, the Ottoman administration extended its control to Hejaz, Yemen, and central

Arabia. The Egyptian power extended southward to Upper Egypt and Sudan. A religious reformer, the Mahdi, kicked out the Egyptians from Sudan in the 1880s and created an Islamic government. Changes were slower and less complete in Iran until the last quarter of the nineteenth century; communications were still limited except for the opening the Karun River valley to international trade.

The establishment of modern communications and railways, the creation of modern armies, and the accompanying military adventures did not come cheaply. To finance these enterprises, the Ottoman and Egyptian governments borrowed heavily from European banks, controlled by the British and the French house of Rothschild. The revenue system of the Islamic countries was not compatible with the usurious Western and Jewish Illuminati banking. A large number of European trading families had accumulated huge amounts of money and gold bullion in close association with the East India Company through slave trade in South Africa, Caribbean Islands, and the American continent. They had made more money in illicit opium trade with China and through the plunder of Indian treasures, industry, and commerce.

With their massive wealth and influence, families such as the Rothschilds and Baring brothers financed wars and trading interests of the royal families and the aristocracy of Germany, France, Austria, Britain, and Russia. The Rothschilds, a secretive Jewish family, conspired to profit by secretly financing the opposing factions of European wars; they financed the Napoleonic army as well as the opposing English armada. They also helped break the blockade of the Southern Confederate states and at the same time financed arms shipment to the army of the North in the American Civil War, which the slave-owning families fought to perpetuate trade in human flesh.

These bankers gathered intelligence about the Middle Eastern regimes for both the British and the French and were the vanguard of the British and French colonial expansion and economic control of Egypt and the Ottoman Empire. In Egypt and the Middle East, the British imperialism and the Jewish capital export worked hand in hand. As with India, the European traders and the moneylenders heralded the arrival of the English and the French occupation forces to control both the trade and natural resources of these countries.

After the Crimean War, the Ottoman sultan and the khedive in Egypt began to accumulate huge debts to the international Jewish bankers. Between 1855 and 1875, the Ottoman debt increased from 9 million Turkish liras to around 251 million. In relation to the financial resources of the Ottoman government, this was a colossal sum; as a percentage of expenditure, interest payments and amortization rose from 15 percent in 1860 to a peak of 50 percent in 1875. Out of the loan of 251 million liras from the international bankers, after commissions and discounts, the Ottoman treasury in Istanbul received a mere 135 million liras. Nor was the borrowed money put to good use. Millions were squandered by the sultan Abdulmecid on his new Dolmabahçe Palace, built to entertain European royals and diplomats, although the official business continued to be conducted from the Topkapi Serai.

Abdulhamid II ascended the throne of the Ottoman Empire in 1876. He was beset with difficulties both at home and abroad from the beginning. In 1877, a disastrous war with Russia followed. The Treaty of San Stefano, after the war, had harsh terms to which Abdulhamid was forced to consent. To maintain his empire in spite of difficulties surrounding him, he employed Germans for organization of his finances and his army. He gradually took all power in his own hands, reducing his ministers to the position of secretaries. Financial embarrassments forced him to consent to a foreign control over his debts, and in 1881, many of the revenues of the empire were handed over to the public debt administration for the benefit of the foreign bondholders. The Ottoman sultans and the khedives of Egypt were unable to distinguish between their personal spending and the revenues of the state. This led to a fiscal disaster and economic enslavement of their peoples, the subsequent disintegration of their empire, and the domination of the international bankers and the English and French colonialism.

During the eighteenth and nineteenth centuries, there was a gradual stagnation of the Ottoman Empire. This decline was caused by many independent factors. The most important was the ascendancy of the *devsirme* class and the incompetence, dishonesty, and lack of integrity of the sultans and the elite. The disappearance of the Turko-Islamic aristocracy led to the debasement of the basic Islamic precept of Allah's covenant of governance by the sultans.

Sultan Abdulhamid was pressured by the British and French governments, at the behest of the London and Paris Rothschilds, to depose the khedive Isma'il Pasha of Egypt. Later, the sultan's lack of astuteness toward 'Urabi Pasha, the would-be savior of Egypt, resulted in the consolidation of English hold over Egypt.

In Egypt, the khedive Isma'il came to power in 1863. In his quest to transform Egypt into a modern Western state, he squandered large sums on palaces, operas, and mistresses. He maintained a harem of nine wives, their children, and extended families in twenty-two palaces. He did much, however, in the line laid down by his predecessors to develop Egyptian industries and culture on European model. During Isma'il's reign, irrigation canals measuring 13,440 kilometers long were dug, four hundred bridges were built, four hundred and eighty kilometers of rail were laid, and eight thousand kilometers of telegraph lines were laid. Towns and cities were modernized by expansion of public services such as water distribution, transport, street lighting, and gas supplies.

Although Isma'il greatly expanded Egypt's revenues and exports mainly of cotton, his infrastructure development entailed far more expenditure than Egypt's income could provide. In the end, through his less than astute fiscal management, he impoverished the country and the peasantry; his despoliation began when Jewish Illuminati moneylenders, and the contractors robbed the khedive. The European contractors engaged in his great works—buildings and irrigation—overcharged him from 80 to 400 percent. For floating loans, he had to pay as much as 25 percent in interest. Of the sixty-eight million pounds that was raised as a national debt, Egypt received only forty-four million, so the nominal interest of 7 percent, in fact, amounted to 12 to 13 percent. Of a loan of thirty-two million pounds in 1873, only twenty-two million ever reached the Egyptian treasury. Behind the bondholders stood the Jewish house of Rothschild of England and France, which gobbled up the remaining funds as commission and discounts. Obviously, the Egyptian people were unable to pay this usurious rate of interest.

Baron Nathaniel Mayer Rothschild of the British house of Rothschild, responsible for financing the Egyptian debt, provided secret intelligence to Benjamin Disraeli, the British prime minister and a fellow Jew, so that Khedive Isma'il could not service his foreign debt and might be induced to sell his stake of 176,602 shares of the Suez Canal Company for four million pounds. The English government was extremely anxious to buy the canal before the French entered their bid. However, the English did not have four million pounds as England's total annual revenue at that time was only ten million pounds. The Rothschild family, the securer of the Egyptian debt, was able to transfer the four-million-pound Egyptian debt at a day's notice to the English government in exchange for the certificate of shares.

Rothschild made a flat £150,000 on this deal and won the irrevocable esteem of the English government and the people.

On the brink of bankruptcy, the khedive's Jewish Illuminati bankers under the influence of the Rothschild family banks refused to extend his credit. Faced with crippling debts and a devastated economy, Khedive Isma'il resorted to an action that brought European, especially British and French, subjugation of Egypt and the Middle East, and it is the basis of the Western economic imperialism that its people have not been able to shake off until today. Isma'il asked for British help in fiscal reform. British responded by sending Stephen Cave, a member of Parliament, to investigate the Egyptian finances. Cave judged Egypt solvent based on its resources and said that all the country needed to get back on its feet was time and proper servicing of its debts. Cave recommended the establishment of a control commission over Egypt's finances to approve future finances.

The European creditors would not allow Egypt time. In 1875, Isma'il suspended payment of interest on the loans. His creditors in Britain and France negotiated the consolidation of debt with Egypt; appointed two European controllers, one British and one French; and established a special department to ensure the service of the debt. By 1877, 60 percent of all Egyptian revenue went to service the national debt. The usurious interest rate remained in effect, and the British and the French kept their hold on Egypt. The khedive was asked by the powers to limit his authority as a first step to solve the country's money problems. He appointed as prime minister Nubar Pasha, an Armenian Christian, to form a cabinet with two Europeans with ministerial responsibility. The khedive was forced to delegate governmental responsibility to his cabinet responsible for running the country independent of the khedive.

The history of Dual Control shows with painful clarity that the agents appointed by Britain and France to manage Egyptian finances acted with no more regard for the interests of the Egyptian people than the thugs of a private moneylender would have shown. In 1877, a year of famine, to pay the interest to the clients of the Rothschilds, taxes were actually collected in advance from the ruined peasants. Instead of reducing the usurious rate of the interest and debt, the Dual Control cut down the Egyptian expenditure. The schools were starved of funds, and two thousand Egyptian Army officers were dismissed from service with eighteen months of arrears of salary unpaid. Many officers of the Egyptian Army and their families were reduced to a state of utter destitution. The efficient military organized by Muhammad Ali was demoralized and reduced to a state that it could no longer stave off any invasion of Egypt.

From such acts of folly and injustice sprung the Egyptian nationalist movement. In 1879, under foreign pressure, Isma'il ordered the Assembly of Delegates dissolved. This assembly had been created by Isma'il in 1866, composed mainly of notables and army officers, and had no legislative authority. Its members refused to relinquish their authority at the orders of the khedive under pressure from foreign powers. On March 29, 1879, they presented a manifesto to the khedive protesting the council of ministers' attempt to usurp their power and authority. They also stated their determination to reject the European minister's demand that Egypt declare itself bankrupt. The leader of the delegation, Muhammad Shariff Pasha, belonged to a secret society, the National Society, that proposed constitutional and financial reform to increase the power of the assembly and resolve Egypt's financial problems without foreign advisers and control. Isma'il then summoned the European consuls and informed them of the discontent of the delegates, disaffection in the army, and the general public uneasiness. Therefore, he rejected the proposal to declare Egypt bankrupt and stated his intent to meet all obligations to Egypt's creditors. He also invited Shariff Pasha to form a government. Shariff Pasha and his all-Egyptian cabinet dismissed the European ministers.

Although these actions made Isma'il popular at home, the European powers—particularly Britain and France—decided that Isma'il had to go. Isma'il refused to abdicate; the European powers put pressure on the Ottoman sultan to dismiss the khedive in favor of his son Tawfiq. Isma'il left Egypt for exile in Naples and subsequently in Istanbul, where he died in 1895.

Tawfiq proved to be weak and pliant in the hands of the European powers. An international commission was appointed with British, French, Austrian, and Italian members. In July 1880, the law of liquidation limited Egypt to 50 percent of its total revenues, and the rest went to the service of debt.

The direct interference of the Europeans in Egypt's affairs and the deposition of Khedive Isma'il forged a nationalistic movement composed of Egyptian landowners, merchants, army officers, and intelligentsia, including the ulema and Muslim reformers. A secret society of Egyptian Army officers also came into existence in 1876. The army society included Col. Ahmed 'Urabi, who would become the leader of the nationalist movement. In 1881, a link was formed between the Arabists and the National Society, and this group took the name *Al-Hizb al-Watani al Ahli*, the National Popular Party. Beginning in 1881, the army officers demonstrated their strength to intimidate the khedive. They began with a mutiny and were able to force a more sympathetic minister of war, and by January 1882, 'Urabi joined the government as undersecretary for war.

These developments alarmed the European powers, especially Britain and France. Britain sent a joint note to Egypt supporting the khedive. The joint note produced an upsurge in anti-European feeling. This produced a shift in the leadership of the nationalist movement from the moderates to the military, with 'Urabi becoming the minister of war. The goal of 'Urabi and his followers became not only the removal of all European influence but also the overthrow of the European puppet, the khedive. The British and the French agreed on a joint show of naval strength and demanded the resignation of the government and the exile of 'Urabi. As a result, violent anti-European riots broke out in Alexandria with considerable loss of life on both sides.

During the summer, the European powers tried to persuade the Ottoman sultan unsuccessfully to send troops to Egypt. Eventually, Britain acted alone. The French withdrew their naval squadron from Alexandria, and in July 1882, the British fleet began bombarding Alexandria.

After the burning of Alexandria, the British marines occupied Alexandria. The British installed the khedive in the Ras-el-Tin Palace. The khedive obligingly declared 'Urabi a rebel and deprived him of his political rights. 'Urabi, in return, obtained a fatwa signed by three Al-Azhar sheikhs deposing Tawfiq as a traitor who brought the foreign occupation of his country and betrayed his religion.

The British, with an army of twenty thousand, invaded and occupied the Suez Canal Zone. A decisive battle was fought at Tell al Kabir on September 13, 1882. The 'Urabi forces were routed and the capital captured by the British. The nominal authority of the traitor khedive was restored. The British occupation that was to last for seventy-two years had begun.

'Urabi was captured; he and his associates were tried by an Egyptian court and sentenced to death. The sentence was later commuted to banishment in Ceylon. With the occupation of 1882, Egypt became part of the British Empire but never officially a colony.

Between 1883 and the outbreak of World War I, Egypt was ruled by three British agents or consuls general; the first one, Sir Evelyn Baring (later called Lord Cromer, 1883–1907), was an autocrat whose control over Egypt was more absolute than that of any pharaoh or khedive. He and his family owned the Barings Bank and was a creditor of Isma'il Pasha, whose debt led Egypt to its loss of sovereignty. The Barings had made their fortune through the plunder of Indian commerce, the African slave trade, the Caribbean slave sugar plantations, and the illicit opium trade with the Chinese peasants. Cromer believed that his first task was the collection of debt on behalf of the European bankers and then the financial solvency of Egypt. He serviced the debt and balanced the budget, and what remained after debt payments was spent on agriculture, irrigation, and railroads. He neglected education and industry. He brought British officials to staff the bureaucracy.

Among major players in Egypt's destiny was a close-knit network of European bankers. The most notable among them was Baron Maurice de Hirsch. He controlled the powerful Anglo-Austrian Bank. Through business mergers and acquisitions, Hirsch was connected to most of the private Illuminati Jewish banks of Europe and through them was related to most of their owners. One of them, Sir Ernest Cassel, was a man who would have a profound impact on Egypt's economy. In June 1898, the khedive Abbas Hilmi, on the advice of his English masters, sold the Daira Sania Estates—Egypt's largest state-run agro-industrial company—to an international consortium led by Cassel for the sum of £6,431,500, representing the Daira's outstanding liabilities to the foreign bankers. This singular transfer of Egyptian-owned enterprise to foreign ownership changed the social and economic face of Egypt for the next sixty years, if not longer. At the same time, Khedive Abbas Hilmi—on Cromer's instigation— issued a decree creating the National Bank of Egypt. The new bank was owned by the Daira's new owners, served as Egypt's regulatory bank, and issued bane until 1960.

Cassel invested heavily in Upper Egypt's desolate regions to build Aswan and Asyut barrages. The building of the barrages enabled Cassel's companies to reclaim thousands of acres to produce cotton and sugar. This also helped the Daira's shares to soar. The National Bank of Egypt was capitalized at one million pounds; the bank's main purpose was to provide means of channeling finance for development projects and to attract British capital and enterprise. What made this bank unique was its charter giving it exclusive right to issue notes.

With the blessing of the Whitehall in London and Lord Cromer in Cairo, Sir Ernest Cassel put up 50 percent of the National Bank of Egypt's founding capital ensuring Britain's lion's share of all major investments in Egypt. To legitimize the bank's position as an Egyptian bank, two "Egyptian" partners were recruited. Ralph Isaac Suares, a Jew, and Constantine Salvagos, a Greek, were offered the remaining shares. A large majority of these *mutamessereen* or pseudo-Egyptians came to Egypt during Muhammad Ali's boom years. With the acquisition of the charter bank, the Cassels, Suareses, and Salvagoses came to possess most of the railways, waterworks, power, and other public utility companies and the biggest landholdings in Egypt. Among the personalities on the board of the National Bank of Egypt, apart from Cassel, was Sir Vincent Caillard; Sir Sidney Cornwallis Peel, the third son of Viscount Peel, the British prime minister; and Carl Meyer, a Rothschild associate. Meyer was also vice president of De Beers Consolidated and a director of the Hongkong and Shanghai Bank.

The complete takeover of the Egyptian economy by the collusion between the Jewish bankers and the English aristocracy is further underlined by the fact that such relationship was and has been the kingpin for control of the wealth of Middle East and Africa during the nineteenth and twentieth centuries and continues until today. It is no accident that the kin of Rothschild, Sir Ernst Cassel's daughter Edwina, married Lord Mountbatten, a cousin of Queen Elizabeth of England and the uncle of the duke of Edinburgh, the queen's husband. To complete the circle of greed and acquisition, the Anglo-Jewish conspirators found willing partners among the Arab Muslim elite, subjecting the Islamic heartlands to 150 years of servitude that is still in progress.

It is of interest to note that, forty years later, the Mountbattens left a lasting legacy in the Islamic world. On the division of India into the Hindu and Muslim parts, Lord Mountbatten—the British viceroy of India—awarded two Muslim-majority districts of the Punjab, Gurdaspur and Firozpur, to Hindu India that gave India a gateway into the Muslim Kashmir. This act enabled Hindu India to annex the Muslim state of Kashmir, igniting a state of ongoing hostilities between India and Pakistan. Edwina Mountbatten had an illicit sexual liaison with the Indian prime minister Jawaharlal Nehru; the intimacy between the Mountbattens and Pundit Nehru decided the fate and enslavement of five million Kashmiris.

The British and other Europeans had their appetites whetted by the plunder of the wealth and the resources of India and Egypt. The capital for the commercial exploitation by the British, French, Dutch, and Danes in India and the Indian Ocean came from the bankers in Amsterdam, London, Paris, Copenhagen, and Lisbon. The Europeans' capital had a stake in the maintenance of European power in the Indian subcontinent and South Asia; for two centuries, a systematic transfer of wealth from India to Europe took place. Although Britain was the primary beneficiary, its allies in Europe, USA, Canada, Australia, and South Africa benefited no less. British banks used their Indian capital to establish industry in the USA,

Germany, and northern Europe. The Industrial Revolution and the modern capitalist world arose from the exploitation and colonization of India and the Middle East. It was the forced pauperization of India, Egypt, and the Ottoman Empire that allowed nations such as Britain and the USA to modernize.

The British and the European colonists learned a valuable lesson in India. While united India had largely held off the Europeans and divided India had temporarily held off divided Europe, divided India was no match for united Europe. The colonists then applied the same principle to the Muslim Middle East. "Divide and conquer" became the maxim of united Europe.

The Muslim rulers, however, never understood the lessons and the guidance of the covenant of Allah and the importance of the unity of the *ummah*. Satan's lure of greed is just too strong.

> Verily this brotherhood of yours is a single brotherhood and I am your Lord and Cherisher: therefore serve Me and no other.
>
> And hold fast, all together by the rope which Allah stretches out for you.
>
> And be not divided amongst yourselves;
>
> And remember with gratitude Allah's favor on you:
>
> For ye were enemies and He joined your hearts in love,
>
> So that by His grace, you became brethren.

Sultan Abdulhamid succeeded to the throne of the Ottoman Empire at the age of thirty-four on August 31, 1876. After Abdulhamid's father, Sultan Abdulmecid died, his uncle Abdulaziz was proclaimed sultan and was shortly afterward deposed and murdered on May

30, 1876. Abdulaziz's son Murad was then made sultan and shortly deposed on August 31, 1876.

Among the conspirators responsible for the murder of Abdulaziz and the deposition of Murad were two members of the Shura Council (Parliament), Midhat Pasha and Avni Pasha. Both men were, as it was later exposed, in the pay of England and other European powers. During that period, Arab and Turkish reformers were trying to curb the autocratic powers of the sultans. After murdering Abdulaziz and deposing Murad, Midhat Pasha took a pledge from Abdulhamid that he would appoint him the grand vizier, support Midhat Pasha's constitution, and promulgate it. And so on December 23, 1876, in an imposing ceremony in Istanbul, the Imperial Rescript (*Hatt-i humayun*) addressed to the grand vizier Midhat Pasha, followed by the text of the constitution, was read. The constitution of 1876 was an outcome of many attempts at Westernizing the institutions of the Ottoman Empire since the beginning of the nineteenth century. Elections were held, and the inauguration of the first historic Ottoman Parliament took place on March 19, 1877.

When Abdulhamid came to power, he saw that his country was too exhausted to undergo any further warfare. He was anxious to continue with the reforms and economic development of the Ottoman Empire. Against his wishes, the parliament on Midhat Pasha's manipulations passed a resolution to go into war against Russia. Abdulhamid was too weak to make any strong protestations, having been put on the throne by the same people who had murdered Sultan Abdulaziz and deposed Murad. The war with Russia was a disaster for the Ottomans. The Russians attacked hoping to control the Thracian straits, but under Western threat, they stopped short of Istanbul. A treaty that would have eliminated Ottoman power from all the Balkan Peninsula was revised by European powers, and in 1878, the Ottomans lost all their Balkan provinces except for a strip of land running from Albania through Macedonia to Thrace.

Muslims now migrated in large numbers from the north to join a large number of Muslims already there. From this point, no province of the remaining Ottoman Empire was without a large number of Muslims. The less advanced but majority Turkish Anatolia began to play a larger part in the Ottoman destiny. Abdulhamid used the military defeat to justify suspension of the constitution, with the ill-conceived war against Russia having been instigated by Midhat Pasha and his parliament. Abdulhamid then embarked on a Pan-Islamic policy that was no doubt aided by the loss of many Christian provinces. For the first time, the Ottoman Empire became an Islamic state, with an overwhelming part of the population being Muslim, and the state could now institute Islamic policies.

The end of the Russian war, however, did not solve the empire's problems. The Ottoman Empire had gone into debt during the Crimean War. Modern wars can no longer be fought at the expense of the taxpayers. In the nineteenth century, the European bankers became rich by lending nine times their original capital to the desperate governments caught in wars at usurious interest rates. During the nineteenth century, the Western governments had learned to wage wars funded by creating paper money to create their own armament industries, instigate wars, and promote international arms trade. The money created out of nothing for the European nations created an industry that began to produce superior arms. These nations with secretive diplomatic maneuvering instigated wars. These wars, in turn, produced a demand for arms to be sold at exorbitant prices. The customers borrowed money from the same institutions that owned the armament industries at usurious interest rates. The impoverished warring nations in the Islamic world ended up losing their sovereignty to the Western governments, ceding their trade, industries, natural resources, ports, and other national interests.

Apart from the debts to fight the Crimean War, which were incurred under Sultan Abdulmecid, still more debts were incurred during the reign of Abdulaziz through extravagance. It became necessary for Abdulhamid to accept a large measure of European control of the Ottoman finances to ensure the payment of these debts.

The Ottoman Empire got involved in the Crimean War due to the maneuvering and diplomatic wrangling between Russia and France. The Ottomans controlled Palestine, Egypt, and a large part of the Middle East. Sultan Abdulmecid had given privileges to protect the Christians and their churches in Palestine to many nations. At that time, England and France had gotten more specific commitments than other nations. France's interest in Palestine was stimulated by domestic crises as both Napoleon II and Napoleon III relied on the support of militant clerical groups in France. The French demanded the key to the Church of Nativity in the old city of Jerusalem, in addition to the right to place a silver star on Christ's birthplace in Bethlehem. The French threatened military action if the Ottomans did not give way, and the Russians threatened to occupy Walachia and Moldavia if he did. The weak Abdulmecid did the best he could under the circumstances and said yes to both the feuding Christian parties. This duplicity was soon discovered, and the French sent warships to Istanbul and to the bay of Tripoli. In December 1852, having no other choice, the Ottomans gave in to the French. In February 1853, the Russians responded by mobilizing two army corps and demanded a secret alliance and Russian protection of all the Orthodox Christians under the Ottoman rule that meant protection of some twelve million Ottoman subjects.

The war for the keys of a Christian church had much deeper significance. Russia and the Ottoman Empire came to blows in the Crimean War (1853–1856). Britain and France joined forces not with Christian Russia but with Muslim Ottomans forces outwardly to stop Russian expansion into the Balkans. However, the subtler agenda was to get a foothold on the Ottoman territory. Britain and France sent troops and funds to the Ottoman sultan as "allies"; with this industrial support, the Ottoman Empire won the war. However, the Ottomans found themselves with powerful British and French troops in their territories, troops that had no intention of leaving.

The Ottoman Empire was now in debt to France and Britain, a debt that simply could not be repaid. Moreover, such debt has been shown in the twentieth century, as in case of Pakistan and Egypt, to lead to vulnerability and submission. Britain and France demanded economic and territorial concessions based on this debt; the Ottoman Empire was forced to open its borders to unrestricted entry of Western goods. Mass-produced goods flooded Ottoman markets, completely swamping the local handcrafted industries. Ottoman debt and subsequent weakness of the Ottoman state enabled Britain and France to move in and take over Ottoman territories. France moved in on North Africa, Morocco, Algeria, and Tunisia. Britain secured control of Egypt, Cyprus, Aden, and Kuwait. Both in Egypt and in Tunisia, Western economic interests befriended the rulers, followed by total control of the economy with impoverishment of the masses. Countries that had no tradition of debt and usury were then swiftly taken over by Britain and France.

The Illuminati Jewish banks lent money at usurious interest rates that the Muslim rulers were unable to pay back, and the European armies came as goons to reinforce the collection and take possession of assets. The Turkish Ottomans maintained their agrarian aristocracy and their political power intact and lost their commercial and industrial lead. The Muslim Ottomans at the end of the eighteenth century, when the great Western industrial transformation had displayed its full implications, found themselves in a particularly exposed situation. In Europe, they were being outdistanced by their own Christian subjects as well as by the Russians in coming to terms with the momentous forces of modernity.

The Ottoman government had no debt before the Crimean War. After the war, the Ottomans needed but had no capital to build its infrastructure. Lacking any resources of its own, the Ottomans turned to those who had capital—France, England, Russia, Germany, and Austria. European interests were willing to supply the networks and systems to the Ottomans based on exclusive concessions. The result was described by a prominent writer, Jacques Benoist-Mechin:

> Each loan was granted on the condition of guarantees and security. Each country had its own banks, monopolies and controllers. Banks railways, mining companies and forestry, gas and waterworks were all foreign built, run and owned. France had seen to it that the tobacco monopoly had been turned over to her in 1883 as well as the docks at Beirut and Istanbul (1890) Smyrna (1892) and Salonika (1896) In 1890 followed the rights to exploit natural resources at Herklion and Salonika as well as running the Jaffa to Jerusalem Railway; in 1891 the Damascus-Homs and Mudanya-Bursa railway rights; in 1892 rights to the Salonika-Constantinople Railway and in 1893 to Smyrna-Kasaba Railway. The English had a healthy share in the "Ottoman Bank". Through the mediation of an Armenian, Calouste Gulbenkian they obtained sole oil rights in Mosul in 1905. The Russians enjoyed various privileges, had secured the rights to all custom duties in Constantinople and Black sea ports. The Germans had secured the rights to free port docks at Haider Pasha (1899), railway shares

and municipal transport and monopoly and the docks at Alexanderetta. Through the operations of diverse combines, the foreign powers sucked the wealth out of the country. The share of the national income that did not flow directly to the Sultans coffers went to London, Paris, Viennese or Berlin banks. European capitalism was at its zenith at the time and drank the blood out of its victim.

With such perfect organization, the people were deprived of the fruit of their labor. Nothing was left for the abandoned cities, the treeless forest which had been over felled or for their fields parched by drought, for the people themselves, who had neither doctors nor teachers.

Abdulhamid, humbled by the defeat of the ill-advised and the poorly planned war against the Russians, set about modernizing the country. The Hejaz Railway was matched by the Baghdad Railway built by the Germans for commercial purposes, extending the western railway systems to Anatolia further to Baghdad and Hejaz. This brought his Muslim subjects within easy reach of Mecca for the pilgrimage. Abdulhamid set out to reform public education modeled on the European system; however, the system did not succeed except in the fields of medicine and military. Modern schools multiplied during his reign, and literature flourished. Translations of Western literature brought Western vision among the educated Turks. Abdulhamid brought modernization in all fields except in the realm of constitutional reform. Institutional changes brought the breakdown of old autonomous, locally rooted solidarities like guilds and local mosque schools, which were replaced by more anonymous, impersonal institutions such as national professional schools untouched by family and neighborhood ties.

Abdulhamid built public amenities like markets, mosques, public baths, and modern hospitals in all major cities. The road system was updated, and seaports were expanded to accommodate steamships. Woolen and cotton textile mills were built. A new sugar-manufacturing industry was established. The armament industry was expanded. The Ottoman armed forces were reorganized. Ottoman artillery was regarded as the strongest in the world, and the navy was the third most powerful in the world. Newspapers and journal publication were encouraged, and before the onset of the First World War, the Ottoman Empire had over thirteen hundred newspapers and journals.

All these improvements, after centuries of philandering and neglect of the populace and public institutions, cost the Ottoman Empire dearly. Wealth had been wasted internally by the wasteful and outdated privileged feudal system of the Muslim empires. Abdulhamid tried to extricate his empire from the immense political and economic problems facing him. He was faced from the beginning of his career with both internal and external enemies, conspiring and collaborating, and he did not know who to trust. The result was concentration of power in his own hands with the crippling of the consultative and constitutional process.

The debt accumulated by the wars forced on his predecessors by fomenting revolts by the Christian subjects of the Balkans and by the maneuverings of the Western powers to create circumstances toward the disintegration of the Ottoman Empire had left the country bankrupt and destitute. In 1870, the management of the state finances was handled by foreigners and their merchant banks. The bank officials and foreign dignitaries in their elegant palaces on the Bosporus were mightier than the sultan and his government. The people, the millions of subjects of the empire, had no say in the governance of their daily life; their only raison d'être was to throw up enough earnings to be able to pay interest every six months to the holders of Ottoman certificates of indebtedness, the foreigners and their banks.

Sultan Abdulhamid was, however, able to pay back most of the Ottoman debt, but at what cost? When Abdulhamid came to power, the debt of the Ottoman Empire stood at 2.53 billion Ottoman gold liras, which was reduced to 106 million liras by the time he was deposed by the Young Turks. To redeem the indebtedness of the Ottoman Empire to the foreign bankers, Abdulhamid had to pay back an additional four billion liras in interest and commissions on top of the two and a half billion liras of the principal debt. During the following ten years, the Young Turks government again borrowed and multiplied the debt by 1,300 percent to 1.38 billion liras.

Ottoman sultans had, over a long period, used the title of caliph as the Sharia ruler. By a combination of historical circumstances with the fall of the Mogul emperor in 1857 and after the ceding of Muslim territories to Russia, Abdulhamid assumed the caliphal leadership of the whole Muslim world. The Muslims universally felt in the nineteenth century, how could the true Muslims be content to lead their lives under brazen infidel rule allowing the Sharia, the sovereign legal code of their world order, to be reduced to a mere personal code? The answer was that even if one substantial Muslim territorial power remained, this would be sufficient to form the base for the Muslims in other lands to look to that power as fulfilling the essential requirements of Muslim conscience. Abdulhamid was glad to assume as head of the Muslim state with most prestige that controlled three of the holiest Muslim shrines. The great symbolic gesture of the new caliphate was the building of a railway in the Hejaz from Damascus to Medina for the hajj pilgrims. Muslims from all over the world contributed to the caliph's project.

For a while, it appeared that the sick man of Europe would finally stand up, but the Western powers were determined to dismember the Ottoman Empire, partition it among themselves, and destroy Islamic unity. The non-Muslim subjects of the state were used by the West to create trouble and instability. The Western states constantly interfered in the domestic affairs of the empire under the pretext of protecting the Christian minorities. The West also launched a campaign of Christian missionary preaching in the Islamic world by building Christian schools and churches. They disseminated un-Islamic social and political mores among the educated Muslim population through lectures and newsprint. The West encouraged the Armenians and financed their revolution against the Ottomans. The English helped the Druze, and the French supported the Maronites in Lebanon to revolt against the Islamic state. Muslims and Christians who had lived in great harmony for centuries now stood apart and squabbled because of the instigations of the Western agents. Western bankers, teachers, missionaries, and archeologists formed the backbone of the Western spy/agent/provocateur network to foment troubles in the Ottoman Empire. Some of the army officer corps trained in Europe, and those trained by the German Army began to conspire against the autocratic rule of the sultan. The educated elite came to confuse modernization with Westernization and liberalization.

While the vultures of Europe hovered overhead, waiting for demise of the Ottoman Empire, the jackals were busy circling the sick victim, whose lifeblood had been sucked out by the leeches—the Jewish bankers. The cowardly but cunning jackals—the Turkish, Arab, Armenian, and minority Christian nationalists—squabbled among themselves but took a nibble off the sick man whenever the opportunity arose. The leeches, not to be outdone, also made a bid for a part of the carcass. In 1901, Jewish banker Mizray Qrasow and a few influential Jewish leaders visited Abdulhamid and offered to pay the debts of the Ottoman Empire, build the Ottoman navy, and provide an interest-free loan of thirty-five million liras in return for Jewish settlements around Jerusalem. Abdulhamid refused and sent them an answer through Tahsin Pasha:

> Tell those impolite Jews that the debts of the Ottoman state are not a shame, France has debt that does not affect it. Jerusalem became a part of the Islamic land when Omer bin Al Khattab took the city and I am not going to carry the historical shame of selling the holy lands to the Jews and betray the responsibility and trust of my people. May the Jews keep their money; the Ottomans will not hide in the castles built with the money of enemies of Islam.

Later in the same year, the founder of the Zionist movement, Theodor Herzl, visited Istanbul and tried to meet Abdulhamid. Abdulhamid refused to meet him. He told his ministers, "Advise Mr. Hertzil, not to take any further steps in his project. I cannot give away a handful of the soil for it is not my own, it is for all the Islamic Nation." At this point, the Zionists turned their attention to the British for dismemberment of the Ottoman state to set up a Zionist state in Palestine. The Jewish money became an important asset in the war against the Ottomans.

Abdulhamid must have been overwhelmed by the storm clouds above him and the thunder in the horizon; Abdulhamid the poet, in his writings, beseeched the Lord:

O mine Allah, You are the Most beloved one,

And no one but You are the most loved.

You are the One and none else,

Oh, mine Allah take my hand in these hard times.

Oh, my Allah be my helper in this critical hour.[32]

The Blue Mosque.

---

[32] Aisha, *My Father Abdul Hamid.*

Chapter Five

The Circle of Evil: The Traitors of Islam

The Islamic nation, the Dar es Salaam, and the *ummah* are united by their belief in the covenant of Allah. Every action of the believer for himself, his family, his community, and most importantly for his nation is carried out in accordance with the covenant of Allah. Every believer, upon profession of his faith, becomes bound by his pledge to abide by the covenant.

Catastrophes in the Islamic world began to occur in the first century of Islam when individuals and groups rebelled against rightful authority and performed treasonable acts that changed the course of Islam's history, from an elected caliph supported by rule through consultation and in consensus and cooperation to self-appointed autocrats through arbitrary coercion, force, and often plunder. The murder of three of the first four caliphs—Umar, Uthman, and Ali—set precedence for bloody succession to the political leadership of Islam. Mu'awiyah, son of Abu Sufyan, an officer of the caliphate and governor of Damascus, revolted against the caliph Ali ibn Abi Talib and set up a dynastic caliphate. Abu Sufyan was the lifelong enemy of the blessed *nabi* and the foe of the nascent Islam.

From then onward, for thirteen hundred years, Muslims had little say in the running of their lives. The caliphs used the name of Islam to tyrannize and subjugate their subjects, plunder their wealth, and perpetuate their personal power. From the time of Umar, who shared his camel with his companion as he traveled to Jerusalem to accept the keys of Jerusalem as the conqueror, to the time of the demise of the caliphate in April 1909, when the caliph Abdulhamid was forced to abdicate, a period of some thirteen hundred years, there were periods of glory when faith (*iman*) flourished, when prosperity and peace reigned with the flowering of arts and sciences; at other times, there was clear loss of faith and open disregard of the covenant of Allah. When disaster struck, there were massacres, famine, epidemics, and wars. Finally, in the second decade of the twentieth century, treason, treachery, and greed brought an ignominious end to the very freedom of the Islamic nation and the *ummah*.

Allah reminds us of the punishment he promised to the ungrateful for their evil and inequities with the words

> Of a city abundantly supplied with sustenance from every place: yet was it ungrateful for the favors of Allah: so Allah made it taste of hunger and terror closing in on it like a garment from every side, because of the evil which its people wrought.

How many were the populations We utterly destroyed because of their iniquities

> Allah sets forth a Parable: a city enjoying security and quiet, abundantly supplied with sustenance from every place: yet was it ungrateful for the favors of Allah: so Allah made it taste of hunger and terror closing in on it like a garment from every side, because of the evil which its people wrought. (Koran 16:112)

> How many were the populations We utterly destroyed because of their iniquities, setting up in their places other peoples? (Koran 21:11)

The Six Principles of Governance in Islam

1. The sovereignty of the Muslim state belongs to Allah.

Through the covenant of Allah, the Muslim community (*ummah*) is the repository of the executive sovereignty through total submission to the will of Allah. The *ummah* has the moral responsibility that is implied in the primordial covenant referred to in the Koran as the viceregency (Koran 2:30–34). Those who uphold the requirements of the covenant are known as Allah's vicegerents (*khulafa*) on the earth. The Koran says:

> To Allah belongs all that is in the heavens and on earth. (3:109)

> Behold thy Lord said to the Angels; I will create a
> vicegerent on earth. (Al-Baqarah 2:30)

The society is made up of such God-fearing people (*muttaqeen*) who constitutes a "middle nation" or axial community (*ummah wast*) whose collective responsibility is to bear witness to the truth and act as an example for the rest of humanity, a nation of moderation that is averse to extremism:

> Thus have We made of you an Ummah of center, that ye might be
> witness over the nation sand the Rasool a witness over you; and we
> appointed the Qibla to which you were used to, only to test those who
> followed the Rasool from those who would turn on their heels. Indeed
> it was a momentous change, except to those guided by Allah. And never
> would Allah make your faith of no effect. For Allah is to all people most
> surely full of Kindness, Most Merciful. (Al-Baqarah 2:143, Koran)

2. The *ummah* is a united community of believers (*Jammaa*).

The *ummah* enjoins good and forbids evil, a community that in its advocacy of truth is a witness over itself and over humankind. This community maintains itself in a permanent state of surrender to Allah (*ummah Muslimah*) as exemplified by the blessed *nabi* Muhammad and his followers in Medina.

Since 661, in spite of fourteen hundred years of soul-searching, devoutness, and piety, the *ummah* has not been able to redeem its right to govern itself and get out of the clutches of transgressors who usurp governance and power over the *ummah*. Twenty-three verses in the Koran mention traits of transgressors that Allah does not love. They are the *Munafiqeen* (truth concealers), *kafirun* (the wrongdoers), *zalimun* (workers of corruption), *mufsidun* (the transgressors), and *ta'adda* (the immoderate, the proud, and the boastful). Humans with these traits do not obey the covenant of Allah. In their lust for power and opulence, these people conspire, lie, steal, kill, and sell the *ummah's* interests for their own benefit. The incidents of 661 were tragic and have been commemorated thousands of times in expression of sorrow. There was the savage murder of Ali ibn Abu Talib and the premature death of thousands of Muslims fighting for a cause, which each party thought was a just cause. In the end, each one lost, with the community of Islam losing the most, and each party forgot to obey the covenant of the Qur'an, to the detriment of their souls.

The Koran is emphatic on the solidarity of the community of Muslims, a community that advocates unity and shuns separation, a community whose hearts Allah has joined in love so that, by Allah's grace, they become brethren unto one another. Allah repeatedly commands believers to call for all that is good, enjoining what is right and forbidding what is wrong. *In the Koran, Allah promises a dreadful penalty (*Azabu azeem*) to those who create schism and division in the community of Muslims. The Muslim community of one and a half billion believers is a single unified* ummah *who are kindred to one another, never to be divided into sects, principalities, states, or kingdoms.* Every person within this community of goodwill, man and woman, is equal in status and enjoys the same rights as everyone else.

Priests, ulema, politicians, kings, and presidents who cause disputes and divisions among the *ummah* have been promised a dreadful penalty by Allah. They have been warned.

And hold fast, all together, by the Rope which Allah (stretches out for you) and be not divided among yourselves; and remember with gratitude Allah's favor on you; for ye were enemies and He joined your hearts in love, so that by His Grace, ye became brethren; and ye were on the brink of the Pit of Fire and He saved you from it. Thus doth Allah make His Signs clear to you: that ye may be guided.

Let there arise out of you a band of people inviting to all that is good, enjoining what is right and forbidding what is wrong: they are the ones to attain felicity.

Be not like those who are divided amongst themselves and fall into disputations after receiving Clear Signs: for them is a dreadful Penalty. (Ali 'Imran 3:103-5, Koran)

3. Murder.

The taking of life is a grievous sin and carries severe reprimand in the Koran. The murderer of a believer earns Allah's curse and an abode in hell. So why would anyone covet dominion over the *ummah* against their will and against the covenant of Allah, unless he is of the *Munafiqeen, kafirun, zalimun,* or *mufsidun* and not among the *Muslimeen,* the servants of Allah and the believers of His covenant?

That if anyone slew a person – unless it be for murder or for spreading mischief in the land – it would be as if he slew the whole people: and if any one saved a life, it would be as if he saved the life of the whole people. Then although there came to them Our Messengers with Clear Signs, Yet, even after that, many of them continued to commit excesses in the land. (Al-Ma'idah 5:32, Koran)

If a man kills a Believer intentionally, his recompense is Hell, to abide therein (forever): and the wrath and the curse of Allah are upon him and a dreadful penalty is prepared for him. (An-Nisa 4:93, Koran)

4. Justice.

Justice (*'adl*) is a divine attribute defined as "putting in the right place." The opposite of *'adl* is *zulm,* which in Koranic terms means "wrongdoing." Wrongdoing is a human attribute defined as "putting things in the wrong place." *Zulm* (wrongdoing) is one of the common terms used in the Koran to refer to the negative acts employed by human beings. Wrongdoing is the opposite of justice, putting everything in its right place, and every act of humans as prescribed by Allah. Wrongdoing is to put things where they do not belong. Hence, wrongdoing is injustice, for example, associating others with Allah; others do not belong in the place for the divine. It is to place false words in place of the truth and to put someone else's property in place of your own. Other examples are taking a life against the divine commandments, replacing people's liberty with oppression, waging war instead of peace, and usurping people's right to govern themselves. The Koran repeatedly stigmatizes men of wrongdoing.

The Koran, when it points out who is harmed by injustice and wrongdoing, always mentions the word *nafs* (self). People cannot harm Allah. By being unjust or by putting things in the wrong place, people harm themselves. They distort their own natures, and they lead themselves astray. Who can one wrong? It is impossible to wrong or do injustice against Allah since all things are His creatures and do His work. Hence, wrongdoing and injustice is an activity against people and Allah's creation. Allah had prescribed His covenant to the humans for the good of human beings. People, tribes, and nations are being helped since Allah leads them into accord, harmony, and justice, which in turn create peace in the world. Allah has laid out all the basic principles for justice in His covenant for the humans to live in harmony. Those who refuse to follow His commandments are therefore ungrateful and hence *kafirs*. Thus, they are wrongdoers (*zalimun*) and only harm themselves. Therefore, there can be no jihad unless it is for justice and against wrongdoing.

An Islamic society and country cannot exist without Allah's umbrella of truth and justice. Yet all Muslim countries today are ruled by *zalimun* who deprive the believers of Allah's mercy through their tyranny and covetousness. There is a clear reason for the glaring weakness of the state-run armies of the Muslim nation-states. The Muslim states are governed by self-appointed kings, dictators, and politicians who are divorced from their *din* and their people. They belong to and serve the interests of the circle of evil.

Two hundred years ago, the circle of evil began its control of the world's wealth through conspiracy, subterfuge, and secrecy by undermining the stability of countries through war, strife, and discord and by weakening governments through creation of confusion in financial markets. The Western armies and intelligence services are the foot soldiers of the circle of evil, and the rulers of both the East and the West are their pawns and puppets to be manipulated at will to control the power and wealth of the world. The intent of the circle of evil has always been to corrupt, divide, and control the wealth of the Islamic land through the manipulation of its rulers, who were initially placed in positions of power by the circle with the help of the Western armies, intelligence, and diplomacy.

The foundation of the regimes of the imperial families of the Arabian Peninsula, Jordan, Brunei, Morocco, and Iran and the imperial government of Hosni Mubarak of Egypt are supported by the British and American armed forces, intelligence, and diplomatic services in opposition to the aspirations of their own people. In return, these regimes provide services to the circle of evil to subvert, undermine, and weaken the neighboring Islamic and Arab countries of Iran, Afghanistan, Iraq, Syria, Libya, Algeria, Sudan, and Mauritania. Turkey and Pakistan are also puppets of the circle of evil; the price tag for the subservience of Turkey is seventeen billion dollars and for Pakistani's dictator a paltry couple of billion dollars in debt relief tagged to some minor trade concessions.

5. Consultation and consensus:

The covenant of the Koran proclaims that the affairs of the community should be conducted through mutual consultation (*ijma*) and decisions reached in consensus. Furthermore, the Koran proclaims consultation as the principle of government and a method that must be applied in the administration of public affairs. The sovereignty of Islamic state belongs exclusively to Allah, whose will and command binds the community and state. The dignified designation in the Koran of the community as vicegerent of Allah on the earth makes the Muslim community, the *ummah*, a repository of what is known as "executive sovereignty" of the Islamic state. The community as a whole, after consultation and consensus, grants people among themselves with authority to manage its affairs (*ulil amri minkum*). Those charged with authority act in their capacity as the representative (*wakil*) of the people and are bound by the Koranic mandate to consult the community in public affairs, and consensus is the binding source of the law. The community, through consultation and in consensus, has the authority to depose any person charged with authority, including the head of state, in the event of gross violation of the law.

> Those who hearken to their Lord and establish regular prayer; who conduct their affairs by mutual consultation; who spend out what We bestow on them for sustenance; and those who when an oppressive wrong is inflicted on them, are not intimidated, but defend themselves. (Koran 42:38–39)

Islam pursues its social objectives by reforming the individual. The individual is seen not just as a member of the community and subservient to the community's will but also as a morally autonomous agent who plays a distinctive role in shaping the community's sense of direction and purpose. The Koran has attached to the individual's duty of obedience to the government a right to simultaneously dispute with rulers over government affairs. The individual obeys the ruler on the condition that the ruler obeys the covenant of the Koran and Allah's commandments, which are obligatory to all Muslims regardless of their status in the social hierarchy. This is reflected in the declaration of the blessed *nabi*: "There is no obedience in transgression; obedience is only in the righteousness." The citizen is entitled to disobey an oppressive command that is contrary to the covenant of the Koran.

6. Solution to disputes:

The Koran is mindful of the likelihood of difference of opinion among the Muslims on matters concerning their community.

> O you who believe! obey Allah and obey the Rasool and those charged with authority among you. If you differ in anything among yourselves, refer it to Allah and His Messenger, if you do believe in Allah and the Last Day: that is best and most suitable for final determination. (Koran 4:59)

Instead of solving such differences through strife, the Koran specifically advises the believers to refer such matters to Allah and His *rasul*, which in the present-day context refers to the covenant of Allah and to the example of the blessed *nabi*. Fighting among Muslims and killing of Muslims is strictly forbidden by the covenant of Allah. All decisions must be achieved through consultation and in consensus within the community. The unity of the *ummah* should be maintained at all cost.

The authority to administer the affairs of the ummah *is granted to people of their choice with conditions and terms based on the covenant of Allah. No individual has the prerogative to take upon himself the right to become the ruler of the believers. Such an action is tantamount to tyranny (*fitnah*). The covenant of Allah commands the believers to fight such tyranny till there is no more oppression and justice prevails everywhere.*

Every believer inherits the Koran, the covenant of Allah, the *din*, and the Dar es Salaam upon his or her submission to Allah. When the blessed *nabi* passed away, the Koran and the *din* were bequeathed to every believer. This custodianship of the Koran, the covenant, the *din*, and the Dar es Salaam rests with every believer individually until the last day. In the Dar es Salaam, individual believers collectively and for a defined period delegate this custodianship to a person of their choice with conditions; in return, that individual is to exercise authority to manage the affairs of the Islamic state. While this authority may be bestowed, it can also be withdrawn if that individual fails to exercise his charge to the satisfaction of the majority of believers. During the period of discharge of his duties, this appointee will be called the caliph. This authority to manage the affairs of the believer and collectively the *ummah* can be bestowed on a person but cannot be exercised by a person unless it has been bestowed in the first place.

Traitors to Islam and the Covenant of Allah

760–800 CE:
The Usurpation of the Sovereignty of the *Ummah*:

When the Islamic armies ventured out to spread the word of Allah, they went out barefoot, half naked, and with no equipment, arms, or provisions against the mightiest nations with the most obvious power, large populations, and great wealth, Persia and Byzantium. The massive windfall of wealth and power to the newly converted Arabs, among whom the new faith of Allah and the teachings of the blessed *nabi* Muhammad had not yet fully assimilated, created problems.

The second caliph, Umar (634–44 CE), was wise and understood the dangers of such a sudden windfall of wealth. He enforced the rule that all lands taken by conquest were to pass into state ownership instead of being distributed among the conquering army. The conquering army was told to stay together in armed camps in garrison cities, where they received stipends paid by the government in return for military service. Agricultural activity was forbidden to the military. This was a farsighted decision by the caliph; this act made the army dependent on the state and accounted for discipline among the enlisted men as they did not have to live off the land of the conquered population.

However, disputes soon arose about the unfair distribution and misappropriation of the revenues from the conquered lands. The conversion to Islam of powerful chiefs and wealthy Meccans undermined the status of the humble men who had risen to leadership of Islam by joining the blessed *nabi* in the early days. The tribal following of the newly converted intensified the competition of the resources in garrison towns and the newly conquered territories. Whereas the enlisted men and the administrators from the prophet's earlier followers had to depend on modest allowance from the government, the powerful chiefs and their followers were getting rich from the resources of the conquest.

Mu'awiyah, as governor of Syria, consolidated his political position by allying himself with the Kalb, the leading tribe of Quda'a, the major confederacy in Syria, by marrying the chief's daughter and allowing the family a substantial share in the government and wealth of Syria. Through the Quda'a tribe and confederacy, Mu'awiyah secured his position and felt secure enough later to pick a fight with the incumbent caliph Ali ibn Abu Talib. Unfair distribution and misappropriation of the *fay* (revenues from conquered lands) in favor of the newly converted tribes and the allies of the governors caused serious disaffection among the veterans who had settled in Iraq, Syria, and Egypt. A group of veterans proceeded to Medina to complain about the situation to the third caliph, Uthman (644–56 CE); and finding him unresponsive, they murdered him brutally and hacked his body into pieces.

Ali ibn Abu Talib was declared the fourth caliph in Medina, but there were other contenders for the position. Ali was based in Kufah, a garrison town in Iraq. Talhah and Zubayr, two early converts supported by the prophet's widow Lady Aishah, were based in Basra, another garrison town in Iraq. Mu'awiyah, a late convert from the family of Uthman whose parents had been bitter enemies of the blessed *nabi* and of Islam, had been appointed governor of Syria by Uthman. Talhah and Zubayr were quickly defeated by Ali, who then fought Mu'awiyah on the plains of Siffin or the west bank of Euphrates on July 28, 657 CE. Ali's forces were on the point of victory when Mu'awiyah and the Syrians asked for a truce and arbitration by fastening copies of the Koran on their lances, interpreted to mean to seek decision from the teachings of the Koran.

Two arbitrators, one appointed by each side, met halfway between Amman and Petra. What exactly happened at this historical conference is difficult to ascertain. The acceptance of the principle of arbitration proved disastrous for Ali; it alienated the sympathy of a large body of his followers, who came to be known as the Kharijites, the Seceders. Adopting a slogan, *La hukma illa lillah* (Arbitration belongs to Allah alone), they rose in arms against Ali. This dispute with Mu'awiyah and the Kharijites dragged on till 661. On January 24, 661, Ali was on his way to the mosque at Kufah when he was struck on the forehead with a poisoned saber by a Kharijite.

With the death of Ali, the republican period of Islam was over. Mu'awiyah was then accepted caliph by the whole community. The year 661 CE was a tragic and defining moment for all Muslims to the present time. Islam lost its innocence and unity; it became divided into its two main sects. More pages have been written about the battles for succession to Uthman than on any other aspect of Muslim history, blaming the opposing sides for the tragic events. These events initiated customs and practices about succession of rulers that challenged the covenant of Allah and, in the long term, have continued to deprive the *ummah* of the divinely granted authority of executive sovereignty and the freedom of activity that goes with it.

Mu'awiyah divided the Islamic empire into several large provinces and appointed his kinsmen as governors. Being a tightly knit small family, they were loyal to Mu'awiyah and above tribal rivalries. He used local officials from the conquered population for assessment and collection of taxes and also relied on them to run the central and provincial bureaucracies. Mu'awiyah kept the Arab tribesmen out of fiscal administration. Ruling the Bedouin was a difficult matter. The solution was to keep them out of centers of power and politics and to rule them indirectly through their chiefs. To maintain law and order among the Bedouin, Mu'awiyah relied on the tribal chiefs who commanded them in war and were responsible for them in peacetime. To keep the tribesmen occupied and away from politics, he organized perpetual warfare and expansion of borders of Islam, which resulted in the conquest in North Africa, Spain, India, and Central Asia. The chiefs were penalized if the Bedouin misbehaved, and they were richly rewarded when they maintained peace between the Bedouin and the government. Only Mu'awiyah and his family had direct political power, only to be shared with the tribe of Quda'a, the backbone of Mu'awiyah's regime.

Mu'awiyah designated his son, Yazid, as his successor. This was an illegal and unpopular move as the caliphate was supposed to be elective. The first two caliphs were elected informally and Uthman formally through an electoral conclave. Nobody had a right to monopolize the caliphate. With the conquests, there was a sudden increase in wealth that inexorably destroyed every feature of the society that the blessed *nabi* had envisaged and the covenant of Allah had commanded.

There was a precipitous stratification of wealth and social and political life, and the state began to assume an un-Koranic imperial form. The Bedouin, the farmer, and the city dwellers lost their freedom and rights when the hereditary caliphate and the state usurped their land and wealth. The common man became excluded from participation in political dialogue and decision-making. The state of the common citizen reverted to the lowly status of the subjects of the Sassanian and the Byzantine Empires of the pre-Islamic era. The sultan and his elite seized control of the centers of power with the aid of a loyal small mercenary army. This began with the control of Damascus and spread out to other centers. The productive land, which was the common wealth of the *ummah*, became the personal property of the sultan, to be distributed to his loyal clients. He used this land to purchase the loyalty of his henchmen, the tribal leaders, and the ulema. The distribution of wealth, estates, and power within a small clan of nominal adherents of the new faith drew a tight circle around the palace and the ruler that inaugurated a 1,400-year tyranny over Islam.

The *fitnah* of Mu'awiyah has come to haunt us today with the un-Koranic practices of present-day rulers who have perpetuated the practices of the Sassanian and Byzantine emperors that Islam had destroyed. Centuries of subjugation, lack of knowledge of the precepts of the Koran, ignorance, and the greed of the ulema have hampered the subject populations to understand their rights bequeathed by Allah. Depriving the peasant and the farmer of the use of land and unjustly taxing the small trader deprived the *ummah* of the entrepreneur class. The greed of the elite restricted the formation of capital, which stymied the improvement on the standard of living of the masses. This deprivation of opportunity killed off the human instinct for self-improvement.

The accumulation of wealth among a few of the elite caused a gradual economic extinction of the masses over the last 1,400 years.

The elite taxed the *ummah* into destitution. The bloated hierarchical bureaucratic elite surrounding the sultan did not create any prosperity or any wealth for the nation but acted like a sponge to the wealth created by the peasantry, the merchants, and the artisans, sucking them dry. Such blame fell not only on the Umayyads but also on every autocratic ruler of Islam.

1095 CE:
The One-Thousand-Year War.

November 25, 1095, is a milestone in the history of Europe and Christendom. On this day at the Council of Clermont, Pope Urban II—addressing a vast crowd of priests and knights and poor folk—declared a holy war against Islam. For Europe, this was a defining moment, and this event has ongoing repercussions until today in the Middle East. This holy war, begun in the twilight of the eleventh century, is still ongoing under various guises and forms into the beginning of the twenty-first century. NATO troops in Afghanistan, Kosovo, Bosnia, and Iraq (the coalition) are the legacy of the Council of Clermont, now called the Council of Europe, and the NATO.

The pope declared the race of Seljuk Turks who had recently converted to Islam to be barbarians. They had swept into Anatolia and seized lands from the Christian empire of Byzantium. The pope declared that the Turks were an accursed race, utterly alienated from God who had not entrusted their spirit to God[33]. Killing these godless monsters was a holy act; it was a Christian duty to "exterminate this vile race from our lands"[34]. Once they had purged the Asia Minor of this Muslim filth, the knights would engage in a still holier task. They would then

---

[33] Robert the Monk, *Historia Iherosolimitana*. Quoted by August C. Krey, *The First Crusade: The Accounts of Eyewitnesses* (Princeton and London, 1921).

[34] Fulcher of Chartres, *History of the Expedition to Jerusalem, 1095–1127*, trans. Rita Ryan (Knoxville, 1969), 66.

march to the holy city of Jerusalem and liberate it from the infidel. It was shameful that the tomb of Christ should be in the hands of Islam.

Since that time, there has been a constant onslaught against Islam by the West. When the Euro-Christian states were not fighting against one another, they grouped together in a pack to attack the Muslim states. On the surface for the public consumption, they fought for their religion to destroy the infidel, but the true motive underlying the thousand-year war was always economic exploitation of the East by the top echelons of Euro-Christianity. The thousand-year incursions of exploitation have changed its stance every so often that the historians have lost the truth between the Crusades; Venetian trade; voyages of discovery; slave trade; colonialism; racism; economic subversion of the natives; piracy in the open seas; maritime ambushes and robbery of coastal cities; plunder of mineral, agriculture, and human resources; opium trade; capitalism; socialism; communism; world wars, both hot and cold; globalization of world trade in the hands of a few nations; and finally the control of oil.

When Damascus fell to the British troops in September 1918, Gen. Edmund Henry Allenby made it a point to visit the tomb of the great warrior Salah al-Din Yusuf ibn Ayyub, the liberator of Jerusalem. Upon approaching the grave of the sultan, he kicked it with his riding boot and uttered, "Finally, the Crusades have been avenged." Allenby, the Christian conqueror of Damascus, had remembered Pope Urban's one-thousand-year-old call to arms against Islam.

1492 CE:
The Fall of Spain.

When the *Muwahhid* dynasty ended, more than half the northern part of Spain and all the western provinces were in Christian hands. Muslim Spain had come under anarchy once again. Muslim territories were broken into small fragments, each at war with the other. Every Muslim chief invited Christian troops against another and offered them some cities and forts in return for their military help. This depravity of Muslim rulers was very pleasing and encouraging to the Christians. By the middle of thirteenth century, many Muslims in Spain had become subject to Christians either by conquest or by treaty. Such Muslims were called Mudejares. They had preserved their religion and the laws but had begun to forget Arabic and to adopt Romance language.

The Nasrid sultans were embroiled in their dynastic quarrels that had been a perpetual curse of the Muslim sultans. The final ruin of the Muslim kingdoms was hastened by the irresponsible move by Sultan Abu al-Hasan 'Ali, who refused to pay customary tribute to Ferdinand and commenced hostilities by attacking Castilian territory. Ferdinand in 1482, in a surprise attack, took Al-Hammah, which stood at the foot of the Sierra de Alhama, and guarded the southwestern entrance of the Granadan domain. At this time, a son of Abu al-Hasan—Abu 'Abd Allah Muhammad—instigated by his mother Fatima, raised the banner of rebellion against his own father. Fatima took revenge against her royal husband for his attachment and attentions toward a Christian concubine and her children. Supported by the garrison, Abu 'Abd Allah in 1482 seized Alhambra and made himself master of Granada.

In the following year, Abu 'Abd Allah—whose name became corrupted to Boabdil in Spanish—had the temerity to attack the Castilian town of Lucena, where he was beaten and taken captive. Abu al-Hasan 'Ali reinstated himself to the Granadan throne, where he ruled till 1485, when he abdicated in favor of his brother Muhammad XII, nicknamed al-Zaghall. Ferdinand and Isabella saw a perfect tool in their prisoner Abu 'Abd Allah in their plan for destruction of Islam and its presence in Spain. Supplied with Castilian men and money, Abu 'Abd Allah in 1486 occupied part of his uncle's capital and once more plunged Granada into a destructive civil war. In the meantime, the Castilian army was advancing. Town after town fell before it. Malaga was captured in the following year, and its Muslim inhabitants were sold in slavery. The noose was getting tighter around the doomed capital. Al-Zaghall made a few unsuccessful stands against the armies of Ferdinand and was defeated. Abu 'Abd Allah fought alongside the Christian armies of Ferdinand against his uncle.

No sooner had al-Zaghall been disgracefully disposed of by his nephew than Abu 'Abd Allah was ordered by Ferdinand to vacate the city and surrender Granada to Isabella and Ferdinand. Abu 'Abd Allah refused to comply. In the spring of 1491, Ferdinand with an army of ten thousand horses marched on Granada and occupied all the land around it. He destroyed crops and farms in a blockade to starve the population into submission. When the winter came, extreme cold and heavy snow barred all access to the outside world. Food became scarce, and the population starved. In December 1491, the hardships of the people had reached their extreme, and the garrison agreed to surrender. The following terms for the surrender were agreed. Abu 'Abd Allah and his officers and people would take an oath of obedience to the Castilian sovereigns. The Castilians entered Granada on January 2, 1492, and supplanted a cross on the crescent on the towers of the fortress.

The sultan Abu 'Abd Allah, with his queen, richly dressed, left his red fortress, never to return. As he rode away, he turned to take a last look at his capital, sighed, and burst into tears. His mother, till then his evil genius, turned to him with the words *"You do well to weep like a woman for what you could not defend like a man."* The rocky eminence where he took his sad farewell look is still known by the name *El ultimo suspiro del Moro* (the last sigh of the Moor).

Ferdinand and Isabella failed to abide by their terms of capitulation. A campaign of forced conversion of Muslims was inaugurated in 1499. All books in Arabic were burned in a bonfire of Arabic manuscripts in Granada. In 1501, a royal decree was issued that all Muslims in Castile and Leon should either convert to Catholicism or leave Spain. In 1526, Muslims of Aragon were confronted with the same choices. In 1556, Phillip II promulgated a law requiring the remaining Muslims to abandon at once their language, worship, and institutions and in 1609 their manner of life. The final order of expulsion of all Muslims from Spain was signed by Phillip III, resulting in forcible deportation en masse of all Muslims from Spanish soil. Some half a million Muslims landed on the shores of Africa or took ships to distant lands of Islam. Between the fall of Granada and the first decade of the seventeenth century, it is estimated that three million Muslims were banished or executed.

1757–1761 CE:
The Battle of Plassey:

In the history of Islam, there are defining moments when an individual's greed left a lasting impact on the freedom of the Muslim community, lasting over several hundred years. Abu 'Abd Allah's avariciousness in conjunction with Isabella and Ferdinand dealt the death blow to seven hundred years of *Islamic* civilization in Spain and the death and expulsion of three million Muslims from Spain.

Half a world away to the east in 1757, the French and the English had been jockeying for primacy of control of trade in the Indian peninsula. The Europeans had brought a powerful navy with guns that the Indians could not match. A small number of well-trained Europeans and European-trained Indian mercenary infantrymen armed with muskets could load and fire with synchronized rapidity that could produce enough firepower to halt a conventional Indian cavalry charge. Armed with this knowledge, the English set out to control revenue-bearing Indian real estate and land. Added to their weapons was the skill to divide, rule, and bribe Indian Muslim noblemen. The covetousness of these noble grandees lost India to Islam.

The English had made Calcutta a wealthy trading post and submitted considerable revenues to the nawab of Bengal. The English provided refuge to some rebels, and the nawab of Bengal Siraj al-Dawlah, a grandson of a previous Mogul governor, demanded their return. When he received no response, Siraj attacked Calcutta and drove the English out. Siraj suddenly found himself the master of Calcutta with an assortment of Englishmen, women, and children who failed to get away with the remaining English who had made a panic-stricken dash to the ships and sailed away. Unharmed, the group was lodged overnight in the detention cell of the fort built by the English for their prisoners. How many were detained is not certainly known, but next morning, only twenty-three staggered out. Dehydration and suffocation had tragically accounted for possibly fifty lives.[35]

The tragedy was apparently unintended. Nevertheless, Siraj was held responsible. Clive, the commander of the British garrison, was thirsting for revenge. Seven months later in 1757, he marched back to the Hugli River and retook Calcutta. He continued the hostilities and marched up the river to Murshidabad, Siraj's capital. In the meantime, Siraj's army took up defensive position at Plassey. Siraj had a well-trained army of fifty thousand; so was the disposition of his troops. Against him were three thousand British troops with slightly superior artillery. Had the battle been fought, the odds would clearly be in Siraj's favor.

Clive had little hope of victory and rested his hopes entirely on the treachery of the dignitaries of the Muslim army. He had already

[35] John Keay, *India: A History* (HarperCollins), 389–91.

negotiated a secret pact with Mir Ja'far, Siraj's commander in chief and a relative. Mir Ja'far deserted with more than half of Siraj's army and joined Clive. Siraj had to run for his life. Clive personally placed Mir Ja'far on the throne of Bengal. British arms had put Ja'far on the throne, and now the British palms waited his greasing. For the British services, Mir Ja'far paid out over £1,250,000 (three billions of dollars in today's money) from the Bengal treasury, of which over £400,000 was paid to Clive in the form of revenue-bearing estates. The demands of the British for more revenue continued to increase. When in 1760–61 Mir Ja'far refused to comply with the British demands, he was promptly replaced on the throne by the British with his son-in-law.

The circle of evil of the *Munafiqun*, hungry for power and wealth, collaborated with the evil of the West in their hunt for power and gold. Mir Ja'far opened the gates of Muslim India to the British for subjugation and plunder, which lasted another two hundred years. The British now discovered that revenue rights were much more profitable than the profits of trade. The revenue receipts from the Indian farmer would quickly eliminate the need to finance imports from India with export of bullion from Britain. In Bengal and later in the rest of India, relieving the ruling princes of revenue rights became a standard practice of the British. In the wake of Plassey, the British traders fanned out into Bengal, Bihar, and beyond to acquire monopoly rights over choice export commodities of saltpeter, indigo, cotton, and opium and over the lucrative internal trade in sea salt. Acquisition of Bengal enabled the British to siphon off the Indian revenue direct from the Indian peasant to the stately homes of Britain, the foundation of the English wealth and power. This wealth was the engine of the industrialization of England, Germany, and the USA, while India was systematically impoverished.

1907–1925:
Traitors Within: The Shame of Islam.

In July 1908, army units of the Ottoman Army in Macedonia revolted against Sultan Abdulhamid II and demanded a return to constitutional rule. Again, on April 24, 1909, troops loyal to the revolution marched from Macedonia and took the capital, Istanbul. The Young Turks were aided in their march onto Constantinople by the Central Powers, especially by the *Neue Freie Presse* of Vienna. And three days later, Sultan Abdulhamid was deposed.

On the twenty-seventh of April 1909, the 240 members of the Ottoman senate agreed under pressure of the national Young Turks to remove Abdulhamid from power. The appearance of four people in the sultan's office on that day—an Arab, a Turk, a Jew, and a Christian—who came to remove him from power was a premonition of the dismemberment of the Islamic world from treachery of the Arabs and the Turks in collusion with Jews and Christians. The caliphate effectively came to an end with the fall of Abdulhamid.

Foreign powers took advantage of the political instability in Istanbul to seize portions of the Ottoman Empire. Austria annexed Bosnia and Herzegovina immediately after the 1908 Turkish revolution, and Bulgaria proclaimed its complete independence. Italy proclaimed war in 1911 and seized Libya. After a secret pact, Greece, Serbia, Montenegro, and Bulgaria invaded and defeated Ottoman forces in Macedonia and Thrace in October 1912.

After a series of disasters, in January 1912 in a coup d'état,[36] the most authoritarian elements of the Young Turks movement took control of the Ottoman government. Kamil Pasha was driven from power and Nazim Pasha was murdered by Enver Bey. The leadership of the Committee

---

[36] John Ridley-Dash, *The Demise of Ottoman* (Girne American University, 1995).

of Union and Progress emerged as a military dictatorship with power concentrated in the hands of the triumvirate of Mehmed Talat Pasha, Ahmed Cemal Pasha, and Enver Bey. Enver, as war minister, was acknowledged as the leader of the group in the government.

On January 13, 1913, Talat and Enver hastily collected about two hundred followers and marched to the Sublime Porte, where the ministers were meeting. Nazim Pasha, hearing the uproar, stepped into the hall, courageously faced the crowd with a cigarette in his mouth and hands thrust in his pockets, and said in good humor, "Come, boys, what is this noise about? Don't you know it is interfering with our deliberations?" The words had hardly left his mouth when he fell dead. A bullet had pierced his heart. The mob led by Enver and Talat then forced their way into the council chamber. They forced Kamil Pasha, the grand vizier, to resign his post by threatening him with the fate that had befallen Nazim.

Assassination became the method by which these conspirators usurped the supreme power. So assassination continued to be the instrument by which they kept their hold on power. The Young Turks destroyed Abdulhamid's regime to restore a democratic constitutional government; instead, they created a reign of terror. Men were arrested and deported by the score, and hangings of opponents became a common occurrence.

Early in January 1914, Enver—then only thirty-two—became war minister. Enver's elevation to the ministry of war was virtually a German victory. He immediately instituted a drastic reorganization of the armed forces. By March 1914, Germans—with the help of Talat, Enver, and Cemal—had tightened their hold on Turkey. Liman von Sanders was first made the head of the first army corps and then the inspector general of all the Turkish armed forces. Another German general, Bronsart von Schellendorf, was appointed the chief of staff, and scores of German officers held commands of first importance. And the Turkish politician Enver Pasha, an outspoken thirty-four-year-old champion of Germany, was minister of war. The kaiser had almost completed his plans to annex the Turkish Army to his own.

Enver secretly signed a treaty of Turko-German alliance on August 2, 1914. Only five people in Turkey knew of this treaty, which brought on the final disintegration of the Ottoman Empire. The puppet grand vizier Said Halim, Talat, and Cemal were convinced by Enver of the wisdom of supporting the Germans in case the war broke out. Enver Pasha chose to ally Turkey with the Central Powers by citing Germany's earlier victories in the war. Thus, the Ottoman Empire joined the Central Powers to form a triple alliance without the knowledge of the cabinet, the parliament, the army generals, and the Ottoman populace. The empire was ruled by three collaborators and puppets of Germany, traitors to Islam, to the Muslims in Turkey, and to the whole of the *ummah.* They acted secretly as collaborators with a foreign government working toward the destruction and disintegration of the only free Islamic state.

Two German warships, the battleship *Goeben* and the cruiser *Breslau,* that were caught in a neutral Turkish port when the war broke out in Europe were handed to the Ottoman Navy. In October, they were put out to sea, flying the Ottoman flag with German officers and crew, and shelled Odessa and other Russian ports. Enver Pasha, as the Ottoman war minister, gave secret orders in a sealed envelope to Admiral Souchon, the commander of the Turko-German fleet, only to be opened when the fleet was deep in the Black Sea. The orders read:

War minister Enver Pasha to Admiral Souchon   *October 25, 1914.*

The entire fleet should maneuver in the Black Sea. When you find a favorable opportunity, attack the Russian fleet. Before initiating the hostilities, open my secret orders given to you personally this morning. To prevent transport of material to Serbia, act as already agreed upon. Enver Pasha.

(Secret Order): The Turkish fleet should gain the mastery of the Black Sea by force. Seek out the Russian fleet and attack her wherever you find her without declaration of war. Enver Pasha.

Souchon now had a surprise for Enver. Rather than causing an incident at sea, the admiral attacked simultaneously the Russian ports of Sebastopol, Theodosia, Novorossiysk, and Odessa on the morning of October 29. This action in effect declared a war on Russia and its allies Britain and France. Once again, Enver acted secretly at the behest of Germany. He did not consult his coconspirators, Talat and Cemal, before ordering the attack on Russia or the declaration of war against the Western allies. He kept his cabinet colleagues, the parliament, and the people of the empire in the dark, who on the morning of October 29, 1914, were surprised to find themselves at war.

The conspiracies, utter stupidity, and lust for power of three men—Talat, Cemal, and Enver—led to the dismemberment of the Ottoman Empire. For another one hundred years, this land of Islam was to know no peace. It became the prey of the circle of evil of the Euro-Christian, Jew, and Arab conspirators.

1914 to the Present:
The Hashemite: From Common Traitors to Kings of Arabs.

According to some sources, Sharif Hussein's son Abdullah had made contacts with the British consul general in Egypt, Lord Kitchener, as early as 1912, if not 1913.[37] Kitchener established a

---

[37] Bruce Westrate, *The Arab Bureau: British Policy in the Middle East, 1916–1920* (Pennsylvania State University Press, 1992).

line of communication with Hussein's family through Hussein's representative, Muhammad al-Faruqi. Kitchener's letters to Hussein contained statements pledging British support in the event of an Arab uprising against the Turks and promising an independent Arabia after the war. In January 1915, Lord Kitchener was replaced by Sir Henry McMahon. In the ensuing correspondence, Hussein set forth a list of demands calling on the British government to support the independence of "Arab countries" within an area bounded on the north by the Mersin-Adana line and the thirty-seventh parallel, on the east by the Persian frontier and the Persian Gulf, on the south by the Indian Ocean (excepting Aden), and on the west by the Red and Mediterranean Seas. Hussein also requested the establishment of an Arab caliphate to supplant the Turkish sultan. In exchange for these concessions, Hussein offered economic preference to Great Britain and a defensive alliance.

In reply, McMahon dispatched on October 24 a letter that more precisely outlined the territorial parameters within which the British were prepared to recognize the Arab independence. These boundaries corresponded roughly with those asked by Hussein earlier with several important differences. In view of Britain's established position and interests, the vilayets of Basra and Baghdad were excluded. Also excluded were the areas of Syria, west of the district of Damascus, Homs, Hama, and Aleppo, as well as districts of Mersin and Alexandretta. Hussein's response on November 5 accepted the exclusion of Mersin and Alexandretta but objected to the exception of what essentially were Lebanon and the coastal Latakia area. Hussein was willing to accept the British claim to the two Mesopotamian vilayets in exchange for monetary compensation, pending the region's eventual return to Arab rule. In his letter on December 14, McMahon held firm to his stance on the Syrian littoral, citing the prior French interests precluding the inclusion of the area to the Arab zone.

Hussein was never promised personal rule of the territory in question. An Arab caliphate was only obliquely referred to in the correspondence. Hussein did not make any attempt to clarify the position taken by the British before he led a revolt against his caliph, sultan, country, and coreligionists under the protection of an alien, infidel, colonial, expansionist power with the full knowledge that parts of the Islamic state—including Syria, Lebanon, Palestine, and Iraq—would pass from Islamic rule to an economic and colonial subjugation of a non-Muslim power. For the sake of his own hunger for power, he used his holy prophetic bloodline to break up the united Islamic state when what its people most needed was a moral and just leadership to steer the state into the path of Allah. He could have drawn on his authority, knowledge, and influence to correct what was wrong in the *ummah* rather than subvert it. He appealed to an infidel power for his own personal elevation to the position of caliph, the spiritual and temporal leadership of the whole Islamic nation.

At that time, there was another player in the treason game with the British. He was the young Bedouin tribal leader 'Abd al-'Aziz (Ibn Sa'ud). He was a master of the *ghazzu*, raiding other tribes to steal their women, camels, sheep, and grain. He was backed by the religious zealots of the Wahhabi sect, who had little regard for life and sought death in the hope of martyrdom and ascent to heaven. Bedouin sheikhs frowned on *ghazzu* as an unwholesome and dishonorable activity. The heads of major Bedouin tribes who claimed hegemony over large tracts of land did not practice it. The way of robbery and plunder as practiced by 'Abd al-'Aziz was contrary to all Koranic teaching and Arab traditions of generosity to the vanquished. 'Abd al-'Aziz prided himself on never taking any prisoners; he murdered all the men of the raided tribe to prevent future retaliation.

Ibn Sa'ud's political emergence began in 1902, when he reclaimed Riyadh[38], the city where his family had been local sheikhs, appointed by local emirs. His first merciless act was to terrorize the population by spiking the heads of his enemies and displaying them at the gates of the city. His followers burned 1,200 people to death. While conducting a raid, he and his followers were very much in the habit of taking young maidens back as slaves and as gifts to friends. This as how Ibn Sa'ud lived at the turn of the century before he became a king when he was a mere head of a small tribe.

The third player was Lawrence. Thomas Edward Lawrence was the illegitimate child of an illegitimate child. His father was Thomas Chapman and his mother, Thomas Chapman's family governess, was the offspring out of wedlock of an English mother and a Norwegian father. In 1913 and 1914, Lawrence worked on a geographical survey of the Negev desert under the archaeological rubric of the Palestine Exploration Fund. Lawrence acquired a great deal of vital cartographic and geographic data for the British intelligence before the venture was terminated by the Turkish authorities in early 1914. When the war began, he found himself as an intelligence officer on the staff of Lord Horatio Herbert Kitchener with David Hogarth, his mentor, a key figure in the British administration in the Middle East. Hogarth later became the head of the Arab Bureau, planning and executing the so-called Arab Revolt. Kitchener, the British consul general in Egypt was in secret contact with Abdullah, son of Sharif Hussein of Mecca, who at the time was a member of Parliament in Istanbul. Sharif Hussein ibn Ali was the Turkish-appointed governor as a caretaker of the Muslim holy shrines of Mecca. Kitchener's strategy was to establish a channel of communication with Hussein to take advantage of the situation in the event of war with Turkey as the Arab lands were

---

[38] Said K. Aburish, *The Rise, Corruption, and Coming Fall of the House of Saud* (St. Martin's Griffin, New York).

critical to the British position in India and Egypt. Winston Churchill underlined the strategic importance of the Persian Gulf oil and the huge refinery at Abadan and made clear the intention of the British government to become the owners and the controllers of the Gulf oil required by the British navy. This vital priority led to the occupation of Basra in 1914 and later the invasion of Mesopotamia.

In June 1916, supported by Abdullah, Faisal, and his other sons, Hussein proclaimed the Arab Revolt against the sultan and the caliph of the Ottoman Empire. For Hussein and sons, it was an act of treason—treason against their religion, people, and sovereign to whom they had sworn allegiance and loyalty. Faisal, who was a serving officer in the Ottoman Army, deserted his post in Syria to join the revolt. It proved to be a dud. Hussein, it turned out, had no following at all. Muslims did not respond to his call, nor did the Arabs. Under his banner, or rather the one that a British official designed for him, those who rallied under him were closer to one thousand rather than one hundred thousand, and they were Bedouin tribesmen and not soldiers. And those who did join were bribed with British gold.

In the make-believe world of Lawrence, Faisal ibn Hussein became Prince Faisal, the field commander of the Arab armies of under one thousand men; and at Faisal's request, Lawrence was assigned to be the British liaison officer with him. With such untrained and undisciplined band of men in Faisal's army, a frontal attack on the Ottoman troops would be suicidal. Some Bedouin men had qualms against fighting face-to-face against fellow Muslims. Over half the Ottoman Army was ethnically Arab. Lawrence, therefore, believed that Faisal's Bedouins would be better employed in fighting a guerilla war than in trying to fight a conventional one. Their object was to take the city of Medina, which lay to the north and blocked Faisal's force from riding to Palestine, where the Middle East war was to be fought.

Faisal's men raided a single-track railway from the Ottoman Palestine, which was the only source of reinforcement and supply to Medina's defenders. A British officer, Herbert Garland, taught Faisal's Bedouins to dynamite the railroad. Garland, Lawrence, and other British officers went on to dynamite it repeatedly. The campaign failed. The Ottoman Muslim forces repaired the railway after each attack and kept it running. Medina never fell to Faisal or to the British. The Ottoman Muslim garrison held on till the end of the war, blocking the land road to Palestine. The Arab and Muslim defenders of Medina and Asir stood their ground to the last day of the war.

June 1916 was a historical moment when, for the first time in the history of Islam since the Battle of Badr in the first year of hijra, the combined forces of the *kafireen* and *Munafiqeen* attacked the city of the prophet of Islam, though unsuccessfully. This attack introduced the combined evil dominion of the *Mutaffifeen*, *kafireen*, and *Munafiqeen* to the heartlands of Islam for the next century to come.

Medina continued to stand in Faisal's way, and had Lawrence not thought of a way around it using the Red Sea route, Hussein's revolt would have stayed bottled up in the Hejaz desert. Now that Lawrence had secured a port in Palestine, General Allenby sent boats to bring Faisal and about a thousand Bedouin followers from Ragheb on the Red Sea to Aqaba. Faisal arrived in Aqaba as a conqueror, and so the world was told by the British media and by Prime Minister Lloyd George's secretariat. In Aqaba, Faisal was reinforced by about twenty-five hundred men, Auda abu Tayi's Bedouins, and some Arab deserters from the Ottoman Army. All together, they formed a camel cavalry corps that harassed the Turkish flank when Allenby's Egypt-based army invaded Palestine and marched into Syria.

Faisal's camel corps presented a pretense that Syria was liberated by the Arabs themselves. In fact, there were a million British troops fighting in the Middle East in 1918 and only thirty-five hundred Husseini troops, and on the face of it was a British war of conquest over the Arabs and not a war of liberation for the Arabs. The British on May 9, 1916, in a secret convention, had already promised Arab Syria to the French (Sykes-Picot Agreement) and on November 2, 1917, in the Balfour Declaration, gave away Arab Palestine to the Jews. The Lawrence-Hussein-sons puppet show was being cleverly orchestrated from London. Each one of the players understood their role and the reward for their part except Hussein and sons. The ambiguous language, willful face-to-face lies, secret agreements, double dealings, deception, flattery, and bribery as a skill and art had become the trademark of English diplomacy over the previous one hundred years. The Arabs and the Bedouins had their own share of guile and cunningness; they were, however, no match for the Anglos as the next one hundred years would reveal. And the Arab leaders never learned.

For his treachery, Sharif Hussein received his first reward in gold sovereigns in March 1916, a shipment in the amount of £53,000, three months before he announced his revolt. Commencing on August 8, 1916, the official allowance was set at £125,000 a month, a sum that was frequently exceeded on Hussein's demand. For example, in November 1916, £375,000 in gold sovereigns was dispatched to Hussein by the British for hajj expenses. The money was to have been used by Hussein to pay his armies and to bribe the sheikhs and the tribes into joining his revolt. The payments were broken down into five categories representing the four armies under the command of Hussein's sons and an allotment for the upkeep of the mosque at Kaaba and for hajj facilities as well as for the operation of Hussein's government in Mecca and Jeddah. Forty thousand pounds was allocated to Faisal, £30,000 to Abdullah, £20,000 each for Ali and Zeid, and £15,000 for expenses at Mecca and Jeddah.

The year 1916 must have been the lowest point in the history of Islam. It was surrounded by powerful enemies around the world and inside; it was being destroyed by self-serving traitors at the very heart of the faith, the Kaaba. For the first time in the history of Islam, the very upkeep of the Holy Mosque of Mecca and the Kaaba and the hajj expenses were being paid for by the *kafireen* at the behest of the *Munafiqeen* under the claim of their lineage from the holy prophet. While claiming their bloodline, they forgot the teachings of the Koran and the example of the prophet.

The British were unable to make all the payments from their London treasury, so in the spring of 1917, the British drew gold out of the rapidly diminishing Egyptian treasury. The source of gold in the Egyptian treasury was the sweat and blood of the Egyptian peasant. Hussein had insisted that he needed additional £75,000 monthly to meet his bloated payroll. The Egyptian peasants were in double jeopardy as they not only had to pay in taxes for Hussein's misadventure but also had to provide free labor of one hundred thousand men for the transport of troops, equipment, and supplies to the British Expeditionary Force of General Allenby from Egypt to Palestine. The British-controlled Egyptian treasury, by June 1917, had only £200,000 in reserve that was available for Hussein. To meet Hussein's demand for additional cash, there was a scramble for alternative source for money. Silver was scarce in India, and agriculture goods were too dear in Egypt. Hussein demanded that the total payment be made in gold; however, he was eventually forced to accept shipments of Indian paper rupees and goods in lieu of precious metals.

1902 to the Present:
The Saudis: From Desert Thugs to Kings of
Arabs and Servants of the *Kafireen*.

The Ottomans, with German finance and technology, planned a railway from Berlin through the Ottoman Empire to end in the Persian Gulf at Kuwait, which was the only deepwater harbor in the region. The railway threatened the growing British influence in the region, and the British quietly preempted the German move by signing an agreement with Sheikh Mubarak al-Sabah of Kuwait. The gist of the agreement signed on January 23, 1899, stated that the sheikh would not receive the agent or representative of any other power without the sanction of the British government, nor would he cede, sell, lease, mortgage, or give for occupation any part of his territory to any other power without the British permission. There was in the treaty no mention of the establishment of a protectorate over Kuwait, although the British Crown assumed that to be the case. Britain then appointed a resident political officer in Kuwait a year after the signing of the treaty.

Ibn Sa'ud, a homeless and hungry tent-dwelling Bedouin youth living in Kuwait, was looking for adventure and a sponsor. At least on two occasions, he wrote to the Ottoman sultan, offering his services; however, he was turned down. The British were looking for influence and contacts in the interior of Arabia and had sent several intelligence agents in the form of explorers. The first British contact with 'Abd al-'Aziz probably occurred soon after the political agent had established himself in Kuwait in 1901. By 1904, 'Abd al-'Aziz was already in the pay of the British and, till 1911, continued to receive small amounts of money. The British scouts had recognized him as potentially useful and kept him in reserve in case hostilities broke out against the Turks.

'Abd al-'Aziz certainly had a mysterious source of support when he raided Riyadh with equipment and camels and with a number of men, which were thought to be beyond his means. After he captured Riyadh, relative peaceful equilibrium of the desert was disturbed by the young Bedouin tribal leader, Ibn Sa'ud. He was a master of the *ghazzu*, raiding other tribes to steal their camels, sheep and grain. He was backed by the religious zealots of the Wahhabi sect, who had little regard for life and sought death in the hope of martyrdom and ascent to heaven. Ibn Sa'ud used much of the money from the British to sponsor colonies of the Ikhwan brotherhood, fanatics of the Wahhabi sect, to which Ibn Sa'ud belonged. The Ikhwan formed the backbone of Ibn Sa'ud's conquering army, whose savagery wreaked havoc across Arabia.

Ibn Sa'ud had no formal education. His literary talent, if any, was extremely restricted; and therefore, his worldview was limited by his own experience of the life of a Bedouin and the tribal code, which had barely changed for fourteen hundred years. His resting place was a tent or under the starlit sky. Food and water were scarce; security and refuge was with the family, clan, and tribe. Intertribal disputes and feuds were frequent and were settled by the sword; raiding the neighboring tribes for their goods and animals was a sport. Killing another Muslim and looting his property in a *ghazzu* was perfectly acceptable and did not cause remorse, slavery was practiced and prevalent, and women were nonentities and not worthy of equality with men. 'Abd al-'Aziz once boasted that he had never had a meal with a woman and that he never looked at the face of the woman he made love. Yet he had been married to over a hundred women and had a similar number of concubines and sex slaves. Religion and spirituality was judged through the narrow tunnel vision of Wahhabi men of religion in a nomadic social setting where neither the Koran nor other religious texts were available to the common man. Any person not following the narrow edicts of the Wahhabi sect of Islam was automatically a heretic and therefore an infidel and punishable by public flogging, amputation, or beheading.

Armed with these moral values and ethics, 'Abd al-'Aziz set out to conquer Arabia with the financial and military assistance of the British. His first victims were the Ibn Rashids of the Ottoman-controlled part of the Arabian Peninsula. The defeat of the Ibn Rashids was, in effect, a British victory. Sir Percy Cox, a British resident in the Persian Gulf, wrote, 'With Ibn-Saud in Hasa (the Gulf Coast of Arabia) our position is very much strengthened.' Percy Cox openly encouraged Ibn Sa'ud to attack the remaining territory of the Ibn Rashids to divert them from reinforcing Turkish troops against the British. Ibn Sa'ud had constant British financial aid, arms, and advisers, initially William Shakespeare and Percy Cox and later Harry Saint John Philby.

After they helped him master eastern Arabia in 1917, the British found another use for Ibn Sa'ud. In 1924, Hussein declared himself caliph of Islam without the consent of the British. Abdullah being entrenched in Amman and Faisal in Baghdad and the elevation of Sharif Hussein to the leadership of whole Islam threatened Britain's growing interests in the Middle East. These interests included strategy to continue to divide and rule the Middle East through subservient local notables. Although Hussein's sons were pliable and obedient to these imperialistic plans, Hussein demanded that Britain live up to its promises to grant Arabs independence and a free hand in all the Arab countries. He objected to British plans to provide Jews with a national home in Palestine. Ibn Sa'ud started his thrust into Hejaz; although the British ostensibly cut off the arms supplies to both sides, most historians believe that the British continued to supply small but crucial amounts of money and arms to Ibn Sa'ud and his merciless Ikhwan. Some of the military equipment used by Ibn Sa'ud was expensive and could not have been obtained without outside help and could not have been used without instructors. At the time, statements by British officials did point to the British hand in Ibn Sa'ud's attack on Mecca. Arthur Hirtzel—a Jew, head of the British India Office at that time—expressed the need for Ibn Sa'ud to establish himself in Mecca.

In 1925, Hejaz fell to Ibn Sa'ud's Ikhwan army. The most advanced and settled part of Arabia with a long history of contact with the outside world, constitutional government, established institutions, and established justice system fell to an anarchist tribal army of religious fanatics. If the British secret planners had wanted to destroy and divide the heart of Islam, they could not have chosen a more competent and effective allies. Ibn Sa'ud's Ikhwan soldiers killed hundreds of males, including children; pillaged homes of the conquered populace for money, gold, and valuable objects; murdered non-Wahhabi religious leaders; and destroyed whole towns. Tolerance of others' beliefs was against Wahhabi and Ikhwan teachings and traditions. They committed massacres in At Ta'if, Bureida, and Al Huda. They tried to destroy the tomb of the prophet and remove the domes of the major mosques. They also desecrated the Sunni graveyards of Mecca. They carried out genocide against Shias of eastern Arabia.

The Ikhwan forces of Ibn Sa'ud indulged in mass killings of mostly innocent victims, including women and children. Ibn Sa'ud's cousin Abdallah bin Mussallem bin Jalawi beheaded 250 members of the Mutair tribe, and Ibn Sa'ud himself set an example for his followers by personally beheading 18 rebels in a public square of the town of Artawaya. The Shammar tribe suffered 410 deaths, the Bani Khalid 640, and the Najran a staggering 7,000. Ibn Sa'ud used massacres to subdue his enemies No less than a 400,000 people were killed and wounded in the Saudi campaign to subdue the Arabian Peninsula. The Ikhwan did not take prisoners and mostly killed the vanquished. Well over a million inhabitants of the territories conquered by Ibn Sa'ud fled to Kuwait, Egypt, Iraq, Jordan, and Syria. By the time Ibn Sa'ud and his family had subdued the country, they had carried out 40,000 public executions and 350,000 amputations, respectively 1 and 4 percent of the estimated population of 4 million.[39]

To summarize the brutality and the insensitivity of Ibn Sa'ud's regime, one has to understand the degree of devastation of the country, which he proudly named after himself in 1932. At the turn of the twentieth century, the population of the territory that became Saudi Arabia was an estimated 3.5 million. By the time, 'Abd al-'Aziz established his control over the kingdom, a million inhabitants had fled the country, 400,000 were killed or wounded, 40,000 were beheaded in public squares, and 350,000 had their limbs amputated for opposing the Saudi regime. Thus, to accommodate 'Abd al-'Aziz in his newfound kingdom, an estimated 30 percent of the population chose exile, 13 percent were killed in war or beheaded in public squares, and 10 percent had their limbs amputated. This left only 47 percent of the population of able-bodied men women and children in the kingdom. Assuming that of the 2.5 million people remaining after the ones who fled the country, 1,250,000 were male and the same number were females, both adult and children, and again assuming that most of the people killed, executed, and dismembered were males, then we are forced to assume that by mid-1930s, the total population of males in Saudi Arabia was only 810,000, of whom 460,000 were able bodied and the remaining 350,000 amputees, mutilated by the state. The ratio of able-bodied men to women was almost 1:3. This would explain the destitution of Saudi Arabia before the discovery of oil when most of the able-bodied, educated, cultured, and enterprising men was eliminated, leaving uneducated Bedouins to run the country. This also explains why after each man took four wives, still, there were plenty of women left to marry. In a culture where women had equality

---

[39] Ibid., 24–27.

with men, suddenly, women were the underdog, unable to resist the inequity. This would also explain the need for foreign workers to man most jobs in the kingdom and why the Saudis have not been able to raise a large enough army, having to depend on the Americans for the defense of their country.

In the hot wind and sand-blown desert, this genocide and iniquity went unnoticed by the world, while similar crimes later during the century in Nazi Germany caused public outcry. It was so because it was a Muslim carrying out genocide against Muslims in the name of Islam with the British-supplied arms for the greater glory of the British Empire. Lord Crewe, a British minister, had proclaimed, "What we want is not a united Arabia, but a disunited Arabia split into small principalities under our suzerainty." With ongoing turmoil within his own kingdom and skirmishes with Hejaz and later with Jordan, Iraq, and Yemen, Ibn Sa'ud afforded Britain the comfort of keeping the Arabs and Muslims divided. This protected its commercial and political interests by opposing a unified Muslim state.

1915 to the Present:
Creation of Israel, a State for the Jews in the Land of Islam.

Alfred Milner, son of a university lecturer, was born in Bonn, Germany, in 1854. After childhood in Germany, he came to England and completed his education at the Oxford University. George Joachim Goschen, who was the chancellor of the Exchequer, brought Milner into the British establishment as his private secretary. On Goschen's recommendation, Milner was appointed undersecretary of finance in Egypt in 1890 and was responsible for the taxation of the Egyptian population to pay off the Egyptian debt to the Jewish bankers.

Cecil Rhodes and Milner were members of a secret society that was patterned on the organization of Jesuits. It was also based on political, personal, and family relationship built over a long period. Financial backing came informally from the fortunes of Cecil Rhodes, the Rothschilds, and other Jewish bankers. There was, by the turn of the century, an acceptance of social mixing among the moneyed Jews and the British aristocracy. Among the first initiates to the Round Table were Rhodes, Lord Rothschild, Milner, Grey, Balfour, Lord Rosebery (Lord Rothschild's son-in-law), and Alfred Beit, a Jewish business genius who handled all of Rhodes's business affairs. Among others to join later was Winston Churchill, who as well as his father, Randolph, before him had been allowed to live a life of opulence, thanks to the benevolence of Lord Rothschild.

The Round Table was originally a major fief within the great nexus of power, influence, and privilege controlled by the Cecil family. The method used to control the center of power was penetrating the fields of politics, education, and journalism; recruitment of men of ability chiefly from All Souls College at Oxford; and linking these men to Cecil and the Round Table block by matrimonial alliances and then granting them positions of power and titles. Milner had recruited Leo Amery, a secret Jew, when he was still at Oxford. Amery was an eminent scholar and, at the time, was regarded as the chief imperial theorist. He served as the *London Times* chief war correspondent during the Boer War and into the period leading to the Great War. Milner actively supported his effort to be elected to Parliament in 1906.

David Lloyd George appointed Milner to his war cabinet in 1916 as secretary of war. Milner, a Jew in league with Cecil Rhodes and Lord Nathaniel (Natty) Rothschild, had intrigued to instigate the Boer War in 1902 to establish British control over the whole of southern Africa. The aim was to exploit extensive mineral wealth of that region. After becoming the secretary of war, Milner brought Leo Amery, another Jew albeit a secret one, as the secretary of the war cabinet. Milner had maintained his contacts with the Rothschilds; in 1912, he had helped Natty Rothschild unify the divided Jewish community of London, less than one spiritual head, Chief Rabbi Joseph Herman Hertz.[40]

British cabinet minister Herbert Samuel, a Jew, wrote a memorandum "The Future of Palestine" in 1915, when Palestine was still a Turkish possession. He argued that Palestine should become a British protectorate, "into which the scattered Jews in time swarm back from all quarters of the globe, in due course obtain home rule, and form a Jewish Commonwealth like that of Canada and Australia." Lord Walter Rothschild, Natty Rothschild's successor as the leader of the British Jews, bent the ears of the prime minister, Lloyd George, and his foreign secretary for a declaration about Palestine. Balfour suggested that "they submit a declaration for the cabinet to consider." The declaration was written by Milner and revised several times. The final version was drafted by Leo Amery, which read,

His Majesty's Government view with favor the establishment in Palestine a national home for the Jewish people and will use their best endeavors to facilitate the achievement of this object, it being clearly understood that nothing shall be done which may prejudice the civil and religious rights of existing non-Jewish communities in Palestine, or the rights and political status enjoyed in any other country.

The British cabinet approved the declaration, which was addressed to Lord Walter Rothschild and signed by the foreign secretary Balfour. The Balfour Declaration, as this Jewish Magna Carta came to be known, gave birth illegitimately to the state of Israel. The document was written by Lord Alfred Milner, a Jew; it was revised and finalized by Leo Amery, another Jew, at the behest of Lord Walter Rothschild. And it was addressed to Lord Walter Rothschild, the leader of the

[40] Ferguson, *House of Rothschild*, 259.

Jews of London, for the purpose of the creation of a state for the Jews in the name of the British government on a land that did not belong to the Jews or to the British. In fact, this was an agreement among a group of conspirators belonging to a secret organization that had a long history of fraud and extortion to grab the world's wealth.

In this case, the plotters made full circle in their relationship. Lord George Joachim Goschen, a German Jew, patronized Alfred Milner, another German Jew, and brought him into the English establishment and introduced him to the Rothschilds. Milner, in turn, brought Leo Amery, a secret Jew, into the war cabinet, and they together wrote the Balfour Declaration for the Lord Rothschild. To complete the circle, George Goshen's daughter Phyllis Evelyn Goschen married Francis Cecil Balfour, Foreign Secretary Balfour's son, on August 31, 1920. From among the same group of conspirators, Herbert Samuel was appointed the high commissioner to Palestine to establish Jewish immigration; Rufus Isaacs (as Lord Reading) was appointed viceroy of India with authority over the affairs over Iraq, Persian Gulf, Palestine, and Arabia.

From this time, Zionists became the allies of the British government, and every help and assistance was forthcoming from each government department. Space was provided for the Zionists in Mark Sykes's office with liaison to each government department. The British government provided financial, communication, and travel facilities to those working in the Zionist office. Mark Sykes, who had negotiated the Sykes-Picot agreement giving Syria to the French, was now working for the Zionists, offering them a part of the same territory. In the meantime, through secret communications, the British, USA, France, Italy, and Vatican had all come to a secret understanding of establishment of a Jewish nation in Palestine. The Balfour Declaration was the culmination of secret negotiations and maneuverings among these powers whose price would be paid to the international Jewry for financial and intelligence support in the war against the Germans and the Turks.

The Koran speaks of the deceivers thus:

> O you who believe! Take not for friends Unbelievers rather than Believers: do you wish to offer Allah an open proof against yourselves? (4:144)

Allah, in the covenant, also reminds the believers repeatedly not to take the *kafirun* (infidels), Jews, and Christians as their *awliya* (friends and protectors) in place of believers. They are friends and protectors unto one another. He who among believers turns to them is one of them. Allah does not guide those who are unjust and evildoers (*zalimun)*. He from among the believers who turns to them is from among the *kafirun, Munafiqeen, mushrikun,* and *zalimun.*

1921–1970 CE:
Treaty of Versailles: The *Munafiqeen,* the Traitors Among Us.

Faisal's camel corps presented a pretense that the Arabs themselves liberated Syria. In fact, there were a million British troops fighting in the Middle East in 1918 and only thirty-five hundred Husseini troops, and on the face of it was a British war of conquest over the Arabs and not a war of liberation for the Arabs. The British, on May 9, 1916, in a secret convention, had already promised Arab Syria to the French (Sykes-Picot Agreement) and on November 2, 1917, in the Balfour Declaration gave away Arab Palestine to the Jews. The Lawrence-Hussein-sons puppet show was being cleverly orchestrated from London. Each one of the players understood their role and the reward for their part except Hussein and sons. The ambiguous language, willful face-to-face lies, secret agreements, double dealings, deception, flattery, and bribery as a skill and art had become the hallmark of English diplomacy over the previous one hundred years. The Arabs and the Bedouins had their own share of guile and cunningness; they were, however, no match for the Anglos and the Franks as the next one hundred years were to reveal. And the Arab leaders never learned.

For his treachery, Sharif Hussein started to receive his reward in gold sovereigns from March 1916 onward, three months before he announced his revolt. The total shipments were in the amount of £1,928,000. The payments were broken down into five categories representing the four armies under the command of Hussein's sons and an allotment for the upkeep of the mosque at Kaaba and for hajj facilities as well as for the operation of Hussein's government in Mecca and Jeddah. Forty thousand pounds per month was allocated to Faisal, £30,000 to Abdullah, £20,000 each for Ali and Zeid, and £15,000 for expenses at Mecca and Jeddah. The year 1916 must have been the lowest point in the history of Islam. At that time, it was surrounded by powerful enemies around the world; and inside, in its very heart, the Kaaba, it was being destroyed by traitors to Islam. For the first time in the history of Islam, the very upkeep of the Holy Mosque of Mecca, the Kaaba, and the hajj expenses were being paid for by the *kafireen* at the behest of the *Munafiqeen* under the claim of their lineage to the holy prophet. In this claim of their bloodline, they forgot the teachings of the Koran and the example of conduct set by the prophet.

The covenant of Allah states:

When you hold secret counsel, do it not for iniquity and hostility and disobedience to the teachings of the Rasool; but do it for righteousness and self-restraint; and fear Allah, to Whom ye shall be brought back.

The Satan inspires secret counsels, in order that he may cause grief to the Believers; but he cannot harm them in the least, except as Allah permits; and on Allah let the Believers put their trust.

No believer, individual, community, or ruler shall make a compact on behalf of the *ummah* or part of it in secret with the unbelievers. Islam regards secret pacts with enemies and hostile actions against one's own people as treason. During the blessed prophet's lifetime in Medina, some people professed Islam yet conspired with the *kafirun* against their fellow Muslims. The Koran has the following description of these *Munafiqeen*.

> Fain would they deceive Allah and those who believe, but they only deceive themselves and realize it not! In their hearts is a disease; and Allah has increased their disease: and grievous is the penalty they incur, because they are false to themselves. When it is said to them: "Make not mischief on the earth," they say: "Why, we only want to make peace!" Of a surety, they are the ones who make mischief, but they do not realize. (Al-Baqarah 2:8-12, Koran)

> Allah will throw back their mockery on them and give them rope in their trespasses; so they will wander like blind ones to and fro. They have bartered guidance for error: but their traffic is profitless and they have lost true direction. Their similitude is that of a man who kindled a fire; when it lighted all around him, Allah took away their light and left them in utter darkness. So they could not see. Deaf, dumb and blind, they will not return to the path. (Al-Baqarah 2:15-18, Koran)

1973 to 1979:
Betrayal of the Covenant: Treason.

Anwar Sadat and the Egyptian Army won partial victory over the Jewish state of Israel in 1973. The victory made Sadat a hero in the eyes of many Arabs, if not equal to then almost comparable to the great Arab hero Gamal Abdel Nasser. Puffed up by success and sycophancy from the likes of Henry Kissinger, Sadat forgot his own roots and began to take advice and comfort from Kissinger and the Israeli lobby in Washington. Against the advice of his closest advisers and the leaders of other Arab countries, he made a secret trip to Israel and addressed the Knesset, the Israeli parliament. Under the American tutelage and patronage, he abandoned his Arab allies, negotiated, and signed a peace treaty with many secret appendices with Israel at the expense of the Palestinians and Syrians. Therefore, all Palestine and the Golan Heights are under Israeli occupation. The Arabs are disunited and in disarray. Sadat sold out Egyptian sovereignty, the Islamic nation, and the holy Islamic places in Jerusalem for four billion dollars a year. Sadat took Jews and Christians as his *awliya* and willfully disobeyed the covenant that every Muslim, if he was a believer, has pledged to obey. He also disobeyed the provisions of the covenant of Yathrib and the prophet's teaching:

> Just as the bond to Allah is indivisible, all the believers shall stand behind the commitment of the least of them. All believers are bonded one to another to the exclusion of other men. This Pax Islamica is one and indivisible. No believer shall enter a separate peace without all other believers whenever there is fighting in the cause of God, but will do so only on the basis of equality and justice to all others. In every expedition for the cause of God we undertake, all parties to the covenant shall fight shoulder to shoulder as one man. All believers shall avenge the blood of one another when any one falls fighting in the cause of God.

1980–2007:
Muslim Complicity in the Invasion of Iran:
The Circle of Evil.

In 1980, Iraq's Saddam Hussein was suddenly a big-time international "player" invited to the gaudy palaces of the Saudi Arabian monarchy. But there was an ulterior motive behind the flattering invitation. Saddam's army was the new protector of the petro-rich against the Iranian hordes.[41]

In summer 1980, Iraq's wily president, Saddam Hussein, saw opportunities in the chaos sweeping the Persian Gulf. Iran's Islamic

---

[41] Robert Parry, Consortium, December 31, 2002.

revolution had terrified the Saudi princes and other Arab royalty who feared uprisings against their own corrupt lifestyles. Saddam's help was sought too by CIA-backed Iranian exiles who wanted a base to challenge the fundamentalist regime of Ayatollah Ruhollah Khomeini. And as always, the Western powers were worried about the Middle East oil fields. Because of geography and his formidable Soviet-supplied army, Saddam was suddenly a popular fellow.

On August 5, 1980, the Saudi rulers welcomed Saddam to Riyadh for his first state visit to Saudi Arabia, the first for any Iraqi president. The Saudis obviously wanted something. At those fateful meetings, amid the luxury of the ornate palaces, the Saudi royal family encouraged Saddam Hussein to invade Iran. The Saudis also passed on a secret message about President Carter's geopolitical desires.

During that summer of 1980, President Carter's failure to free fifty-two American hostages held in Iran was threatening his political survival. This multisided political intrigue shaped the history from 1980 to the present day. Iraq's invasion of Iran in September 1980 deteriorated into eight years of bloody trench warfare that killed and maimed an estimated one million people. This war generated billions of dollars in profits for the West and their well-connected arms merchants.

Haig's Talking Points. Robert Parry in his article in the Consortium on December 31, 2002, states that he gained access to the Iran-Contra investigation documents, including papers marked secret and top secret, that apparently had been left behind by accident in a remote Capitol Hill storage room. Those papers filled in twenty years of missing pieces of the intrigue that led to the Iraqi invasion of Iran. The papers clarified President Reagan's early strategy for a clandestine foreign policy hidden from Congress and the American people. One such document was two-page talking points prepared by Secretary of

State Alexander Haig for a briefing of President Reagan. Marked top secret/sensitive, the paper recounted Haig's first trip to the Middle East in April 1981.

In the report, Haig wrote that he was impressed with bits of useful intelligence that he had learned. Both Egypt's Anwar Sadat and Saudi prince Fahd explained that Iran was receiving military spares for US equipment from Israel. This fact might have been less surprising to President Reagan, whose intermediaries allegedly collaborated with Israeli officials in 1980 to smuggle weapons to Iran behind President Carter's back.

But Haig followed that comment with another stunning assertion. It was also interesting to confirm that President Carter gave the Iraqis a green light to launch the war against Iran through Fahd. In other words, according to Haig's information, Saudi prince Fahd, later King Fahd, claimed that President Carter, apparently hoping to strengthen US hand in the Middle East and desperate to pressure Iran over the stalled hostage talks, gave clearance to Saddam's invasion of Iran. If true, Jimmy Carter, the peacemaker, had encouraged a war. Haig's written report contained no other details about the green light. The paper represented the first documented corroboration of Iran's long-held belief that the United States backed Iraq's 1980 invasion.

The Iraqi invasion did make Iran more desperate to get US spare parts for its air and ground forces. Yet the Carter administration continued to demand that the American hostages be freed before military shipments could resume. But according to house task force documents that Parry found in the storage room, the Republicans were more accommodating.

Secret FBI wiretaps revealed that an Iranian banker, the late Cyrus Hashemi who supposedly was helping President Carter on the hostage talks, was assisting Republicans with arms shipments to Iran and peculiar money transfers in fall 1980. Hashemi's elder brother, Jamshid, testified that the Iran arms shipments via Israel resulted from secret meetings in Madrid between the GOP campaign director William J. Casey and a radical Islamic mullah named Mehdi Karroubi.

For whatever reasons, on Election Day 1980, President Carter still had failed to free the hostages, and Ronald Reagan won in a landslide. Within minutes of President Reagan's inauguration on January 20, 1981, the hostages finally were freed. In the following weeks, the new Reagan administration put in place discreet channels to Middle East powers as Haig flew to the region for a round of high-level consultations. Haig met with Iraq's chief allies, Saudi Arabia and Egypt, and with Israel, which was continuing to support Iran as a counterweight to Iraq and the Arab states.

On April 8, 1981, Haig ended his first round of meetings in Riyadh. After Haig's return to Washington, his top secret talking points fleshed out for President Reagan the actual agreements that were reached at the private sessions in Saudi Arabia, as well as at other meetings in Egypt and Israel. "As we discussed before my Middle East trip," Haig explained to President Reagan, "I proposed to President Sadat, Israel's Prime Minister Menachem Begin and Crown Prince Fahd that we establish a private channel for the consideration of particularly sensitive matters of concern to you. Each of the three picked up on the proposal and asked for early meetings."

Haig wrote that, upon his return, he immediately dispatched his counselor, Robert Bud McFarlane, to Cairo and Riyadh to formalize those channels. He held extremely useful meetings with both Sadat and Fahd, Haig boasted. These early contacts with Fahd, Sadat, and Begin solidified their three countries as the cornerstones of the administration's clandestine foreign policy of the 1980s: the Saudis as the moneymen, the Israelis as the middlemen, and the Egyptians as a ready source for Soviet-made equipment.

Although President Carter had brokered a historic peace treaty between Egypt and Israel, Sadat, Begin, and Fahd had all been alarmed at signs of US weakness, especially Washington's inability to protect the Shah of Iran from ouster in 1979. Haig's talking points captured that relief at President Carter's removal from office. "It is clear that your policies of firmness toward the Soviets have restored Saudi and Egyptian confidence in the leadership of the US," Haig wrote for the presentation to his boss.

Both Fahd and Sadat went much further than ever before in offering to be supportive. Haig said Sadat offered to host a forward headquarters for the rapid deployment force, including a full-time presence of US military personnel. Sadat also outlined his strategy for invading Libya to disrupt Mu'ammar al-Gaddhafi's intervention in Chad. Haig reported that Prince Fahd was also very enthusiastic about President Reagan's foreign policy. Fahd had agreed in principle to fund arms sales to the Pakistanis and other states in the region, Haig wrote. The Saudi leader was promising too to help the US economy by committing his oil-rich nation to a position of no drop in production of petroleum. "These channels promise to be extremely useful in forging compatible policies with the Saudis and Egyptians," Haig continued. "Both men value the 'special status' you have conferred on them and both value confidentiality."

In the following years, the Reagan administration would exploit the special status with all three countries to skirt constitutional restrictions on executive war-making powers. Secretly, the administration would tilt back and forth in the Iran-Iraq War between aiding the Iranians with missiles and spare parts and helping the Iraqis with intelligence and indirect military shipments. According to a sworn affidavit by a former Reagan national security staffer, Howard Teicher, the administration enlisted the Egyptians in a secret Bear Spares program that gave the United States access to Soviet-designed military equipment. Teicher asserted that the Reagan administration funneled some of those weapons to Iraq and also arranged other shipments of devastating cluster bombs that Saddam's air force dropped on Iranians troops.

In 1984, facing congressional rejection of continued CIA funding of the Nicaraguan contra rebels, President Reagan exploited the special status again. He tapped into the Saudi slush funds for money to support the Nicaraguan contra rebels in their war in Central America. The president also authorized secret weapons shipments to Iran in another arms-for-hostages scheme, with the profits going to off-the-shelf intelligence operations. That gambit, like the others, was protected by walls of deniability and outright lies.

When Parry interviewed Haig several years ago, he asked him if he was troubled by the pattern of deceit that had become the norm among international players in the 1980s. "Oh, no, no, no, no!" he boomed, shaking his head. "On that kind of thing? No. Come on. Jesus! God! You know, you'd better get out and read Machiavelli or somebody else because I think you are living in a dream world! People do what their national interest tells them to do and if it means lying to a friendly nation, they are going to lie through their teeth."

But sometimes the game playing did have unintended consequences. In 1990, a decade after Iraq's messy invasion of Iran, an embittered Saddam Hussein was looking for payback from the sheikhdoms that he felt had egged him into war. Saddam was especially furious with Kuwait for slant drilling into Iraq's oil fields and refusing to extend more credit. Again, Saddam was looking for a signal from the US president, this time George Bush. When Saddam explained his confrontation with Kuwait to US ambassador April Glaspie, he received an ambiguous reply, a reaction he apparently perceived as another green light. Eight days later, Saddam unleashed his army into Kuwait, an invasion that required five hundred thousand US troops and thousands more dead to reverse.

This document is a window into the workings of the circle of evil, the agents of Euro-Christianity, Zionism, and *Munafiqeen* that are out to destroy Islam. Saddam, Fahd, Sadat, Begin, and the agents of the West started a chain reaction in 1980 that set off the Iran-Iraq War, the Israeli invasion of Lebanon, the Iraqi invasion of Kuwait, the subsequent multination invasion of Iraq, the UN embargo of Iraq, the NATO invasion of Afghanistan, the ongoing occupation of Iraq, the second Israeli war against Lebanon, and the ongoing occupation and massacre of the Palestinians.

During the last twenty-seven years, the turmoil initiated by Saddam, Fahd and his Saudi clan, and Sadat in collaboration with the West and Israel has killed four million Muslims, both Arab and Iranians. This circle of evil has, in the last twenty-seven-years, prevented Islam from freeing itself from the clutches of slavery of the West. Once again, the *Yahudi-Salibi* ingenuity enrolled and used a *Munafiq* to sow the seeds of discord in the Islamic world.

1979 to 1991:
Saddam, the Servant of the *Kafireen*, Traitor to Islam.

Saddam Hussein replaced al-Bakr as president of Iraq in July 1979. The bloodbath that followed eliminated all potential opposition to him. Saddam was now the master of Iraq with no one around him daring to question his actions. Two actions that he initiated led the Islamic community to disastrous disunity and debt. He attacked his fellow Muslims, Iran in 1980 and Kuwait in 1990.

The Iran-Iraq War turned out to be a battle between two egomaniac personalities, each with a Messiah complex, with neither of them willing to call a truce and a halt to the hostilities. The result was emaciation and bleeding of both countries to near bankruptcy. The Iraqi troops launched a full-scale invasion of Iran on September 22, 1980. France supplied high-tech weapons to Iraq, and the Soviet Union was Iraq's largest weapon supplier. Israel provided arms to Iran, hoping to bleed both the nations by prolonging the war. At least ten nations sold arms to both warring nations to profit from the conflict.

The United States followed a more duplicitous policy toward both the warring parties to prolong the war and cause maximum damage to them. The United States followed a more duplicitous policy toward the warring parties to prolong the war and cause maximum damage to both of them. The United States and Iraq restored diplomatic relations in November 1984. Washington extended a $400 million credit guarantee for the export of US goods to Iraq. The CIA established a direct Washington-to-Baghdad link to provide the Iraqis with faster intelligence from US satellites.[42] The satellite data provided to Iraqis was some factual and some misleading information. Casey, the CIA director, was urging Iraqi officials to carry out more attacks on Iran, especially on economic targets.[43]

The US policy toward Iran was two faced as it followed two tracks at the same time. On the one hand, the US government carried out a covert program to undermine the government of Iran[44]. Starting in 1982, the CIA provided $100,000 a month to a group in Paris called the Front for the Liberation of Iran, headed by Ali Amini,

---

[42] Stephen Engelberg, "Iran and Iraq Got Doctored Data, US Officials Say," *New York Times*, Jan. 12, 1987, A1, A6.

[43] Bob Woodward, *Veil*, 480.

[44] The Tower Commission, *President's Special Review Board* (Bantam Books, New York), 294–95.

who had presided over the reversion of Iranian oil to foreign control after the CIA-backed coup in 1953. The United States also provided support to two Iranian paramilitary groups based in Turkey, one of them headed by Gen. Bahram Aryana, the Shah's army chief.[45] The United States also carried out clandestine radio broadcasts into Iran from Egypt, calling for Khomeini's overthrow and urging support for Bakhtiar. Simultaneously, the United States pursued the second track of clandestinely providing arms and intelligence information to Iran in 1985 and 1986. In 1984, Washington launched Operation Staunch in an effort to dry up Iran's sources of arms supplies by pressuring US allies to stop supplying arms to Iran. While Washington was pretending to be neutral in the war and trying to make everyone else stop selling arms to Iran, the United States made secret arms transfers to Iran and encouraged Israel to do the same.[46] The United States provided intelligence to Iranians, which was a mixture of factual and bogus information. The USA did, however, provide full critical data to Iran before its critical victory in the Fao Peninsula in February 1986.

The Iran-Iraq War was not between good and evil. Islam forbids fighting among the Muslims and forbids murder and the taking of life unless it is in the cause of justice. Saddam Hussein launched a murderous war to regain a few square miles of territory that his country had relinquished freely in 1975 border negotiations. There were one and a half million Muslim casualties in this senseless fraternal war. The war ended in a cease-fire that essentially left prewar borders unchanged. The covenant of Allah not only forbids such an internecine war but also provides a mechanism for dispute resolution. Instead of condemning the aggressor, the Arab states

---

[45] Leslie H. Gelb, "US Said to Aid Iranian Exiles in Combat and Political Units," *New York Times*, March 7, 1982, A1, A12.

[46] Leslie Gelb, "Iran Said to Get Large-Scale Arms from Israel, Soviets and Europeans," *New York Times*, March 8, 1982, A1, A10; Anthony Cordesman, *The Iran-Iraq War*, 31.

sided with Saddam Hussein, providing him with funds for further bloodletting. Saddam Hussein used banned chemical weapons against fellow Muslims, the Iranians and Kurds. The eight-year-long war exhausted both countries. The primary responsibility for the prolonged bloodletting must rest with the governments of the two countries, the ruthless military regime of Saddam Hussein and the ruthless clerical regime of Ayatollah Khomeini in Iran. Whatever his religious convictions, Khomeini had no qualms about sending his followers, including young boys, to their deaths for his own greater glory. This callous disregard for human life was no less characteristic of Saddam Hussein.

Saudi Arabia gave $25.7 billion and Kuwait $10 billion to Iraq to fuel the war and the killing of Muslims by Muslims. Saddam Hussein also owed the Soviets, USA, and Europe $40 billion for the purchase of arms. The cost of war to the Iranians was even greater. The rest of the world community sold arms for eight and a half years and watched the bloodletting. The USA sold arms and information to both sides to prolong the war strategically and to profit and gain influence and bases in the Gulf countries. Ayatollah Khomeini, in particular, was a hypocrite in dealing with Israel in secret, especially when his public pronouncements were venomously anti-Israel.

Iran, Iraq, and all the Arab states of the Persian Gulf took the Western countries, the Soviet Union, and Israel as their *awliya*, in contradiction to the commandments of the covenant. The ayatollah and his clerics should have known and understood their obligations to Allah and to their people as spelled out in Allah's covenant. The uncontrolled Arab-Iranian hostility left a deep, festering wound in the body of the nation of Islam. The West made gains by setting up permanent bases in Saudi Arabia, Oman, the United Arab Emirates, Bahrain, Qatar, and Kuwait. This is the land that Muhammad, the Blessed messenger of Allah, freed from the infidels, only to be handed over to infidels by the *Munafiqeen.*

1990 to 2006:
Saddam Opens the Gateway of Islam to the *Kafireen.*

On August 2, 1990, Saddam Hussein was into mischief again. He invaded and occupied Kuwait. The sheikh of Kuwait and his family fled to Saudi Arabia. A coalition of Arabs, NATO, and many other countries carried a massive bombardment of Baghdad and other parts of Iraq on January 17, 1991, destroying the military installations, industrial units, and civilian infrastructure of Iraq. On February 24, 1991, American-led forces launched a ground offensive into Iraq and defeated the Iraqi Army. A United Nations resolution placed Iraq under an embargo till Iraq gave up all its biological and chemical weapons and also all nuclear weapon-making material.

After the Kuwait war at the invitation of King Fahd, the USA has continued to maintain large operational army and air force bases and command and control facilities that enable them to monitor all air and sea traffic as well as all civilian and military communications in the Middle East. Bahrain, in the meantime, has become the headquarters of the naval fleet command. Qatar has the longest runways in the Middle East and host to the United Stated Central Command Center. The Middle East, at the beginning of the twenty-first century, is under the absolute military and economic grip of the USA and NATO. The circle of evil—the *Yahudi, Salibi,* and *Munafiqeen*—continues to dominate the lives of the Muslims.

1992 to the Present:
The American Empire:

The Circle of Evil.

After Saddam Hussein's Iraq was thoroughly trounced by the United States and its NATO and Arab allies in February 1991, the Western countries used their power in the United Nations Security Council to set up an embargo on Iraq. No food, medicines, or equipment for use in the reconstruction of the destroyed power and water purification plants was allowed into Iraq. Over the following twelve years, over half a million Iraqi children died and five million children suffered from malnutrition and disease. Iraq suffered from depravation and disease created by the United Nations, a world body established to bring about peace and reduce suffering in the world. Eventually, when the UN did start the oil-for-food program, the funds were skimmed by the United Nations to pay for war reparations, and the food aid meant for the victims of the embargo did not always get to them.

The New American Century.

Iraq was thoroughly humiliated and defeated in February 1991. This was considered by the Americans to be a magnificent victory. In fact, the war was between a war-weary Iraq, with a population of eighteen million people, and a coalition of the world's most developed countries and the wealthy Arabs. The Arabs supplied over a hundred billion dollars and all the air, land, and naval bases to fight this war. After its humiliating defeat in Vietnam, the USA had avoided any frontal assault on any country till the war on Iraq. Actually, the Americans had been bold enough to attack two ministates, Granada and Panama, which had only parade ground armies and won hands down.

In early 1990s, emboldened with these victories and by the fall of Soviet Russia from internal decay, a group of Republican politicians founded the Project for the New American Century. They planned and conspired to take the White House and the two other branches of government as well. They began to lay on the drawing board their vision about how the United States should move in the world when the time came.

Donald Rumsfeld, Dick Cheney, James Woolsey, Paul Wolfowitz, Richard Perle, Bill Kristol, James Bolton, Zalmay M. Khalilzad, William Bennett, Dan Quayle, and Jeb Bush led the Project for the New American Century. They were representing ideas and ideologies of faceless, influential, wealthy individuals and corporations that helped them set up think tanks and provided them funds to buy up media outlets—newspapers, magazines, TV networks, radio talk shows, and cable channels. Through the inside manipulations of the governor of Florida, Jeb Bush, and through the friendship of Dick Cheney with his fishing pal, justice of the Supreme Court Antonin Scalia, George W. Bush was selected the president of the United States. The new president was a foreign policy novice and described by some as intellectually incurious who had struggled with alcoholism all his life. The Western governments have powerful diplomatic, economic, and military alliance that has an edge over the rest of the world.

Beyond what has been stated, more than the diplomatic, economic, and military strength of their alliance is the power provided to United States, Britain, and Israel by the traitors of Islam. In our age, we have people who think that they can get the best both the worlds by compromising their nations and Islam's interests with the enemy. They constitute the other half of the circle of evil that is destroying Islam. They pretend to be Muslims. They pray, they fast, and they go for the hajj pilgrimage. Their fingers robotically sift through their prayer beads. Allah has bestowed on them so much wealth and power that their next one hundred generations will be able to live lavishly off their wealth. They love the luxury of their private Gulf Stream jets and granite places with silken rugs and gold plumbing fixtures. Dozens of attendants rush to their raised brow. Are they happy? Moreover, are they in peace with Allah's grace upon them? No. Wealth and power is not enough; they want more of it.

Nine countries collectively have acted as the Muslim part of the circle of evil. They are Egypt, Pakistan, Bahrain, Kuwait, Qatar, United Arab Emirates, Oman, Jordan, and Saudi Arabia. In the Afghanistan and Iraq invasions of 2002–2006, an estimated 260,000 Muslim men, women, and children were killed and hundreds of thousands injured and millions made homeless by bombing. Two sovereign Islamic nations have been decimated, their state structure shattered, and economies annihilated. It would take at least thirty years to rebuild these nations and rehabilitate their citizens. The loss was not to the Taliban or to Saddam Hussein. The loss is to the unity of the *ummah*, the unity that has been ordained in the covenant with Allah. Who will assist in the destruction of Islam perpetrated by a secret cabal of *Yahudi-Salibi* conspirators in Washington? In the twenty-first century, treason is hard to hide but hard to explain.

Pakistan: Pakistan's illegitimate dictator Musharraf, who had stolen the government by force of arms, craved for legitimacy. Power corrupts, and absolute power corrupts absolutely. Any power and wealth acquired with *harramma* will continue to be maintained with *harramma*. Those who promote disunity of the *ummah* are promised severe retribution. Disobedience of the covenant of Allah is haram and is cursed. Haram will breed more haram and Allah's wrath. It reminds us of how the scales of Allah's justice, the two hands of Allah—His mercy and His wrath—are reflected in the human domain, where people have been appointed Allah's vicegerents. Deeds of goodness and wholesomeness are associated with mercy, paradise, and the beautiful. Evil and corruption is rewarded with wrath, hell, and the ugly.

The other "Muslims" who perpetrate evil association with the *kafireen* are princes and kings of Arabia, the land of Islam, Allah's blessed prophet, and the holy shrines of Mecca and Medina. Bahrain, Kuwait, Qatar, United Arab Emirates, Jordan, Oman, and Saudi Arabia united with the evil to destroy the lives of 50 million Muslims in Iraq and Afghanistan and the faith of 1.5 billion believers.

Bahrain: Although Bahrain is a constitutional monarchy, it is run like a family enterprise by the Al Khalifah family. In 1992, the sheikh gave himself the title of king. The king, the crown prince, the commander in chief, the prime minister, the defense minister, housing minister, the interior minister, the oil and development minister, and the foreign ministers are related through blood and marriage, and they all are kith and kin of the Al Khalifah family, afraid to share governance with their 724,000 subjects. This family has carved most of Bahrain's agriculturally fertile land for their own private use. Members of the Al Khalifah family control over 80 percent of the agriculture land in Bahrain. They have allocated themselves virtually all the coastal land. Thirty-three percent of all oil revenue goes to the members of the Al Khalifah family; the instruments of the state are run on the rest. Two percent of the population owns 90 percent of the wealth of the islands. To safeguard the wealth and position of this family, the Al Khalifah clan has secret treaties with the United States to protect the family from their subjects and from their neighbors. They act as the springboard for the United Stated Army, Marines, and Navy in their two invasions of Iraq and Afghanistan and in the ongoing hostilities against Iran. The Al Khalifah family has permitted the American Fifth Fleet to be based in Bahrain. The Fifth Fleet, for over thirty years, has menaced the Persian Gulf and has worked against the freedom of Iran and Iraq.

Kuwait: Kuwait, an oil-rich patch of desert, was carved out of the Basra district of the Ottoman Empire through the connivance of the British to circumvent the German plan to build railways from Berlin through the Ottoman Empire to Kuwait in the Persian Gulf. Kuwait, being the only deepwater harbor on the western edge of the Persian Gulf, provided the British with a supply and refueling center for its navy. It has continued to be subservient to the *kafireen* to maintain the Sabah family's power and riches. The Sabah family, like other Arab monarchies, runs their country as a family incorporation, all ministries being run by the family. Most of the country's wealth reverts to the royal family.

2003 to Present:
Muslim Complicity in the Invasion of Iraq:
Saudi Arabia.

Bahrain, Kuwait, Qatar, United Arab Emirates, Oman, Jordan, Pakistan, and Saudi Arabia willingly provided Britain and the United States facilities for overflight, air operations, basing, port facilities, and facilities to preposition equipment for the Iraq invasion. It should come as no surprise to Muslims around the world that the Saudi royal family directly participated in the American invasion of Iraq and the slaughter of about 260,000 Iraqis and in the destruction of Iraq's infrastructure.

Treason Among Us.

On Friday, November 15, 2002, the Saudi ambassador Prince Bandar bin Sultan came to the Oval Office to see Pres. George W. Bush. Dick Cheney and Condoleezza Rice were also there. Bandar had been a long-term fixture in Washington, having served during four

American presidencies. He had a ready access to American presidents, particularly the first President Bush, and the Bush family regarded him as a member of the family, where the prince had acquired the name Bandar Bush. On the same token, the Saudis had reputedly invested $1.4 billion in the Bush family, and the American president could safely be named George Bush Ibn Sa'ud. In this relationship, the Saudis do the American bidding in the Middle East, and the Americans protect the royal family interests and investments. In spite of this deep relationship and $3 trillion Saudi investment and support to the American economy, the Saudis do not have the resolve and will to use their clout to solve the Palestinian problem.

Bandar handed the president a private letter from Prince Abdullah, the de facto ruler of Saudi Arabia, and provided an English translation of the text. The text, in summary, congratulated the president's victory achieved by the Republican Party under his leadership. It stated that Prince Bandar was authorized to convey and discuss his message to the president face-to-face. As instructed Bandar then said formally, "Since 1994, we have been in constant contact with you at the highest level regarding what needs to be done with Iraq and Iraqi regime. Now, Mr. President, we want hear from you directly on your serious intention regarding this subject so we can adjust and coordinate so we can make right policy decision."

In 1994, King Fahd had proposed to President Clinton a joint US-Saudi covert action to overthrow Saddam, and Crown Prince Abdullah in April 2002 had suggested to Pres. George Bush that they spend up to $1 billion in a joint operation with the CIA. "Every time we meet, we are surprised that the United States asks us to give our impression about what can be done regarding Saddam Hussein," Bandar said, suggesting that the repeated requests caused them to "begin to doubt how serious America is about the issue of regime change. Now tell us what you are going to do."

Bandar read, "If you have a serious intention, we will not hesitate so that our two military people can then implement and discuss in order to support the American military action or campaign. This will make Saudi Arabia a major ally for the United States."

President Bush thanked the ambassador and said that he always appreciated the crown prince's views; he was a good friend and a great ally. Bush added that when he made up his mind on the military option, he would contact the crown prince before his final decision.[47]

On January 11, 2003, Dick Cheney invited Prince Bandar bin Sultan, the Saudi ambassador, to his West Wing. Present on this occasion were Defense Secretary Don Rumsfeld and Joint Chief of Staff Chairman Gen. Richard Myers. The American defense officials appraised Bandar, a foreigner, of their battle plans against Iraq, even before Colin Powell, the US secretary of state, knew of them. General Meyers unfurled a large map of the area and explained the first part of the battle plan. The plan involved a massive bombing campaign over several days. The United States would drop on Iraq four times the bombs that destroyed it during the forty-two days of the Gulf War. And during those days, Americans dropped more bombs on Iraq than were dropped by all the combatants during the Second World War. Bandar was informed that his fellow Arab and Muslim Iraqis were to be exploded, incinerated, and blown to bits with four times the explosives than had ever been used on this planet previously. Special forces, intelligence teams, and air strikes would be launched through the five-hundred-mile Saudi border with Iraq.

The next day, Bandar met George W. Bush. The Saudis wanted an assurance that, this time, Saddam would be totally finished, and the president reminded the ambassador of his briefings from "Dick, Rummy, and General Meyers," in which they had assured Bandar that,

---

[47] Woodward, *Plan of Attack*, 228–30.

this time, Saddam indeed would be toast.[48] Bandar flew to Riyadh and provided a verbatim report of the battle plan to Crown Prince Abdullah. Abdullah advised Bandar to maintain strict secrecy till they could figure out their next move.

On Friday, March 14, 2003, Bandar was shown into the Oval Office; Cheney, Rice, and Card were there. Bandar was unshaven, he had put on weight, and the buttons on his jacket were straining. He was tired, nervous, and excited. He was sweating profusely. "What's wrong with you?" the president asked Bandar. "Don't you have a razor to shave with?"

"Mr. President," Bandar replied, "I promised myself I would not shave until this war starts."

"Well, then, you are going to shave very soon."

"I hope so," Bandar said. "By the time this war starts, I will be like bin Laden." He then indicated a long beard of a foot or two.

On Wednesday, March 19, 2003, at 7:30 p.m., Condoleezza Rice told Bandar, "The president has asked me to tell you that we are going to war. At about 9:00 p.m., all hell will break loose."

"Tell him he will be in our prayers and hearts," Bandar said. "God help us all."

Bandar then called Crown Prince Abdullah in a prearranged code in reference to an oasis, Roda outside Riyadh. "Tonight the forecast is there will be heavy rain in the Roda," Bandar said from his car phone to Saudi Arabia.

Abdullah asked, "Do you know how soon the storm is going to hit?"

Bandar replied, "Sir, I don't know, but watch TV."

---

[48] Ibid., 263–68.

The American air campaign against Iraq was essentially managed from inside Saudi Arabia, where American military commanders operated an air command center and launched refueling tankers, F-16 fighter jets, and sophisticated intelligence-gathering flights, according to American officials.[49] Senior officials from both countries told the Associated Press that the royal family permitted widespread military operations to be staged from inside the kingdom during the invasion of Iraq.

Between 250 and 300 air force planes were staged from Saudi Arabia, including AWACS, C-130s, refueling tankers, and F-16 fighter jets, during the height of the war, the officials said. Air and military operations during the war were permitted at the Tabuk air base and the Arar regional airport near the Iraq border. "We operated the command center in Saudi Arabia. We operated aeroplanes out of Saudi Arabia, as well as sensors and tankers," said Gen. T. Michael Moseley, a top air force general who was the architect of the campaign. During the war, US officials held a media briefing about the air war from Qatar although the air command center was in Saudi Arabia—a move designed to prevent inflaming the Saudi public.

When the war started, the Saudis allowed cruise missiles to be fired from navy ships across their airspace into Iraq. The Saudis provided tens of millions of dollars in discounted and free oil, gas, and fuel for American forces. During the war, a stream of oil delivery trucks, at times, stretched for miles outside the Prince Sultan air base, said a senior US military planner. The Saudis were influential in keeping down the world oil prices during the run-up to the Iraq War by pumping 1.5 million barrels a day. The Saudis kept Jordan supplied with cheap oil for its support in the Iraq War. Although King Abdullah of Jordan had met with the leaders of Turkey, Syria, and

[49] "New Details on Saudi Help in Iraq War," Associated Press, April 25, 2004, http://wwwfoxnews.com/story/0,933,118084,00.html.FoxNews.

Egypt and made well-publicized statements against the war on Iraq, he had secretly committed to support the American war effort against Iraq. American troops and intelligence services operated from inside the Jordanian borders in their invasion of Iraq.

Saddam Hussein was a traitor to Islam and a tyrant and deserved humiliation. However, at the eve of the war, he contacted Egypt for asylum. The Egyptians, at the behest of the Americans, refused. Prince Bandar had been informed directly by Hosni Mubarak. Yet Iraqis were attacked and the country decimated.[50]

The Saudis, Egyptians, and other Arab rulers were aware of the magnitude of the planned air attack on the Iraqi people. The invasion of Iraq ostensibly was to depose Saddam and his regime. Saddam tried to abdicate, leave Iraq, and sought asylum in Egypt. Yet the Arab rulers let the invasion go unchallenged and, in fact, assisted a *kafir* power to occupy a sovereign Muslim country. They allowed 560,000 Iraqis to be blown to bits and hundreds of thousands civilians to be maimed. Eighty percent of the population lost their jobs. The country was decimated. The infrastructure had been blown into stone age, and the desert had been poisoned with radioactive waste from spent ammunition for thousands of years to come.

2001 to the Present:
After Eighty-Seven Years, History Repeats Itself:
More Traitors.

Enver Pasha secretly signed a treaty of Turko-German Alliance on August 2, 1914. Only five people in Turkey knew of this treaty, which brought on the final disintegration of the Ottoman Empire. The puppet grand vizier Said Halim, Talat, and Cemal were convinced by Enver of the wisdom of supporting the Germans in case the war

---

[50] Woodward, *Plan of Attack*, 312.

broke out. Enver Pasha chose to ally Turkey with the Central Powers by citing Germany's earlier victories in the war. Thus, the Ottoman Empire joined the Central Powers to form a triple alliance without the knowledge of the cabinet, the parliament, the army generals, and the Ottoman populace. The empire was ruled by three collaborators and puppets of Germany, traitors to Islam, to the Muslims in Turkey, and to the whole of the *ummah*. They acted secretly as collaborators, with a foreign government working toward the destruction and disintegration of the only free Islamic state.

Two German warships, the battleship *Goeben* and the cruiser *Breslau*, that were caught in a neutral Turkish port when the war broke out in Europe were handed to the Ottoman Navy. In October, they were put out to sea, flying the Ottoman flag with German officers and crew, and shelled Odessa and other Russian ports. Enver Pasha, as the Ottoman war minister, gave secret orders in a sealed envelope to Admiral Souchon, the commander of the Turko-German fleet, only to be opened when the fleet was deep in the Black Sea. The orders read:

War minister Enver Pasha to Admiral Souchon   *October 25, 1914.*

The entire fleet should maneuver in the Black Sea. When you find a favorable opportunity, attack the Russian fleet. Before initiating the hostilities, open my secret orders given to you personally this morning. To prevent transport of material to Serbia, act as already agreed upon. Enver Pasha."

(Secret Order): The Turkish fleet should gain the mastery of the Black Sea by force. Seek out the Russian fleet and attack her wherever you find her without declaration of war. Enver Pasha.

The admiral attacked simultaneously the Russian ports of Sebastopol, Theodosia, Novorossiysk, and Odessa on the morning of October 29.

The first cannon shot from the Turkish fleet, in effect, declared a war on Russia and its allies Britain and France. Once again, Enver acted secretly at the behest of Germany. He did not consult his coconspirators, Talat and Cemal, before ordering the attack on Russia or the declaration of war against the Western allies. He kept his cabinet colleagues, the parliament, and the people of the empire in the dark, who on the morning of October 29, 1914, were surprised to find themselves at war.

The conspiracies, utter stupidity, and lust for power of three men—Talat, Cemal, and Enver—led to the dismemberment of the Ottoman Empire. For another one hundred years, this land of Islam was to know no peace. This land of Islam became the prey of the circle of evil of the Euro-Christian, Jew, and Arab conspirators.

The New American Century: The *Yahudi-Salibi* Conspiracy.

At the end of the twentieth century, American planners formulated a new doctrine for the deployment of American might. It reads:

> Unites States will rule the world. United States will turn into the centre of global empire. Washington will decide the fates of governments divide up riches of foreign economies and impose democracy in American sense of the world. With overwhelming military superiority United States will prevent new rivals to from rising up to challenge it on world stage. United States will have dominion over friends and foes alike. United States will be the bully on the block. If required its armed forces will use preemptive overwhelming military force. It will prevent and discourage development of nuclear programs in other countries.

In the American view, Iran, Iraq, and North Korea are the *axis of evil*, and the destruction of their military and economic prowess is a priority. Wars and military adventures benefit from coalitions, but the United States must determine and control all missions and lead the fights. The United States will not only be the most powerful but must be powerful to deter the emergence of rival powers.

After the wane of the Soviet Union, there was no threat to the security of the United States and its people; therefore, the American people demanded reduction in the defense expenditure. The defense industry and the financial institutions demanded continuing spending on armaments and defense industry to keep the economy running. America needed a threat to replace the Soviet Union. Inexplicably, this threat suddenly appeared from the caves in the Hindu Kush Mountains of Afghanistan. From a cave lit with a kerosene lantern in Tora Bora, on September 11, 2001, a man called Osama bin Laden directed and launched four massive airliners full of innocent passengers, which crash-landed into the Twin Towers of the World Trade Center and the Pentagon. The US Air Force shot down the fourth plane on the way to the White House. Three thousand people died. This catastrophe shook America and the world.

The Pentagon boosted its budget in increments from $260 billion to $480 billion over a period of twenty months. To the surprise of most people who were not aware, almost all the planners of the new American century were Jews. The conspirators Abram Shulsky, Robert Martinage, Paul Wolfowitz, Lewis Libby, James Lasswell, Mark Lagon, Phil Meilinger, Robert Kilebrew, William Kristol, Steve Rosen, Robert Kagan, Dov Zakheim, Fred Kagan, Donald Kagan, Devon Gaffney Cross, Stephen Cambone, Elliot Cohen, Alvin Bernstein, and Richard Perle are all Jews, and most of these men have spent some part of their life in Israel. They hold Israeli citizenship and are active in promoting pro-Israeli and anti-Arab and anti-Muslim causes. A few are right-wing Christian Zionists. All are committed to Israel and the Likud Party of the former Israeli prime minister Sharon.

This Jewish-Israeli transplant in Washington and the Christian right movement want to decisively shift the balance of power in the Middle East in favor of Israel so that it could effectively impose peace terms on Palestinians and Syrians, divide and fragment Arab and Muslim countries, and impose American/Israeli hegemony and economic and military control over the Middle East. They want to demonstrate to the world that America does have the will and power to disarm any rogue state that attempts to acquire weapons of mass destruction. They also want to demonstrate to any future rival powers that America could invade the Persian Gulf and deny any rival supplies of oil. In other words, comply with the American/Israeli wishes or else.

To achieve these objectives, the conspiring hawks planned to dominate the oil-rich arch of Islam extending from Syria on the Mediterranean to Afghanistan in the Hindu Kush Mountains. They planned to set up military bases in Iraq and link those to bases in Central Asia, Horn of Africa, Persian Gulf, and the Mediterranean.

The planning of invasion of Iraq and its execution were carried out secretly by a group of Jews working inside the Pentagon, namely, Paul Wolfowitz, Richard Perle, Douglas Feith, and Paul Nitze. In July 2001, at the Group of Eight summit held in Genoa, Italy, plans were discussed for the ouster of the Taliban from power. Wolfowitz, Perle, and Nitze were the people pushing for the American occupation of Afghanistan and Iraq. Bush's cabinet intended to take military action to take control of the Persian Gulf whether or not Saddam Hussein was in power. The blueprint written in September 2000 was supported by an earlier document written by Wolfowitz and Libby recommending maintaining American bases in Saudi Arabia and Kuwait to keep American control over the Arab oil. Another member of this team was the propagandist William Kristol, a Council on Foreign Relations (CFR) member.

Donald Rumsfeld (secretary of defense) and Paul Wolfowitz (deputy secretary of defense) set up a secret bureau within in the Pentagon. The Office of Special Plans (OSP) in the Pentagon dealt with the Middle East. Douglas Feith headed the Near East South Asia Center (NESA). Retired intelligence officers from the State Department, the Defense Intelligence Agency, and the Central Intelligence Agency had long charged that this office exaggerated and doctored the intelligence from Iraq and the Middle East before passing it along to the White House. Key personnel who worked in the OSP and NESA under the control of Douglas Feith were part of a broader network of Jews and Zionists who worked with similar Bush political appointees scattered around the American national security network. Their assignment was to move the country to war, according to the retired lieutenant colonel Karen Kwiatkowski. Kwiatkowski was assigned to NESA from May 2002 through February 2003.[51] Other political appointees who worked with them were William Loti, Abram Shulsky, Michael Rubin, David Schenker, Michael Makovsky, and Chris Lehman.

Along with Feith, all the political appointees have a common close identification with Ariel Sharon and the Likud Party in Israel. This group works closely with Richard Perle, John Bolton, Michael Wurmser, and Elizabeth Cheney. There are published reports that this group works with a similar group in the Israeli prime minister Ariel Sharon's office in Jerusalem. The OSP and the NESA personnel are already discussing and planning "going after Iran and Syria" after the war in Afghanistan and Iraq. Political plans of the Likud Party and the Council for Foreign Relations work on behalf of the Jewish finance

---

[51] Jim Lobe, "Pentagon Now Home to Neoconservative Network," *Dawn*, Aug. 9, 2003.

and defense industry to facilitate borrowing by the governments. It is amazing how in banking and wars Jewish names keep coming up.

In the arch of Islam, Iran is the keystone; and Syria, Iraq, Afghanistan, and Pakistan constituted the western and eastern halves of the arch. If Iran fell, the whole Muslim world would come tumbling down into the American lap. The planners decided to work on the weakest link of the chain. Afghanistan and Iraq had been devastated by twenty-five years of war, and Iraq had further been bled through the United Nations sanctions. Once Iraq and Afghanistan had been decimated and removed from the arch, then Iran and Syria would come tumbling down too.

After the fall of the Soviet Empire, the world was settling down to a slumber of peace, and the people of the world looked forward to a disarmed world. The planners of the new American century wanted an event so overwhelming and catastrophic that would propel the American people's psyche into a prolonged period of perpetual warfare. The assistance for such an event came from a very unsuspecting source.

Pakistan: The *Munafiq* Connection.

Gen. Pervez Musharraf, in a bloodless coup d'état on October 12, 1999, ousted the elected Pakistani government, arrested the prime minister Nawaz Sharif, and installed his own military regime. Accusing the previous government of corruption and ruining the economy, Musharraf promised to bring economic progress and political stability, eradicate poverty, build investor confidence, and restore democracy as quickly as possible. Two years later, none of these promises had been fulfilled. The economy was on a knife-edge, and there was growing, popular discontent with falling living standards and lack of basic democratic rights. The regime was under fire not only from the political opposition but also from its supporters in the ruling military elite. The schisms in the military reflected the pressure that the regime was under both domestically and internationally.

While the USA and other major powers tacitly accepted the coup, they had become increasingly critical of Musharraf's failure to carry out the economic measures demanded by the International Monetary Fund and his failure to crack down on Islamic fundamentalism. The USA had effectively blocked IMF loans and had not lifted economic sanctions imposed on Pakistan after its 1998 nuclear tests. The USA also demanded that Musharraf put pressure on the Taliban regime in Afghanistan to hand over Osama bin Laden, whom the USA blamed for the terrorist bombing of US embassies in Kenya and Tanzania.

Musharraf's junta confronted serious debt problems as a result of the IMF's repeated delays in disbursing $1.56 billion in loans. Without the IMF's backing, Pakistan had been unable to reschedule its $38 billion in foreign loans and was at the risk of defaulting on repayments of $5 billion of its loans that were due by the end of the year. According to official records, Pakistan's foreign exchange reserves were down to a bare one-third of a billion dollars.

To impose its policies, the military regime resorted to an outright repression, making a mockery of its claims of returning Pakistan to democracy by 2002. All the evidence pointed to a regime with a rapidly dwindling base of support. Its only answer to protests and opposition was more repression and seeking respite from foreign sources.

There was evidence that Musharraf's junta was secretly cooperating and cozying up with the US military and intelligence services and covertly helping the USA in its operations in Afghanistan. With CIA backing and with the injection of massive amounts of US military aid, Pakistan's Inter-Services Intelligence (ISI) had, in the 1980s and 1990s, developed into a major intelligence network wielding enormous power over all aspects of Pakistani civilian and military life. The ISI had a staff of military and intelligence officers, bureaucrats, undercover agents, and informers estimated at 150,000.[52] With this active collaboration with the CIA, the ISI continued to perform covert intelligence operations in the interests of the United States in Afghanistan and Central Asia. The ISI had directly supported and financed a number of terrorist organizations, including al-Qaeda. This cooperation with the al-Qaeda began as an extension of American interest in the region, and it could not have continued without the consent and the knowledge of the CIA.

The Sequence of Events: April 4, 2000. ISI director Gen. Mahmood Ahmed visited Washington. He met officials at the CIA and the White House. In a message meant for both Pakistan and the Taliban, US officials told him that al-Qaeda had killed Americans and "people who support those people will be treated as our enemies." However, no actual action, military or otherwise, was taken against either the Taliban or Pakistan.

May 2001. CIA director Tenet made a quiet visit to Pakistan to meet with Pres. Pervez Musharraf in May 2001. While in Islamabad, Tenet had an "an unusually long meeting" with General Musharraf. He also met with his Pakistani counterpart, ISI director Lt. Gen. Mahmood Ahmed.

July 2001. The BBC's George Arney reported on September 18 that American officials had told former Pakistani foreign secretary Niaz Naik in mid-July of plans for military action against the Taliban regime: "Mr. Naik said US officials told him of the plan at a UN-sponsored international contact group on Afghanistan which took place in Berlin. Mr. Naik told the BBC that at the meeting the US

---

[52] Ahmed Rashid, "The Taliban: Exporting Extremism," *Foreign Affairs*, November–December 1999. See also Michel Chossudovsky, "Who Is Osama bin Laden?" *Global Outlook* no. 1 (2002).

representatives told him that unless Bin Laden was handed over swiftly America would take military action to kill or capture both Bin Laden and the Taliban leader, Mullah Omar." The wider objective, according to Mr. Naik, would be to topple the Taliban regime and install a transitional government of moderate Afghans in its place, possibly under the leadership of the former Afghan king Zahir Shah. "Mr. Naik was told that Washington would launch its operation from bases in Tajikistan, where American advisers were already in place. He was told that Uzbekistan would also participate in the operation and that 17,000 Russian troops were on standby. Mr. Naik was told that if the military action went ahead it would take place before the snows started falling in Afghanistan, by the middle of October at the latest."

July 2001. The FBI confirmed in late September 2001, in an interview with ABC News, that the 9/11 ringleader, Mohammed Atta, had been financed from unnamed sources in Pakistan in July 2001:

As to September 11th, federal authorities have told ABC News they have now tracked more than $100,000 from banks in Pakistan, to two banks in Florida, to accounts held by suspected hijack ring leader, Mohammed Atta. As well . . . "Time Magazine" is reporting that some of that money came in the days just before the attack and can be traced directly to people connected to Osama bin Laden. It's all part of what has been a successful FBI effort so far to close in on the hijacker's high commander, the money men, the planners and the mastermind.[53]

The FBI had information on the money trail. They knew exactly who was financing the terrorists. Less than two weeks later, the findings of the FBI were confirmed by Agence France-Presse and the *Times of India*, quoting an official Indian intelligence report. According to these two reports, the money used to finance the 9/11 attacks had

---

[53] Statement of Brian Ross reporting on information conveyed to him by the FBI, ABC News, September 30, 2001.

allegedly been "wired to WTC hijacker Mohammed Atta from Pakistan, by Ahmad Umar Sheikh, at the instance of ISI Chief General Mahmood Ahmad."[54]

July 2001. At the Group of Eight summit held in Genoa, Italy, plans were discussed for the ouster of the Taliban from power. Wolfowitz, Perle, and Nitze were the people pushing for the American occupation of Afghanistan and Iraq. Bush's cabinet intended to take military action to take control of the Persian Gulf whether or not Saddam Hussein was in power. The blueprint written in September 2000 was supported by an earlier document written by Wolfowitz and Libby recommending maintaining American bases in Saudi Arabia and Kuwait to keep American control over the Arab oil.

Late August 2001. Barely a couple of weeks before September 11, Rep. Porter Goss, together with Sen. Bob Graham and Sen. Jon Kyl, were on a top-level intelligence mission in Islamabad. They held meetings with Pres. Pervez Musharraf and with Pakistan's military and intelligence brass, including the head of Pakistan's Inter-Services Intelligence, Gen. Mahmood Ahmed. Porter Goss, a Florida Republican and former CIA operative, was chairman of the House Intelligence Committee. He also chaired, together with Sen. Bob Graham, the Joint Senate House Committee on the September 11 attacks.

Amply documented, Porter Goss had an established personal relationship to the head of ISI, Gen. Mahmood Ahmed, who according to the *Washington Post* "ran a spy agency notoriously close to Osama bin Laden and the Taliban" (May 18, 2002).

According to the Council on Foreign Relations, the ISI had over the years supported a number of Islamic terrorist organizations while maintaining close links to the CIA:

---

[54] *Times of India*, Delhi, October 9, 2001.

Through its Inter Services Intelligence agency (ISI) Pakistan has provided the Taliban with military advisers and logistical support during key battles, has bankrolled the Taliban, has facilitated trans shipment of arms, ammunition and fuel through its territory and has openly encouraged the recruitment of Pakistanis to fight for the Taliban.

Pakistan's army and intelligence services, principally the Inter-Services Intelligence Directorate (ISI), contribute to making the Taliban a highly effective military force In other words, up to and including September 11, 2001, extending to December 2001, the ISI had been supporting Taliban net work.

And that was precisely the period during which Porter Goss and Bob Graham established a close working relationship with the ISI chief, Gen. Mahmood Ahmed. The latter had, in fact, "briefed" the two Florida lawmakers at ISI headquarters in Rawalpindi, Pakistan:

*Senator Bob Graham's first foreign trip as chairman of the Senate Intelligence Committee, in a late-August 2001, with House intelligence Chairman Goss and Republican Senator Jon Kyl of Arizona, focused almost entirely on terrorism. **It ended in Pakistan, where (ISI Chief) General Mahmoud Ahmed's intelligence agents briefed them on the growing threat of al Qaida while they peered across the Khyber Pass at an obscure section of Afghanistan,** called Tora Bora. The Americans also visited General Ahmed's compound and urged him to do more to help capture Osama bin Laden. The general hadn't said much, but the group had agreed to discuss the issue more when he visited Washington on September 4, 2001.*

September 4, 2001. Gen. Mahmood Ahmed arrived in the USA on an official visit.

September 4–9, 2001. He met his US counterparts, including CIA head George Tenet, according to official sources. He also held long parleys with unspecified officials at the White House and the

Pentagon. But the most important meeting was with Marc Grossman, US undersecretary of state for political affairs.

September 9, 2001. The leader of the Northern Alliance, Gen. Ahmad Shah Masoud was assassinated on the ninth of September 2001. The ISI, headed by General Ahmed, was allegedly involved in ordering the assassination of General Masoud. Ahmad Shah Masoud was the last hurdle in the Northern Alliance's cooperation with the USA in the coming invasion of Afghanistan. The kamikaze assassination took place two days before the attacks on the Twin Towers and the Pentagon during Gen. Mahmood Ahmed's official visit to Washington (September 4–13, 2004). The official communiqué of the Northern Alliance pointed to the involvement of the ISI.

September 10, 2005. According to Pakistani journalist Amir Mateen in a revealing article published one day before the 9/11 attack[55]:

ISI Chief Lt-Gen. Mahmoud's week-long presence in Washington has triggered speculation about the agenda of his mysterious meetings at the Pentagon and National Security Council. Officially, he is on a routine visit in return to CIA Director George Tenet's earlier visit to Islamabad. Official sources confirm that he met Tenet this week. He also held long parleys with unspecified officials at the White House and the Pentagon. But the most important meeting was with Marc Grossman, U.S. Under Secretary of State for Political Affairs. One can safely guess that the discussions must have centred on Afghanistan and Osama bin Laden. What added interest to his visit is the history of such visits. Last time Ziauddin Butt, Mahmoud's predecessor, was here, during Nawaz Sharif's government, the domestic politics turned topsy-turvy within days.

---

[55] Amir Mateen, "ISI Chief's Parleys Continue in Washington," *News*, September 10, 2001.

Morning of September 11, 2001. The three lawmakers Bob Graham, Porter Goss, and Jon Kyl and General Mahmood *all met in a top-secret conference room on the fourth floor of the US Capitol.* Also present at this meeting were Pakistan's ambassador to the USA Maleeha Lodhi and several members of the Senate and House intelligence committees. According to Graham's copious notes, they discussed "poppy cultivation" before they discussed terrorism. But then the Americans pressed Ahmed even harder to crack down on al-Qaeda. And then at "9:04 — Tim gives note on 2 planes crash into World Trade Center, NYC" (*Washington Post*, May 4, 2003).

However, at no time since 9/11 had Rep. Porter Goss and his Senate counterpart, Bob Graham (chairman of the Senate Intelligence Committee), acknowledged the role of Pakistan's ISI in supporting al-Qaeda. In fact, quite the opposite. One year after the attacks, the former head of the ISI continued to be described as a bona fide intelligence counterpart supportive of the US "war on terrorism." In an interview in the *New York Times* on the first anniversary of 9/11, Sen. Bob Graham described his August 2001 encounter with General Ahmed:

I had just come back a few days before September the 11th from a trip [to] Pakistan and [a] meeting with President Musharraf and with the head of the Pakistani intelligence service.
While we were meeting with the head of the intelligence service, a general whose name was General Ahmed, he had indicated he would be in Washington in early September, we — Porter Goss, myself — had invited him to meet with us while he was there.

It turned out that the meeting was a breakfast on September 11. The head of the ISI arrived in the USA on the fourth. Graham stated in the interview that he got back a few days before 9/11, which suggested that the Goss-Graham mission could well have returned to Washington on board the same military plane as General Ahmed.

So we were talking about what was happening in Afghanistan, what the capabilities and intentions of the Taliban and Al Qaida were from the perspective of this Pakistani intelligence leader, when we got the notices that the World Trade Center towers had been attacked.

September 12–13, 2001. At 10:00 a.m. a day after the devastating terrorist attacks on New York's World Trade Center and Pentagon headquarters in Washington, Gen. Mahmood Ahmed, ISI chief, arrived at the State Department for an emergency meeting with the US deputy secretary of state, Richard Armitage. "General, we require your country's full support and cooperation," Armitage told Pakistan's spymaster and member of the triumvirate that ruled the country. "We want to know whether you are with us or not, in our fight against terror." The meeting was adjourned for the next day after the general had assured Armitage of Pakistan's full support.

"We will tell you tomorrow what you are required to do," Armitage said as they left the room.

Meanwhile at 1:30 p.m., Colin Powell spoke to President Musharraf on the phone. "The American people would not understand if Pakistan did not cooperate in this fight with the United States," Powell said candidly as one general to another. President Musharraf promised to cooperate fully with the United States.

It was 12:00 p.m. on September 13, 2001, when General Mahmood returned to the State Department for the second meeting. "This is not negotiable," said Armitage as he handed over a single sheet of paper with seven demands that the Bush administration wanted him to accept.

The general glanced through the paper for a few seconds and replied, "They are all acceptable to us."

The swift response took Armitage by surprise. "These are very powerful words, General. Do you not want to discuss with your President?" he asked.

"I know the president's mind," replied General Mahmood.

A visibly elated Armitage asked General Mahmood to meet with George Tenet, the CIA chief, at his headquarters at Langley. "He is waiting for you," said Armitage.

The American demands, to which General Mahmood acceded to in no time, required Pakistan to abandon its support for the Taliban regime and provide logistical support to the American forces. The list of demands included the following:

1. Stop al-Qaeda operations on the Pakistani border and intercept arms shipments through Pakistan and all logistical support for bin Laden.
2. Give blanket overflights and landing rights for US planes.
3. Provide access to Pakistan's naval bases, airbases, and borders.
4. Give immediate intelligence and immigration information.
5. Curb all domestic expression of support for terrorism against the United States and its friends and allies.
6. Cut off fuel supply to the Taliban and stop Pakistani volunteers going into Afghanistan to join the Taliban.
7. Break diplomatic relations with the Taliban and assist the USA to destroy bin Laden and his al-Qaeda network.

September 13, 2001. General Ahmed met Sen. Joseph Biden, chairman of the Senate Foreign Relations Committee.

The Decision to Go to War

At meetings of the National Security Council and in the so-called war cabinet on September 11, 12, and 13, CIA director George Tenet played a central role in persuading Pres. George Bush to launch the "war on terrorism."

September 11, 2001, 3.30 p.m. A key meeting of the National Security Council (NSC) was convened, with members of the NSC communicating with the president from Washington by secure video.[56] In the course of this NSC videoconference, CIA director George Tenet fed unconfirmed information to the president. Tenet stated that "he was virtually certain that bin Laden and his network were behind the attacks.[57]"

The president responded to these statements quite spontaneously, off the cuff, with little or no discussion, and with an apparent misunderstanding of their implications. In the course of this videoconference (which lasted for less than an hour), the NSC was given the mandate by the president to prepare for the "war on terrorism." Very much on the spur of the moment, the green light was given by videoconference from Nebraska. In the words of President Bush, "We will find these people. They will pay. And I don't want you to have any doubt about it."[58]

4:36 p.m. (one hour and six minutes later). Air Force One departed for Washington. Back in the White House, that same evening at nine, a second meeting of the full NSC took place, together with Secretary of State Colin Powell, who had returned to Washington from Peru. The NSC meeting (which lasted for half an hour) was followed by the

---

[56] *Washington Post*, January 27, 2002.

[57] Ibid.

[58] Ibid.

first meeting of the so-called war cabinet. The latter was made up of a smaller group of top officials and key advisers.

9:30 p.m. At the war cabinet, "Discussion turned around whether bin Laden's Al Qaida and the Taliban were one and the same thing. Tenet said they were."[59]

11:00 p.m. By the end of that historic meeting of the war cabinet, the Bush administration had decided to embark on a military adventure that began the war on Afghanistan and Iraq. Astonishingly, within a course of forty-eight hours, the military junta of Pakistan took an about-turn to become a lynchpin in the US-led military operation in Afghanistan that ousted the Taliban regime. The speed of the quick about-turn surprised even the American authorities.

Events after September 11 during the week in Washington and Islamabad provided an interesting insight into the ad hoc and arbitrary decision-making process of military dictatorships on crucial national security and foreign policy issues. Like the policy to support the Taliban regime, the decision to surrender the country's sovereignty was also taken just by two generals. There were no consultations at any level when President Musharraf abandoned support for the oppressive and reactionary regime in Afghanistan, gave the American forces complete access to Pakistani territory, and assisted in the invasion of an ally and an independent Muslim state. A similar sequence of events had occurred in the history of Islam eighty-seven years earlier when Enver Pasha secretly signed a treaty of Turko-German alliance on August 2, 1914.

On the evening of September 12, General Musharraf received a phone call from General Mahmood in Washington, who briefed him about his meeting with Armitage. Later, US ambassador Wendy Chamberlain met with him and conveyed a formal message from

---

[59] Ibid.

the American leaders for cooperation. The president assured her of Pakistan's full support.

As it occurred in Turkey eighty-seven years earlier, in Pakistan, there was no consultation with political leaders on the paradigm shift in the strategic discourse of the nation. General Musharraf took his handpicked, unelected cabinet into confidence, almost three days after his ISI chief had already signed on the dotted line to the US demands. He told the ministers that the decision to cooperate with the United States was necessary to safeguard Pakistan's nuclear assets and its Kashmir policy.

General Musharraf did not find it hard to convince his cabinet, but it was not so simple when it came to his corps commanders and members of his military junta. At least seven senior officers, including Lieutenant General Mahmood, who had earlier in Washington signed on the dotted line, showed reservations on the decision to pull out support for the Taliban regime. The people of Pakistan and the owners of the land were astonished when they found themselves involved in a long war on behalf of the *kafireen* against their own countrymen in Waziristan and against other Muslims in Afghanistan.

Musharraf acted swiftly and fired the dithering general Mahmood and the other reluctant generals who disagreed with him. Through a series of purges at the top level, General Musharraf consolidated his position with the new commanders backing him fully on the new policy on Afghanistan. The shift in Pakistan's Afghan policy and the decision to support the United States brought minor economic and political benefits to General Musharraf's regime. From a pariah state, Pakistan became the center of focus of the international community. Never before had so many head of states traveled to Pakistan as they did in the few weeks after September 11. Pakistan was, once more, the USA's strategic partner.

According to senior American sources, the US-led coalition could not have achieved its swift success in Afghanistan without the ISI's intelligence support. The agency, which had been deeply involved with the Taliban from its inception, guided the American forces to the bombing and the massacre of the Taliban, its own creation. For this treachery, Musharraf's junta extracted paltry economic aid and concessions from the USA and other Western countries. Pakistan sold its honor for a $1 billion loan write-off, $600 million in budgetary support, and debt rescheduling. Pakistan was sold for $1.6 billion. Musharraf sold the heritage of each Pakistani man, woman, and child for US$10 each, equivalent to five hundred Pakistani rupees.

Munafiqeen in Pakistan assisted a kafir power to occupy two sovereign Muslim countries, Afghanistan and Iraq. They allowed 560,000 Afghans and Iraqis to be blown to bits and hundreds of thousands civilians to be maimed. Eighty percent of the population lost their jobs. The countries were decimated. Their infrastructure had been blown into stone age, and the desert and the mountains had been poisoned with radioactive waste from spent ammunition for thousands of years to come.

Yet this is not the end. And yet to come is the invasion of Iran, Libya, and Syria. Do the Saudis, Pakistanis, and Egyptians feel that they will be spared of this fate when the *kafireen* will decide to go for them?

Carefully Planned *Yahudi-Salibi-Munafiq* Intelligence Operation

The 9/11 attacks on New York and Washington were carefully planned intelligence operations. The 9/11 terrorists did not act on their own volition. The suicide hijackers were instruments of a carefully planned international intelligence operation. The evidence confirmed that al-Qaeda was the brainchild of the CIA and supported by Pakistan's military intelligence, the Inter-Services Intelligence. And the ISI, in turn, was an arm of the CIA in South Asia and owed its existence to the CIA. The ISI is the foreign flag of the CIA.

The spontaneity of the discovery of the culprits and the instant declaration of war against the Taliban and al-Qaeda is a play written long time ago by the authors of the new American century in which the actors recited the long-memorized lines. The prologue was the act in which the Twin Towers exploded in a haze of smoke and dust, a real smoke screen of deception and lies foreshadowing what was yet to come.

The ISI and the CIA began planning the Massacre of the Twin Towers in April 2000. Such a gigantic explosive event was meant to be shown alive on every television screen around the world to arouse sympathy for America the victim and revulsion against the perpetrators of the ghastly event. It was the opening scene of America's war against the world.

May 2001. CIA director Tenet made a quiet visit to Pakistan to meet with Pres. Pervez Musharraf in May 2001. While in Islamabad, Tenet had an "an unusually long meeting" with General Musharraf. He also met with his Pakistani counterpart, ISI director Lt. Gen. Mahmood Ahmed.

June and Subsequent Months of 2001. Money used to finance the 9/11 attacks was wired to WTC hijacker Mohammed Atta from Pakistan by Ahmad Umar Sheikh at the instance of ISI chief, Gen. Mahmood Ahmed.[60] Both Mohammed Atta and Ahmad Umar Sheikh are now known to have been the intelligence assets of both the CIA and the ISI for many years. The FBI had information on the money trail. They knew exactly who was financing the terrorists. Less than two weeks later, the findings of the FBI were confirmed

---

[60] *Times of India*, Delhi, October 9, 2001.

by Agence France-Presse and the *Times of India*, quoting an official Indian intelligence report.

July 2001. At the Group of Eight summit held in Genoa, Italy, plans were discussed for the ouster of the Taliban from power. Wolfowitz, Perle, and Nitze were the people pushing for the American occupation of Afghanistan and Iraq. Bush's cabinet intended to take military action to take control of the Persian Gulf whether or not Saddam Hussein was in power. The blueprint written in September 2000 was supported by an earlier document written by Wolfowitz and Libby recommending maintaining American bases in Saudi Arabia and Kuwait to keep American control over the Arab oil.

Late August 2001. Barely a couple of weeks before September 11, Rep. Porter Goss, together with Sen. Bob Graham and Sen. Jon Kyl, were on a top-level intelligence mission in Islamabad. They held meetings with Pres. Pervez Musharraf and with Pakistan's military and intelligence brass, including the head of Pakistan's Inter-Services Intelligence, Gen. Mahmood Ahmed. Porter Goss, a Florida Republican and former CIA operative, was chairman of the House Intelligence Committee. He also chaired, together with Sen. Bob Graham, the Joint Senate House Committee on the September 11 attacks. Porter Goss since then has replaced George Tenet as the director of the newly reformed and empowered CIA.

September 4, 2001. Gen. Mahmood Ahmed arrived in the USA on an official visit. Bob Graham stated in the interview that he got back a few days before 9/11, which suggested that the Goss-Graham mission could well have returned to Washington on board the same military plane as Gen. Mahmood Ahmed.

Between September 4 and 9, 2001. Gen. Mahmoud Ahmed met his US counterparts, including CIA head George Tenet. Official sources confirmed that he met Tenet this week. He also held long parleys with unspecified officials at the White House and the Pentagon. But the most important meeting was with Marc Grossman, US undersecretary of state for political affairs. On September 9, the leader of the Northern Alliance, Gen. Ahmad Shah Massoud, was assassinated by the ISI, headed by Gen. Mahmood Ahmed. Ahmad Shah Massoud was the last hurdle in the Northern Alliance's cooperation with the USA in the coming invasion of Afghanistan. The kamikaze assassination took place two days before the attacks on the Twin Towers and the Pentagon during General Ahmed's official visit to Washington (September 4–13, 2004). The official communiqué of the Northern Alliance pointed to the involvement of the ISI while Mahmood Ahmed was still on US soil.

Morning of September 11, 2001. The two lawmakers Bob Graham and Porter Goss, the chairman of the Joint Senate House Intelligence Committee Jon Kyl, and General Mahmood all met in a top secret conference room on the fourth floor of the US Capitol. Also present at this meeting were Pakistan's ambassador to the USA Maleeha Lodi and several members of the Senate and House intelligence committees. And then at "9:04 — Tim gives note on 2 planes crash into World Trade Center, NYC" (*Washington Post*, May 4, 2003).

The evidence showed an intense collusion and collaboration between the president of Pakistan and his top intelligence staff and the senior American officials, the overseers of US intelligence services from the House and the Senate of the United States, and the director of the CIA. And Mahmood Ahmed traveled to the United States for the final fine-tuning of the planned operation between his men and the US side. There is little doubt that the 9/11 episode was a well-orchestrated, well-planned, and technically high-precision job undertaken by skilled people in collaboration with those within the aviation authority, the air force, the FBI, the immigration services, and a centralized secret group of planners with international intelligence connections with the CIA, ISI, and others.

And finally, the perpetrators sat down all together to watch the results of their handiwork in a top secret room on the fourth floor of the US Capitol. Mahmood's presence in Washington was to ensure that the Pakistani intelligence chief delivered all that he had promised and did not crawl out of his part of the bargain.

In this conspiracy of the circle of evil, over three thousand innocent men and women lost their lives. And it was just the opening shot in a long war against humanity.

If anyone slew a person – unless it be for murder or for spreading mischief in the land – it would be as if he slew the whole people: and if any one saved a life, it would be as if he saved the life of the whole people. (Al-Ma'idah 5:32, Koran)

Take not life, which Allah hath made sacred, except by the way of justice or law: This He commands you, that you may learn wisdom. (Al-An'am:151–53, Koran)

The covenant of Muhammad written in Medina is the first constitution of Dar es Salaam. The covenant is a brief summary of the covenant of the Koran underlining the fundamental obligations of the individual believers to their community in times of conflict.

The Muslims constitute one Ummah to the exclusion of all other men.
All believers shall rise as one man against anyone who seeks to commit injustice, aggression, crime, or spread mutual enmity amongst the Muslims even if such a person is their kin.
Just as the bond to Allah is indivisible, all the believers shall stand behind the commitment of the least of them. All believers are bonded one to another to the exclusion of other men.
The believers shall leave none of their members in destitution without giving him in kindness that he needs by the way of his liberty.
This Pax Islamica is one and indivisible. No believer shall enter a separate peace without all other believers whenever there is fighting in the cause of God, but will do so only on the basis of equality and justice to all others.

In every expedition for the cause of God we undertake, all parties to the covenant shall fight shoulder to shoulder as one man.
All believers shall avenge the blood of one another when any one falls fighting in the cause of God. No believer shall slay a believer in retaliation for an unbeliever, nor shall he assist an unbeliever against a believer. Whoever is convicted of killing a believer deliberatively but without righteous cause shall be liable to the relatives of the killed. Until the latter are satisfied, the killer shall be subject to retaliation by each believer. (The Covenant of Muhammad)

During the last two hundred years, Muslims have lost in the battlefield in every conflict against the West; and in doing so, they have been subjected to humiliation and colonization lasting more than a century. Why did that happen? Muslim communities are beset with traitors and *Munafiqeen*. They look like Muslims, dress like Muslims, and pray like Muslims. They frequently go for *umrah* and hajj, yet for a price, they disobey every article of the covenants of Muhammad and of the Koran. For the price of a kingdom and a fiefdom, they betray their *din* and the *ummah*.

During the last three centuries, the Muslim states had had many external enemies whose motives were varied. All of them used disgruntled Muslim princes, noblemen, and tribes with the temptation of wealth and territory in fostering their aim. Once the conquering armies managed to gain a stranglehold on the Muslim territory, the traitors were discarded like rags once their usefulness was over. Yet in Muslim history, there had never been shortage of such traitors. In recent history, those who invited and aided the infidels in the occupation of the lands of Islam are the generals of the Pakistan Army, Northern Alliance of Afghanistan, Kurds of Iraq, the Shias of Iraq, the Saudi royal family, the Jordanian royals, and the sheikhs of Qatar, Kuwait, Bahrain, United Arab Emirates, and Oman. The result is the occupation and decimation of Palestine, Afghanistan, Iraq,

Syria, Somalia, and Libya with the resulting loss of life of millions of believers.

The loss of life of more than one million Iraqis caused by the United Nations sanctions was aided and abetted by the rulers of the Arabian Peninsula, Turkey, Jordan, and Iran. In fact, all the Islamic states combined are in no better position now to solve their problems of defense, disunity, infighting, poverty, illiteracy, and poor world image than they had in 1909, when Caliph Abdulhamid was deposed by their ilk. When the Koran says the following, it might as well have been addressed to the present rulers of Islam:

> When the Hypocrites come to thee, they say, "We bear witness that thou art indeed the Rasul of Allah". Yes, Allah knows that you are indeed His Rasool and Allah bears witness that the Hypocrites are indeed liars.
>
> They have made their oaths a screen (for their hypocrisy), thus they obstruct (men) from the Path of Allah: truly evil are their deeds.
>
> That is because they believed, then they disbelieved: so their hearts are sealed, therefore they understand not.
>
> When you look at them, their figures please you and when they speak and you listen to their words, they are as worthless as decayed pieces of wood propped up. They panic that every shout is against them. They are the enemies, beware of them. Let the curse of Allah be on them! How they are perverted! (Al-Munafiqun 63:1–8)

How apt and fitting are Allah's words with regard to rulers of Islam. You see them sitting on their grandiose gold-covered chairs with thick velvet cushions, dressed in silken robes with gold embroidery, attending meetings of the Arab League and the Organization of Islamic Cooperation. We say, "Wow, these are our princes of Islam, all of them meeting to seek ways and means of our deliverance from tyranny and oppression." After their hard and difficult deliberations, they speak out gently in soft tones of their anguish and concern about the state of the *ummah*. Their words are as worthless as a rotten, hollow, and crumbling log unable to support the truth. Their hypocrisy and lies have dogged the *ummah* year after year for the last three hundred years. They are insecure and panic stricken in case the believers seek justice and retribution. The Koran says:

When you look at them, their figures please you and when they speak and you listen to their words, they are as worthless as decayed pieces of wood propped up. They panic that every shout is against them. They are the enemies, beware of them. Let the curse of Allah be on them! How they are perverted!

We have seen in this chapter that there is a distinct circle of evil that does Satan's bidding. A circle of smart financiers, usually Jews, and secret societies like the Illuminati spin the web of the devil or sets the trap using the Christian armies to snare the Muslims. There are traitors among the Muslims, the *Munafiqeen*, who finally snap shut the trap door. Throughout the history of man, this story has been repeated over and over again. The trap can be set only with deception and guile.

On the eve of the Iraq War while the Jews in the Pentagon were planning and the Pentagon and the White House were carrying on the troop deployment, the whole world knew what was happening. The Arab kings, the third dimension of the evil, were doing the bidding of the *kafireen*; the only people being fooled were the Arab and Muslim people. Yet the people who drove the fuel tankers to the air bases, the Saudi and Jordanian armies, the diplomats, and the news reporters knew the game plan. If anyone was deceived by Bandar and Abdullah and their royal kin, they wanted to be deceived.

In this day and age of paper and pen and electronic communication, every believer has access to the guidance of Allah and their covenant with Him. In Islam, there are no professional kings or rulers, nor are there professional politicians. Today the whole world knows of the *fitnah,* corruption, dishonesty, *Fahasha,* treachery, and disobedience to the covenant of Allah by the Muslim ruling classes and politicians. The kings and rulers of Islam cannot rule unless the believers want to be ruled by them. The *Munafiqeen* and the *Fahasha* cannot be the guardians of *beit el Allah* and the guardians of the rites of hajj unless the Muslims allow them. If "Muslims" follow the lead of the *Munafiqeen,* disobey the covenant, and do evil, they themselves become tainted by the same evil. Every believer is reminded by his covenant to invite others to all that is good and right and forbid what is wrong.

> Let there arise out of you a band of people inviting to all that is good, enjoining what is right and forbidding what is wrong: they are the ones to attain happiness. (Ali 'Imran 3:103–5, Koran)

The Koranic principle of enjoining good and forbidding what is evil is supportive of the moral autonomy of the individual. This principle authorizes the individual to act according to his or her best judgment in situations in which his or her intervention will advance a good purpose. The following saying of the blessed prophet supports individual action by a believer:

> If any one of you sees an evil, let him change it by his hand and if he is unable to do that, let him change by his words and if he is still unable to do that let him denounce it in his heart, but this is the weakest form of belief.

This principle assigns to the individual an active role in the community in which he or she lives. *The Koran annunciated the principle of free speech fourteen hundred years ago.* Believing men and women are reminded that they are the best of people, witnesses over other nations. Such a responsibility carries with it a moral burden of an exemplary conduct of one who submits to the divine truth and whose relationship with Allah is governed is by *taqwa,* the consciousness of humankind's responsibility toward its Creator. With that knowledge and faith, the believer is well equipped to approach others to enjoin what is right and forbid that is wrong. This moral autonomy of the individual, when bound together with the will of the community, formulates the doctrine of infallibility of the collective will of the *ummah*, which is the doctrinal basis of consensus.

When the blessed *nabi* died, he left behind the Koran, the *din*, and the Dar es Salaam. The blessed *nabi* wisely did not nominate a successor to his spiritual and worldly legacy. The believers all together inherited the Koran, the *din*, and the Dar es Salaam till the end of time. Allah addresses individual believers, both men and women, in His covenant, guiding them to the conduct of this spiritual and worldly legacy of the blessed *nabi*. Every believer has the autonomy of their conduct of their spiritual and the earthly affairs. Humans have enough freedom to make their own choices: if they make the choice to do beautiful and wholesome deeds (*saalihaat*) motivated by faith (*iman*) and God-wariness (*taqwa*), they please Allah and bring harmony and wholesomeness to the world, resulting in peace, justice, mercy, compassion, honor, equity, well-being, freedom, and many other gifts through Allah's grace. Others choose to do evil and work corruption (*mufsidun*), destroying the right relationship among the creation, causing *fitnah*, hunger, disease, oppression, pollution, and other afflictions. In the universal order, corruption is the prerogative of the humans, and vicegerency gives the humans the freedom to work against the Creator and His creation. Allah measures out the good and the evil, the wholesome and the corrupt. Allah commands the humans to be righteous.

In the commandments of the covenant, Allah addresses individual men and women who in unity form a community, the *ummah*. Nevertheless, the emphasis of the guidance is to the individual believer for his and her own conduct. The concept of a covenant also

338

symbolizes the relationship between humans, among Allah's creatures, and the rest of His creation. They all share one God, one set of guidance and commandments, the same submission and obedience to Him, and the same set of expectations in accordance with His promises. They all can therefore trust one another since they all have similar obligations and expectations. In view of the Koran, humans, communities, nations, and civilizations will continue to live in harmony and peace so long as they continue to fulfill Allah's covenant.

Evil has companions—those who conspire and scheme, the ones who execute, those who condone, and finally everyone who sees evil and does nothing to avert it. When believers refuse to follow the evildoers and unjust rulers, the latter cannot rule over the *ummah*. Every believer has the power and authority to speak out against deceit, injustice, treason, and evil among his community. The believers in unity have the power to cast out deceit, injustice, treason, and evil from their community. This moral autonomy of the individual, when bound together with the will of the community, formulates the doctrine of infallibility of the collective will of the *ummah*, which is the doctrinal basis of consensus. This consensus is in good as opposed to evil. When the Islamic rulers and the state fall into degradation and depravity because of the actions of those in authority, the burden of preventing such perpetration of evil rests with every individual believer and in unison with the community. When evil occurs in the Islamic society, those who bear the ultimate responsibility are the believers for not acting against it and letting it occur.

The Fate of Treason

Talat Pasha, Enver Pasha, and Cemal Pasha formed the triumvirate that seized the Ottoman government and led the Ottoman Empire into the First World War, which essentially a war of Christians against Christians fought for the control of wealth and trade of Europe and the world. Neither the people of the empire nor the cabinet, parliament, or the army had been informed of the decision to go to war. They were the tools of the German emperor and had no interest in the welfare of their own people. Germany lost the war, and as a result, the Turks were badly defeated. Mustafa Kemal abandoned Syria, Iraq, and Arabia, leaving the Islamic nation to the mercy of the British and the French. Talat Pasha, Enver Pasha, and Cemal Pasha abandoned the field and made a run for their lives. Syria, Iraq, and Arabia were captured by the British, the French, and their Arab tools. What was once a united empire was divided into Azerbaijan, Turkey, Syria, Lebanon, Iraq, Saudi Arabia, Yemen, Oman, Kuwait, Aden, and the Trucial States by the Turks, the British, and the French in the name of Turkish and Arab nationalism under the control of Western tools.

What was the fate of the traitors to Islam and Allah's covenant? In July 1919, a Turkish court-martial investigating the conduct of the government during the war period condemned the three—Talat Pasha, Enver Pasha, and Cemal Pasha—to death. At the time the sentence was pronounced, Talat had already fled to Germany, in which country Enver Pasha and Cemal had also taken refuge. Enver had since returned to Turkey and joined the nationalists.

Talat Pasha: An unsuccessful attempt to assassinate Talat was made in Constantinople early in 1915, at which time he was seriously wounded by the would-be murderer's bullet. Talat Pasha, former grand vizier of Turkey and one of the three leaders of the Young Turk movement, was murdered in Berlin on March 15, 1921, in an act of revenge by an Armenian assassin. He was walking in a street in a western suburb with his wife when a young man who had been following overtook them and, tapping Talat on the shoulder, pretended to claim acquaintance with him. Then drawing a revolver, the man shot Talat through the head and with a second shot wounded the wife. Talat fell to the pavement and was killed instantly. He had been on the run in fear for his life. He had been living as a fugitive under assumed names, first in Switzerland and later in Germany. He evidently feared the fate that had now overtaken him, for he had frequently changed his address in Berlin and, at the time of his death, was living at a pension in the West End.

Cemal Pasha: The fall of Jerusalem in December 1917 sent Cemal back to Constantinople, where he remained in office until the collapse of the Young Turk administration in October 1918. He subsequently fled Constantinople along with other ministers aboard a German ship. Cemal thereafter served as liaison officer in talks between the newly established Soviet Union and the postwar Turkish government. He also spent a brief period acting as a military adviser to Afghanistan. He was murdered by Armenian assassins at Tbilisi on July 21, 1922.

Enver Pasha: Enver died on August 4, 1922, in hiding near Baljuan, in present-day Republic of Tajikistan, of a wound that he sustained while fleeing from Russian cavalry. The ambitions and treachery of this forty-one-year-old soldier and adventurer led to the overthrow of the authority of the Ottoman sultan. As a tool of the German monarch, his actions resulted in the defeat and dismemberment of the Ottoman Empire and enslavement of the Muslims for over hundred years.

Sharif Hussein of Mecca: In June 1916, supported by Abdullah, Faisal, and his other sons, Sharif Hussein proclaimed the Arab Revolt against the sultan and the caliph of the Ottoman Empire. For Hussein and sons, it was an act of treason—treason against their religion, treason against their people, and treason against his sovereign to whom they had sworn allegiance and loyalty. Faisal, who was a serving officer in the Ottoman Army, deserted his post in Syria to join the revolt. The revolt proved to be a dud. Hussein, it turned out, had no following at all. Muslims did not respond to his call nor did the Arabs. Under his banner, or rather the one that a British official designed for him, those who rallied under him were closer to one thousand rather than one hundred thousand, and they were Bedouin tribesmen and not soldiers. And those who did join were bribed with British gold.

Faisal's camel corps presented a pretense that Syria was liberated by the Arabs themselves. In fact, there were a million British Indian troops fighting in the Middle East in 1918 and only thirty-five hundred Husseini troops, and on the face of it was a British war of conquest over the Arabs and not a war of liberation for them. The British, on May 9, 1916, in a secret convention, had already promised Arab Syria to the French (Sykes-Picot Agreement) and on November 2, 1917, in the Balfour Declaration, gave away Arab Palestine to the Jews. The Lawrence-Hussein-sons puppet show was being cleverly orchestrated from London. Each one of the players understood their role and the reward for their part except Hussein and sons. The ambiguous language, willful face-to-face lies, secret agreements, double dealings, deception, flattery, and bribery as a skill and art had become the trademark of English diplomacy over the previous one hundred years. The Arabs and the Bedouin had their own share of guile and cunningness; they were, however, no match for the Anglos as the next one hundred years would reveal. And the Arab leaders never learned.

After the war, Sharif Hussein—the commoner from Istanbul—declared himself the king of Hejaz and the caliph of Islam. The Muslim world ridiculed the king. The British had no further use for him and dropped him like a dirty rag. Angry with the British for their deception, Hussein sank into deep depression. He abdicated his pretend throne in favor of his son Ali. Ali, in turn, was driven out from Mecca by Ibn Sa'ud with the British help in 1925.

As a compensation for his loyalty and services, the British granted Hussein a villa in Cyprus and a pension. For his treasonable services against Islam, this caliph of Islam and a gallant servant of the British was elevated to the rank of a Knight of the Grand Cross in the Most Honorable Order of the Bath by the English sovereign. Hussein died a broken man in 1933.

Faisal ibn Hussein: Faisal deserted his post in the Ottoman Army and a seat in the Turkish Senate to join the revolt against the Ottomans. The English, in their duplicity, had promised parts of Syria to the Arabs, the French, and the Jews. The English proclaimed Faisal the king of Syria on March 8, 1920. The French chased him out of Damascus on July 27, 1920, with English connivance. The English, unable to control the restive population of Iraq in need of a willing sheikh for hire, selected Faisal as a good pliable tool to control Iraq. Faisal was proclaimed king of the British protectorate of Mesopotamia on August 21, 1921. He ruled over Iraq as the nominal ruler under the British protection and guidance till his death of heart disease in Bern, Switzerland, on September 8, 1933. Till the end, he hung on to his puppet strings. For his loyalty to the British Crown, this son of the pretender to the caliphate was awarded the title of the rank of a Knight of the Grand Cross in the Most Honorable Order of the Bath, three months before he died.

Faisal was installed king of an artificial country in which different clans had enjoyed historic rights. In 1922, the Kurdish leader Mahmood declared an independent Kurdistan as had been originally envisioned by the Paris Peace treaties of 1919. Originally Britain's choice to govern in the Sulaymaniyah region, Mahmood had fallen out with the British in 1919 and had been captured but later pardoned. His second revolt in 1922 came at a time when Turkey was pressing hard its claims to Mosul. The British, with the complicity of Faisal, responded by suppressing the revolt in 1924. Under Faisal's sovereignty, the British Royal Air Force bombed the Iraqi villages, tribes, and crops repeatedly for over two and a half years. The British aircraft used poison and mustard gas to put down the peoples fight for independence.

Meanwhile, at the time Britain was creating the throne for Faisal, Kurdistan was deeply divided. Kirkuk and Arbil demanded separate governorates and opposed the Arab rule of Iraq. Nevertheless, faced with potential for continuing revolts, Faisal's government agreed not to appoint Arab officials in Kurdish provinces.

In 1925, a major Kurdish uprising inside Turkey led by Sheikh Sa'd had repercussions in Iraqi Kurdistan, but violence did not break out again until 1927. In the meantime, Kurdish leaders had been increasingly frustrated by their powerlessness in Parliament, where Arabs dominated. In 1927, a new uprising was led by Sheikh Ahmad Barzani, the uncle of the present head of the Kurdistan Democratic Party in Iraq, Mas'ud Barzani. Sheikh Ahmad had been ruling his own area pretty much without government interference, and as control from Baghdad increased, so did his resistance. His revolt continued until 1932, when he surrendered to Turkish troops rather than to Arabs in Baghdad. In the meantime, a massacre in Sulaymaniyah in 1930 had helped cement the rise of Kurdish nationalism.

In 1933, in Faisal's last year on the throne, the Iraqi government clashed with the Assyrian minority, and the Iraqi Army carried out a full-scale massacre of Assyrians in the north, many of whom had already been driven out of Turkey. Faisal was succeeded by his son King Ghazi, a playboy of sorts, and reputed to be a homosexual.

In 1934 and 1935, there were tribal uprisings along the middle Euphrates, some of them quite serious. A new Kurdish uprising occurred in August of 1935, and soon after this, the Yezidis—a small, syncretistic, isolated sect living in northern Iraq—also rose. Further uprisings occurred in the Basra area in 1935 and 1936.

In October 1936, Gen. Bakr Sidqi—the army commander—staged a coup. This was the first military coup in the modern Arab world (though it had Ottoman and Iranian models in the early twentieth century to emulate). Sidqi, of Kurdish origin but not a Kurdish nationalist, had been commander of the northern region army units during several of the revolts and made his name putting down the Assyrian "troubles"; in alliance with the so-called Ahali Group political faction, he took power, and King Ghazi accepted the coup. By now, the army was a central player in politics. Nuri as-Said would play a key role in the years that followed, usually as the British puppet.

In 1939, young king Ghazi was unexpectedly killed in an automobile accident. Some believe that he was murdered. There was a deliberate cover-up of circumstances leading to Ghazi's death. The speculation was that Nuri as-Said and the English collaborated in Ghazi's murder. Ghazi's son, Faysal, became king as Faysal II; but as he was only four years old, regency was established under Emir 'Abd al-Ilah, a cousin on the Hashemite side and also a maternal uncle of the young king.

Azza, the daughter of Faisal ibn Hussein and the granddaughter of Hussein ibn Ali, the pretender to the caliphate, renounced Islam in 1936 to marry a Greek hotel waiter.

Faysal II: The last British puppet on the Iraqi throne was murdered by army mutineers on July 14, 1958, bringing an inglorious end to the dynasty of treason and treachery.

Nuri as-Said: The pillar of British rule in Iraq was recognized by the people of Baghdad while on the run in a woman's garb. He was captured by the people and slaughtered. In July 1958, as tensions and mass demonstrations against the regime mounted, a military group known as the Free Officers overthrew Britain's venal political agents, the Hashemite monarchy of Faysal II and the government of Prime Minister Nuri as-Said, in a military coup. The royal family and Nuri were assassinated. Such was the loathing for Nuri that his naked body was dragged ignominiously through the streets of Baghdad until it was reduced to a pulp. Forty years of brutal exploitation and political repression by the British and their Hashemite collaborators had come to an end.

Abdullah ibn Hussein: He was appointed an emir as an instrument of British policy to help moderate and dampen the Palestinian opposition to the Jewish settlement in Palestine. Sir Herbert Samuel was appointed the high commissioner to direct Abdullah in this direction. At the Cairo conference, Lawrence summed up the British position by declaring, "It will be preferable to use Transjordan as a safety valve, by appointing a ruler who would bring pressure to bear, to check anti Zionism[61]." The West used Abdullah to undermine Arab efforts against Israel in 1948. Abdullah secretly met Zionist leaders from 1922 onward, merely a year after the creation of Transjordan. These meetings continued during the Palestinian disturbances in 1932 and 1936. The amity between the two conspiring sides was so total that, in a meeting, Abdullah and the Jewish envoy discussed ways of eliminating the mufti of Jerusalem, the leader of Palestinians, and the enemy of both sides[62]. He secretly conspired with Chaim Weizmann for the partition of Palestine in 1947. Abdullah was murdered in the Al-Aqsa Mosque in July 1951 by a nationalist Palestinian.

Hussein: Abdullah's grandson started his secret contacts with the Israeli leaders in 1957, and by 1963, regular meetings[63] with the leaders became a regular occurrence. In 1963, Hussein made secret visit to Tel Aviv. In the period preceding 1967, Hussein performed

[61] Dann, *Great Powers*, 94.

[62] Shlaim, *Partition*, 203.

[63] Raviv and Melman, *Every Spy*, 213.

several treasonable acts, which were openly anti-Arab. In response to the creation of PLO, which wanted to replace him as the Palestinian representative, Hussein's[64] intelligence service provided the names and location of the Palestinian fighters infiltrating and battling the Israelis. Hussein did not stop here. His intelligence service also provided Israeli's information about other Arab countries.[65]

From 1970 onward, there were several secret meetings between Hussein and the Israeli defense minister Moshe Dayan and with Israeli prime minister Golda Meir.[66] This extensive period of secret Jordanian Israeli cooperation produced the most treasonable act of Hussein's life, informing Israel of the impending Egyptian-Syrian attack of October 1973.[67]

Hussein ibn Talal narrowly escaped several assassination attempts. Throughout their long career of treason and treachery to Islam, the descendants of Sharif Hussein boasted of their holy prophetic bloodline. In Islam, the only thing that a believer requires is Allah's hand over his hand. Respect of the bloodline is the old relic from the days of priesthood of gods bequeathed on Islam through the pagan Quraish. Remember Abu Jahl? He was of the same bloodline as the blessed prophet, yet he had been condemned in the Koran to the posterity.

Of the seven members of the Hashemite clan who became kings, Hussein ibn Talal was the only one who escaped assassination or eviction from his throne. Hussein ibn Ali, Ali ibn Hussein, Faisal ibn Hussein, and Talal ibn Abdullah were forced to abandon their throne and kingdom. Faisal had the good fortune to gain another kingdom.

---

64 Black and Morris, *Secret War*, 238.

65 Raviv and Melman, *Every Spy*, 214.

66 Heikal, *Secret Channels*, 310.

67 Black and Morris, *Secret War*, 265.

Ghazi, Faysal II, and Abdullah were murdered by their subjects. Treachery and glory carry their price.

Anwar Sadat: Sadat forgot his own roots and began to take advice and comfort from Kissinger and the Israeli lobby in Washington. Against the advice of his closest advisers and leaders of other Arab countries, Sadat offered himself as a servant and a tool the circle of evil, the *Yahudi-Salibi* confederation. He made a trip to Israel and addressed the Knesset, the Israeli parliament. Under the American tutelage and patronage, he abandoned his Arab allies, negotiated, and signed a peace treaty with many secret appendices with Israel at the expense of the Palestinians and Syrians and Muslims in general. As a consequence, all Palestine and the Golan Heights are under Israeli occupation. The Arabs are disunited and in disarray. Sadat sold out Egyptian sovereignty, the Islamic nation, and the Islamic holy places in Jerusalem for three billion dollars a year. He took Jews and Christians as *awliya* and willfully disobeyed the covenant that every Muslim, if he was a believer, has pledged to obey. He also disobeyed the provisions of the covenant of Yathrib and the prophet's teaching:

Just as the bond to Allah is indivisible, all the believers shall stand behind the commitment of the least of them. All believers are bonded one to another to the exclusion of other men. This Pax Islamica is one and indivisible. No believer shall enter a separate peace without all other believers whenever there is fighting in the cause of God, but will do so only on the basis of equality and justice to all others.

Puffed by the stature the Americans gave Anwar Sadat, he began to behave like a pharaoh. This son of an impoverished petty official began to live in opulence. He moved from palace to palace. He also loved to be saluted by thousands of parading soldiers. During a military parade in Cairo in 1981, Lt. Khaled Istambouli of the Egyptian Army, along with accomplices, jumped out of an armored vehicle opposite the presidential dais and sprayed the dais with hundreds of bullets with their automatic weapons. instantly killing Anwar Sadat, the modern pharaoh.

Saddam Hussein: On December 30, 2006, on the holy Muslim day of Eid, Saddam Hussein—the former president of Iraq—was hanged by a puppet court of the American occupation in Iraq. The execution was recorded on a cell phone camera, and the grisly images were broadcast around the world. Millions of people throughout the world, including Iraq, denounced the execution as an outrage and miscarriage of justice. This was the revenge of the circle of evil, the *Yahudi-Salibi-Munafiq* connection, and an example to those who dared cross the dictates of the circle.

Chapter Six

The Present World Order: Craving, Usury, Banking, Fake Money, and Secrecy

From the beginning, man has had an ingrained instinct for greed, envy, and covetousness. Tribes raided their neighbors for their food stock, cattle, and women. Chieftains and kings invaded others for their gold and land. Greed, war, and plunder became enshrined as nobility, chivalry, bravery, courage, valor, pluck, and heroism. Odes of old, songs of the brave, and poems of the battle, in time, became epics of history carved in stone of the greatness of thugs, plunderers, destroyers of civilizations, and mass murderers such as Alexander of Macedonia, Genghis Khan, Tamerlane, Mahmud Ghaznavi, Christopher Columbus, Vasco da Gama, Napoleon Bonaparte, Harry Truman, Saddam Hussein, and the two Bushes, to name a few.

Yet thousands more reaped from plunder and mass murder behind the great trading corporations—the East India, North American, and African trading companies of Europe—which in the name of commerce enslaved thousands and pillaged African, American, aboriginal, and South Asian wealth and devastated their cultural heritage built over thousands of years. Greed also wiped out entire civilizations in the Americas, killing millions with deliberate inoculation of smallpox into the populations of Native Americans in the plunder for their gold and land. Deliberate introduction of strong European liquor into native societies devastated their civilization, from which they have not recovered.

The Koran has given clear guidance to mankind on equitable and just share of earthly wealth:

And in nowise covet those things in which Allah hath bestowed His gifts more freely on some of you than on others: To men allotted what they earn and to women what they earn: But ask Allah for His bounty. (An-Nisa 4:29–32)

In the old days, city-states of Babylon and later Rome and Damascus manufactured consumer goods and traded them in the city for profit. People from the countryside brought their produce to the market and exchanged it for manufactured goods. The city-states bought the raw material from the countryside, manufactured it, and sold it back to the countryside at great profit. At the time, the city and countryside communities were autonomous and bartered with each other to their mutual benefit. The farmers and countrypeople saw the simple manufacturing tools in the cities, returned to the countryside, and promptly set up their own industries in competition with the cities. In Europe in the Middle Ages, the resources were scant. For the cities to survive, they had to control the resources and the trade of their countryside. Raiding parties from the cities attacked the countryside, destroyed their primitive industrial structure, and carried their wealth back to the city. The comparative advantage of the adjoining villages was eliminated by the use of force to maintain the dependency of the countryside on city manufacturing.

One city would become more efficient in their mercantile enterprise and set off a struggle for the markets and resources of other city-states. City-states fought city-states. These imperial city-states evolved into nations that continued to fight over the source of their wealth, control of their resources, and trade.

The imperial nations of Europe sought and began to control markets and wealth over the oceans in the Americas and on the Asian coastline. They colonized all continents and continued to battle over who would control the wealth-producing process, the sea-lanes, and the trade of their colonies, their countryside. Europe had been in a state of perpetual war for control over world resources.

The plunder of the colonies of the Americas and India provided them capital to industrialize their countries and force their mass-produced goods onto their colonies in exchange for their wealth in raw products and food, which helped them accumulate more capital. More capital generated more wealth. Trade with the colonies necessitated the creation of a mercantile fleet. Protection of the sea-lanes, in turn, necessitated the buildup of a large naval fleet. Capital required by the European monarchies to wage wars and by the merchants for trade began to be financed by merchant bankers. These bankers, from the mid-eighteenth century onward, began to accumulate a massive amount of wealth. They were instrumental in financing private armies and opposing parties in wars. Most bankers were Jews, with intricate family and communal network of business built over many generations. Usury among Jews, Christians, and Muslims was forbidden. However, Jewish merchants had no difficulty with such restriction on usury and in charging usurious interest rates as long as the borrowers were non-Jews.

Mayer Bauer, the sire of the Rothschild merchant banking family, learned from experience that with deposits of *one thousand* marks in his bank with some judicious manipulation, he was able to loan out ten times the principal, that is, *ten thousand marks*, and make for himself a similar amount of wealth as the original deposit within a very short period. Soon such bankers were able to finance industries and railways all around the world. These bankers also began to wield an inordinate amount of influence with the centers of power in Europe. They were also a valuable source of intelligence about the Middle Eastern lands to their governments. The Western powers, in the meanwhile, were conspiring to partition the Ottoman Empire. The vast territorial, geographic, and economic advantages of the Ottoman Empire tempted the English, French, Germans, and Russians to plan its dismemberment.

These imperial nations were exhausted and flat broke after battling over the world's wealth during the two world wars and no longer had the power to keep the world under their control. After the First World War, the imperial countries converted the captive Islamic lands into a patchwork of sixty or so principalities, small patches of land, and *imperial countryside*, each to be drained of their resources systematically by a designated imperial power. A submissive emir was designated the autocratic ruler by the imperial powers to control the populace. Without exception, all the emirs acted as imperial puppets, to the detriment of Islam and the Muslims.

The entire colonial world, the *countryside* of the imperial nations, started breaking free after the Second World War. The only country left with enough wealth and power after the Second World War was the United States, to whom all the warring nations were beholden either through defeat or through debt. The hundred or so colonized countries had been left impoverished, uneducated, and with little or no infrastructure. With no more resources in manpower or in tangible wealth, Britain, France, the Netherlands, and the lesser colonial powers abandoned the resource-rich former colonies to the United States. The United States, which to that point had the reputation of a benevolent, freedom-loving country, gained control of the cheap resources of what became the third world through the subtle mechanizations of the Cold War.

Every believer and every person with an ambition to free mankind from oppression and tyranny is duty bound to learn a lesson from the history of the downward slide of colonized people on political, economic, educational, social, and cultural fronts. With the knowledge of the workings of such exploitation, they are duty bound to remedy the conditions that caused such a catastrophe.

Monopolizing Money:

Before the widespread use of money, trading involved the simplest use of commercial transaction—barter, the exchange of two or more products of roughly equal value. Gold and silver became accepted as money nearly five thousand years ago in most cultures. The earliest gold coins were found in the ruins of Sumer, minted nearly five thousand years ago. Coins of measured value had been routinely minted from precious metals in most cultures. The value of such coins was equal to the labor required to produce any other item that this treasure could buy. Over thousands of years, gold had been regarded as money, known as commodity money.

In the Islamic world, Umar ibn al-Khattab established the known standard relationship between the weight of the dinar and the weight of the dirham. The dinar weighed 4.3 grams of gold and the dirham 3.0 grams of silver. The first dated coins assigned to the Islamic era were the copies of the silver dirham of the Sassanian Yazdegerd struck during the caliphate of Uthman with an Arabic inscription, "In the name of Allah." In the year 75 (695 CE), Caliph 'Abd al-Malik ordered the minting of all dirham according to the standard set by Umar ibn al-Khattab. Gold and silver coins remained the official currency of the Moguls, Safavids, and Ottoman Empire till their disintegration in recent times.

In the West, when the rulers became strapped for cash, they resorted to debasing their currency by lowering the gold or silver content. The use of gold as money was handicapped by its weight and bulk and the need of protection against debasement. In the nineteenth century, the problems of bulk and debasement were eliminated by printing paper money that could be redeemed for a stated amount of gold and silver. As the paper money was backed by gold, there remained the complication of accumulating and storing this valuable commodity.

The next step in the evolution of money was the use of pure paper money. The First and Second World Wars greatly weakened the old imperial countries' economies as almost all their gold had been traded for war material, purchased from the United States. Having lost their gold reserves, the imperial European powers kept on printing money to continue their wars of acquisition. Their colonial populations were drained of their resources with a systematic pillage of their wealth through subtle trading maneuvers. Colonial produce from India, Africa, and the Middle East was first bought with printed paper money. A million pound sterling notes—which cost less than twenty pounds to print, money created out of nothing—was used to purchase cotton, rubber, oil, and metal ore among other items and exported directly to Britain, for instance, or to the United States of America. The US goods purchased from the proceeds were then sent to Britain either for the war effort or for rebuilding the shattered cities. The colonial people were left to use the counterfeit state notes to buy their daily needs from whatever was left in the country. Excessive amount of paper money in the colonies caused rampant inflation.

During the second half of the nineteenth century and the twentieth century, there was a systematic transfer of wealth from the third world countries to the West. The Western countries—through their monopolies in shipping, insurance, banking, and manufacturing industries—further multiplied their acquired wealth a hundredfold. The British used Indian paper money, rupees, to bribe and arm the Bedouins of Sharif Hussein to fuel the war against the Ottomans after Britain's Arab Bureau exhausted all its gold stock in the Egyptian treasury.[68] The British used Indian rupees, created out of nothing, to bribe the sheikhs of the Persian Gulf and Emir 'Abd al-'Aziz (Ibn Sa'ud).

---

[68] The Arab Bureau.

The Banking System:

Among the first bankers in the Western world were the Knights Templar after their return from their Crusades against the Muslims. They had accumulated an immense amount of wealth; they were given enormous riches by the Christians supporting the Crusades against Islam by bestowing legacies, hoping to buy their place in heaven. The Knights Templar also obtained an enormous amount of wealth through loot and plunder of Christian gold and treasures of Constantinople on their way to the Holy Land. More gold and riches were accumulated by them during the rape and plunder of the Muslim lands of Syria and Palestine. The Knights Templar set up their temples in Paris and London and turned them from sleepy hamlets into great financial centers. King Phillip IV of France, in league with Pope Clement V, destroyed the Knights Templar and stole their fortune. The Order of the Knights Templar then went underground to work and plot secretly within other organizations. The world had a strict ban on usury, and as the time passed, this was forgotten, and banking began to develop, which now holds a tight clutch on humanity.

The currency at that time was gold and silver, and for safety reasons, the owners began to deposit their wealth with the goldsmiths, who had suitable strong rooms for storage and safekeeping. The goldsmiths issued paper receipts for gold and silver deposited with them. The depositors would pay their debts and expenses by withdrawing a portion of their gold and silver deposits as necessary. It was obviously a cumbersome process to move all the precious metals, and paper receipts slowly became accepted as currency. Gold and silver were rarely moved, but the ownership changed with the issuing of receipts to pay the debts. Goldsmiths charged storage fee and transaction charges for each receipt. In the same manner today, vast fortunes are made by simply moving numbers between one computer file to another.

The goldsmiths and other owners of the strong rooms began to realize that, at any one time, only a fraction of gold and silver was being withdrawn by the owners. So they began to issue notes (money) to people who did not own gold and silver and charge them interest on the notes. The only way their dishonesty would be discovered was if they issued too many notes and if every one of the gold and silver depositors tried to withdraw it at the same time. They began to issue notes for the ownership of the gold and silver greatly more than what they had deposited in their vaults. They began to issue an increasing number of notes depending on the gold and silver that the "banks" did not even have in their vaults. And they earned interest on the fictitious gold that did not exist. They could issue lots of bits and pieces of paper for gold and silver that did not exist and charge interest in doing so. In other words, a trick was perpetrated by lending gold and silver that did not exist and that they did not own. And profit was made out of nothing. This whole system of transactions was based on fraud and deceit. In summary, this is the description of modern banking.

In the eighteenth century, there was a major leap in the banking system's influence over world finance. This occurred with the emergence and rapid rise of dominance of one Jewish family, the house of Rothschild. Mayer Amschel Bauer was born in 1743 in Frankfurt, Germany. He worked briefly for the Oppenheimer Bank in Hanover and later became a moneylender. He acted as an agent for William IX, landgrave of Hesse-Kassel. Williams's family made a fortune by hiring out troops to Britain to fight in the American War of Independence. The Rothschild empire was built on money embezzled by Mayer Amschel from William, who in turn had stolen it from the soldiers he had hired out to the British. The money, said to have been around three million dollars, was paid by the British government to William to be paid to the soldiers but was kept by William for himself.[69]

---

[69] George Armstrong, *Rothschild Money Trust* (1940), 22.

William gave the money to Mayer Amschel Bauer to hide it from Napoleon's armies, but instead, Bauer sent it to England hidden in casks of wine with his son Nathan to establish a London branch of the family empire.

Nathan used the money to buy vast quantities of gold looted by the East India Company from India (Battle of Plassey) and used this gold to finance the Duke of Wellington's military adventures. Nathan was able to brag later that, in the five years he had been in England, he increased his original investment given by his father by 2500 times to 50 million pounds, comparable to purchasing power of billions of dollars today. It was around the time of Nathan's arrival in London that Mayer Bauer changed his name to Rothschild after the red shield emblem on the ghetto home of his ancestors to avoid anti-Semitism, prevalent in Europe in those days.

Mayer and his eldest son, Amschel, supervised the family banking business from their Frankfurt bank, son Nathan Mayer established the London branch in 1804, and the youngest son joined the Paris banking circles in 1811 while son Solomon started operating in Vienna and Karl in Naples. To prevent prying eyes, the family wrote all correspondence in *Judendeutch*, German written in Hebrew characters.

According to the *New Encyclopedia Britannica*, "Mayer set a pattern that his family was to follow so successfully, to do business with reigning houses by preference and to father as many sons as possible who could take care of the family's many business affairs abroad."

"From the earliest days, the Rothschild appreciated the importance of proximity to politicians, the men who determined not only the extent of budget deficit but also the domestic and foreign policies," wrote biographer Niall Fergusson. "Rothschild influence extended to royalty as well. Nathan first came into contact with British royalty thanks to his father's purchase of outstanding debts owed by George, Prince Regent, Later King George IV and his brothers."[70]

Ferguson traced the Rothschilds' influence through British royalty to Queen Victoria's consort, Prince Albert, and his son. The Rothschilds were quite close to most prominent British politicians such as Lord John Russell, Lord William Gladstone, Benjamin Disraeli, Arthur Balfour, Joseph Chamberlain, Lord Randolph Churchill, and his son Winston Churchill. The Rothschilds ingratiated themselves with the British politicians financially, and in return, most subtly influenced British foreign and fiscal policies. The Churchill family had a long-standing relationship with the Rothschilds. Winston Churchill's father, Randolph Churchill, was funded by the house of Rothschild while he was the British chancellor of the exchequer in the mid-1800s. Randolph died owing sixty-five thousand pounds to the Rothschilds when, in comparison, the total British government annual revenue was only ten million pounds.[71] Not only was the loan forgiven but more funds were also advanced to his son Winston by his good friend Lord Victor Rothschild. In return, Lord Victor Rothschild was granted full run of the British intelligence during the Second World War.[72]

The Rothschilds lent money that did not exist to finance wars, lending money to the opposing sides of the war, making immense profits from the interest. They also owned and controlled the armament industries from which the warring countries purchased weapons of destruction. The profits of war continued to multiply with the interest on the loans, commissions, sale of weapons, training of troops, and transport of weapons to the battlegrounds in Rothschild ships. When the warring countries have devastated each other with the help of money and weapons supplied by the bankers, the same banks then

[70] Ferguson, *House of Rothschild*, 9.

[71] *The Churchills*, Independent Television, May 1995.

[72] *Secret Societies*, 208.

lent more money that did not exist to rebuild their shattered nations and economies. The reconstruction produced even greater profit than the sale of weapons of destruction. And through debt, the bankers controlled those countries' governments and their commerce and economy. The Rothschild Empire became highly skilled in such manipulations as did those in America, such as JPMorgan, and many others in Europe. Behind the smokescreen of the global banking empires, armament industries, oil companies, and global corporations conspiring to gain control of the world's wealth are the same few families and individuals. There is evidence to suggest that the house of Rothschild was behind the resurgence of both the great American banking empires, the Morgans and the Rockefellers.

When Nathan Rothschild died, his eldest son, Lionel, became the head of the London Rothschilds. He advanced massive loans to the British and American governments as well as to the Egyptians. He lent eighty million pounds to the British government to finance the Crimean War, in which the Ottomans fought the Russians. Interestingly, he also acted as an agent to the Russian government for twenty years and loaned Russia the money to fight the Turks and the British during the Crimean War. The Ottomans received armaments and military assistance from the British in the Crimean War, which was engineered by Russia, France, and Britain in a dispute over which of the Christian churches would administer the holy Christian sites in Jerusalem. The Turkish populace paid for fifty years in gold and commodities, many times multiplied, the money lent by the Rothschilds in the Western-engineered war in which thousands perished. As a result, Egypt was occupied by the British on the pretext of nonpayment of this loan at the instigation of the Rothschilds. Turkey was drained of its lifeblood over usurious loans, the benefits of which never touched the population; the wars imposed caused suffering, poverty, humiliation, and in the end disintegration of the Ottoman Empire.

Lionel Rothschild was succeeded by his son Nathan Mayer, who became the first Lord Rothschild when he was raised to the peerage by Queen Victoria in 1885. He went on to become the governor of the Bank of England with untold power to influence the world's financial system. The Bank of England has always been an arm of the global elite who plotted and conspired to seize the wealth and territories of the world. The Rothschild representatives around the world continued to manipulate world events to expand their power and achieve world domination.

Al-Mutaffifeen: The Purveyors of Fraud

A group of global elite bankers created a network of central banks in each country working together to manipulate the financial system across Europe and the United States. These bankers—*al-Mutaffifeen*, dealers in fraud—have been described in the Koran:

> Woe to those that deal in fraud, those who, when they have to receive by measure, from men, exact full measure, but when they have to give by measure or weight to men, give less than due. Do they not think that they will be called to account?
>
> On a Mighty Day, a Day when (all) mankind will stand before the Lord of the Worlds? Nay! Surely the Record of the Wicked is (preserved) in Sijjin. (Mutaffifeen 83:1-7, Koran)

A central bank in each country was an idea of the *Mutaffifeen*, the purveyors of fraud. The earlier central banks were opened in Amsterdam and Hamburg. The Bank of England soon followed. This bank, owned privately by the *Mutaffifeen*, started by lending money to the British government. The owners of the bank made fantastic profits, which came from the pockets of the common man, through income tax and the exploitation of the poor people of the British Empire. This was the beginning of the national debt, when nations began to be indebted to moneylenders who owned the banks.

The kings and politicians did not understand the workings of money. Therefore, the minting of money was given over to a committee that also had the authority to base the country's wealth on gold that was controlled and held by the *Mutaffifeen* bankers. The aristocrats and merchants who created the Bank of England and the East India Company also began to control the country's wealth. With this wealth, they rapidly created a merchant fleet and a private army. The trading corporations expanded their mercantile empires and began to control whole countries in South Asia and the Far East for the European kings and aristocracy. In time, these empires of the *Mutaffifeen* merchant bankers became the greatest drug operations the world has ever seen.

The *Mutaffifeen*—usurious, thieving drug barons—plundered gold, silver, and jewels from India, Burma, Ceylon, Indochina, China, Indonesia, Malaya, and the Philippines and used their ill-gotten wealth to influence world events. The *Mutaffifeen* bankers were involved in the American Civil War, in which they financed both sides. The London Rothschilds funded the North, and the Paris Rothschilds funded the South.

In the earlier part of the twentieth century, these bankers began planning the takeover of the world's largest economy, that of the United States. They wanted two things, a new central bank like the Bank of England to control the American nation's borrowing and the introduction of a federal income tax to give them control over the government's finances. There was serious opposition to this, but in classic *Mutaffifeen* fashion, in a clearly well-planned strategy, they duped the American Congress and the public. First, the *Mutaffifeen* bankers supported the election of Pres. Woodrow Wilson in 1909.

He was a front man and a political puppet. The real power of the Wilson administration was in the hands of a man called Col. Edward Mandell House. Mandell House got the instructions from the banking conspirators, and he, in turn, instructed Woodrow Wilson, who did as he was told.

In 1902, the Rothschilds sent one of their agents, Paul Warburg, to America with his brother Felix to rearrange US banking to suit the Rothschilds and the *Mutaffifeen* interests. Another brother, Max Warburg, stayed at home in Frankfurt to run the family banking business there. Upon arrival in the United States, Paul Warburg married Nina Loeb of the Rothschild-controlled Kuhn, Loeb & Co. while Felix married Frieda Schiff, the daughter of Jacob Schiff, the head of Kuhn, Loeb & Co. Both brothers became partners in the company, and Paul was given a salary of half a million dollars. When Jacob Schiff arrived in America to join Kuhn, Loeb & Co., he married the daughter of Solomon Loeb. Schiff was to become the manipulator of American banking for over half a century. Schiff and the Rothschild family had shared the same house in Frankfurt in the days of Mayer Amschel.

The conspiring bankers met at a place called Jekyll Island in Georgia in greatest secrecy to put together the bill for the introduction of the new US central bank, the Federal Reserve System. For years, those who participated denied that such a gathering ever took place. The time of the meeting that supposedly "did not take place" was when the conspiring *Mutaffifeen* bankers took over the US economy and its people with an organization called the Federal Reserve System, which is neither federal nor does it have any reserves.

The secret seven who met in secrecy in Jekyll Island at J. P. Morgan's island resort off the coast of Georgia were Frank A. Vanderlip, Abraham Piatt Andrew, Henry P. Davison, Charles Norton, Benjamin

Strong, Paul Warburg, and Sen. Nelson Aldrich. Frank A. Vanderlip represented William Rockefeller and Jacob Schiff's investment firm of Kuhn, Loeb & Co. Vanderlip later was to become the president of New York's National City Bank; Abraham Piatt Andrews the assistant secretary of the United States Treasury; Henry P. Davison a senior partner of J. P. Morgan and Company; Charles Norton the president of First National Bank of New York(a JPMorgan company); Benjamin Strong a Morgan lieutenant; Paul Warburg a partner of Kuhn, Loeb & Co.; and Rhode Island Republican senator Nelson Aldrich the chairman of the National Monetary Commission, the only nonbanker in the group. Aldrich was an associate of banker J. P. Morgan and father-in-law of John D. Rockefeller Jr. Warburg, a representative of the European Rothschilds, was brother to Max Warburg, chief of the M. M. Warburg & Co. banking consortium in Germany and the Netherlands.[73]

The conspirators representing the houses of Morgan, Rockefeller, and Rothschild came up with a plan to take control of the US banking system. These seven men, under the guidance of Paul Warburg, concluded not to have one central bank in the United States but several. They agreed that no one was to utter the words *central* or *bank*. Most importantly, they decided that their creation would be made to look like an official agency of the US government. This proposal came to be known as the Aldrich plan. From the beginning, the plan was ill fated and seen as a transparent attempt to create a system of bankers by the bankers and for the bankers. The proposal never got off the committee stage, and the bill was doomed.

A new tactic was then used by the banking *Mutaffifeen*. Congressman Carter Glass of Virginia was given the task of writing a new bill. Glass attacked the Aldrich plan and stated that it lacked government control and created a banking monopoly in the hands of the New York

---

[73] Jim Marrs, *Rule by Secrecy* (HarperCollins), 70.

bankers; it opened the door to inflation. Glass then said that what the country needed was an entirely fresh approach, a genuine reform bill that was not written by the agents of the money trust. He then went on to draft an alternative, the Federal Reserve Act, which in every aspect was an exact image of the Aldrich plan.

Vanderlip and Aldrich spoke venomously against the Glass bill, even though Glass had cleverly incorporated entire sections of the Aldrich plan. It was clearly an effort to garner public support for the Glass bill by the appearance of banker opposition. President Wilson signed the Federal Reserve Act on December 23, 1913, just two days before Christmas, with some of the congressmen already home for the holidays and the average citizen's attention clearly elsewhere.

"Congress was outflanked, outfoxed and outclassed by a deceptive, but brilliant psycho-political attack," commented author Griffin in his well-researched book about the most blatant scam in history, the creation of the Federal Reserve System[74].

The Federal Reserve System is composed of twelve Federal Reserve banks, each serving a section of the United States but each dominated by the New York Federal Reserve bank. The Federal Reserve System is such a pivotal force in the world economic system that financial experts in every nation pay close attention to any action it takes. Even the slightest interest rate change it makes can shake markets and create or destroy millions of jobs. It is important to know who controls the Fed. By using a central bank to create alternate periods of inflation and deflation and thus squeezing the public for vast profits, it has been worked out by international bankers into an exact science.

An examination of the major stockholders of New York banks shows clearly that a few families related by blood, marriage, or business interests still control New York City banks and, in turn,

---

[74] Griffin, *Creature.*

hold the controlling stock of the Federal Reserve Bank of New York. Eustace Mullins, in his 1983 book, *The Secrets of the Federal Reserve*, presented charts connecting the Federal Reserve Bank of New York and its member banks to the families of the Rothschilds, Morgans, Rockefellers, Warburgs, and others. The private control of the Federal Reserve continues till today. The Federal Reserve Bank of New York completely dominates the other eleven branches through stock ownership, control, and influence by having the only permanent voting seat in the Federal Open Marketing Committee and handling all open market bond transactions. Two banks, Chase Manhattan Bank (merged with the Chemical Bank) and Citibank, own 53 percent of shares. These facts point to the reality that a handful of determined families control the economies of America and the world.

In the Islamic monetary system, gold and silver coins were minted at the command of the sovereign and used as legal tender in trade and commerce. The value of gold over the centuries continued to be stable among trading nations. Gold and silver coins were traded in exchange for commodities, services, and government expenditure. Soldiers were paid in gold or silver coins, and meritorious services rendered were rewarded with titles to estates owned by the state. Wars were expensive and therefore, by necessity, short. State revenue was collected through taxation of the populace in gold or commodities. In just societies, the subjects were protected with justice, and education, health, and social services were provided through voluntary donation of zakat by the population. Warfare was only defensive. All the offensive wars perpetrated by Muslim rulers against one another were for self-aggrandizement, conquest, and plunder and all strictly forbidden by the Koran. History of such rulers showed that most were gangsters who, along with a few armed followers, took control of the centers of power and terrorized their subjects and neighboring states.

From the beginning, coveting an increased amount of money supply led to fraudulent practices that, in turn, caused destruction to honest trade and commerce. Unscrupulous merchants began to shave a tiny portion of each coin they received and then melted it down into new coins. Before long, the king's treasury started doing the same to the coins it received in taxes. In this way, money supply was increased, but the amount of gold was not. This subterfuge initially succeeded, but the end result was what always happens when money supply is artificially expanded—there was inflation. Whereas one coin previously would buy twelve sheep, now it was accepted for only ten. The total amount of gold needed for twelve sheep never really changed. Everyone knew that one coin did not contain the same amount of gold.

The governments became bolder in their plans to exploit their subjects. They began to dilute the amount of gold and silver content in the coins by adding base metals in the coins; thus, the coins appeared to be of the same size and color. People wisely discounted the coins, and the real value of goods and services and gold stayed the same.

Governments do not like to be thwarted in their plans to exploit people. So they found a way to force people to accept these tokens of money. This led to the first legal tender laws. By royal decree, the *coin of the realm* was declared legal for the settlement of debts and payment of taxes. Anyone who refused it at face value was subject to fine or imprisonment.

The business of banking began Europe in the fourteenth century. Its function was to evaluate exchange and safeguard people's coins. In the beginning there were notable examples of total honest banks that operated with remarkable efficiency considering the vast variety of coins they handled. They also issued paper receipts that were so dependable they freely circulated as money and cheated no one in the process. But there was more demand for more money and more loans and the temptation soon caused the bankers to seek easier paths. They began lending out pieces of paper that *said* that they were receipts, but which in effect were counterfeit. The public could not tell one from the other and accepted both of them as money. From that point forwards the receipts in circulation exceeded the gold held in reserve and the age of *fractional reserve banking* had dawned. This led immediately to what would become the unbroken record from then to the present: a record of inflation, booms and busts, suspension of payments, bank failures and repudiation of currencies and recurring spasms of economic chaos.

The Bank of England was set up in 1694 to institutionalize fractional-reserve banking. As the world's first central bank, it introduced the concept of partnership between bankers and the politicians. The politicians would receive spendable money (created out of nothing by the bankers) without having to raise taxes. In return the bankers would receive a commission on the transaction-deceptively called interest, which would continue in perpetuity. Since it all seemed to be wrapped up in mysterious rituals of banking which the common man was not expected to understand there was practically no opposition to the scheme. The arrangement proved to be so profitable to the participants that it soon spread to so many other countries in Europe and eventually to the United States.[75]

The international banking system is based on the system developed in Europe over the last two hundred years and then grafted into the American economy. At the end of the Second World War, the

[75] G. Edward Griffin, *The Creature from Jekyll Island* (American Media), 183.

economies of both the victors and the defeated in Europe and Japan were devastated and depleted of all gold reserves. The plans for a new international economic system were worked out by delegates from forty-four countries at the White Mountain Resort of Bretton Woods, New Hampshire, in 1944. No sovereign Islamic states were present.

The new economic system was the product of the collaboration between John Maynard Keynes, representing Britain, and Harry White of the US Treasury. Instead of an international economy where each nation's economy was backed by its stock of gold, the new system made the US dollar the centerpiece of the new structure. The dollar was supported by 75 percent of the world's stock of monetary gold. The US economy had been boosted by 30 percent during the Second World War, while the economies of Europe, Russia, China, Japan, and the colonial world had been thoroughly devastated. While rearming the allies and the conquest of the enemies, most of the world's monetary gold was transferred to the United States through arms sales and as rewards of the conqueror.

The Bretton Woods arrangements provided that the United States would be the only nation with a currency freely convertible into gold at a fixed value. All other countries were. Before this conference, currencies were exchanged in terms of their gold value, and the arrangement was called the "gold exchange standard," determined by how much gold they could buy in the open market. The Bretton Woods arrangements sought to recapture the advantage of gold standard while minimizing the pain imposed by the gold standard on countries that were buying too much, selling too little, and losing gold. The method by which it was to be accomplished was the same as the method devised in Jekyll Island to allow American banks to create money out of nothing without paying the penalty of having their currencies devalued by other banks. It was the establishment of a world central bank that would create common fiat money based on the dollar for all nations and then require them to inflate together at the same rate. There was to be a kind of common insurance fund that would rush that fiat money to any nation that temporarily needed to face down a run on its currency.

Fiat money is defined as "paper money decreed legal tender, not backed by gold or silver." Therefore, it does not represent anything of intrinsic value, and it is legal tender. Thus, the only way the governments can exchange its worthless paper money for tangible goods is to give its citizens no choice.

United States, the kingpin of the world monetary order, went on a spending spree after the Second World War. As the economies of Europe and Asia revived, the lure of profit drove a massive amount of banking capital from the United States into thousands of enterprises across the seas and attracted rising foreign imports to America's shores. The United States deployed American military might around the globe and fought two hot wars in Asia as well as a cold war against the Russians. The war in Vietnam alone cost the Americans dearly, a sum of $180 billion. Before the game was over, Americans would find themselves besieged by their economic competitors and forced by gold onto their knees before their friends. As Americans spent their dollars abroad, foreign ownership of bank deposits in American banks and of short-term US Treasury obligations increased from $8 billion in 1950 to over $20 billion in 1960. If foreigners at that moment had decided to convert all their dollar assets into gold, the US gold stock would have been exhausted[76].

On August 15, 1971, Richard Nixon signed an executive order declaring that the United States would no longer redeem its paper dollars for gold. The IMF had to depend on the central banks of its member nations to provide cash and so-called credits, but since these

---

[76] Peter L. Bernstein, *The Power of Gold*, 334.

banks could print as much money as they wished, from then on, there would be no limit. When the dollar broke loose from gold, there was no longer a ready standard for measuring currency values.

When a country spends more than it earns in international trade, a trade deficit exists. This is similar to the situation of a person who spends more than he earns. In both cases, the process cannot be sustained unless (a) earnings are increased, (b) money is taken out of savings, (c) assets are sold, (d) money is counterfeited, or (e) money is borrowed.

Increasing the money is the best solution. All else is temporary at best. The second option is not feasible as virtually no government in the world today has any savings. Selling of assets as an option also is not available to most governments. The only government asset that is readily marketable is gold, and only a few countries today have a stockpile of gold from which to draw. Governments have also sold nationalized industries, mineral rights, and real estate to foreign investors.

The counterfeit option is available to a country in a unique position of having its currency accepted as the medium of international trade. Such countries include the United States, Great Britain, France, Italy, Japan, Germany, and the Netherlands. In that event, it is possible to create money out of nothing, and other nations have no choice but to accept it. Thus, for years, a country like the United States has been able to spend more money than it earns in trade by having the Federal Reserve, a privately owned organization, create as much money whenever it needs.

The United States is one of the safest places in the world to invest one's money. But to do so, one had to convert his native currency into dollars. This gave the dollar greater value in the international markets than it otherwise would have merited. In spite of the fact that the

Federal Reserve was creating huge amounts of money, the demand for it by foreigners was seemingly limitless. Thus, America has been able to finance its trade deficit with fiat money, in real terms fraudulent and counterfeit money, a feat no other nation in the world has been able to achieve.

After the 1973 Yom Kippur War, the Middle Eastern oil producers raised oil price with the connivance of the *Mutaffifeen* bankers and the oil companies by 400 percent. There was a widespread economic collapse around the world that allowed these banks to accumulate yet more land, businesses, and control of wealth. The Rockefeller-controlled Exxon became the largest corporation. The deal behind the scenes with the Arab producers was that oil would only be purchased in dollars, and a large percentage of billions of dollars the Arabs were receiving in extra revenues would be invested in the global *Mutaffifeen* banks. The recipients were Chase Manhattan, Citibank, Manufacturers Hanover Trust of New York, Bank of America, Barclays, Lloyds, and Midland. These banks then set about lending and investing these dollars in Asia, Africa, and South America, who were forced to borrow to prevent starvation in the wake of oil price shocks.

In 1974 alone, Arab producers invested $57 billion in financial institutions in New York and London. To date, there is an estimated six trillion dollars of Arab money invested in America and Europe that could have raised the living standards of Muslims around the world twenty-five-fold. The banks controlled by the Rockefellers, Rothschilds, Morgans, and other related families, in turn, lent ten times their deposit of Arab money to third world countries. Today the Muslim world is reeling in debt, paying out an estimated $122 billion annually in interest and principal to these half-dozen banking families.

Islamic Countries: External Debt in Million Dollars (2006 CE)

Country		Country		
Afghanistan	not known	Lebanon	6,725	
Albania	821	Libya	not known	
Algeria	30,665	Malaysia	44,773	
Azerbaijan	693	Maldives	180	
Bahrain	0	Mali	3,201	
Bangladesh	16,376	Mauritania	2,589	
Bosnia	not known	Morocco	20,687	
Brunei	0	Niger	1,659	
Burkina Faso	9,907	Nigeria	30,315	
Chad	1,019	Oman	3,629	
Comoros	203	Pakistan	32,229	
Djibouti	288	Palestine	not known	
Egypt	31,964	Qatar	0	
Eritrea	not known	Saudi Arabia	0	
Ethiopia	10,352	Senegal	3,861	
Gambia	477	Sierra Leone	1,243	
Guinea	3,546	Somalia	2,635	
Guinea-Bissau	964	Sudan	16,843	
Indonesia	150,876	Syria	22,435	
Iran	14,391	Tajikistan	1,070	
Iraq	not known	Tanzania	7,603	
Jordan	8,486	Tunisia	11,078	
Kazakhstan	5,714	Turkey	102,074	
Kyrgyzstan	1,148	Turkmenistan	2,266	
Kuwait	0	UAE	0	
		Uzbekistan	not known	
		Yemen	4,138	
Total	287,890	+	321,233	=$609.12 billion

The combined interest paying debt of the world of Islam to the *Mutaffifeen* bankers today stands at $609.12 billion. With 10 percent return of principal annually along with 10 percent interest compounded daily, the annual repayment to the lenders collected from the Muslim citizens, the taxpayers, will amount to a whopping sum of *$122 billion annually*, an indebtedness of the sum of one hundred US dollars for every living Muslim man, woman, and child for the rest of their lives. An estimated 40 percent of the money borrowed by the Muslim countries never reached the people, whose standard of living it was supposed to raise. Out of this amount of $250 billion, half went into commissions, bribery, and the pockets of politicians, ministers, presidents, and kings. The other half, $120 billion, was rolled over into the debt for the interest, compounded daily, which had remained delinquent because of budget shortfalls.

Of the remaining $360 billion borrowed, around $180 billion were put into state-owned and state-operated industries that are constipated by bureaucracy, corruption, and graft. Doomed to economic failure from the start, they consumed the loans with no possibility of repayment. These industries served as a rotating employment exchange for the friends, families, and supporters of the politicians and green pastures for the retired generals of the military governments. The rest of the $180 billion dollars had been consumed to keep the military and intelligence agencies well greased and the politicians, generals, and kings in power.

The Western loans can only be paid in hard currency. Therefore the Muslim countries have to raise $122 billion a year in hard currency in dollars, Eurodollars, pound sterling, or yen simply to service the debt. Most Muslim countries do not have a surplus trade balance and therefore have fallen into a perpetual debt trap from which they will never ever be able to escape in the present global system.

To accumulate hard currency reserves, the governments encourage their farmers to grow cash crops that can be merchandised overseas as raw products for the Western industries. As a result, domestic agriculture is unable to feed the countries' population, necessitating cereal imports, causing further debt burden. Muslim countries import seventy-five million tons of cereals per annum. Historically, all Muslim nations had been self-sufficient in food and cereals. The pressure to grow cash crops, inefficient agricultural practices, poor seed, high cost of fuel and fertilizer, absentee owners of land, poor technology, and poor irrigation practices are responsible for the food shortage and therefore trade deficits. Cereals are bought from the European common market and the United States, where the farmers are subsidized to grow cereal and other agriculture products in surplus. These two areas of the world produce 140 million tons of surpluses in grains stimulated by subsidies to their farmers. The export of all the surplus grain to the third world countries, plus the freight, shipping, handling, and commissions, nets the producers—the European common market and the USA—$60 billion annually, of which half is spent by Muslim countries. The cereal imports by Muslim countries amounts to $300 billion over ten years, which accounts for 40 percent of the external debt of the Muslim world.

This food shortage is astonishing as the landmass of the Islamic world covers an area of 30,605,212 square kilometers of some of the most fertile land in the world. This land, since prehistoric times, has been the breadbasket of the world.

Cereal Imports to Muslim Countries in Metric Tons Annually

Country	Metric tons	Country	Metric tons
Afghanistan	242,000	Lebanon	647,704
Albania	278,000	Libya	1,993,860
Algeria	6,291,538	Malaysia	3,569,469
Azerbaijan	655,321	Maldives	31,369
Bahrain	185,000	Mali	115,437
Bangladesh	3,684,072	Mauritania	801,448
Bosnia	Not known	Morocco	3,340,314
Brunei	35,297	Niger	98,798

Burkina Faso	54,646	Nigeria	2,955,325
Chad	48,348	Oman	509,292
Comoros	41,407	Pakistan	2,527,375
Djibouti	89,936	Palestine	Not known
Egypt	10,589,395	Qatar	166,445
Eritrea	580,920	Saudi Arabia	7,293,459
Ethiopia	580,920	Senegal	856,168
Gambia	127,690	Sierra Leone	311,529
Guinea	288,179	Sudan	758,790
Guinea-Bissau	69,947	Syria	597,845
Indonesia	2,691,499	Tajikistan	Not known
Iran	6,339,974	Tunisia	1,953,172
Iraq	3,455,169	Turkey	2,970,779
Jordan	1,766,139	Turkmenistan	755,159
Kazakhstan	18,591	UAE	1,658,261
Kyrgyzstan	154,532	Uzbekistan	Not known
Kuwait	699,307	Yemen	2,554,262
	38,967,827	**+**	**36,466,260 = 75,434,087 metric tons**

A glance at the major borrowers of the Muslim world tells a story of unstable, corrupt regimes with human rights abuses, poor democratic record, warfare, and subservience to the command of the Western powers. There is a strange correlation among unstable, repressive, undemocratic regimes; human right abuses; civil unrest; arms imports; food shortage; foreign debt; and collusion with Western governments against Islamic interests.

Foreign Debt as Compared with Cereal Imports

Country	Foreign debt	Annual grain imports
	Million dollars	Metric tons
Algeria	30,665	6,291,538
Egypt	31,964	10,589,395
Ethiopia	10,352	580,920
Indonesia	150,876	2,691,499

Jordan	8,486	1,766,139
Malaysia	44,773	3,569,469
Morocco	20,687	3,340,314
Nigeria	30,315	2,955,325
Pakistan	32,229	2,527,575
Sudan	16,843	758,790
Turkey	102,074	2,970,779
Total	479,264	38,041,743

These countries, no doubt, have larger proportion of the population, but they also have some of the world's greatest resources and a fertile landmass. These countries have a record of 80 percent of the Muslim world's external debt, and they import an estimated 50 percent of the grain brought into the Islamic world. Their economies are in shambles. They all have a history of human rights abuses and have all been (except for Malaysia) saddled with corrupt robber leadership subservient to outside political and monetary forces.

Rule by Secrecy

Throughout the history of man, the route to power and control of people and their riches has been through a maze of secrecy, deceitful manipulation, subterfuge, and conspiracy. During and after the European Crusades into the Islamic heartland, various Christian organizations from diverse lands of Europe began to band together into secret organizations to achieve different agendas. In time, they began to control and influence the ruling houses of Europe, the papacy and the church, and the centers that controlled commerce and wealth. Wars between the kingdoms of Europe rarely had to do with the interest of people, justice, freedom, or human rights. Wars were fought to promote the interests of these secret organizations, which were the power behind the kings and the church.

All royal dynasties of the world originated from a band of robbers who invaded a land and came to control the centers of power and wealth. Their first act of governance was to eliminate all opposition (execution, massacres), control the population through brute force (army and secret services), and control the wealth of the land (rob the previous holders of their gold, precious stones, mansions, and estates through taxation of peasants and merchants). The rulers put on fancy garb and sat on a raised platform. The collaborators were given gaudy robes, high-sounding titles, and estates. To perpetuate the largesse from the rulers, the hangers-on supported the prolongation of the dynasty. Such was the beginning of the "establishment," a system of control of instruments of political and military power and acquisition of wealth in the hand of a select few.

With new invaders and the turnover of dynasties, the hangers-on, the courtiers, and the conspirators, the power behind the new rulers never changed. The clans behind the throne, the elite, the parasites, and the leeches honed their skills through greed and lechery, programmed their genes through marriage and social connections, and kept their power through secret organizations and conspiracy. The British Empire and the European royalty are a clear example of this inherited and aristocratic control lasting over a thousand years. The sovereigns of Europe sent their armies to the East and the West to loot and rob. The marauding armies presented the monarch with the pick of the robbed gold, diamonds, and treasures that had been hoarded by generations of Indians and other Asians over thousands of years. In return, the grateful sovereign rewarded his thugs with knighthoods, lordships, and earldoms of the realm. Thugs were ennobled over the meaner subjects to create nobility that would be the backbone of the dynasty. The nobility was presented with charters to fleece Her Majesty's loyal subjects around the world through constitutional pillage by taxation and unjust monopolistic trading practices.

After the Second World War, with the total economic ruin of European colonial powers, there occurred involuntary emancipation of the colonial subjects. The European heartland was in total ruins; with no military might to control the world's wealth, Europe faced further economic and industrial disaster. Nations of Europe and the United States then got together to establish a world order to maintain their hegemony over the rest of the world. The United Nations was created on the corrupted foundation of the League of Nations. Through a carefully crafted world order and a preordained power structure, the United States, Russia, Britain, and France—through a veto power over the rest of the world—reigned supreme. The Security Council became the instrument of the big four to control the world. At that time, the only Islamic countries totally independent of foreign domination were Turkey and Afghanistan. Saudi Arabia, Iraq, Iran, Jordan, and Egypt were beholden to the British apron strings.

Other arrangements of control—the Bretton Woods Agreement, the International Monetary Fund, and the World Bank—were established to strengthen the Western grip over the world's resources. Toward the same end, the American Marshall Plan was inaugurated to rebuild and establish a united Europe with a single unified army, currency, and purpose meant for world domination. Such immaculate and secretive planning, coordination, and cooperation gave birth to the organization of the so-called G8 nations. The United States, Canada, Russia, Britain, France, Italy, Germany, and Japan formed the G8, a grouping of countries with a population of seven hundred million people dominating the world through superior technology, military power, economics, industrial manufacturing, trade, education, and transport. These countries are resource poor, and their economies will crumble if their access to cheap resources of the underdeveloped world is severed.

The greatest threat to the international and Islamic economy is the fiscal system designed at Bretton Woods that made the United States dollar the kingpin of the world's monetary order whereby the world has to acquire the dollar or the currency of G8 countries to buy the West's industrial goods or pay their debts. When Richard Nixon severed the link between gold and the dollar, the G8 countries began a bonanza of printing paper money twenty times their 1971 economic base. The United States Federal Reserve System, a privately owned banking system, was set up in the image of Bank of England to control the country's fiscal system. The USA, being the world's largest economy, influences the world's commercial base. The money supply of the USA and G8 countries is based on consumer demand. The money is printed by the Treasury and handed over to the central bank, or the Federal Reserve service, which in turn lends these notes created out of ink and paper at an interest rate determined by the Federal Reserve service. The commercial banks then loan out this "money made out of nothing" to the consumers at an additional interest rate generally calculated at prime rate fixed by the federal bank plus 1 to 5 percent, making a huge profit. The paper note printed by the treasury becomes *money* only when it is lent out to someone as the principal to be paid back with interest.

Almost all Western governments conduct business on deficit basis, meaning that they spent far greater money than they receive in revenue. The United States government had, by 1999, borrowed and accumulated a debt of $5.7 trillion. By 1997, the US government was paying out $350 billion in interest payments, amounting to the total revenues collected through personal income tax. The current US government debt is eight trillion dollars. The debt of the American people is another thirty-three trillion dollars. With the printing of additional currency, the purchasing power of the dollar has continued to devalue by 5 percent each year since 1973. Therefore, the 2002 dollar has only 20 percent purchasing power of the 1972 dollar. In 2005, the third world farmers and workers had to labor fifteen hours to purchase industrial products produced by a European or American worker in one hour. In the same vein, the populations of the third world have to work five to seven times longer to service their international debt compared with what they did thirty years ago.

The G8 summitry and its move for globalization of the world's trade and economy aims to perpetuate the control of the resources and labor of the third world and the Islamic nations. The aim of the G8 and their elite who dictate their policies of the West is to prevent the unification of the Islamic world through internal subversion, military coups, and creation of discord among Muslim nations (Iran and Iraq, Iraq and Kuwait) and through the perpetuation of the Palestinian-Israeli conflict. Western support of incompetent and corrupt leaders of the Middle East—Reza Shah, Anwar Sadat, Hosni Mubarak, King Hussein of Jordan, Saddam Hussein, Fahd, and Abdullah has muzzled the voice of the believer for the last three generations. For the price of a bit of flattery, a subtle threat, and a pocketful of money, Muslim generals, politicians, and princes sold their country's interests to the West. Musharraf put up for sale the sovereignty of Pakistan, Afghanistan, Central Asia, and Iraq to the Americans, renewing Western control over the resources and sovereignty of Islam for another century. Leaders of Islamic nations are watched for their vanity, submissiveness, megalomania, corruption, and lack of principles. Their weaknesses are scrutinized and analyzed. Accordingly, they are pampered with flattery, cash, and gifts and occasionally with blackmail and subtle threats till they singly or collectively become thoroughly emasculated, reminiscent of eunuchs prostrating in the presence of the king of the West in Washington. Before they know it, they have sold out their people's unity, sovereignty, resources, and dignity. All this does not occur accidentally. It is planned with care for years and executed by skillful players who have carefully studied the psyche and weaknesses of the Middle Eastern upstarts.

Conspiracy and intrigue for power and wealth has been with us since prehistoric times. Modern history is woven with the thread of intricate secrecy and planning that has affected the life of every person on this planet for the benefit of the few who control the wealth of the world. Cecil Rhodes, a fabulously wealthy Englishman, exploited the continent and peoples of Africa through gold and diamond mines in southern Africa. Rhodes, as a student of Oxford University, came under the influence of John Ruskin. Ruskin, a professor of fine arts, created a revolution in the thinking of the privileged undergraduates of Oxford and Cambridge Universities. Most of these students, upon graduation, went on to administer and govern far-flung colonies of the British Empire. For the rest of his life, Rhodes remained obsessed with Ruskin's philosophy of the creation of a world government centered on Britain.

As Rhodes's wealth grew with the exploitation of South African gold and diamonds, he established companies like De Beers Consolidated Mines and Consolidated Gold Fields. He became the prime minister of the Cape Colony and used his wealth to influence the parliamentary seats in Britain and South Africa. By the 1890s, he had a yearly income of a million pounds (when Britain's annual revenue was ten million pounds), most of which went to furthering his aims of a world government centered on Britain.

Rhodes planned and set up a secret society that would manipulate events in a way that led to the introduction of a centralized global control in the hands of a few select elite. The society came to be known by several names; one of them was the Round Table and another the Committee of Three Hundred. The society was structured on Illuminati and Freemasonic lines. There was an inner circle, the Society of the Elect, that knew exactly what the game and aim was; and the outer circle of friends, made up of influential people, could help the cause but did not always know the full implications or the ambitions of the Round Table. The Round Table's real manipulators were mostly those with real power rather than those with the *appearance* of power. Their names were not recorded in history like those of the famous politicians and generals, but they controlled the events far more than those documented by history books.

Lord Astor (Comm. 300) was a member of the inner circle of the Round Table. He owned the *Times* newspaper and controlled the flow of information to the public. The power lies not with the politicians but with the shadowy figures in the background that advise and control them through the manipulation of news and events. The Astor family had made its fortune smuggling opium into China and had instigated the British fleet to control Chinese ports to facilitate their drug smuggling into China in the nineteenth century. Their ships picked up lead and mercury in Gibraltar and opium from Smyrna in Turkey and then sold it in China.

The Rothschilds, through their membership and added influence in the inner circle of the Round Table, plotted the Boer War in South Africa in 1899–1902, in which tens of thousands of men women and children were killed, many in concentration camps established by Lord Kitchener (Comm. 300). The prime minister and the foreign minister at that time was Lord Salisbury (Comm. 300) of the elite Cecil family, a close friend of Winston Churchill (Comm. 300). Lord Salisbury and the Cecil family were key players in the Rhodes Round Table operation, which secured the enormous gold and diamond and other mineral wealth of South Africa for the British and, in particular, the Rothschilds.

The Cecil family, at that time, held a strong grip on the English government. No fewer than seven sons, nephews, and cousins sat on the government benches and four more in the cabinet. The House of Commons came to be known as Hotel Cecil. One of them, Arthur J. Balfour, was preparing to take over as prime minister when his uncle Lord Salisbury retired. Baron Nathan Rothschild was member of the Round Table, which represented the interests of the house of Rothschild and the bankers they controlled, such as the Warburgs, Schroeders, and Lazards.

J. P. Morgan (Comm. 300) joined the Round Table in 1899. When Rhodes died, he left his wealth to the cause, although in one of his earlier wills he had bequeathed his wealth to the Rothschilds. It has been stated that his mining activities had been financed by the Rothschilds.

After Rhodes, Alfred Milner (Comm. 300)—a Rothschild agent—took over the leadership of the Round Table. Under Milner's stewardship, the Round Table influence grew, and it went on to enjoy tremendous power at the heart of the British government. Among its inner membership were Arthur Balfour (Comm. 300), the foreign secretary, and the prime minister whose Balfour Declaration would, in effect, bring the state of Israel into being.

The Round Table controlled the *London Times* newspaper and other publications that controlled the British and Commonwealth public opinion. The house of Rothschild bought interest in three leading European news agencies: Wolff in Germany, Havas in France, and Reuters in England. These news agencies provide news stories to all newspapers and media outlets, so what they say is repeated by the whole media. So people believe that because they are all printing the same information with the same slant, it must be the true occurrence without realizing that the information is being fed from the same source. People are manipulated by a few hidden hands that control world events.

Alfred Milner was the chief influence in the British war cabinet of Lloyd George (Comm. 300). He would dominate the British delegation at the Paris Peace Conference of 1919, when the shape of the postwar world was decided. He was also the major player behind the division of the spoils of the remnants of the Ottoman Empire and the creation of League of Nations, an attempt to create a world government under the British rule.

The Round Table decided the policy in Ireland, Palestine, and India from 1917 to 1945. The Round Table also "controlled the sources and writing of history of British Imperial and foreign policy since the Boer War[77]." The dissemination of their version of world events and the rewriting of history were used to brainwash their citizens and the youth in schools and universities. Such manipulations of the Round Table have, to some extent, affected the life of almost every human being during the last one hundred years, not through a democratic process but through the maneuverings of a handful, nameless, and faceless people working for their own secret agenda.

Carroll Quigley, a professor at Georgetown University, was an insider who had been given access to papers on the *new world order* conspiracy. He broke ranks and revealed in great detail what was happening behind the scenes in the first fifty years of this century. He wrote in his book *The Anglo-American Establishment*:

The picture is terrifying because such power, whatever goals at which may be directed, is too much to be entrusted safely to any group.

No country that values its safety should allow what the Milner group accomplished— that a small number of men would be able to wield such power in administration and politics, should be given complete control

---

[77] Carroll Quigley, *The Anglo-American Establishment* (New York: Books in Focus, 1981), 312.

over the publication of documents relating to their actions, should be able to exercise such influence over the avenues of information that create public opinion and should be able to monopolize so completely the writing and teaching of the history of their own period[78].

The Round Table network was not only directing the policies of the most powerful country and empire in the world but also extending its influence across the Atlantic to the United States. It was there that the power blocs that would control the political and economic policy and the communication industry were being assembled. The central players and the financial supporters of the Round Table in the United States were the Carnegie United Kingdom Trust; the companies and the trusts controlled by the Rockefeller, J. P. Morgan, and Whitney families; and others linked to international financiers in London, the Rothschild and Lazard brothers. All these were supporters of a unified new world order with the world financial system beholden to them. The Round Tables were interconnected through secret network to the Freemasonry and sinister secret societies like the Skull and Bones.

Out of this skillful group of plotters and operators of secret diplomatic maneuvering came the dismemberment of the Ottoman Empire and the creation of the state of Israel. The Arab pawns of this chess game did not even realize that they were being taken for a ride. A hundred years later, the descendants and successors of the same Arab and Muslim elite are still dancing to the same puppeteers' tune, completely oblivious of the whole story of the replay they are participating in. A hundred years later, the Turks, the Arabs, and the other players in the drama of the First World War are still entangled in the web cast by the Round Table, unable to find their way out of the net.

---

[78] Quigley, *Anglo-American Establishment*, 197.

Part Three

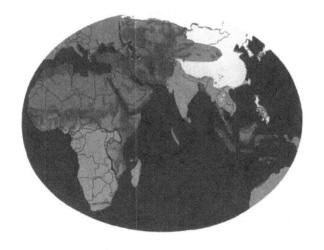

The Dar es Salaam:
The Renewal of Islam's World Order:
The Key to the Abode of Peace

Chapter Seven

The Dar es Salaam

Reading and writing skills in the sixth century around the world were limited. Literacy was perhaps limited to less than five percent of the population in the courtesan and clerical circles. Among the population, in general, knowledge was transmitted through oral tradition and was limited to practical matters of livelihood, trade, and religion. Books and scriptures were not accessible to the population at large. Therefore, concepts and principles were based on cultural experience that was hard to change. This situation caused diversity among neighborly communities. Unity of ideas occurred often through compulsion from above when conquerors pushed through the ideas of their culture to the subject people.

Had the blessed *nabi* Muhammad in the year 610 of the Common Era opened an office across from the Kaaba and from there distributed printed and bound copies of the Koran to the pilgrims coming from all across Arabia, he would have made no impact on the psyche of that population. The people did not possess the know-how to grasp the concepts and precepts of knowledge of unity of Allah, tawhid, *taqwa* of Allah, and the criterion to distinguish between good and evil (*husna* and *Fahasha*) at that time.

The Precept of Tawhid

The Koran laid the foundation of the idea of one universal God, and from this fount arose all that is known and all that will ever be known. It laid this foundation of the knowledge of one universal Allah for the believers in the first twelve years of Blessed Muhammad's prophecy, and it took another ten years to establish the precepts of truth, justice, covenant, equality, good, and evil. The Koran laid out these principles in clarity for all time to come.

In the sixth-century Arabia, at the time of the birth of the blessed *nabi*, the Arabian Peninsula was steeped in ignorance, superstition, spirit, and idol worship. There was no belief in or concept of one universal God. In the Mediterranean world, the one God was a tribal deity of the Jews, while the God of Christians was accessible to man through the creed of Trinity, in which God had incarnated into the human Jesus and Jesus into the divine God. Abraham, who had lived in the mists of time somewhere in the Middle East, believed in one universal God, the Creator of the universe. He placed his absolute trust in the universal God, Allah. He faithfully obeyed Allah's commands and did Allah's bidding, offering his most loved son in sacrifice. Allah's bidding was only a test for Abraham and an example for mankind. Those who followed Abraham, submitting their whole selves to Allah, and those who placed all their faith and trust in Him became Muslims, the believers. With time, Abraham's life story became an oral folktale; and by the time it came to be written in testaments, it had changed greatly. Other prophets thousands in number followed, giving the same message of Abraham to all mankind: submit to your Lord and Maker, believe in Him, and place your trust in Him always. People forgot the message, and the Messenger became the Lord, and in their minds, the Lord became their tribal deity to be worshipped at an altar or in a shrine. Thus, their god became their tribal and personal savior. The priesthood took over guardianship over their god and prescribed dogma and creed for the god and the worshippers to obey.

The blessed *nabi* Muhammad taught that everything in the universe originates from the one and the only reality of Allah and that man's ultimate salvation rests with the recognition of his total dependence on Him. This entails conscious submission to the will and the law of Allah. Muhammad, the *rasul* and *nabi* of Allah, received the revelation of the word, law, and commandments of Allah, which he was commanded to spread to all mankind. Today we believe that the universal God is the center of the belief of all the three monotheistic religions—Judaism, Christianity, and Islam. Nothing could be farther from the truth; for the Jews, God continues to be a tribal deity with His favorite children, and those who call themselves Christians, can only access God through His favorite son, Jesus. Yet God the Creator of the universe is the God of every particle and of every organism that was ever created. God, Allah, through the act of creation and sustenance, is connected to and is within reach of all His creation.

Islam is a way of life, a *din*, in the straight path to Allah. There is an implicit assumption in the Koran that there exists an agreement between Allah and His creation, portrayed as a covenant, a mutual understanding in which Allah proposes a system of regulations for the guidance of the humans. This guidance is presented in the form of commandments to be accepted and implemented by people. Allah then makes promise of what He will do in the event that man willingly abides by these commands and regulates his life in accordance with them. The concept of promise is clearly conditional on man's obedience. The covenant of the Koran symbolizes the relationship between Allah and man; man becomes His steward, vicegerent, or custodian on the earth through submission and obedience to His will (*islam*) as expressed in His commands and is able to take the advantage of Allah's promises and favors.

The commandments of Allah, addressed to the believers (men and women), are the fundamental values of the covenant between Allah and man, which become obligatory to man when the fire of love for Allah is kindled in his heart and he submits to the will of Allah and becomes His servant (believer) and the steward on the earth.

This commandment, similar to the Ten Commandments of Moses, emphasizes tawhid and respect for parents; prohibits infanticide on the grounds of poverty, taking of life, lewd acts, adultery, fornication, and embezzlement of orphan's property; stresses honesty in trade; and emphasizes the individual's responsibility to be just. Allah commands humans to be righteous. In the commandments of the covenant, Allah addresses individual men and women who in unity form a community, the *ummah*. Nevertheless, the emphasis of the guidance is to the individual believer for his and her own conduct.

The concept of a covenant also symbolizes the relationship between humans, among Allah's creatures, and the rest of His creation. They all share one God, one set of guidance and commandments, the same submission and obedience to Him, and the same set of expectations in accordance with His promises. They all can therefore trust one another since they all have similar obligations and expectations. In view of the Koran, humans, communities, nations, and civilizations will continue to live in harmony and peace so long as they continue to fulfill Allah's covenant.

After calling on the believers of their individual responsibility of submission to the will and command of Allah (*islam*), Allah reminds them of the other two dimensions of the *din*, *iman* and *ihsan*. The Koran then sums up the faith of a Muslim as follows: belief in Allah, in the last day, in the angels, in the Koran, and in the messengers of Allah. Believers are told to spend for the love of Allah on one's kin, the needy, the orphans, the wayfarer, and the ones who ask; to be steadfast in prayer; to practice regular charity; to fulfill their covenant (with Allah); to be firm and patient in tribulation, adversity, and times of stress, pain, and panic; and to perform wholesome and beautiful deeds.

The last part of this sura reminds the believer of his and her responsibility to the community, the *ummah*.

It is not righteousness that you turn your faces towards East or West; but it is righteousness to believe in Allah and the Last Day and the Angels and the Book and the Messengers; to spend of your substance, out of love for Him, for your kin, for orphans, for the needy, for the wayfarer, for those who ask and for the ransom of slaves; to be steadfast in prayer and practice regular charity, to fulfill the Covenant which you have made; and to be firm and patient, in pain suffering and adversity and throughout all periods of panic. Such are the people of truth, the God-fearing. (Al-Baqarah 2:177, Koran)

In the covenant of Allah, believers are shown their responsibility toward the three dimensions of their din, that of submission, faith, and performance of wholesome and beautiful deeds. Once the individual has become cognizant of the precepts of the unity, Tawhid of one universal God; has submitted to Him; and has faith and trust in Him, he knows that Allah loves those who perform beautiful deeds for the Creator and His creation. Islam reforms the individual. The covenant of Allah provides guidance to the believers individually, who then collectively fulfill their role as a community, the *ummah*. The commandments on the role of the believers in the service of the *ummah* are as follows:

Verily this brotherhood of yours is a single brotherhood and I am your Lord and Cherisher: therefore serve Me and no other,

amongst yourselves; and remember with gratitude Allah's favor on you, for you were enemies and He joined your hearts in love, so that by His grace, you became brethren.

Enjoining what is right and forbidding what is wrong. Let there arise out of you a band of people, inviting all that is good,

Be not like those who are divided amongst themselves and fall into disputations after receiving clear signs; for them is a dreadful penalty.

Ye are the best of the peoples evolved for mankind, enjoining what is right, forbidding what is wrong and believing in Allah.

Thus have We made of you an Ummah of the center, that ye might be witness over other nations and the Messenger, a witness over you. And We appointed the Qibla to which you were used to, only to test those who followed The Rasool from those Who would turn their heels.

Whoever submits his whole self to Allah and is a doer of
good, has grasped indeed the most trustworthy handhold and
with Allah rests the end and decision of all affairs.

Take not the Jews and the Christians for your friends and protectors, they are but friends and the protectors to each other. And he amongst you that turns to them is of them. Verily Allah does not guide the people who are unjust.

While the covenant defines the believer's submission to Allah, it also provides insight into Allah's commandments about man's economic life in this world and in the hereafter.

Economics plays a significant role in the social structure of Islam, so significant that Allah did not leave the economic aspect of life to be solely determined by human intellect, experience, caprice, and lust. Allah made it subject to revelation. Thus, Muslims prosper when they follow Allah's laws and subject themselves to scarcity when they turn to the human systems. Koran promises peace and plenty to those who obey their covenant with Allah, and to those who turn away from His covenant, the Koran portends a life of need, scarcity, and want.

But whosoever turns away from My Message, verily for him is a life narrowed down and we shall raise him up blind on the Day of Judgment." Thus do We recompense him who transgresses beyond bounds and believes not in the Signs of his Lord: and the Penalty of the Hereafter is far more grievous and more enduring. Is it not a warning to such men how many generations before them We destroyed, in whose haunts they now move? Verily, in this are Signs for men endued with understanding. (Taha 20:124, 127–28, Koran)

In the above *ayah* of the Koran, there is the word *ma'eeshat*, which comes from the word *ma'ashiyyat*, which is the recognized meaning

394

of the word "economics." The consequences of the rejection of Allah's covenant and guidance are clearly portrayed: a life narrowed down or constricted is a miserable one—one of need, scarcity, unhappiness, poverty, hunger, disease, pestilence, and famine occurring individually or all of them at one time.

The covenant of Allah does not put off the realization of the fruits of obeying or ignoring Allah's guidance until after death, nor does it hide it in spiritual abstractness. Observance of the covenant makes life on the earth economically, physically, and spiritually rich and happy. Nonobservance makes it economically miserable and physically and spiritually depressing. In fact, the economic, physical, and spiritual condition of a people provides a pragmatic test of the soundness of the revealed guidance.

Furthermore, the Koran declares that the people who transgress Allah's guidance and are economically deprived in this world will also be worse off in the hereafter.

> Verily for him is a life narrowed down and We shall
> raise him up blind on the Day of Judgment.

Allah created the earth and then bestowed on man His favor to extract sustenance from it. He also created the sun, moon, and stars for a just equilibrium and harmony in the universe. The sun provides energy for the growth, sustenance, and well-being of humans, plants, and animals. Gradually, man began to extract more than his personal needs from the earth; and the boom of economics, trade, and commerce started, creating cycle imbalance, disharmony, wars, poverty, and injustice throughout the globe. This disharmony caused by greed not only blemished the humans but the animal life also suffered with disappearance of species. Pollution and contamination of the environment resulted from the race to accumulate and hoard the world's wealth in a few hands. Man disobeyed Allah's universal laws and Allah's covenant.

According to the Koran, economics and the observance of the moral code of Allah's covenant go hand in hand, and they cannot be separated from each other:

> He has created the heavens and the earth for just ends: far is
> He above having the partners they ascribe to Him!

> He has created man from a sperm-drop; and behold
> this same (man) becomes an open disputer!

> And cattle He has created for you (men): from them you derive
> warmth and numerous benefits and of their (meat) you eat.

> And you have a sense of pride and beauty in them as you drive them home
> in the evening and as you lead them forth to pasture in the morning.

> And they carry your heavy loads to lands that you could not (otherwise) reach
> except with souls distressed: for your Lord is indeed Most Kind, Most Merciful.

> And (He has created) horses, mules and donkeys, for you to ride and use for
> show; and He has created (other) things of which you have no knowledge.

> And unto Allah leads straight the Way, but there are ways that turn
> aside: if Allah had willed, He could have guided all of you.

> It is He Who sends down rain from the sky. From it you drink and
> out of it (grows) the vegetation on which you feed your cattle.

> With it He produces for you corn, olives, date palms, grapes and every
> kind of fruit: verily in this is a Sign for those who give thought.

> He has made subject to you the Night and the Day; the
> Sun and the Moon; and the Stars are in subjection by His
> Command: verily in this are Signs for men who are wise.

And the things on this earth which He has multiplied in
varying colors (and qualities): verily in this a Sign for men
who celebrate the praises of Allah (in gratitude).

It is He Who has made the sea subject, that you may eat thereof flesh
that is fresh and tender and that you may extract there from ornaments
to wear and You see the ships therein that plough the waves, that you
may seek (thus) of the bounty of Allah and that you may be grateful.

And He has set up on the Earth mountains standing firm, lest it should
shake with you; and rivers and roads; that you may guide yourselves;

And marks and sign-posts; and by the stars (Men) guide themselves. Is then
He Who creates like one that creates not? Will you not receive admonition?

If you would count up the favors of Allah, never would you be able to number
them; for Allah is Oft-Forgiving, Most Merciful. (An-Nahl 16:3–18)

Sama in the Koran signifies the universe and *ardh* man's domain on
the earth pertaining to his social and economic world. Allah is the
Lord of the heavens and the earth and what is in between. The divine
laws under which the universe functions so meticulously and smoothly
should also apply to the economic life of man so that he might achieve
a balanced, predictable, equitable, and just financial life. *Sama* is the
source of Allah's benevolence to humanity and of His universal laws
that govern human subsistence and sustenance on the earth. *Ardh* is
controlling man's economic life in this world. Allah's kingdom over the
heavens and the earth sustains man's economic life and directly affects
man's conduct and his obedience to Allah's covenant.

Ayahs in Sura An-Nahl are explicit. Allah created the heavens and
the earth for just ends, to bring peace, harmony, equilibrium, and
justice to the universe. He is Allah the One, Lord of the creation.
He sends water from the heavens for sustenance of life on the earth—
humans, plants, and animals. Allah sends sunshine to the earth to

provide warmth and light to sustain human, plant, and animal life. Allah fashioned moon and stars to create equilibrium in the universe, every object in its intended place revolving in its fixed orbit in perfect harmony and balance. Allah knows the secrets and mysteries of the heavens and the earth, the so-called sciences, and the knowledge of particles, elements, cells, mitochondria, chromosomes, gravity, and black holes, only an infinitesimal portion of which he revealed to man, yet man is arrogant and boastful.

He also emphasizes on the unity and brotherhood of the believers, the *ummah*. This unity is the unity of goodness, enjoining what is right, forbidding that is wrong, and believing in Allah. Allah has made this brotherhood an *ummah* of the center. Allah has appointed the *ummah* a witness and an example to other nations as He appointed the *rasul* a witness over the *ummah*. Allah proclaims a code of conduct for the *ummah* in the covenant. Without fulfilling the covenant of Allah, for the believers, all acts of submission, faith, and worship are meaningless and of little consequence.

Insignificant raindrops fall on parched land singly and disappear forever; however, the same raindrops coalesce in strength to form little streams and then little rivulets and then join together to become mighty rivers flowing further, dropping into powerful and majestic waterfalls, yet again joining together with other rivers, lakes, and more hill torrents, to end up in mighty oceans ever increasing in size, in length, in depth, and in power yet at all times obedient to the will of Allah. Similarly, an insignificant man without faith is like a drop of water on parched land. Yet the same man, a believer, strengthened by his covenant with Allah, joins others with the covenant to form a little community that, again, with other believers in unity with Allah unites to form a single united *ummah* of all the Muslims around the world, a powerful, united people witnessing over other nations, with Allah and His prophet witnessing over them.

The united Islamic community has the moral responsibility that is implied in the primordial covenant referred to in the Koran as Allah's vicegerency on the earth. The Islamic society is made up of such God-fearing people and constitutes a "middle nation" or axial community (*ummah wast*) whose collective responsibility is to bear witness to the truth and act as an example for the rest of humanity. It is a nation of moderation that is averse to extremism. The community of believers enjoins what is right and forbids what is wrong.

Allah promises an Abode of Peace, the Dar es Salaam to those on the straight path, those who submit to and believe in Allah and perform wholesome and beautiful deeds. Beautiful deeds are rewarded by Allah with a place in Jannat (place of peace and plenty), in the afterlife. Life of Jannat is attained in this world too by those submit to and believe in Allah and perform wholesome and beautiful deeds and fulfill the Covenant of Allah.

The Dar es Salaam

But Allah does call

To the Abode of Peace: Dar es Salaam

He does guide whom He pleases

To a way that is straight. (Yunus 10:25)

In Allah's Dar es Salaam, believing men constitute 750 million individuals of the *ummah*, and women constitute the other 750 million. And between them, they form one solid, united *ummah*. Together in partnership, men and women have produced the progeny of Adam to carry out the divine and omnipotent will of Allah. The Koran addresses all believers, both men and women, together:

The Covenant and the Dar es Salaam

And you Believers (men and women)! Turn you all
together towards Allah, that you may attain bliss.

The world of the believers, the Dar es Salaam, is spread across the
globe, covering every dwelling and place of prostration where Allah's
name is praised and loved: Afghanistan, Albania, Algeria, Bahrain,
Bangladesh, Benin, Bosnia, Brunei, Burkina Faso, Cameroon,
Chad, Chechnya, Comoros, Djibouti, Egypt, East Turkistan,
Gabon, Gambia, Guinea, Guinea-Bissau, Guyana, Indonesia, Iran,
Ivory Coast, Iraq, Jordan, Kashmir, Kazakhstan, Kosovo, Kuwait,
Kyrgyzstan, Lebanon, Libya, Malaysia, Maldives, Mali, Mauritania,
Morocco, Mindanao, Mozambique, Niger, Nigeria, Oman, Pakistan,
Palestine, Qatar, Saudi Arabia, Senegal, Sierra Leone, Somalia,
Sudan, Suriname, Syria, Tajikistan, Tanzania, Togo, Tunisia, Turkey,
Turkmenistan, Uganda, United Arab Emirates, Uzbekistan, and
Yemen. In other political domains—Russia, China, India, Serbia,
Macedonia, and in the rest of the world—every household and place
of prostration where Allah, the God of the universe, is praised and
worshipped is the abode of peace the Dar es Salaam. Therein, the
covenant of Allah is enshrined as guidance to mankind.

Constitution of the Dar es Salaam

The covenant of Allah is enshrined in the Koran. Every believer, upon
his submission to Allah, makes a compact with Allah to obey His
covenant. The covenant of the blessed *rasul* of Allah (Yathrib) affirms
the covenant of Allah and pronounces the criterion of conduct of the
ummah and that of the Islamic state, the Dar es Salaam. These two
covenants form just basis of the code of conduct of each believer and
their community. Together, they constitute the constitution of the
Islamic state not to be tampered with by ordinary humans, whether

400

they come under the guise of kings, sultans, sheikhs, presidents, generals, or ordinary citizens.

The Covenant of Allah: The Covenant of the Koran

Verily those who pledge their allegiance unto you, (O Muhammad) swear it unto none but Allah; the Hand of Allah is over their hands. Thereafter whosoever breaks his Covenant does so to the harm of his own soul and whosoever fulfils his Covenant with Allah, Allah will grant him an immense Reward. (Al-Fath 48:10, Koran)

He is Allah, there is no Deity but He; Knower of the hidden and the manifest. He is the Rahman (the Most Gracious), the Rahim, (Most Merciful.)

He is Allah; there is no Deity but Him,
The Sovereign, the Pure and the Hallowed,
Serene and Perfect,
The Custodian of Faith, the Protector, the Almighty,
The Irresistible, the Supreme,
Glory be to Allah, He is above all they associate with Him.

He is Allah, the Creator, the Sculptor, the Adorner of color and form. To Him belong the Most Beautiful Names: whatever so is in the heavens and on earth, Praise and Glory Him; and He is the Almighty and All-Wise. (Al-Hashr 59:18–24, Koran)

Allah. There is no god but He, the ever Living, the One Who sustains and protects all that exists. No slumber can seize Him or sleep.

His are all things in the heavens and on earth. Who is there to intercede in His presence except as He permits?

He knows what happens to His creatures in this world and in the hereafter. Nor do they know the scope of His knowledge except as He wills.

His Throne extends over the heavens and the earth and He feels no fatigue in guarding and protecting them.

The Covenant and the Dar es Salaam

He is the Most High, Most Great. (Al-Baqarah 2:255, Koran)

Say, "Come I will recite what your Lord has prohibited you
from: Join not any thing in worship with Him.

Be good to your parents: kill not your children because of
poverty, We provide sustenance for you and for them.

Come not near to shameful deeds (sins and illegal
sexual activity) whether open or secret.

Take not life, which Allah hath made sacred, except by the way of justice
or law: This He commands you, that you may learn wisdom.

And come not near the orphan's property, except to
improve it, until he attains the age of full strength.

And give full measure and full weight with justice. No burden
We place on any soul but that which it can bear.

Whenever you give your word speak honestly even if a near relative is concerned.

And fulfill the Covenant of Allah. Thus He
commands you that you may remember.

Verily, this is My Way leading straight: follow it: follow not (other)
paths for they will separate you from His path. This He commands
you that you may remember. (Al-An'am 6:151–53, Koran)

Believe in Allah, His Rasool and the Book that He has sent to His
Rasool and the Scriptures that He sent to those before him. Any
who deny Allah, His angels, His Books, His Rasools and the Day of
Judgment has gone far far astray. (An-Nisa 4:136, Koran)

Bow down, prostrate yourself and serve your Lord and do wholesome deeds
that you may prosper. Perform Jihad, strive to your utmost in Allah's cause
as striving (jihad) is His due. He has chosen you and Allah has imposed
no hardship in your endeavor to His cause. You are the inheritors of the

faith of your father Abraham. It is He who has named you Muslims of the times before and now, so that Allah's Rasool may be an example to you and that you are an example to mankind. (Al-Hajj 22:77–78, Koran)

> But Allah doth call to the Abode of Peace
> Dar es Salaam
> He doth guide whom He pleased to a Way that is straight.
> To those who do right and in abundance neither
> darkness nor shame shall cover their faces!
> They are the heirs of Paradise, they will abide
> therein forever. (Yunus 10:25, Koran)

It is not righteousness that you turn your faces towards East or West; but it is righteousness to believe in Allah and the Last Day and the Angels and the Book and the Rasools; to spend of your substance, out of love for Him, for your kin, for orphans, for the needy, for the wayfarer, for those who ask and for the ransom of slaves; to be steadfast in prayer and practice regular charity, to fulfill the Covenant which you have made; and to be firm and patient, in pain (or suffering) and adversity and throughout all periods of panic. Such are the people of truth, the God-fearing. (Al-Baqarah 2:177, Koran)

Verily fellowship of yours is a single brotherhood and I am your Lord and Cherisher: therefore serve Me (and no other). (Al-Anbiya 21:92, Koran)

And hold fast, all together by the rope which Allah (stretches out for you).

> And be not divided amongst yourselves;
> And remember with gratitude Allah's favor on you:
> For you were enemies and He joined your hearts in love,
> So that by His grace, you became brethren and a community.

Let there arise out of you a band of people enjoining what is right and forbidding what is wrong. They are the ones to attain felicity.

> Be not like those who are divided amongst themselves,
> And fall into disputations after receiving clear signs
> For them is a dreadful penalty. (Ali 'Imran 3:103–5, Koran)

The Covenant and the Dar es Salaam

You are the best of the peoples evolved for mankind,
Enjoining what is right, forbidding what is wrong and
believing in Allah. (Ali 'Imran 3:110, Koran)

Thus have We made of you an Ummah of the center,
That you might be witness over other nations,
And the Rasool a witness over yourselves.
And We appointed the Qibla
To which thou wast used,
Only to test those who followed
The Rasool from those
Who would turn their heels. (Al-Baqarah 2:143, Koran)

Whoever submits his whole self to Allah and is a doer of good,
Has grasped indeed the most trustworthy handhold,
And with Allah rests the end and decision of [all] affairs. (Luqman 31:22, Koran)

Take not the Jews and the Christians for your friends and protectors,
They are but friends and the protectors to each other.
And he amongst you that turns to them is of them.
Verily Allah does not guide the people who are
unjust and evil. (Al Ma'idah 5:51, Koran)

Oh you who believe!
Take not for friends and protectors those who take
your religion for a mockery or sport,
Whether among those who received the scripture before you, or
among those who reject faith. (Al-Ma'idah 5:57, Koran)

O you who believe!
Take not infidels (kafireen) for Awliya (friends and protectors)
in place of believers. Would you offer Allah a clear warrant
against yourselves? (An-Nisa 4:144, Koran)

O you who believe! Take not for friends and protectors (Awliya those
who take your religion for mockery, whether from amongst people
of the book or from amongst the kafireen. Be in taqwa of Allah,
fear Allah if you have faith indeed. (Al-Ma'idah 5:57, Koran)

Your (real) friends are Allah, His Rasool and the Fellowship of Believers, those who
Establish regular prayers and regular Charity and
they bow down humbly in worship.
As to those who turn for friendship to Allah, His
Rasool and the fellowship of Believers, it is
The Fellowship of Allah that must certainly triumph. (Al-Ma'idah 5:55–56, Koran)

Oh you who believe obey Allah and obey the Rasool,
And those charged with authority among you. If you differ in any thing
among yourselves, refer it to Allah and His Rasool if
you do believe in Allah and the last Day
That is the best and the most suitable for the final
determination. (An-Nur 4:59, Koran)

And the firmament has He raised high,
And He has setup the balance of Justice, in order
that you may not transgress due balance.
So establish weight with justice and fall not short in the balance
Of those We have created are people who direct others with truth
and dispense justice therewith. (Al-A'raf 7:181, Koran)

Those who hearken to their Lord and establish regular prayer;
Who conduct their affairs by mutual consultation;
Who spend out what we bestow on them for sustenance;
And those who when an oppressive wrong is inflicted on them, are not
intimidated but defend themselves. (Ash-Shura 42:38–39, Koran)

The recompense for an injury is an injury equal thereto (in degree): but if
a person forgives and makes reconciliation, his reward is due from Allah:
for (Allah) loves not those who do wrong. (Ash-Shura 42:42, Koran)

There is no compulsion in religion: Truth stands out clear from error,
Whoever rejects evil and believes in Allah hath grasped the
most trustworthy Handhold, which never breaks.
And Allah hears and knows all things. (Al-Baqarah 2:254–57, Koran)

For men and women who surrender unto Allah,
For men and women who believe,

The Covenant and the Dar es Salaam

For men and women who are devout
For men and women who speak the truth,
For men and women who persevere in righteousness,
For men and women who are humble,
For men and women who are charitable,
For men and women who fast and deny them selves
For men and women who guard their chastity,
For men and women who remember Allah much,
For them Allah has forgiveness and a great reward.
For men and women who surrender unto Allah,
For men and women who believe,
For men and women who are devout
For men and women who speak the truth,
For men and women who persevere in righteousness
For men and women who are humble,
For men and women who are charitable,
For men and women who fast and deny them selves,
For men and women who guard their chastity,
For men and women who remember Allah much,
For them Allah has forgiveness and a great reward.
(Al-Ahzab 33:35, Koran)

It is not fitting for a Believer, man or woman, when a matter has
been decided by Allah and His Messenger, to have any option about
their decision: if anyone disobeys Allah and His Messenger, he is
indeed on a clearly wrong Path. (Al-Ahzab 33:36, Koran)

Say to the:
Believing men that they should lower their gaze and guard their modesty:
That will make for greater purity for them: And Allah is acquainted
with all that they do. And say to the Believing women that they should
lower their gaze and guard their modesty; That they should not display
their adornments except what is ordinarily obvious, That they should
draw a veil over their bosom and not display their adornments
(Except to the immediate family)
And that they should not strike their feet in order to
draw attention to their hidden adornments.
And O you Believers!

406

Munawar Sabir

Turn you all together Toward Allah that you may
prosper. (An-Nur 24:30–31, Koran)

The Believers, men and women, are protectors, one of another: they enjoin
what is just and forbid what is evil: they observe regular prayers, practice
regular charity and obey Allah and His Rasool. On them will Allah pour
His Mercy: for Allah is Exalted in power, Wise. (At-Tawbah 9:71, Koran)

Fight in the cause of Allah those who fight you but do not transgress
limits: for Allah loves not transgressors and slay them wherever you
catch them and turn them out from wherever they have turned
you out for tyranny and oppression are worse than slaughter.
But fight them not at the Sacred Mosque, unless they (first)
fight you there but if they fight you, slay them.
Such is the reward of those who suppress faith. But if they
cease, Allah is oft Forgiving, Most Merciful. And fight them
on until there is no more tyranny or oppression,
And there prevail justice and faith in Allah: but if they cease let there be no
hostility except to those who practice oppression. (Al-Baqarah 2:190–93, Koran)

Those who devour usury will not stand except as stands one whom the Satan
by his touch hath driven to madness. That is because they say: Trade is like
usury, But Allah hath permitted trade and forbidden usury. Those who after
receiving direction from their Lord, Desist, shall be pardoned for the past:
their case is for Allah to (judge); But those who repeat (the offence) are the
companions of fire; They will abide therein (forever). Allah will deprive usury
of all blessing, However, will give increase for the deeds of charity: For He does
not love those who are ungrateful and wicked. (Al-Baqarah 2:275–76, Koran)

And eat not up your property among yourselves for vanities, nor use
it as a bait for judges, with intent that you may eat up wrong fully and
knowingly some of other peoples property. (Al-Baqarah 2:188, Koran)

Oh you who believe! Guard your souls, if you follow right guidance,
No hurt can come to you from those who stray; The goal of you all is
to Allah, It is He who will show you the truth of all that you do. [79]

The Covenant of Yathrib:

The Covenant of the Blessed Rasul of Allah, Muhammad

In the name of Allah the compassionate and the merciful.

1. No believer shall slay a believer in retaliation for an unbeliever, nor shall
    he assist an unbeliever against a believer. This is a covenant given by
    Muhammad to the believers.

2. They constitute one Ummah to the exclusion of all other men.

3. The believers shall leave none of their members in destitution without
    giving him in kindness that he needs by the way of his liberty.

4. No believer shall take as an ally a freedman of another Muslim without
    the consent of his previous master. All believers shall rise as one man
    against anyone who seeks to commit injustice, aggression, crime, or
    spread mutual enmity amongst the Muslims even if such a person is
    their kin.

5. Just as the bond to Allah is indivisible, all the believers shall stand behind
    the commitment of the least of them. All believers are bonded one to
    another to the exclusion of other men.

6. This Pax Islamica is one and indivisible. No believer shall enter a separate
    peace without all other believers whenever there is fighting in the cause of
    God, but will do so only on the basis of equality and justice to all others.
    In every expedition for the cause of God we undertake, all parties to the

---

[79] Al-Baqarah 2:143, 156, 177, 188, 190–92, 275–76, 278, 279; Ali 'Imran
3:103–5, 110; An-Nisa 4:59; Al-Ma'idah 5:51, 57, 105; Al-A'raf 7:181; At-
Tawbah 9:71; Yunus 10:25–26; Al-Anbiya 21:92; An-Nur 24:30–31; Luqman
31:22; Al-Ahzab 33:35; Ash-Shura 42:38–39; Ar-Rahman 55:79.

covenant shall fight shoulder to shoulder as one man. All believers shall avenge the blood of one another when any one falls fighting in the cause of God.

7. The pious believers follow the best and the most upright guidance.

8. Whoever is convicted of killing a believer deliberatively but without righteous cause shall be liable to the relatives of the killed. Until the latter are satisfied, the killer shall be subject to retaliation by each and every believer.

9. Any Jew who follows us is entitled to our assistance and the same rights as any one of us, without injustice and partisanship. As the Jews fight on the side the believers, they shall spend their wealth on equal par with the believers. The Jews are an *Ummah* along side the believers. The Jews have their religion and the Muslims theirs. Both enjoy the security of their populace and clients except the unjust and the criminal amongst them. The unjust and the criminal destroy only himself and his family.

10. None of the Jewish tribes may go to war without the permission of Muhammad, though none may be prevented from taking revenge for a wound inflicted upon them. Whosoever murders anyone will have murdered him self and the members of his family, unless it be the case of the man suffering a wrong, for God will accept his actions. The Jews shall bear their public expenses and so will the Muslims. Each shall assist the other against any violator of this covenant. Their relationship shall be one of mutual advice and consultation and mutual assistance and charity rather than harm and aggression. Assistance is due to the party suffering an injustice not to one perpetrating it.

11. Yathrab shall constitute a sanctuary to the parties of this covenant. Whatever the difference or dispute between the parties to this covenant remains unsolved shall be referred to God and to Muhammad. The Jews are entitled to the same rights as this covenant has granted to other parties together with the goodness and charity of the latter. Allah is the guarantor of the piety and the goodness that is embodied in this covenant. The people in this covenant come to the assistance of one another against any aggressor.

12. Allah is the guarantor of the truth and goodwill of this covenant Allah grants his protection to whosoever acts in piety, charity goodness.

The Role of Islam in the Twenty-First Century

The miracle of the twenty-first century is that, in spite of warfare, turmoil, and *fitnah*, Islam is the fastest-spreading religion in the world. Three large regions of spiritual osmosis and spiritual regeneration are in India, sub-Saharan Africa, and the Euro-Christian world of Americas and Europe. The Koran is the most recited book every day in the world. Islam continues to influence other beliefs toward the belief in one universal God. Because of Islam's silent influence in the contemporary world, there are now more believers in the unity of God among Jews, Christians, Hindus, Buddhists, and other religions than any other time in history.

As in the times past, in the present, the believers of the *ummah wast*, the *ummah* of the middle path, seek their salvation in communion with Allah. The believers march in the path of Allah, the path of moderation guided by their covenant with Him in silence, peace, fortitude, and humility. The *ummah* is the best of the peoples evolved from mankind, enjoining what is good and forbidding all that is evil. The blessed *nabi* delivered the message of peace and love to the world. He came as an inspiration, a beacon of light, a bearer of glad tidings, to invite humanity to Allah's grace and mercy. Strengthened by this inspiration, when Islam advances, the world gains tranquility, love, and knowledge. With the role of Islam, there is truth, honesty, justice, equality, and prosperity for all. The precepts of the covenant of Allah ensure human dignity, equality, justice, consultative government, a state where there is realization of lawful benefits to people, prevention of harm, and removal of hardship. The covenant of Allah educates individuals by inculcating in them self-discipline, patience, restraint, and respect for the rights of others.

The believers constitute one *ummah* to the exclusion of all other men. Just as the bond with Allah is indivisible, all believers shall stand in commitment with the least of them. All believers shall rise as one against anyone who seeks to commit injustice, aggression, or crime or spread mutual enmity among the Muslims. The believers shall leave none of their members in destitution without giving him in kindness and liberty what he needs. In every expedition in the cause of Allah, the *ummah* undertakes to fight shoulder to shoulder as one man. All believers shall avenge the blood of one another when anyone falls fighting in the cause of God. Whoever is convicted of killing a believer deliberatively but without righteous cause shall be liable to the relatives of the killed. Until the latter are satisfied, the killer shall be subject to retaliation by each and every believer.

When one and a half billion people of Islam ignore Allah's commandments, they bring on themselves *fitnah* and oppression of the *Munafiqeen*. Life of delusion and self-deception in search of the material things of the world brings on *fitnah*, oppression, and loss of hope. Allah helps those who help themselves. When people choose to be led by falsehood to live in disunity, disharmony, and subjugation, they have no hope. Hope is in Allah and in His covenant. Hope is in tawhid, truth, and justice for humanity. When the believers among the one and a half billion Muslims practice their *din* in the path of Allah, goodness in the world outweighs all evil, and there is peace in the world. There is no hunger, war, or oppression. There is hope, and Allah's *din* reigns supreme.

Seven Simple Steps to Freedom

In Islam, life is a chain of good intentions and good deeds. Submission to Allah is in tawhid, which is the proclamation of the unity of the believer with Allah and the communion of believers in one *ummah* under the grace of the one merciful Lord, Allah. This unity is proclaimed in every call to prayer (*adhan*) five times a day from sunrise to sunset around the world day after day. And in this communion, Allah declares:

> Your real friends are Allah, His Rasool and the Fellowship of Believers, those who establish regular prayers and regular charity. And they bow down humbly in worship. As to those who turn for friendship to Allah, His Rasool and the fellowship of Believers, it is the Fellowship of Allah that must certainly triumph.

This unity is ordained by Allah. To enforce this unity of the *ummah*, each Believer must determine his intention with an action. This action is to show the power and the resolve of the *fellowship of Allah* to those opposed to the unity of Islam, the *Munafiqeen* and the *kafireen*. Each believer will raise the standard of the *ummah* over his home, his mosque, and every Muslim institution everywhere in the world.

This standard is the crescent and the star of Islam over the background of blue sky, the sign of the universe of Allah. This is the standard of the Dar es Salaam. This standard represents tawhid and the precepts of the covenant of Allah that ensure human dignity, equality, justice, consultative government, a state where there is realization of lawful benefits to people, prevention of harm, removal of hardship, and education of every individual by inculcating in him self-discipline, patience, restraint, and respect for rights of others. It is a standard under which there is restitution of all wrongs and imbalances in society.

The show of the standard of the Dar es Salaam is a reminder to the believers of Allah's promise that His fellowship will certainly triumph.

Each believer will act to ensure that his kin, his neighbors, his fellow citizens, his government, his leaders, the media, the universities, all Islamic organizations, political parties, and parliaments reaffirm their oath of obedience to the following declaration of Allah:

> Verily fellowship of yours is a single brotherhood and I am your Lord and Cherisher: therefore serve Me and no other,

> And hold fast, all together by the rope which Allah (stretches out for you). And be not divided amongst yourselves; and remember with gratitude Allah's favor on you: For you were enemies and He joined your hearts in love, So that by His grace, you became brethren.

> Enjoining what is right and forbidding what is wrong. Let there arise out of you a band of people, inviting all that is good,

> Be not like those who are divided amongst themselves and fall into disputations after receiving clear signs For them is a dreadful penalty. (Ali 'Imran 3:103-5, Koran)

You are the best of the peoples evolved for mankind, Enjoining
what is right, forbidding what is wrong and believing in Allah.

Thus have We made of you an Ummah of the center, that you might be
witness over other nations and the Rasool a witness over yourselves. And
We appointed the Qibla to which you were used to only to test those
who followed the Rasool from those who would turn their heels.

Whoever submits his whole self to Allah and is a doer of good, has
grasped indeed the most trustworthy handhold. And with Allah rests
the end and decision of [all] affairs. (Al-Baqarah 2:143, Koran)

And following the reaffirmation their faith in Allah and their oath
to obey the His declaration, every believer will declare and affirm the
political unity of the Islamic world by the twenty-seventh of April
2009, the one-hundredth anniversary of the forced abdication of the
last genuine caliph, Abdulhamid.

1. One and a half billion believers, the fellowship of Allah,
   have the resolve, authority, and power to physically remove
   the un-Koranic rulers who oppose the unity of the *ummah*.
   The believers will peacefully march through their palaces and
   offices to remove from places of authority all vestiges of *fitnah*,
   treachery, and oppression. Fewer than fifty families responsible
   for the decadence in the governance of the *ummah* represent
   the circle of evil in the Islamic state. With the *ummah's* resolve,
   these fifty or so families will be made to step down from their
   positions of authority and relinquish their ill-gotten assets to
   the people.

2. One and a half billion believers, the fellowship of Allah, have
   the authority, power, and resolve to physically remove all
   Western and foreign military bases and intelligence services
   from the lands of Islam. The believers will peacefully march
   through the offices, barracks, hangars, ammunition dumps,

armories, and installations of all foreign military bases and remove from there all vestiges of *fitnah,* treachery, and oppression. Opposition to such eviction will meet the peril of fire of thousands of remotely controlled aerial, terrestrial, and maritime explosive vehicles that will vaporize the power of the un-Koranic external *fitnah* and its agents from the land of Islam.

3. All pacts, treaties, and agreements, both covert and open, signed by Muslim rulers with the Western powers have been extinguished with the invasion of Afghanistan and Iraq. Today all such treaties are void.

4. The organizations of the *ummah* and the existing Islamic states will coordinate the following:

   a) Establish a rapid deployment mobile expeditionary force of believers under a unified command from the armies of all Islamic states to fight *fitnah,* conspiracy, and aggression against every part of Islam. This force will defend every inch of the land of Islam from *fitnah* and oppression. This force will comprise a mechanized army of one million men and women with one thousand frontline aircraft and modern naval fleets in all Muslim waters. They will defend all the land, seas, and oceans of Islam.

   b) Train and arm a volunteer mobile commando force of twelve million mujahideen men and women organized in three hundred autonomous armies with their own armor, air force, and ships. Their loyalty will be to Allah and the precepts of His covenant and the Dar es Salaam.

   c) Establish a unified foreign policy for all Islamic lands under a unified organization. All current treaties and pacts signed will automatically extinguish. Relations and agreements with the rest of the world will be renegotiated

under the name of the one unified state of the Dar es
Salaam.

d) Establish a unified currency supported by gold. No fiat
money will be accepted in trade. Usury will be abolished
and banking and trade reorganized. Pricing of products
for trade and commerce will be based on a just and
standardized unit of hourly work performed by every
human around the world.

5. The Dar es Salaam, the Islamic union, will exit the Western-
controlled United Nations and its subsidiary organizations and
sponsor the formation of a new world organization based on
justice and equality rather than power and riches. This world
organization will represent the people of the world rather
than nations. It will be run by the people for the well-being
of the peoples of the world. The Dar es Salaam will exit the
World Bank, the International Monetary Fund, the World
Trade Organization, and the Breton Woods Agreement.
New agreements will be negotiated with the Euro-Christian,
Chinese, Hindu, and African civilizations on the basis of
equality and justice for all the people of the world.

6. Organize unified intelligence services to defend the Dar es
Salaam.

7. A unified structure of governance of the Dar es Salaam shall
be established based on the precepts of the covenant of Allah.

Within one year of the of the renewal of Islam's world order,
establishment of the structure of Dar es Salaam's governance will take
place. In Islam, there are no professional or hereditary rulers. And in
Islam, there are no priests and no politicians.

Every believer inherits the Koran, the law, and the blessed *nabi's*
legacy. And each believer is the guardian and the executor of the law.

In Allah's Dar es Salaam, men constitute 750 million individuals of the *ummah*, and women constitute the other 750 million. And between them, they form one solid, united *ummah*. Together in partnership, men and women have produced the progeny of Adam to carry out the divine and omnipotent will of Allah. The Koran addresses all believers, both men and women, together: *"And you Believers (men and women)! Turn you **all together** towards Allah, that you may attain prosperity."*

The Dar es Salaam constitutes the following territories of the *ummah*: Afghanistan, Albania, Algeria, Bahrain, Bangladesh, Benin, Bosnia, Brunei, Burkina Faso, Cameroon, Chad, Chechnya, Comoros, Djibouti, Egypt, Ethiopia, East Turkistan, Gabon, Gambia, Guinea, Guinea-Bissau, Guyana, Indonesia, Iran, Ivory Coast, Iraq, Jordan, Kashmir, Kazakhstan, Kosovo, Kuwait, Kyrgyzstan, Lebanon, Libya, Malaysia, Maldives, Mali, Mauritania, Morocco, Mindanao, Mozambique, Niger, Nigeria, Oman, Pakistan, Palestine, Qatar, Saudi Arabia, Senegal, Sierra Leone, Somalia, Sudan, Suriname, Syria, Tajikistan, Tanzania, Togo, Tunisia, Turkey, Turkmenistan, Uganda, United Arab Emirates, Uzbekistan, and Yemen. Other Muslim domains within the boundaries of countries of Russia, China, India, Serbia, and Macedonia will have an extraterritorial association with the Dar es Salaam through their large Muslim populations.

Every Muslim, whether residing in or outside the bounds of the Dar es Salaam, is a member of the *ummah* and has the right and the obligation to the citizenship of the Dar es Salaam. Equally, every non-Muslim residing within the bounds of the Dar es Salaam who has sworn allegiance to the state will have the same citizenship rights and obligations, as well as all freedoms prescribed by the Koran to the Muslims, in short absolute and complete equality (Document of Yathrib: First Year of Hijra).

The extent of the Islamic world at the advent of the
European awakening in the fifteenth century CE.

Step One: Sovereignty

To Allah belongs all that is in the heavens and on earth. (Koran 3:109)

The sovereignty of the heavens and earth and what is in between belongs to Allah.

> Allah's command and the covenant of Allah
> bind the *ummah* and the state.

Step Two: Allah's Viceroy on the Earth

Behold thy Lord said to the Angels; I will create a vicegerent on earth.
(Al-Baqarah 2:30, Koran)

It is Allah who has subjected the sea to you that ship may sail through by His command that you may seek His bounty and that you may be grateful.
(Koran 45:12)

We have honored the children of Adam; provided them with transport on land and sea; given them for sustenance things good and pure; and conferred on them special favors, above a great part of Our Creation. (Koran 17:70)

When I have fashioned him in due proportion and breathed into him of My spirit, so the angles prostrated themselves, all of them together. (Koran 38:72–73)

Allah created the progeny of Adam, both men and women; breathed His Spirit into them; bestowed dignity on them; honored them; and conferred on them special favors above a great part of His creation. The covenant of Allah has established a simple code of conduct for the believers to follow in their daily lives. The same conduct applies to the community of Islam, the *ummah*, and their state. Muslims disobey the covenant at their peril.

The Chain of Authority:

Allah addressed the believers and ordained a chain of authority in the management of their affairs.

Obey Allah and obey the Rasool and those charged amongst you with authority in the settlement of your affairs. If you differ in any thing among yourselves, refer it to Allah and His Rasool. (The Koran and the prophet's teachings)

The sovereignty of Islamic state belongs exclusively to Allah, whose will and command binds the community and state. The dignified designation in the Koran of the community as vicegerent of Allah on the earth makes the Muslim community, the *ummah*, a repository of the "executive sovereignty" of the Islamic state. The community as a whole, after consultation and consensus, charges people from among themselves with authority to manage its affairs (*ulil amri minkum*). Those charged with authority act in their capacity as the representative (*wakil*) of the people and are bound by the Koranic mandate to consult

419

the community in public affairs, and consensus is the binding source of the law. The community, by consultation and in consensus, has the authority to depose any person charged with authority, including the head of state, in the event of gross violation of Allah's law.

The believers will, from time to time, choose their *wakil* to manage the affairs of the Dar es Salaam. Such affairs will be administered on the basis of the commandments of Allah in accordance with His covenant.

> All Muslims are one brotherhood, one *ummah*, in one land, all servants of one Allah, the First and the Last, fulfilling His covenant, witnessed over by Allah's *rasul*, an *ummah* that witnesses over other nations.

Step Three: *Muslimeen, Iman,* and Deeds

It is not righteousness that ye turn your faces to towards East or West, but it is righteousness to believe in God and the last day and the Angels and the Book and the Messengers.
To spend of your substance, out of love of Him, for your kin, for orphans, for the needy, for the wayfarer, for those who ask and for the ransom of the slaves. To be steadfast in prayer, and to practice regular charity. To fulfill the contracts, which you may have made. And to be firm and patient, in tribulation and adversity and in times of stress. Such are the people of truth the God fearing.
(Al-Baqarah 2:177, Koran)

The type of surrender is a deliberate, conscious, and rational act made by a person who knows with both intellectual certainty and spiritual vision that Allah is the Real. The knower of God is a Muslim, one who submits to the divine truth and whose relationship with Allah is governed by *taqwa*, the consciousness of humankind's responsibility toward its Creator. The concept of *taqwa* implies that the believer has the added responsibility of acting in a way that is in accordance with three types of knowledge: *ilm al-yaqin, ain al-yaqin,* and *haqq al yaqin* (knowledge of certainty, eye of certainty, and truth of certainty). The believer must endeavor at all times to maintain himself or herself in a constant state of submission to Allah and obey His covenant with the believers.

Iman and Deeds: Allah's covenant reminds the believers of their duty to their Creator and to their fellow man; only those who *have faith and do righteous acts* will have success in their earthly lives and in the hereafter. The phrase *amilu al saalihaat* (to do good, to perform wholesome deeds) refers to those who persist in striving to set things right, who restore harmony, peace, and balance. The other acts of good works recognized in the covenant of the Koran are to show compassion, to be merciful and forgive others, to be just, to protect the weak, to defend the oppressed, to be generous and charitable, to be truthful, to seek knowledge and wisdom, to be kind, to be peaceful, and to love others.

Alladhina aaminu wa 'amilu al saalihaat[80].

> On those who believe and do good will
> Allah Most Gracious bestow love.

Step Four: The *Ummah*

Verily this brotherhood of yours is a single brotherhood and I am your Lord and Cherisher. Therefore serve Me (and no other) and hold fast, all together by the Rope which Allah stretches out for you. And be not divided amongst yourselves; and remember with gratitude Allah's favor on you; for you were enemies and He joined your hearts in love, so that by His grace, you became

---

[80] Koran 2:25; 2:82, 277; 4:57, 122; 5:5; 7:42; 10:9; 11:23; 13:29; 14:23; 18:2, 88, 107; 19:60, 96; 20:75, 82, 112; 21:94; 22:14; 23:50, 56; 24:55; 25:70–71; 26:67; 28:80; 29:7, 9, 58; 30:15, 45; 31:8; 32:19; 34:4, 37; 38:24; 41:8; 42:22–23, 26; 45:21, 30; 47:2, 12; 48:29; 64:9; 65:11; 84:25; 85:11; 95:6; 98:7; 103:3.

brethren. Let there arise out of you a band of people inviting all that is good, enjoining what is right and forbidding what is wrong. They are the ones to prosper. Be not like those who are divided amongst themselves and fall into disputes after receiving clear signs. For them is a dreadful penalty. Ye are the best of the peoples evolved for mankind, enjoining what is right, forbidding what wrong and believers in Allah. Thus have We made of you an Ummah of the center, That ye might be witness over other nations and the Rasool a witness over yourselves. Whoever submits his whole self to Allah and is a doer of good, has grasped indeed the most Trustworthy handhold. And with Allah rests the end and decision of all affairs. (Al-Baqarah 2:143)

The *ummah* is a community of believers that

- is united as one people and one nation whose heart Allah has joined in love so that they are brethren to one another;
- enjoins good and forbids evil;
- is committed to truth and administers justice on the basis of truth as the *ummah* has been commanded by Allah to act justly to others and to one another and, in its advocacy of truth, is a witness over itself and over mankind;
- observes due balance and moderation in all its actions, avoids extremism, and does not transgress due bounds in anything where men and women are straight and honest in all their dealings;
- maintains itself in a permanent state of surrender to Allah;
- is united in a single brotherhood, not to be divided into sects, schisms, principalities, states, or kingdoms as Allah has promised *Azabu azeem* (a dreadful penalty) to those causing divisions among the *ummah*;
- looks after its own members in peace, tribulation, and adversity and in times of stress.

The Islamic society, as envisioned in the Koran and the Sunna, is a just and moral society—a society in which every individual—man and woman, from the highest to the lowest, from the first to the last—has equal, unimpeded, and unquestionable right and freedom to practice his faith in accordance with his beliefs as, in Islam, there is no compulsion in matters of religion; right to life, which includes mental and physical and emotional well-being; right to safeguard one's property; right to intellectual endeavors, acquisition of knowledge, and education; right to make a living; and right to free speech and action to enjoin good and forbid evil. In enjoying his freedoms, the individual ensures that his activities do not impinge on the similar rights of others.

The ruler (*amri minkum*) and his bureaucracy will deal with every individual and his or her problems with empathy, sympathy, and compassion. The word *compassion* is commonly translated to mean "sympathy," which is not quite correct. One with compassion does have empathy or sympathy with a subject, but when an injustice is committed, his inner self will compel him to correct the injustice with an action as opposed to just a feeling of passive sympathy.

The just and moral society is the *ummah*, made up of community upon community like a pyramid that gradually tapers to an apex where justice and administration is carried on according to the Koran and the covenant of Allah. At the apex of this pyramid, under the guidance of the covenant of Allah, sits as the *ummah's* representative (*wakil*) the caliph or the imam. The governance is based on open, transparent, honest, truthful statecraft where justice is practiced by the *ummah's* *wakil* at the top and is seen by all. The community at the base of the pyramid ensures that its appointed *wakil* and the community bureaucracy are just and honest, free from moral and economic corruption. Each community also acts as the guardian of the covenant of the Koran and acts on the precepts dictated therein.

> Verily this brotherhood of yours is a single brotherhood and I am your Lord and Cherisher: therefore serve Me (and no other).

Step Five: the Community's Mutual Welfare: Zakat

All wealth belongs to Allah, who bestows it on some people more than others. This wealth is given in trust, whereby the possessor is obliged to give the surplus to Allah's cause, to his kin, to the widows and orphans, and to the needy first in his community and then in other communities around him. Wealth is to be shared so that no single individual of the *ummah* or the world should go hungry or be without education, shelter, and treatment against illness.

It is not righteousness that ye turn your faces to towards East or West, but it is righteousness to Believe in God and the last day and the Angels and the Book, and the Messengers, to spend of your substance, out of love of Him, for your kin, for orphans, for the needy, for the wayfarer, for those who ask and for the ransom of the slaves; to be steadfast in prayer and to practice regular charity, to fulfill the Covenant, which you have made; and to be firm and patient, in tribulation and adversity and in times of stress. Such are the people of truth the God fearing. (Al-Baqarah 2:177, Koran)

Every Muslim, male or female, who at the end of the year is in possession of about fifteen dollars or more in cash or articles of trade must give zakat at the minimum rate of 2.5 percent. Zakat is incumbent on all liquid, visible, movable, and immovable properties belonging to Muslims. Two and a half percent in zakat was suggested by the *masha'ikhs* of the old schools of jurisprudence, over a thousand years ago. It is indeed not applicable to the circumstances of the present day. Two and a half percent of all the liquid assets of a Muslim adult after deduction of a reasonable amount of expenses for the maintenance of the person's family and other dependents is not an excessive amount of money. Allah constantly reminds the believers to practice regular charity. Giving to the needy with love and respect out of love of Allah is a profound act of spiritual cleaning. The more one gives in wealth and in kindness, the higher is his status with Allah.

In the united Muslim lands of the Dar es Salaam, if every adult man and woman gives minimum of *$15* in *zakat*, the total collected will amount to *$12 billion*. If every one of the one thousand billionaires and one million millionaires in the Islamic world contributes a minimum of 2.5 percent of their liquid wealth in the way of Allah, the total collected will be in the tune of another *$50 billion*. If we approach another ten million prosperous businesspeople with liquid assets of $500,000 to pay their minimum zakat, the sum collected from them will amount to another *$125 billion*. The total sum thus collected amounts *$187 billion*. Now we appeal to the same population that, in this twenty-first century, 2.5 percent is not really enough to feed and house the large disadvantaged population of the *ummah* and ask for 5 percent of their liquid assets. The total collected will amount to *$379 billion*. Half of this sum may then be used to feed, clothe, house, and educate the poor and needy population and the remaining half to create industries and jobs and training for the people who have not been able to exit the cycle of poverty.

When we become passionate and fulfill Allah's commandments and do, at the behest of the blessed *nabi*, what the Muhajirun and the Ansar did in Medina—empty our coffers at one time in the cause of Allah and give away to the *ummah* 20 percent of all the substance that we have accumulated and do not use, this gift in the way of Allah will amount to *$2.5 trillion*.

There is an estimated forty-five thousand tons of accumulated gold hoardings in the Islamic countries in the form of jewelry, gold bricks, gold bars, gold artifacts, and national treasures in museums of an estimated value of $548 billion. In addition, there is a hoard of precious stones worth another $100 billion. Twenty percent of gift from this hoard of the bullion and precious stones will amount to another *$130 billion.*

Even though the Islamic states have been milked dry by our elite and their colonial cohorts, the *ummah*—acting in accordance with Allah's covenant—shall be able to eradicate all poverty and destitution within the Dar es Salaam within *one year.* The resources will come from within the community of believers; the generosity of the *ummah* will provide a start-up gift of *$2.5 trillion* and an annual levy of $500 billion. So why is the *ummah* so destitute? The destitution comes from stinginess, craving, and greed. The wealth thus generated will create the infrastructure of hospitals, schools, highways, bridges, harbors, industries, and agriculture, which will provide jobs, security, wealth, and social services.

Were the precepts of the covenant of Allah applied to the rest of the humanity, all poverty, depravation, and disease would disappear from the world in one year. Less than 10 percent of the world's population owns 80 percent of the world's wealth. This disparity is caused by unbridled feudalism and capitalism in man's history.

The total wealth of the world is estimated to be $330 trillion. If every human gave away 2.5 to 5.0 percent of their surplus income in zakat to eradicate poverty, disease, and hunger in the global village, *$7.5 to $15.0 trillion* will become available; half this amount can be used to eradicate, hunger, illiteracy, unemployment, and disease annually and the remaining amount to build the world's infra-structure for environmentally sustainable agriculture and industrial production to sustain mankind. In no time, the world will be a stable place with the eradication of wars, famines, epidemics, ignorance, and hunger.

> The Believers have the Power and the Knowledge
> to end poverty and destitution in the world.
> What they need is intention and action.

Step Six: Equality and Freedoms

Allah's covenant provides equality to every individual within the community, both men and women. Allah has elevated the rank and dignity of the children of Adam, both men and women, with special favors above that of most of His creation, including the angels. The dignity and favors promised by Allah include six special values: faith, life, intellect (education), property, lineage, and freedom of speech and action.

Equality of Men and Women:

The Koran addresses men and women who submit to Allah, who believe, who are devout, who speak the truth, who are righteous, who are humble, who are charitable, who fast and deny themselves, who guard their chastity, and who remember Allah much and promises them a great reward and forgiveness for their transgressions. In this address, Allah treats individual men and women equitably with a promise of similar reward for their good acts. In Allah's eyes, all men and all women who do good deeds carry the same favor with Him.

Allah admonishes both the believing men and women to lower their gaze in modesty and guard their chastity. Allah is well acquainted with all that men and women do. Allah commands believers, men and women, to turn *all together* toward Allah so that they may prosper. This can happen only when the believers, men and women, turn to Allah collectively as a community in a mosque as was customary during the lifetime of the *nabi* of Allah.

According to the Koran, men and women are autonomous and answerable to Allah for their own deeds and actions, and only they as individuals are rewarded or punished for their deeds. In a community, men as a group or the state has no sanction from the Koran to enforce any restrictions on the freedom of righteous and believing women. To every man and to every woman, Allah has bestowed rights to freedom, faith, life, intellect, property, and education. The authority of a ruler who denies these basic freedoms to men or to women is openly disputable. The individual obeys the ruler on the condition that the ruler obeys the Koran and Allah's covenant.

For men and women who surrender unto Allah,
for men and women who believe,
for men and women who are devout,
for men and women who speak the truth,
for men and women who persevere in righteousness,
for men and women who are humble,
for men and women who are charitable,
for men and women who fast and deny them selves,
for men and women who guard their chastity,
for men and women who remember Allah much,
for them Allah has forgiveness and a great reward.

Say to the

Believing men that they should lower their gaze and guard their modesty; that will make for greater purity for them; And Allah is acquainted with all that they do.

And say to the

Believing women that they should lower their gaze and guard their modesty; that they should not display their adornments except what is ordinarily obvious, that they should draw a veil over their bosom and not display their adornments

(Except to the immediate family)
And that they should not strike their feet, in order to draw attention to their hidden adornments.
And O you Believers!
Turn you all together Toward Allah that ye may prosper. The believer's men and women are protectors one of another. They enjoin what is just and forbid what is evil. They observe regular prayers, practice regular charity obey Allah and His messenger. On them will Allah pour His mercy, for Allah is exalted in power, wise.

Oh ye who believe!
Guard your souls. If ye follow (right) guidance, no hurt can come to you from those who stray. The goal of you all is to Allah, it is He who will show you the truth of all that you do.

Women were regarded as inferior beings in most pre-Islamic cultures, including among the Arabs, Persians, Greeks, and Romans as well as the Hindus. Their status was not any higher among the Turkish and the Mongol tribes of Central Asia. In Judaism, women were forbidden from the inner sanctuary of the temple; and in the early Pauline Christianity, their position was relegated to the entrance of the church for worship. Islam brought dignity and grace to the status of women—the mothers, wives, and daughters. Women had their rights established and their social status elevated as equal to that of men. They attended prayer services at the Prophet's Mosque; they held regular and frequent discourse with the *nabi* of Allah on religious, women's, and family issues. They participated in battles alongside their men. Women worked outside their homes. The first person to convert to Islam, Khadijah, was a successful international trader and owned an import and export business, dealing goods from India, Persia, Africa, Yemen, and the Byzantine Empire. She employed several men to assist her in her business. Other women memorized the Koran and taught other Muslims. A'ishah gave regular talks and discourses on religious matters. Other women led the ritual prayers and *dhikr-e-Allah* gatherings.

The Koran, as in the sura above, addresses men and women equally, subjecting them together to similar obligations of submission to Allah, regular prayer, giving in charity, modesty in dress and behavior, righteousness, humility, chastity, worship, truthfulness, remembrance of Allah, and being kind and just. Allah blessed mankind (*insan*), both men and women, with dignity, justice, and equality. He promised them the same rewards and gave them the same obligations. *Be steadfast in prayer and practice regular charity* is an ongoing and repetitive theme in the Koran. Allah calls those who believe, both men and women, to hasten to the congregation prayer on Friday, the day of assembly.

O you who believe! (Men and women) When the call is proclaimed to prayer on Friday, the Day of Assembly, hasten earnestly to the Remembrance of Allah and leave off business and traffic that is best for you if you only knew!

And when the Prayer is finished, then you may disperse through the land and seek of the Bounty of Allah: and celebrate the Praises of Allah frequently, that ye may prosper. (Al-Mumtahanah 62:9–10, Koran)

Women attended obligatory prayers, *jum'ah* prayers, and Eid prayers in the Prophet's Mosque. Whenever the apostle of Allah finished his prayers with *Taslim*, the women would get up first, and he would stay in his place for a while before getting up. The purpose of staying was that the women might leave before the men who had finished their prayer.

Soon after the *nabi* died, there occurred an enormous expansion of the Islamic domain. Women, for a while, enjoyed their newly won freedom and dignity given by Islam and proclaimed by the blessed *nabi* Muhammad. Soon afterward, the Arabs reached an unprecedented level of prosperity and began to accumulate large harems of wives, concubines, and female slaves and servants. These women were increasingly confined to their quarters and not allowed to go out unchaperoned. Subsequently, the architecture of the Middle East dwellings changed to suit the new circumstances. The courtyard of the house had high walls, and the only entrance was where the master of the house sat. The master of the harem was so jealous of the chastity of his women that he only employed eunuchs as his servants and guards at his house. The institution of eunuchs was a peculiar Middle Eastern practice related to the institution of the harems of the elite.

The trampling of women's rights was and is a betrayal of the blessed *nabi* Muhammad's emancipation of women. As more Arabs, Romans, Persians, Hindus, Turks, and Mongols embraced Islam, they brought with them their peculiar bias against women and female infants. The Islamic emancipation of women was ignored; women were confined within their houses, covered head to foot in cloth, denied spiritual growth, and denied access to education and to places of worship. Shamefully, the scholars and the ulema encouraged this state of affairs. Women were gradually discouraged from praying in the mosque and were excluded from congregational worship. Thus, the Muslims for centuries have betrayed the *nabi* of Allah and disobeyed Allah's covenant.

Pre-Islamic Arab and other cultures regarded women as their chattel and possession. Abduction and rape of opponents' women was a favored pastime of those victorious in battle to humiliate the vanquished. Thus, the birth of a female child was regarded as a matter of shame, which led to the practice of infanticide. This practice was forbidden earlier on during the prophet's mission. However, the primordial masculine instinct resurfaced in the new Muslim. His subconscious shame and embarrassment of the female in his household was sublimated into gentler and more socially acceptable alternative. As the Koran points out, he chose to retain the female child on sufferance and contempt rather than bury her in the dust. And the Koran points out, *"What an evil choice they decide on!"* The shame and cultural burden in some of the Muslim societies is so intense that the female infant is buried in the coffin of yashmak (burka) in the confines of her brick house. She is not killed off physically but intellectually and spiritually by withholding the intellectual and spiritual sustenance that Allah had provided for her.

> Indeed Lost are those who slay their children, foolishly and without knowledge and have forbidden that which Allah has provided for them and inventing lies against Allah. They have indeed gone astray and heeded no guidance. (Al-An'am 6:140, Koran)

> When news is brought to one of them, of the birth of a female child, his face darkens and he is filled with inward grief!

> With shame does he hide himself from his people, because of the bad news he has had!

> Shall he retain it on sufferance and contempt, or bury it in the dust? Ah! What an evil choice they decide on? (An-Nahl 16:58–59, Koran)

Women should have the freedoms bestowed by Allah's covenant. They should enjoy their birthright to life, which includes mental, physical, and emotional well-being; right to safeguard property; right to intellectual endeavors, acquisition of knowledge, and education; right to make a living; and right to free speech and action to enjoin good and forbid evil. In enjoying their freedoms, every individual, man and woman, ensures that their activities do not impinge on the similar rights of others. Every civilized society grants its women—mothers, sisters, wives, and daughters—a place of dignity and honor. In this station of dignity, every woman has the rite of passage through homes, streets, bazaars, and mosques. Every woman should have free access to the sites, services, and amenities in her community without fear of interference to her dignity and honor or harm to her mental, physical, and emotional well-being. Any society that does not afford its women such freedom, dignity, and honor does not belong to the fellowship of Allah. A community in which women are forced to shelter under the cover of a curtain, chador, and burka to escape indignity and molestation by its men cannot be a society that has submitted to Allah, nor does it receive the mercy of Allah.

> And O you Believers (men and women)!
> Turn you all together Toward Allah that ye may prosper. The believer's men and women are protectors one of another. They enjoin what is just and forbid what is evil. They observe regular prayers, practice regular charity obey Allah and His messenger. On them will Allah pour His mercy, for Allah is exalted in power, wise. (At-Tawbah 9:71, Koran)

> To every man and to every woman Allah has bestowed equal rights to faith, life, intellect, property, education, and freedom of speech and action, enjoining what is right and forbidding what is wrong, and to make a living.

Step Seven: Conduct of Affairs of the Islamic State through Consultation and Consensus

> Those who hearken to their Lord and establish regular prayer; who conduct their affairs by mutual consultation; who spend out of what We bestow on them for sustenance; and who when oppressive wrong is inflicted on them dot flinch and courageously defend themselves. (Ash-Shura 42:38–39, Koran)

The dignified designation of the community as vicegerent of Allah on the earth makes the Muslim community, the *ummah*, a repository of the "executive sovereignty" of the Islamic state. The Koran teaches that all affairs of individuals and the community should be conducted by mutual consultation (*ijma*) and decisions reached through consensus. Furthermore, the Koran proclaims consultation as a principle of government and a method that must be applied in the administration of public affairs. The sovereignty of Islamic state belongs exclusively to Allah, whose will and command binds the community and state.

> The sovereignty of the Islamic state rests with the *ummah* through the participation of individual believers, both men and women, through mutual consultation and decisions reached in justice and consensus.

Step Eight: The Executive

The Khalifah, Imam, or the Wakil of community's affairs: ulil amri minkum.

Oh You who believe! Obey Allah and obey the messenger and those charged with authority among you. If you differ in any thing among yourselves, refer to Allah and His Messenger. If you do believe in Allah and the last day: that is the best and most suitable for final determination. (Koran 4:59)

> Upon the death of the blessed *nabi*, each believer in Allah, man and woman, inherited the Koran, the covenant of Allah, the din, and the Islamic state on the earth, the Dar es Salaam. Every individual believer, collectively with other believers, therefore has the authority to appoint for a defined period a suitable person to administer the affairs of his din and the ummah. With this authority to bestow the custodianship of the affairs of the ummah, the believer also has the power to revoke such an appointment if the appointed person fails to discharge his mandate to the satisfaction of the majority of believers.

The community, the *ummah,* as a whole, after consultation and consensus, grants people among themselves with authority to manage its affairs (*ulil amri minkum*). Those charged with authority act in their capacity as the representative (*wakil*) of the people and are bound by the Koranic mandate to consult the community in public affairs, and general consensus is a binding source of the law. The community, by consultation and in consensus, has the authority to depose any person charged with authority, including the head of state, in the event of gross violation of Allah's law and disobedience of the covenant of the Koran.

Islam pursues its social objectives by reforming the individual. The ritual ablution before prayer, the five daily prayers, fasting during the month of Ramadan, and the obligatory giving of charity all encourage punctuality, self-discipline, and concern for the well-being of others. The individual is seen not just a member of the community and subservient to the community's will but also as a morally autonomous agent who plays a distinctive role in shaping the community's sense of direction and purpose. The Koran has attached to the individual's duty of obedience to the government a right of to simultaneously dispute with rulers over government affairs. The individual obeys the ruler on the condition that the ruler obeys the covenant of the Koran and Allah's commandments, which are obligatory to all Muslims regardless of their status in the social hierarchy. This is reflected in the declaration of the blessed *nabi*:

There is no obedience in transgression; obedience is only in the righteousness.

The citizen is entitled to disobey an oppressive command that is contrary to the Islamic law according to the covenant of the Koran.

Step Nine: The Dar es Salaam:

The Pax Islamica

But Allah does call

To the Abode of Peace: Dar es Salaam

He does guide whom He pleases

To a way that is straight.

(Yunus 10:25, Koran)

In every Islamic land, there sits a tyrant gouging the freedoms of the people. The Dar es Salaam is the abode of peace that Allah has promised to His righteous servants who follow His straight path. Dar es Salaam is the home of the *ummah*, which extends in the west from the Atlantic coast of Africa to the Muslim population of the Philippines in the east. In the north, its domains extend from the Muslim population of Russia to those of Indonesia in the south. Every country where the Muslim population forms a majority is the geographic part of the domain of Islam, the abode of peace. Every member of the *ummah* within and outside the boundaries of the domain of the Dar es Salaam shall have the right of citizenship of and shall enjoy all the benefits and the obligations that go with it. The home and place of worship of every believer on the globe is the primary unit of the Dar es Salaam.

A united Dar es Salaam has been denied to the *ummah* by self-proclaimed rulers who usurped the land of Islam by conquest and force of arms. These rulers have ruled over the land for the last fourteen centuries with the support of tribal, slave, and mercenary armies along with the cooperation of corrupt and self-serving elite and ulema. The *ummah* has been denied its God-given right to control its destiny. It had been left destitute, impoverished, and in ignorance by these rulers and the elite. By Allah's grace, the *ummah* is now ready to roll over the borders and barriers within the Dar es Salaam and assume its executive sovereignty over the land of Islam, flush out the anthill of despots from their termite palaces, and establish the covenant of Allah under one *ulil amri minkum* with the authority to conduct governance with justice, consultation, and consensus of the community.

The greatest miracle in Islam is the revelation and the preservation of Allah's divine word, the Koran. The next greatest miracle is not only the survival but also the expansion of the *ummah* during the turbulent centuries of tyrannical sultanic and colonial rule. In spite of the alien systems of governments of the sultans and the dictators based on self-aggrandizement and perpetuation of power, the common people and the community of Islam have continued to receive nurturing and spiritual enlightenment from within the community through the love of Allah and His blessed *rasul*, Muhammad. Holy men, sages, Sufis, and other humble religious teachers have continued to nurture the love of Allah in the heart of the people. They have sought to teach and preach *taqwa* and the knowledge of Allah in humility and sincerity.

The ulema and religious scholars, having served as the elite and the functionaries of the sultans and the state, have continued to claim the sole custodianship of the knowledge of the Koran and Hadith. As the self-proclaimed holders of divine knowledge, they have continued to dissect, debate, and quarrel on insignificant matters of the *din* while forgetting that such matters did not lead the *ummah* any further to the path of Allah. The path to Allah's *din* is through the heart in humility and sincerity. The scholars and the ulema established priesthood over Islam, even though Islam does not recognize priesthood or its hierarchical structure. These priests became the founders and keepers of man-made dogma and creed in Islam. Their influence on society has led to divisiveness, to the detriment of society, in education and equality of men and women in both temporal and religious matters. It has been said that you educate a boy to educate a man, and you educate a girl to educate a whole nation. Women have been, over the centuries, squeezed out of communal worship of Allah. The sultans, ulema, and elite made women a decoration of the harem and excluded them from all civic functions, denying women the dignity and rights sanctioned to them by Allah in the Koran.

There is no priesthood, clergy, or hierarchical ecclesiastical structure in Islam. Muftis, ulema, religious scholars, ayatollahs, and their religious police have given themselves a right to guide and control the *ummah* in matters of religion. Any opinions and interpretations outside the authority of the Koran are the personal thoughts of these scholars, and they do not constitute the sanction of Allah or that of the blessed prophet. The believers, men and women, pledged obedience to the covenant of Allah. The Koran teaches moderation and humility in all affairs of the *din* and the world. Self-proclaimed religious figures with militant views of Islam forget that the path to Allah is moderation as defined by the Koran and in the blessed prophet's teachings. Scholars who preach against other Muslim groups holding convictions different from their own cause division among the Muslims; they fail to realize that it is not the Islamic political history that forms the path to the worship of Allah; it is the Koran, Allah's covenant, that is supreme. It is the acceptance of Allah's mercy and grace in one's heart that counts. In spite of these continuing setbacks, Islam and the *ummah* have survived, and both are getting stronger.

In Allah's Dar es Salaam, men constitute 750,000,000 individuals of the *ummah*, and the women constitute the other 750,000,000; between them, they form one solid, united *ummah*. Together in partnership, men and women have produced the progeny of Adam to carry out the divine and omnipotent will of Allah. The Koran addresses all believers, both men and women, together:

And you Believers (men and women)! Turn you all together towards Allah, that ye may attain bliss.

The Dar es Salaam constitutes the following: Afghanistan, Albania, Algeria, Bahrain, Bangladesh, Benin, Bosnia, Brunei, Burkina Faso, Cameroon, Chad, Chechnya, Comoros, Djibouti, Egypt, Ethiopia, East Turkistan, Gabon, Gambia, Guinea, Guinea-Bissau, Guyana, Indonesia, Iran, Ivory Coast, Iraq, Jordan, Kashmir, Kazakhstan, Kosovo, Kuwait, Kyrgyzstan, Lebanon, Libya, Malaysia, Maldives, Mali, Mauritania, Morocco, Mindanao, Mozambique, Niger, Nigeria, Oman, Pakistan, Palestine, Qatar, Saudi Arabia, Senegal, Sierra Leone, Somalia, Sudan, Suriname, Syria, Tajikistan, Tanzania, Togo, Tunisia, Turkey, Turkmenistan, Uganda, United Arab Emirates, Uzbekistan, and Yemen. Other Muslim domains within the boundaries of countries of Russia, China, India, Serbia, and Macedonia have an extraterritorial association with the Dar es Salaam through their large Muslim populations.

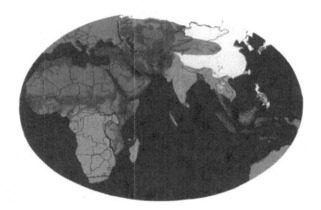

The place of the Dar es Salaam among the Euro-Christian, Hindu, Chinese, and African civilizations.

Every Muslim, whether residing in or outside the bounds of the Dar es Salaam, is a member of the *ummah* and has the right and the obligation to the citizenship of the Dar es Salaam. Equally, every non-Muslim residing within the bounds of the Dar es Salaam who has sworn allegiance to the state will have the same citizenship rights and obligations, as well as all freedoms prescribed by the Koran to the Muslims, in short absolute and complete equality (Document of Yathrib).

Step Ten: Organization and Electoral College of the *Ummah*

At the grass roots, the *ummah* has been, through divine guidance, a democratic society governing itself justly in consultation and consensus through its intrinsic resources. Historically, however, the *ummah* has been consistently denied the means of a participatory democratic system of government at higher levels by ongoing upheavals in their lands caused by marauding armies in search of power and booty. The democratic and humane social system at the basic level could not be transformed into a viable democratic political order of consultation and consensus at the upper level because of the tribal, feudal, and sultanic monarchical order of the ruling classes. For over one thousand years, the rulers and their governments were estranged and cut off from their people. Troops and civil servants came from the tribal formations, slaves, and *devsirme* classes. Land- and revenue-bearing estates were allocated to the military commanders and revenue agents, and the people were merely sharecroppers. Such un-Koranic autocratic feudalism has continued to exist in all Islamic lands. The covenant of Allah is the code of conduct for the Muslims. Without fulfilling the covenant of Allah, all acts of submission, faith, and worship become meaningless and of little consequence.

The *Ummah*:

Verily this brotherhood of yours is a single brotherhood and I am your Lord and Cherisher; therefore serve Me and no other. And hold fast, all together the Rope which Allah stretches out for you and be not divided amongst yourselves. And remember with gratitude Allah's favor on you, for ye were enemies and He joined your hearts in love. So that by His Grace, you became brethren. Let there arise out of you a band of people inviting all that is good, enjoining what is right and forbidding what is wrong. Be not like those who are divided amongst themselves and fall into disputations after receiving clear signs for them is a dreadful penalty.

Ye are the best of the peoples evolved for mankind, enjoining what is right, forbidding what is wrong, and believing in Allah.

Thus have We made of you an Ummah of the center, that you are witness over other nations and the Rasool a witness over yourselves. Whoever submits his whole self to Allah and does wholesome and good deeds, has grasped indeed the most trustworthy handhold. And with Allah rests the end and decision of all affairs. (Al-Baqarah 2:143, Koran)

The sovereignty of the Dar es Salaam rests with the Muslim *ummah*, which is the aggregate of individual believers. For the aggregate to believe in and to comply with the divine commandments, the individual has to be reformed and taught his responsibilities as the member of a divinely ordained indivisible brotherhood.

Insignificant raindrops fall on parched land singly and disappear forever; however, the same raindrops coalesce in strength to form little streams and then little rivulets and then join together to become mighty rivers flowing further, dropping into powerful and majestic waterfalls, yet again joining together with other rivers, lakes, and more hill torrents, to end up in mighty oceans ever increasing in size, in length, in depth, and in power yet at all times obedient to the will of Allah. Similarly, an insignificant man without faith is like a drop of water on parched land. Yet the same man, a believer, strengthened by his covenant with Allah, joins others with the covenant to form a little community that, again, with other communities in unity with Allah form a single united *ummah* of all the Muslims around the world, a powerful, united people witnessing over other nations, with Allah and His prophet witnessing over themselves.

The *Ummah el Nuqta*:

The basic unit of the *ummah* is the *ummah el nuqta*, consisting of about one thousand adults over the age of fifteen years, comprising around five hundred families of a neighborhood. This unit is an autonomous, self-help neighborhood administered in consultation and with consensus from within the *nuqta* by the community itself. The community will ensure the well-being of each member of this community unit in matters of nutrition, spiritual and worldly education, health, housing, clean water, waste disposal, social planning, and development. The community will ensure that none of their members go without food, shelter, health care, and education.

The *ummah el nuqta* community will select or elect from among themselves an *ulil amri minkum*, a *sheikh al nuqta* and a committee of four members—*mushirs*, two men and two women—to administer the affairs of the *nuqta* every two years for a tenure of four years. The *sheikh al nuqta* will run the affairs of the community and will act as the chairperson of the committee. The *sheikh al nuqta* will run the day-to-day affairs of the community with the help of his committee with ongoing consultation with the community. The *sheikh al nuqta* may be a man or a woman in accord with the community's will. The *mushirs* will represent their community on various administrative boards related to education, health, transport, and municipal affairs and in matters of interest to the community at the next higher level of the administration, the *ummah el haraf.*

1. The *sheikh al nuqta* will be responsible for the civic discipline and law and order within the community. He will mediate any disputes within the community and will act as a magistrate at the community level. The community will police itself without interference from the outside except at the request of the committee.

2. Each *nuqta* community will aim for the highest possible standard of public health, education, health care, housing, and nutrition for its members. It will promote universal literacy for its members within a short period of four years, to be achieved with the maximum effort on the part of each member, assisting one another. Such mutual assistance will also be carried out in matters of education, trade, business, and housing and in every other matter of civic and social concern within the community.

3. The community will appoint a scholar as a spiritual guide or an imam for a designated period, whose appointment may or may not be renewed at the end of that period according to the community's will. The imam will provide spiritual guidance to those seeking it, as well as religious services to the community.

4. As with the sheikh and the *mushirs*, the tenure of the imam will depend on his character, ability, and performance at the will of the community.

5. Community welfare and developmental projects will be funded through a voluntary contribution of 20 percent of everyone's income. Every man and woman will contribute in money, commodities, or labor. The provincial government will provide funding for the administration of *ummah el nuqta*.

Individual families, cooperative associations, and women's groups within the *nuqta* will utilize their dormant and nonproductive wealth to create industry, jobs, and productivity within their community. It is estimated that an average couple in the Middle East and South Asia owns one hundred grams of gold ornaments, the rich own several kilograms of gold, and the poor own just a few grams; nevertheless, the average amount is estimated to be about a hundred grams per couple. The *nuqta* community (500 families × 100 g = 50 kg) will have access to 50 kg of gold for investment, converting a dormant hoard into a personal and a community asset.

Ummah el Haraf

One hundred *nuqta* communities will get together and authorize the next level of administration, the *ummah el haraf,* which will run the rural communities comprising about one hundred thousand adults or twenty-five thousand families. Some communities may merge where geographic or ethnic interests dictate such a merger. One *mushirs* from the *ummah el nuqta* will represent his or her community on the *ummah el haraf* executive council, and another representative will sit on the *ummah el haraf* planning committee charting out the future course of the communities. In urban areas and cities, similar arrangements will constitute a city municipality executive council and city municipality planning council. The two *mushirs* from the *ummah el nuqta* will represent their community in the two *ummah el haraf* councils, the executive and the planning. Care will be taken to balance gender equality of the members on the councils. The *mushirs* sitting on the executive and planning committees of the *ummah el haraf* will, in consultation with their communities, select the *sheikh el haraf* from among themselves as the head of the *ummah el haraf.* The *sheikh* will be the chairperson of both the executive and the planning councils.

1. The *mushirs*, along with experts from a variety of disciplines, will sit on various committees dealing with hospitals, schools, highways, finance, police, water, garbage disposal, planning,

business, commerce, and so on. Recognizing the sovereignty of the *ummah*, the sheikh and the *mushirs* will consult the community before coming to any decisions, which will be made in consensus with the community. The decision-making will of necessity be slow and will require the assent of the community. The planning council will look at the needs of the community in the years ahead and will also act as the lawmakers in tune with the laws of Allah and as a check on the executive. The executive council will run the day-to-day affairs of the *ummah el haraf* and execute the decisions and planning of the planning council. A council of the *sheikhs el nuqta* will ensure that none of the councils and their functionaries abuse their authority nor misappropriate public assets.

2. The *ummah el haraf* is an autonomous body acting in a role assigned to them by the *ummahs el nuqta* and *el haraf* as enshrined in the constitution.

3. The communities of *ummah el haraf*, consisting of twenty-five thousand families, will in consultation and in consensus select from among themselves one able person of impeccable character, ability, and experience every two years for a four-year term to represent their interests at the provincial and national levels.

4. A Council of ten *sheikhs el haraf* from ten *ummahs el haraf*, ten representatives of the *sheikh el nuqta* from these communities, ten representatives of the *mushirs* of these communities, along with twenty-five representatives of various organizations, guilds, ulema, professions, universities, and so on will constitute a *majlis-e-ijma*. *Majlis-e-ijma* will act as the consultative body acting as the eyes, ears, and voice of an adult population of one million people of the region. This *majlis* will

comprise an equal number of men and women. Each *majlis-e-ijma* will select two of its members to sit on the national and the *villayat ijma* councils to coordinate the national consensus on policy matters, which will be binding on the executive.

5. This *majlis-e-ijma* will, on an ongoing basis, consult the communities in their area in matters of mutual interest and arrive at a consensus of opinion on that matter and continually liaise with their *naibs* on the *majlis-e-watanniya, majlis-villayat,* as well as the provincial and the national executives, the ministries of these governments, and the officials and functionaries of these two levels of government.

6. The *majlis-e-ijma* will, every two years, appoint the ten elected representatives, the *naibs*, to one of the following task forces as assigned by the constitution of the *ummah el haraf*:

   a) The lower house of the national legislature, the *majlis-e-watanniya.*

   b) The provincial legislature, the *majlis-villayat.*

   c) The national executive.

   d) The provincial executive.

   e) The planning council, formulating strategies and policies concerning the nation in all spheres such as defense, foreign policy, fiscal matters, trade and commerce, population, education, health issues, Sharia and legal matters, transport, ports, cultural affairs, agriculture, mining, industry, civic planning, scientific research, and so on, delineating the course of the country in the short and long terms.

   f) The security commission, *majlis-e-naazir,* a watchdog and oversight bureau watching unobtrusively all the functions of the national and provincial governments, the government ministries and agencies, intelligence services, the armed forces, and the law enforcement agencies and the courts.

The *naibs*, as a body, will create and strengthen institutions based on Koranic democratic principles that the sovereignty of the *ummah* and the Dar es Salaam devolves from the individual believer to a collective repository of executive sovereignty of the whole *ummah* as a trust from Allah. The people entrusted with authority to administer the *ummah*'s affairs by contract are the *wakil* and the servants of the *ummah* and not the masters or the rulers. The legislative, executive, policy and planning, and security institutions will in clear and no uncertain terms derive their authority from individual believers, collectively from the *ummah*, as prescribed by the Koran. This authority will be passed from below upward through the *mushirs* and the *naibs*. The *majlis-e-ijma* in the middle—being the eyes, ears, voice, and conscience of the *ummah*—will in consultation with the community, the *ummah*, and the institutions of the legislature, the executive, the policy and planning bureau, and the security council on an ongoing process develop a consensus of opinion to formulate the policy for the government to act on. The Muslim society, which has always been democratic, will for the first time universally have a democratic government with solid legislative and executive institutions. The authority will, in effect, evolve from the common man and woman believer at the base through their appointed representatives to the top, the head of state and his executive, as in a pyramid, the base being a solid foundation and the top being the apex, resting there on a secure and firm institutional structure.

Political Structure: Based on Consultation and Consensus at the Grass Roots:

The political structure will be without political parties. An untrammeled democratic system will be maintained with the election and appointment of only *five* positions by any single citizen of the Dar es Salaam.

1. Two *mushirs*, one man and one woman, to be appointed by a thousand adults of the *nuqta* community from among themselves for a four-year term every two years. The community will find people of faith; of impeccable character, track record, and ability; and in particular of honesty from among themselves in consultation and arrive at a full consensus before making an appointment. The choice may be made from a short list of people forwarded by various citizen groups. Emphasis will be on the citizens' choice rather than self-recommendation and self-aggrandizement by individuals.

2. The *sheikh el nuqta*, man or a woman, to be selected by the *nuqta* community for a four-year term from among people of impeccable character and proven ability.

3. One *naib*, a man or a woman, to be elected alternatively every two years for a four-year term by the aggregate of ten *nuqta* communities, the *ummah el haraf*, constituting one hundred thousand adults.

4. A *raiis*, a man or a woman, will be elected by universal suffrage for a four-year term to run the administration of the vilayet as its chief executive.

5. An *emir* or a *caliph*. The whole adult population of the *ummah* from around the world will, for a six-year term, elect an emir or a caliph, the chief executive of the Dar es Salaam, from a list of people prepared by the national council of the

majlis-e-ijma in consultation with all major organizations and ordinary citizens. The candidate nominated for this position should be of impeccable reputation and character, administrative ability, and communication and interpersonal skills. He should be recognized as having submitted to the absolute and omnipotent will of Allah, and he should have a relationship with Him that is governed by *taqwa*, the responsibility of the humankind toward the Creator, and consciously act in accordance with the three types of knowledge: *ilm al-yaqin*, *ain al-yaqin*, and *haqq al-yaqin* (knowledge of certitude, eye of certitude, and truth of certitude). He should be known to be in a state of constant submission to Allah. The caliph should be a natural leader, leading through example, piety, and humility through the guidance of his covenant with Allah. The caliph will guide and administer but will not rule. He and his family will have no privileges other than those defined by his office.

6. A council of the states composed of the *raiis* of every state or his deputy will form the upper house of the *majlis-e-watanniya* to protect the rights of each state.

7. There will be no obvious opposition party in the *majlis-e-villayats* or in the *majlis-e-watanniya* as in the Western democracies. The Islamic system has a built-in check and balance system within the framework of consultation and consensus at all levels of the government. The *majlis-e-ijma* and its national and state councils as well as the policy and planning councils are, at all times, open to the special interest and lobby groups to present their viewpoint. The security council and the *majlis-e-ijma* will unobtrusively oversee the conduct of the governments and their functionaries, putting an end to any irregularities before they take root and become entrenched.

Ummah el Villayat:

The autonomous Muslim states that exist today will become the autonomous vilayets of the Dar es Salaam. All Muslim countries that function today as independent states will amalgamate into one united country. The population will form one united *ummah*, the *ummah wast* as proclaimed by Allah in the Koran, and their present rulers will cease to exercise every form of authority. Their authority will revert to the *ummah* as commanded by Allah. The sixty or so countries will become vilayets—states that will unite to form the Dar es Salaam, with autonomy to run their own affairs internally in the fields of health, education, agriculture, irrigation, highways, law and order, forestry, fisheries, municipalities, industry, internal trade, and commerce.

1. The states or the vilayets will be totally autonomous in the internal affairs as described above.

2. The legislative assembly, the *majlis-e-villayats*, will have authority to enact legislation in accordance to the tenets of the covenant of the Koran. It will also act as watchdog over the executive. The *naibs* appointed by the *ummah el haraf* will constitute the *majlis*, will derive their authority from the *ummah el haraf*, and will act in consultation and in consensus with *ummah el haraf* and the *majlis-e-ijma* of their district in the best interests of the nation.

3. The head of the executive, the *raiis*, and his deputy will be elected directly by the *ummah el villayat* in consultation and in the consensus from a number of people recommended by the council of *majlis-e-ijma* of the vilayet for a four-year term.

4. The *raiis* will administer with the help of a cabinet of his selection from the *naibs* and other experts approved by the *majlis-e-villayats* for a four-year period.

5. A policy and planning bureau composing of *naibs* and experts in their fields will on an ongoing basis formulate alternate policies in every sphere of the jurisdiction of the vilayet. The policies will be discussed by the legislature and the executive in an open forum of the legislature; modified, accepted, or rejected by the *majlis* and the executive; and then implemented by the executive.

6. Task forces composing of the representative *naibs* and experts in various fields will research and collect information to advise various ministries on policy matters concerning their subject. Various interest groups will be invited for their opinions on the subject matter, and their advice and interest should be given due consideration in formulating a policy.

7. The *raiis* will derive his authority from the *ummah* and will act according to Allah's covenant and with the consent and the consensus of the *ummah* through the *majlis-e ijma, majlis-e-villayats*, policy and planning council, and various interest groups.

8. All citizens of any race, caste, creed, religion, gender, age, and wealth shall stand equal in the eyes of the law, same as in the eyes of Allah. There shall be no elite in the state, and no one shall use a title or a name to show superiority over other beings. All titles bestowed, inherited, or self-assumed shall extinguish.

9. The services of every person to the *ummah* and to the nation given selflessly will be recognized to be as such, and no person shall have precedence in recognition of such services in the form of land grant or with funds from the public treasury, which are not available to other citizens.

10. For the purposes of law and citizenship, any person declaring his submission to Allah and His covenant is a believer and a

Muslim. For the purposes of the state, there will be no sects, and the rights of all citizens will be protected.

Ummah el Dar es Salaam:

The Dar es Salaam is the composite political reality that represents the home and the place of worship of every believer in the world. It is an amorphous land mass in which every home and every place of worship of the believer is the Dar es Salaam. The state of Dar es Salaam will nurture each man under the commandments of the covenant of Allah. In the Dar es Salaam, every human—man and woman, from the highest to the lowest, from the first to the last—shall have equal, unimpeded, and unquestionable right to liberty; right to practice his faith in accordance with his beliefs as, in Islam, there is no compulsion in matters of religion; right to life, which means intellectual, physical, and emotional well-being; right to safeguard one's property; right to intellectual endeavors, acquisition of knowledge, and education; right to earn a living; and right to free speech and action to enjoin good and forbid evil. In enjoying these freedoms, the individual will ensure that his activities do not impinge on the rights and freedom of others.

Every believer inherits the Koran, the covenant of Allah, the *din*, and the Dar es Salaam after his or her submission to Allah. When the blessed *nabi* died, the Qur'an and the *din* were bequeathed to each Believer. This custodianship of the Koran and the *din* were bequeathed to every believer. This custodianship of the Koran, the covenant, the *din*, and the Dar es Salaam rests with every believer individually until the last day. In the Dar es Salaam, individual believers collectively and for a defined period delegate this custodianship to a person or persons of their choice with conditions; in return, that individual is to exercise authority to manage the affairs of the Islamic state. While this authority may be bestowed, it can also be withdrawn if that individual fails to exercise his charge to the satisfaction of the majority of believers. During the period of discharge of his duties, this appointee will be called the caliph.

At the top of the pyramidal hierarchy of the *ummah*, the head of state and the successor to the temporal power of the blessed *nabi* of Allah is the caliph, appointed to office by universal suffrage by every adult believer for a period of six years. Suitable candidates will be nominated by the national council of *majlis-e-ijma* and other organizations after consultation with citizens. Those nominated for the position of caliph will be presented to the people by the *majlis-e-ijma*. For this position, there will be no electioneering and no self-recommendation. The lessons of schism and disunity of Islam caused by Mu'awiyah's seizure of the caliphate in the sixty-sixth year of hijra will not be forgotten.

Ten *naibs* or deputies elected by the composite of fifty *haraf* communities every two years will be assigned to serve on the following bodies for a four-year term:

1. *Majlis-e-watanniya* (national parliament).
2. *Majlis-e-villayats* (provincial parliament).
3. National executive.
4. Provincial executive.
5. The planning councils formulating strategies and policies concerning the nation in all spheres such as defense, foreign policy, trade and commerce, fiscal matters, population, education, agriculture, health issues, Sharia and legal matters, transport, ports, cultural affairs, mining, civic planning, scientific research, security and intelligence, and so on. This committee will plan the possible course for the nation in the short and the long terms.
6. The security commission (*majlis-e-naazir*), a watchdog and an oversight bureau watching unobtrusively all functions of

the provincial and national governments, the government ministries and agencies, the intelligence services, the armed forces, the law enforcement forces, and the courts. One member will represent their *haraf* community on the advisory committee of the caliph and the *raiis*. These members' services will be allocated to various subcommittees as required by the needs of the day.

7. One member appointed to the *ijma council*. The function of this council will be to consult with the *ummah* and assess the consensus of public opinion on various issues in the public domain. The committee's function will also include education of the public opinion through provision of true and honest information on the state matters of concern to the citizens. The Dar es Salaam's modus operandi shall be based on truth and trust as advocated by the covenant of Allah.

8. These *haraf* community representatives will represent the public consensus on issues under consideration to their assigned committees, commissions, and the *majlis*. These ten members from their communities will be the best education tools to enlighten their communities on the workings of an Islamic system of governance based on Allah's covenant. Honest two-way communication from the base to the apex of the pyramid of governance and vice versa will smash any barriers of misunderstanding between the levels of administration and the people. This web of communication will unify the *ummah*. Rules, laws, and conduct of governance based on the thirty-seven commandments of the covenant of Allah will drive away Satan and humans controlled by him. These ten representatives of *haraf* communities, representing a population of five million, will meet regularly with the citizen groups to deal with their questions and problems in a formal,

documented setting to find the solutions to the questions from the officialdom of the state.

the solutions to the questions from the officialdom of the state.

The *nuqta* communities of one thousand adults, totaling a population of about twenty-five hundred, will be the basic community of the Dar es Salaam. This community holds the executive sovereignty of the Dar es Salaam. Six hundred thousand such autonomous communities form the basis of consultation and consensus of decision-making in all issues relating to the Dar es Salaam, where the democratic control over the nation begins at the grass roots and disseminates all the way to the apex.

The believer's covenant with Allah reforms the individual by setting him or her to Allah's straight path. Similarly, reformed individuals in the community reinforce one another's resolve and actions in accordance with the straight path. Every believer when reciting *shahadah* in the daily prayer also pledges obedience to the covenant of Allah:

> Verily those who pledge their allegiance unto you (O Muhammad), pledge it unto none but Allah; the Hand of Allah is over their hands. Thereafter whosoever breaks his Covenant does so to the harm of his own soul and whosoever fulfils his Covenant with Allah, Allah will grant him an immense Reward. (Al-Fath 48:10, Koran)

The actions of believers reflect their faith and total submission to Allah—the only Reality; the Knower of the hidden and the manifest; the *Rahman* and the *Rahim*; the Sovereign; the Pure; the Hallowed, Serene, and Perfect; the Protector; the Almighty; the Supreme; the Creator; the Most High; the Most Great. Allah sent the blessed Muhammad and other blessed *rasuls* as witnesses to mankind, bearing glad tidings that Allah is the only reality and that everything else is dependent on Allah. Allah revealed the divine message, the Koran, to Blessed *Nabi* Muhammad as guidance and a covenant to humankind. Those who obey the covenant and Allah as guidance and hold on to Allah receive His grace, mercy, benevolence, and protection. The believers are conscious of Allah's presence with them at all times. And all their actions are with the awareness that Allah is with them; though they may not see Him, He sees them.

The believers in Allah pledge to

- fulfill their covenant with Allah;
- serve Allah and His creation with generous, beautiful, and *righteous* deeds, pledging to provide their kin, neighbors, community, and those in need with sustenance from their means and wealth;
- be just and truthful;
- shun shameful deeds, *Fahasha*;
- be united within the *ummah*;
- seek protection of Allah as the *Waliy* and reject Jews, Christians, and the infidels as their *awliya* or protectors;
- fight in the cause of Allah;
- fight injustice, unbelief in Allah, *fitnah*, and tyranny until there is no more and until justice prevails altogether and everywhere;
- not take life. Allah has made life, which Allah has made sacred;
- not betray the trust of Allah and his *nabi* with theft, deception, fraud, corruption, and dishonesty;
- not devour usury nor hoard wealth;
- be good, kind, and caring to their parents;
- not kill or deprive their children because of poverty (abortion and murder);

- treat one another in kindness and on the basis of equality and justice;
- not crave those things of what Allah has bestowed His gifts more freely on some than others as men and women are assigned what they earn;
- be just and stand firmly for justice and truth as witness to Allah;
- always speak the truth and always deal justly that he shall not be dealt with unjustly;
- invite others to what is good and right and forbid what is wrong;
- avoid suspicion, which leads to sin;
- not ridicule other believers;
- avoid secret counsels, which are inspired by Satan;
- not use intoxicants, gambling, carrion, blood, flesh of swine, and any food on which a name other than that of Allah has been invoked;
- not prohibit and make unlawful the good things that Allah has made lawful;
- commit no excess as Allah does not love people given to extremism;
- respect other people's privacy and enter not their houses without first asking permission.

On ninth day of *Zul-hajj* in tenth year of hijra, Allah in His mercy proclaimed to humankind through His blessed *rasul* that *Allah had perfected the* din *of the believers,* bestowed on them His blessings, and decreed Islam as the *din* of believers.

In Sura Al-Kahf, Allah proclaims, *"We have explained in detail in this Qur'an, for the benefit of man kind every kind of similitude,* but man is in most things contentious."

In Taha, it says, "So *We have made the Qur'an easy in your own tongue* that with it you may give glad tidings to the righteous and warnings to people given to contention."

And in Ad-Dukhan, it says, "Ha Mim. *By the Book that makes matters lucid;* We revealed it during blessed night, verily We are always warning against Evil. Therein is proclaimed every wise decree, by command from Our Presence, for We are ever sending Revelations, as a Mercy from Your Lord, for He is the Hearer and the Knower."

In these suras, Allah proclaims that His message to mankind in the Koran "is perfect, detailed, easy and lucid." Accordingly, Allah's *din* is not to be tampered by humans at any time. After that day, any additions and alterations to the *din* of the believers are a man-made innovation.

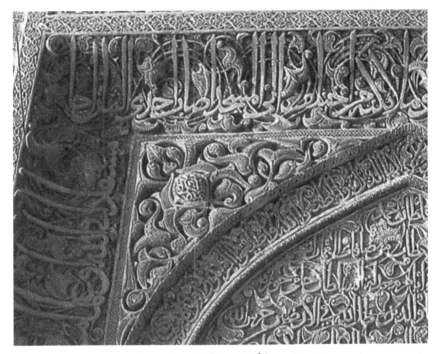

Friday Mosque, Isfahan.

Chapter Eight

The Autonomy and Economy of the *Nuqtaeen*

The twenty-five hundred members of each *nuqta* community, in fulfillment of their covenant with Allah, guided and protected by Him, form the solid foundation of the fellowship of Allah and the Dar es Salaam. In the world of believers, every individual is in communion with Allah and thus has pledged to the covenant of Allah. The faith of the believer thus makes him autonomous and responsible for his own actions and well-being; at the same time, through his allegiance to the covenant, he is responsible for the welfare of his community. Armed with the covenant of Allah, with Allah as his protector, every *nuqtaeen* becomes the defendant of the Dar es Salaam. As the fundamental unit of the *ummah*, each *nuqtaeen* community is autonomous politically and economically but merges with the neighboring communities to become economically and politically self-sufficient to provide required services to the community.

This fundamental autonomy of the individual and that of the basic community provides the criterion of Islamic democracy where every man, woman, and child has God-given, equal, and unimpeded right to liberty; right to practice their faith in accordance with their beliefs as, in Islam, there is no compulsion in matters of religion; right to life, which means, intellectual, physical, and emotional well-being; right to safeguard one's property; right to intellectual endeavors, acquisition of knowledge, and education; right to earn a living; and right to free speech and action to enjoin good and forbid evil. In enjoying these freedoms, the individual will ensure that his activities do not impinge on the rights and freedom of others.

Upon this premise is then built the union of community upon community, where the dignity of human beings is considered to have five special values—faith, life, intellect, property, and lineage—that must be protected by the law as a matter of priority. Although the basic interests of the community and those of the individual coincide within the structure of these values, the focus is nevertheless on the individual. This principle assigns to the individual an active role in the community in which he or she lives. The Koran annunciated the principle of free speech fourteen hundred years ago. Believing men and women are reminded that they are the best of people, witnesses over other nations. Such a responsibility carries with it a moral burden of an exemplary conduct of one who submits to the divine truth and whose relationship with Allah is governed is by *taqwa*, the consciousness of humankind's responsibility toward its Creator. The believer has the responsibility of acting in accordance with the three types of knowledge—the knowledge of certitude (*ilm al-yaqin*), the eye of certitude (*ain al-yaqin*), and the truth of certitude (*haqq al-yaqin*). With that knowledge and faith, the believer is well equipped to approach others to enjoin what is right and forbid what is wrong. This moral autonomy of the individual, when bound together with the will of the community, formulates the doctrine of infallibility of the collective will of the community (*ummah*), which becomes the doctrinal basis of consensus.

Economic and Social Structure

Every *nuqta* community will own its own agriculture land of ten thousand acres or more of productive land to be used for communal food production, animal husbandry, and dairy production. The *nuqtaeen* will take possession of the land currently owned by their governments and lease and purchase other land from within or outside their community. This communal farm will be operated on a cooperative and commercial basis. All surplus commodities, after the needs of the community are met, will generate income for the community.

The *nuqtaeen* community will ensure that each member is adequately housed and fed. The community will own a land bank for housing, and every family will be entitled to a plot of land for their dwelling and voluntary help from the members of their community. Every member will provide a free voluntary service of eight hours a week or thirty-two hours each month in labor or in kind to the community. The services may include teaching, adult literacy, house building, street cleaning, community beautification, or care of the elderly and children.

Each community will operate its own schools, organize the curricula, and supervise teaching and the education standard of its children. The curricula will include an amalgamation of the teachings of the Koran, linguistics, mathematics, social and general sciences, and modern technology. The education will be in Arabic, vernacular, and an international language. Highest standards will be maintained. There will be organization and maintenance of free health services at the community level and operation of general and specialized hospitals in cooperation with the neighboring communities.

The *nuqta* community will be responsible for the availability of clean and potable water, sewage and waste disposal, local town planning, and beautification of the town. The *nuqta* communities will jointly create jobs in service industries, agriculture, commerce, education, manufacturing, transport, construction, professions, administration, civil service, and so on. Elders of the *nuqtaeen* will ensure correct conduct in accord with the covenant of Allah to set an example for the younger generation in matters of daily living, community affairs, and governance of the *ummah*. Each elder will mentor the next generation to ensure that the younger generation will grow up in a loving, nurturing community where every person is treated with respect, politeness, and love. In the *nuqta* community, every child is the child of the community, nurtured and taught in love, peace, and harmony. The *nuqtaeen* live, work, and play under the guidance and protection of Allah. There will be no want and therefore no craving, greed, violence, hostility, nor any crime. From such *nuqta* communities will arise an *ummah* of the Dar es Salaam, the fellowship of Allah as envisaged by Allah and His blessed *nabi* Muhammad.

Wealth in the modern capitalist world is created by usurious banking systems supported and owned by corporations on the backs of the common man already impoverished by the usurious banking and corporate systems and the tax-grabbing governments that are, in turn, indebted to the satanic, usurious Illuminati banking and corporate conglomerates. The wealth created by the usurious banking and corporate circle rapidly circulates through the population of workers and consumers but essentially returns to the usurious banking corporation coffers. The result is that 80 percent of the wealth stays with the closed circle of the banks and corporate amalgam, and the rest of the world subsists on the remaining 20 percent. The Koran was cognizant of such inequity when it declared fourteen hundred years ago:

> What Allah has bestowed on His Rasool from the people of the townships, belongs to Allah, to His Rasool and to the near of kin and orphans, the poor and the homeless; in order that it may not merely make a circuit between the wealthy among you. So take what the Rasool assigns to you and deny yourselves that which he withholds from you. And fear Allah; for Allah is strict in Punishment. (Al-Hashr 59:7, Koran)

In the *Nuqtaeen* community, economic, and industrial infrastructure, there will be a partnership between four equal partners working according to a usury-free Islamic financial system where profits will

463

come from production and sale of commodities and not from trading and lending of money. This partnership will be between the following:

- The *nuqta* community, which will provide investment of money, land managerial expertise, and workforce.

- Investors groups: Wealthy people from various communities will be encouraged to invest in the infrastructure and industry of the *nuqta* communities. Wealthy sheikhs and other financiers from Islamic lands who have invested over seven trillion dollars in the Western countries will be encouraged to invest in the Dar es Salaam.

- A national machine tool manufacturing organization, which will be set up to manufacture and acquire industrial machinery and equipment to help establish and maintain industrial plants in the country. Youth with initiative and skills will be trained on the technology of manufacturing. This complex will provide homegrown solutions to correct the industrial backwardness of Muslim lands.

- Merchandizing and export corporation, which will in partnership with the *nuqtaeen* provide expertise in export and merchandising of goods around the country and the world.

Promoting the Koranic way of life in the fulfillment of the covenant at home, school, and place of work will encourage conformity to the covenant's thirty-seven steps. In places of business, integrity of investment managers, managerial staff, and workers is of utmost importance as it promotes spirituality, growth, and prosperity of the community. Each *nuqta* community will be recognized for its work ethics, honesty, achievements in knowledge and education, industry, beautiful deeds, unity, and love and care.

Each *nuqta* community, in association with one another, will be self-sufficient in the fields of basic education, provision of health care, welfare of those in need, and production of its own food, building materials, power, clean water supply, and public health and public transport systems. Community farms will produce grain, vegetables, dairy, and meat products. Ponds, canals, and lakes will enhance aquaculture and fish production. Communities, in cooperation, will establish their own brick kilns, quarries, cement factories, and stone, granite, and timber industries to achieve affordable housing for all. Tree plantations within the community will provide lumber for building material and furniture.

Domestic animal organic waste from animal husbandry and dairy farms with organic waste from sawdust and plant material will provide methane and other fuel for household power and energy and prevent deforestation for firewood. All communities will harness power from wind, sun, and water. Scarce water will be conserved. Water for irrigation will be preserved with piped drip irrigation system and further conserved with the use of plastics and greenhouses.

Innovations in agriculture and industry will require experimentation and knowledgeable agriculture managers with initiative. Science and knowledge will be for community benefit rather than for the acquisition of futile certificates and degrees. Schools and universities will experiment and observe for the community's benefit. The *nuqtaeen* will ensure a safe and clean environment and preservation and renewal of the world's resources.

The *Nuqtaeen*: The Foundation of the Islamic State

Upon the death of the blessed *nabi*, each believer in Allah, man and woman, inherited the Koran, the covenant of Allah, the *din*, and the Islamic state on the earth, the Dar es Salaam.

- The *ummah el nuqta* is the basic Islamic state. It is autonomous and free to conduct its own affairs. Sixty thousand such autonomous states voluntarily join together under the protection of Allah to form the *ummah el wast* and the Dar es Salaam.

- In the affairs of Allah, in the communities of Islam, there are no sultans, no kings, nor any dictators.

- In the affairs of Allah, there are no priests, nor can the ulema proclaim themselves to be the spokespersons of Allah. There are wise people among the *ummah* who are endowed with knowledge and wisdom, which is sought by people in their own free will. However, knowledge and opinions of scholars cannot be imposed on people against their wishes. The priests and ulema can never become spokespersons of Allah.

- In Islam, there are no mercenary armies. Every believer shall have military training, knowledge of military tactics, and military technology. Every believer has the obligation to defend his *nuqta* community and the Dar es Salaam.

- Each believer is free.

Inside the dome of Lutf Allah Mosque.

Chapter Nine

Education of the *Nuqtaeen*

The education system in most Islamic countries is a relic of the colonial era. This came about after the willful destruction of the precolonial madrassa system, some of which was good, while the rest was warped by the ravages of time. Learning and acquisition of knowledge had become anchored to the fossilized systems of the *masha'ikhs* of the schools of jurisprudence and subject to the fatwas of ulema with a dubious knowledge of Islam. The introduction of a foreign system of education in foreign languages delayed the reintroduction of mass education and literacy in the lands of Islam for five generations over 150 years. The colonial curricula was based on the need for subordinate workers, and it discouraged initiative and inquiring and innovative minds. The rote system of teaching and learning was developed in the era when the only teaching aids were slate and chalk.

In the ideal education system, the child is initiated into the discipline of learning by laying a foundation on which the child will embark on a lifelong journey of acquisition of learning and knowledge. The child is taught to acquire knowledge and information from the sources in nature and from those readily available to humans worldwide. Knowledge may be given or imparted through close association and constant mentoring, an apprenticeship that results in molding of character and acquisition of wisdom. Wisdom is acquisition of knowledge with understanding, perception, insight, and judgment that comes with age and experience. However, a good master can pass on this gift to his apprentices through close association, mentoring, and guidance. This was the knowledge of the early Muslim scholars, Sufi saints, Christian monks, and Greek philosophers.

In contrast, we have today's knowledge of mass education where information is imparted to the pupil in a politically motivated random curriculum, only to be regurgitated at examination time. This knowledge lacks insight, skills, humility, and judgment; it also fails to impart awareness of Allah's grace and magnificence. This knowledge promotes an ability to collect data and facts without endowing on the student the necessary equipment required to apply the data to the community's needs in practical matters. This is today's science and literature.

Today's mass system has become so impersonal that a young scholar on entrance to school is lost and is at the mercy of the environment within the school; it may be wholesome or malevolent depending on his peers and the quality of the instruction. Six hours at school deprive the child of parental influence, which needs to be substituted with an equally nurturing and character-molding atmosphere. This scholarship should impart love of knowledge and embark the pupil on a lifelong journey of spirituality, learning, acquisition of knowledge, and self-improvement. On this journey, the pupil should recognize the love of Allah, commune with his Creator, and come to understand his obligations to his covenant with Allah and his fellow humans. The student needs to understand the *iman*, his *din*, truth, justice, peace, and love of humans. On this foundation of spirituality, truth, justice, peace, respect, love, and equality of humans, the pupil will embark on the learning of languages, mathematical skills, social and general sciences, technology, and other skills required for work for his family and his community.

In secular education, religion and moral values are deliberately devalued, resulting in lying, fraud, and dishonesty in the political, business, and judicial systems, which have taken an art form of deception. Moral values are calibrated in accord with the adversarial legal system and human laws devised by crooked politicians in line with the corrupted secular world. A witness in law is expected to take an oath on the Bible or the Koran and stretch the truth into deception. Muslim, Jewish, and Christian leaders alike stand on the world stage and speak blatant untruth and simultaneously preach high morality to the world. The world's forum, the United Nations, has become the greatest showcase of lies, deceit, and duplicity in the history of mankind. This is the world today.

In the "Muslim" world of politics and business, deceit, fraud, dishonesty, and injustice have subdued common morality and decency. The perpetrators are no longer bothered by their conscience and make no effort to disguise their actions. This state is the product of unbridled hypocrisy practiced over generations of mentors and role models. "Muslims" have gone astray and have lost their soul. They have lost *furqan*, the ability to distinguish between right and wrong. This state occurs with loss of *taqwa* of Allah in the daily life of the Muslims. The world has become a small globe where rapid communication has dimmed the cultural divide. The indecent, shameful, and profane travel fast around the world, traversing the cultural and linguistic barriers at the speed of light. The good and the wholesome sink into the dust, hardly causing a stir. The distinction between good and evil has become dimmed in the glare of mass communication. To err is human. To recognize the error and find a straight path is a blessing. To recognize the error and continue to repeat it is like poking one's finger into Allah's eye—the eye of the divine law, the covenant of Allah. It is sin.

The average child unknowingly faces two situations. Two hundred years of Islamic decadence and the influence of modern Western culture given to cravings and immediate gratification of desires have spread the rot in the "Muslim" world. As a backlash to this decadence, there is a resurgence of extremism among the mullahs and so-called ulema. Instead of taking an evenhanded approach of moderation, truth, justice, reform of individuals, and teaching of equality of humans, men and women, their approach is of vengeance, brutality, and isolation. The Holy Koran is open to interpretation and action by individual believers. Why should it not be so when Allah so often addresses the believers directly in seventy-five verses of the Koran with advice? Instead, the mullah circles command the right to interpret and dictate their version of Islam to the believers. Islam is not a religion; therefore, it has no man-made dogma nor creed. Islam is a way of life as shown by Allah in the Koran. Man's interference in the divinely ordained *din* has ended up in the *fitnah* of the clerics and rulers in Afghanistan, Pakistan, Saudi Arabia, and Iran on one hand and the profanity of modernity on the other.

Accordingly, to reform the social order in line with the dictates of the Koran, the educational system should be equipped with the values of a just society—truth, honesty, justice of humans, peace for all, and an equitable distribution of Allah's grace. The education of the child and, for that matter, that of an adult must be the composite of six powerful factors of equal importance:

1. *Strong moral and spiritual values shall be inculcated as commanded by Allah in His covenant.* This is accompanied by the practice of such values in daily life with a strong daily reinforcement of the values of a just society. There is the customary practice of salat and dhikr and the teaching of Arabic language, the Koran, catechism of Islam, the life and legacy of the blessed prophets, comparative religion, and Islamic history. Every school should have a spiritual section in which the student is taught the practice of religious rites. There should be a traditional environment in the religious section as in the

traditional mosque and madrassa. Submission comes with prostration in humility and cleanliness. This prostration, humility, and submission can appropriately take place in *sajdah* and prayer.

From the ages of five to thirteen years, the student should spend a third of his time in this section of the school. The child will require a counselor or a parent figure in this section to teach and reinforce traditional family, spiritual, and moral values. The counselors, parents, and teachers will require regular consultation and liaison with regard to the child's progress in accordance with the goals set by the school and the parents. These counselors will, in a gentle and matter-of-fact way, promote moral and spiritual values and counsel boys and girls about the distinction between right and wrong behavior and between good and evil, what is shameful (*Fahasha*), and the criterion to distinguish between what is good and bad (*furqan*). Shameful deeds should be discouraged. Tolerance and respect for other humans and their beliefs should be reinforced. The emphasis should be on moral conduct, truth, honesty, justice, and respect for other people and their property.

2. *The remaining two-thirds of the time in school to the age of thirteen is to be spent in the academic and technical sections.* The pupil will learn languages, mathematical skills, and social and general sciences. Language studies in this section will involve learning a vernacular and an international language, in addition to Arabic.

3. *The third part of education starting right at the beginning is the mastery of skills in technology and artisanship.* These include computer sciences, metalworking, woodworking, electrical and plastic manufacturing, agriculture, horticulture, and animal husbandry.

4. *After school hours, sports, physical exercise, public speaking, martial arts, hobbies, music, and other activities will be sponsored by the schools.* All students, through their school years, will be given the responsibility for maintenance, upkeep, and cleanliness of their classrooms, school, and its gardens. Children will learn to take pride in manual work and cleanliness.

The secondary education system therefore needs to be reformed to accommodate Islamic moral values, the political and economic changes in the Islamic world, and the need of Islamic people to keep up with the latest scientific discoveries and technology and absorb the proliferation of information. Secondary school education will be the modified continuation of the principles set in primary schools. At the end of their school years, students should have grounding in the moral values of their covenant and practice of faith, mastery of at least three languages and their literature, mathematics, social and general sciences, social skills, computer sciences, technology, and sports. Each student will be a moral person with literary, technological, and physical skills to serve himself, his family, and his community.

5. *Secondary school students and all men and women will have an awareness of their rights under the covenant of Allah and their obligation and social responsibility to their community, country, and Allah's creation.* With this education and awareness of the teachings of the Koran, they will never again be subject to tyranny of the mullah, the aristocrat, nor the ruler. Nor will their community and country fall subject to tyranny and oppression, foreign or domestic. For the last fourteen hundred years, the believers have lived under the tyranny, oppression, and *fitnah* of the sultans, aristocrats, foreign oppressors, and military and civilian *Munafiq* dictators.

6. *Every Muslim should know that every man, woman, and child has God-given, equal rights.* In enjoying these freedoms, the

individual will ensure that his activities do not impinge on the rights and freedom of others. To reiterate, every believer, man and woman, has freedom and equality. No one is superior to the other except in righteousness and virtue.

The downfall of the Islamic state during the nineteenth and twentieth centuries was caused by the life of ease and loss of faith among the ruling classes of the Muslim states. Such ruling classes never had a sanction from Allah to rule the Muslims. They professed to abide by the covenant of Allah in words but not with their deeds. The rulers imposed themselves on the believers and began the plunder of the wealth of the people through treachery, deceit, injustice, murder, and the help and manipulation of the ecclesiastical hierarchy and establishment of the mosque. With the misappropriated wealth of their subjects came the decline of moral values, use of alcohol, gambling, shameful deeds, cheating, and killing of their fathers, their brothers, and their own children in their quest for the throne. The wealth required for obscene luxury was at first plundered from their subjects and then from the neighboring principalities.

When these riches were exhausted, the rulers turned to borrow from the usurious Western Illuminati, Masonic, and satanic Jewish bankers. Familiarity with the Western financial system brought further indebtedness, followed by secret alliances with the Western powers against their fellow Muslims. This caused disunity among the Muslims and finally capitulation and total political and economic collapse. All this occurred because the rulers disobeyed the covenant of Allah. The believers abdicated their executive sovereignty over the Dar es Salaam, permitting their rulers a free rein to disaster. Muslims and their rulers failed to observe their covenant with Allah.

The Dome of the Rock.

Chapter Ten

The Dar es Salaam: Economy

The Dar es Salaam, the vast land of the Muslims, extends east to west from Indonesia to the west coast of Africa and north to south from Kazakhstan to Mozambique. It stretches from twenty degrees east to one hundred degrees east longitude and from fifty degrees north to thirty degrees south latitude. It takes the sun twelve hours to lighten up the earth from one end of the Dar es Salaam to the other. The northern steppes develop freezing temperatures in the winter; the desert lands are unbearably hot in the summer. The coastal regions are awash with all the blue oceans and the seas of the world.

Historically, this land has enriched the world with its produce, industry minerals, and culture. The heritage of all civilizations of the ancient worlds arose from the dust of the Dar es Salaam. The great civilizations, those known to history and those obscure, arose in the lands now inhabited by the believers. The Dar es Salaam once was home to the Babylonians, Sumerians, ancient Egyptians, Phoenicians, Romans, Trojans, Greeks, ancient Indus valley inhabitants, Carpathians, and many others. Those who believed did not always inhabit these lands, a habitation where people lived in peace and security, receiving sustenance in abundance, unappreciative of Allah's gifts; and in their scorn for the divine grace, Allah made them taste hunger and fear. These populations fell victims to their own caprice; they gave up divine guidance and found other gods to worship besides Allah. They became ungrateful and began to regard Allah's bounty as their rightful due from the idols they followed. Many habitations of the ingrate fell into depredation and turned to dust; their place was taken over by the people of *taqwa*, those who were god-wary. And

476

thus, the wheel of Allah's mercy turns, and so the cycle of humanity goes on.

Islam is a way of life in the straight path to Allah. There exists an agreement between Allah and His creation, portrayed as a mutual understanding in which Allah proposes a system of regulations for the guidance of man. This guidance is presented in the form of commandments to be accepted and implemented by people. Allah promises prosperity and protection in this world and in the hereafter when man is willing to abide by the commandments and regulate his life according to them. The concept of promise is clearly conditional on human obedience. The covenant of Allah symbolizes the relationship between Allah and man; man becomes His steward and vicegerent on the earth through submission and obedience to His will (*islam*) as expressed in Allah's commandments. Man is then able to take advantage of Allah's promises and favors.

The concept of the covenant also symbolizes the relationship between humans among Allah's creatures and the rest of His creation. They all share in one God, one set of guidance and commandments, the same submission and obedience to Him, and the same set of expectations in accordance with His promises. They all can, therefore, trust one another since they all have similar obligations and expectations. In view of the Koran, humans, communities, nations, and civilizations will continue in harmony and peace so long as they continue to fulfill Allah's covenant.

Economics plays a significant role in the social structure of Islam, so significant that Allah did not leave the economic aspect of life to be solely determined by human intellect, experience, caprice, and lust. Allah made it subject to revelation. Thus, Muslims prosper when they follow Allah's laws and are subjected to scarcity when they turn to human systems.

The Koran promises peace and plenty for those who obey their covenant with Allah; for those who turn away from Allah's covenant, the Koran portends a life of need, scarcity, and want.

> But whosoever turns away from My Message, verily for him is a life narrowed down and We shall raise him up blind on the Day of Judgment. And thus do We recompense him who transgresses beyond bounds and believes not in the Signs of his Lord: and the Penalty of the Hereafter is far more grievous and more enduring. It is not a warning to such men (to call to mind) how many generations before them We destroyed, in whose haunts they (now) move? Verily, in this are Signs for men endued with understanding. (Taha 20:124, 127–28)

In the above *ayah* of the Koran, the word *ma'eeshat* comes from the word *ma'ashiyyat*, which is the recognized meaning of the word *economics*. The consequences of rejection of Allah's guidance are clearly portrayed: a life narrowed down or constricted is a miserable one—one of need, scarcity, unhappiness, poverty, hunger, disease, pestilence, and famine all occurring together or separately.

The Koranic covenant does not hold over the realization of the fruits of obeying or ignoring Allah's guidance until after death, nor does it hide it in spiritual abstractness. Observance of the covenant makes life on the earth economically, physically, and spiritually rich and happy. Nonobservance of the covenant makes life on the earth economically, physically, and spiritually miserable. In fact, the economic, physical, and spiritual condition of a people provides a pragmatic test of the soundness of the revealed guidance.

Furthermore, the Koran declares that people who transgress Allah's guidance are economically deprived in this world and will be worse off in the hereafter.

> Verily for him is a life narrowed down and We shall raise him up blind on the Day of Judgment. (Taha 20:124, 127–28)

According to the Koran, economics and the observance of the moral code of Allah's covenant go hand in hand, and they cannot be separated from each other.

> Glory to the Lord of the heavens and the earth, the Lord supreme! Exalted is He from all that they ascribe to Him. So leave them to talk nonsense and amuse themselves until they meet that Day of theirs, that they have been promised. It is He Who is God in heaven and God on earth; and He is the Wise, the Knower. And blessed is He, whose is the kingdom of the heavens and the earth and all that is between them: with Him is the knowledge of the Hour: and to Him shall ye return. And those whom they invoke besides Allah have no power of intercession; except those who bear witness to the truth and are aware.

Sama in the Koran signifies the universe and *ardh* man's domain on the earth pertaining to his social and economic world. Allah is the Lord of the heavens and the earth and all that is in between. The divine laws under which the universe functions so meticulously and smoothly should also apply to the economic life of man so that he might achieve a balanced, predictable, equitable, and just financial life. *Sama* is the source of Allah's benevolence to humanity and also of His universal laws that govern human subsistence and sustenance on the earth. *Ardh* controls man's economic life in this world. Allah's kingdom over the heavens and the earth sustains man's economic life and directly influences man's conduct and his obedience to Allah's covenant.

Ayahs in Sura An-Nahl are explicit: Allah created the heavens and the earth for just ends to bring peace, harmony, equilibrium, and justice to the universe. He is Allah the One, Lord of the creation. He sends water from the heavens for sustenance of life on the earth—the life of humans, plants, and animals. Allah sends sunshine to the earth to provide warmth and light to sustain human, plant, and animal life. Allah fashioned the moon and stars to create equilibrium in the universe, every object in its intended place, revolving in its fixed orbit in perfect harmony and balance. Allah knows the secrets and mysteries of the heavens and the earth, the so-called sciences, and the knowledge of particles, elements, cells, mitochondria, chromosomes, gravity, and black holes. He revealed only an infinitesimal portion to man, yet man is arrogant and boastful.

> He has created the heavens and the earth for just ends: far is He above having the partners they ascribe to Him! (An-Nahl 16:3, Koran)

> It is He Who sends down rain from the sky. From it you drink and out of it (grows) the vegetation on which you feed your cattle. (An-Nahl 16:10, Koran)

> He has made subject to you the Night and the Day; the Sun and the Moon; and the Stars are in subjection by His Command: verily in this are Signs for men who are wise. (An-Nahl 16:12, Koran)

> To Allah belongs the mystery of the heavens and the earth. And the Decision of the Hour (of Judgment) is as the twinkling of any eye, or even quicker: for Allah hath power over all things. (An-Nahl 16:77, Koran)

In other *ayahs* of Sura An-Nahl, Allah recounts the bounties and comforts He bestowed on man for the sustenance of life and for his economic well-being. Allah created cattle for humans for warmth, food, and transport and horses, mules, and donkeys for riding and for display. With the moisture from the skies, He produces corn, olives, date palms, grapes, and every type of fruit for man. Allah made good things for humans in different colors and quantities so that they may eat fresh and tender seafood, obtain beautiful ornaments from the ocean, sail their ships, and plow the oceans around the world. From the cattle, Allah produces milk, pure and wholesome to drink; and from the fruit of the date palm and vine, one gets food and drink and from the bees honey of varying colors that heals ailments.

> And cattle He has created for you (humans): from them ye derive warmth and numerous benefits and of their (meat) ye eat.

And ye have a sense of pride and beauty in them as you drive them home
in the evening and as you lead them forth to pasture in the morning.

And they carry your heavy loads to lands that you could not (otherwise) reach
except with souls distressed: for your Lord is indeed Most Kind, Most Merciful.

And (He has created) horses, mules and donkeys, for you to ride
and use for show; and He has created (other) things of which
you have no knowledge. (An-Nahl 16:5–8, Koran)

It is He Who sends down rain from the sky. From it ye drink and
out of it (grows) the vegetation on which ye feed your cattle.

With it He produces for you corn, olives, date palms, grapes and every
kind of fruit: verily in this is a Sign for those who give thought.

He has made subject to you the Night and the Day; the
Sun and the Moon; and the Stars are in subjection by His
Command: verily in this are Signs for men who are wise.

And the things on this earth which He has multiplied in
varying colors (and qualities): verily in this a Sign for men
who celebrate the praises of Allah (in gratitude).

It is He Who has made the sea subject, that ye may eat thereof flesh that
is fresh and tender and that you may extract there from ornaments to
wear and you see the ships therein that plough the waves, that you may
seek (thus) of the bounty of Allah and that you may be grateful.

And He has set up on the earth mountains standing firm, lest it should
shake with you; and rivers and roads; that ye may guide yourselves;

And marks and signposts; and by the stars (Men) guide
themselves. (An-Nahl 16:10–16, Koran)

And verily in cattle (too) will ye find an instructive Sign. From what
is within their bodies, between excretions and blood, We produce,
for your drink, milk, pure and agreeable to those who drink it.

And from the fruit of the date palm and the vine, ye get out wholesome
drink and food: behold, in this also is a Sign for those who are wise.

And thy Lord taught the Bee to build its cells in hills,
on trees and in (men's) habitations;

Then to eat of all the produce (of the earth)and find with skill the
spacious paths of its Lord: there issues from within their bodies a
drink of varying colors, wherein is healing for men: verily in this is a
Sign for those who give thought. (An-Nahl 16:66–69, Koran)

Allah created the earth and then bestowed on man His favors to
extract sustenance from it. He also created the sun, moon, and stars
to create a just equilibrium and harmony in the universe. The sun
provides energy for the growth, sustenance, and well-being of humans,
plants, and animals. Gradually, man began to extract more than his
personal needs from the earth; and the boom of economics, trade,
and commerce started, creating cycles of imbalance, disharmony,
wars, poverty, and injustice throughout the globe. Not only did
this disharmony caused by greed blemish humans but animal life
also suffered by the disappearance of whole species. Pollution and
contamination of the environment resulted from the race trying
to accumulate and hoard the world's wealth in a few hands. Man
disobeyed Allah's universal laws and covenant.

In return for all of Allah's favors, Allah commands the following:

- Justice (al-'adl). Justice, fairness, honesty, integrity, and
  evenhanded dealings are a prerequisite of every Muslim's
  conduct when dealing with others whether socially or in a
  business transaction.
- Doing what is good and beautiful (al-ihsan). This attribute
  includes every positive quality such as goodness, beauty, and
  harmony. Human beings have an obligation to do what is

wholesome and beautiful in their relationship with Allah and His creatures.

• Providing for those near you (*qurba*) and your kith and kin. Help them with wealth, kindness, compassion, humanity, and sympathy

Allah forbids *Fahasha*—all evil deeds, lies, false testimony, fornication, selfishness, ingratitude, greed, and false belief. Whosoever fulfills the covenant of Allah performs beautiful and righteous deeds, and Allah will give him or her a new life and reward them with greater wages.

Allah commands justice, the doing of good and liberality to kith and kin and He forbids all shameful deeds and injustice and rebellion: He instructs you, that ye may receive admonition. Fulfill the Covenant of Allah when ye have entered into it and break not your oaths after ye have confirmed them: indeed you have made Allah your surety; for Allah knows all that you do. (An-Nahl 16:90–91, Koran)

Whoever works righteousness, man or woman and has Faith, verily, to him will We give a new Life, a life that is good and pure and We will bestow on such their reward according to the best of their actions. (An-Nahl 16:97, Koran)

Tawhid, the main pillar of Islam, signifies that man's economic life depends wholly on Allah's laws of the universe and that their relationship to those who believe is through the obedience to the covenant of Allah. Allah maintains in the Koran that there is no creature on the earth whose sustenance is not provided by Allah.

No creature moves on earth that Allah does not nourish.
He knows its essential nature and its varying forms, every detail has its place in the obvious plan. (Koran 11:6)

How Are the People in Need Provided for Their Sustenance and Needs of Daily Lives?

All wealth belongs to Allah, who bestows it on some people more than others. This wealth is given in trust, whereby the possessor is obliged to give the surplus for Allah's cause, to his kin, to the widows and orphans, and to the needy first in his community and then in the other communities around him. Wealth is to be shared so that not a single individual of the *ummah*, or indeed in the world, should go hungry or be without education and shelter.

> It is not righteousness that you turn your faces towards East or West; but it is righteousness to believe in Allah and the Last Day and the Angels and the Bookend the Messengers; to spend of your substance, out of love for Him, for your kin, for orphans, for the needy, for the wayfarer, for those who ask and for the ransom of slaves; to be steadfast in prayer and practice regular charity, to fulfill the Covenants which you have made; and to be firm and patient, in pain (or suffering) and adversity and throughout all periods of panic. Such are the people of truth, the God-fearing. (Al-Baqarah 2:177, Koran)

> And when they are told, "Spend you of (the bounties) with which Allah has provided you," The Unbelievers say to those who believe: "Shall we then feed those whom, if Allah had so willed, He would have fed, (Himself)? Ye are in nothing but manifest error. (Koran 36:47)

> Alms are for the poor and the needy and those employed to administer the (funds); for those whose hearts have been (recently) reconciled (to the truth); for those in bondage and in debt; in the cause of Allah; and for the wayfarer: (thus is it) ordained by Allah and Allah is full of knowledge and wisdom. ((At-Tawbah 9:60, Koran)

The above two verses clearly indicate that a human is given bounty by Allah. In return, his obligation is to distribute the surplus after his needs have been met to the needy. The Koran specifies that the zakat be distributed to the *fuqara* (the poor who ask), to *al-masakin* (the poor and the needy who do not ask), to zakat administrators, to those who spread the light of Islam to those inclined, for freedom of those in bondage, to those in debt, for the cause of Allah, and for the wayfarer who treads the path for Allah's service.

In the covenant, the believer surrenders to Allah his life and belongings in return for His guidance, a place in paradise in the hereafter, and peace with prosperity in this world. Every believer according to his or her covenant with Allah has the obligation to extend the benefits that He has provided him or her to those who did not receive the same. Such acts of generosity will be rewarded by Allah with a place in *Jannat* (place of peace and plenty) in the afterlife. Life of *Jannat* is to be attained in this world also, provided the compact with Allah is adhered to. The believer is Allah's instrument in fulfilling His promise to Adam that

> none will remain without food or clothes and none will
> suffer from heat or thirst. (Koran 20:118)

In the verses below, Allah has promised believers and those who fulfill His covenant the reward for their acts of charity. He will double the harvest of their labors, forgive their sins, and provide them with His bounties. They shall not have fear, nor shall they grieve. Fear and grief arise from misfortunes, which cause anxiety and depression. Allah promises that He will safeguard believers from misfortunes. And to those devouring usury, Allah will deprive them of all blessings. Obedience of Allah's covenant provides *Jannat* in the hereafter and a life of *Jannat*, peace and plenty, in this world. It also brings balance, harmony, and stability to the economic life of the world in that it meets the necessities of each person and eliminates unnecessary suffering.

> O you who believe! Do no render in vain your charity by reminders of
> your generosity or by injury, like him who spends his wealth to be seen
> of men, but he does not believe in Allah nor in the Last Day. His likeness

is the likeness of a smooth rock on which is a little soil; on it falls heavy rain, which leaves it bare. They will not be able to do any thing with what they have earned. And Allah does not guide the disbelieving people.

And the he likeness of those who spend their substance, seeking to please Allah and to strengthen their souls, is as a garden, high and fertile; heavy rain falls on it but makes it yield a double increase of harvest and if it receives not heavy rain, light moisture suffices it. And Allah is seer of what you do. (Al-Baqarah 2:264–65, Koran)

O you who believe! Give of the good things that you have (honorably) earned and of the fruits of the earth that We have produced for you and do not even aim at giving anything which is bad, when ye yourselves would not receive it except with closed eyes. And know that Allah is free of all wants and worthy of all praise.

The Evil One threatens you with poverty and bids you to conduct unseemly. Allah promises you His forgiveness and bounties. And Allah cares for all and He knows all things.

He grants wisdom to whom He pleases; and he to whom wisdom is granted receives indeed a benefit overflowing; but none will grasp the Message but men of understanding.

And whatever ye spend in charity or devotion, be sure Allah knows it all. But the wrongdoers have no

Those who (in charity) spend of their goods by night and by day, in secret and in public, have their reward with their Lord: on them shall be no fear, nor shall they grieve.

Those who devour usury will not stand except as stands one whom the Satan by his touch hath driven to madness. That is because they say: "Trade is like usury," but Allah hath permitted trade and forbidden usury. Those who after receiving direction from their Lord, desist, shall be pardoned for the past; their case is for Allah (to judge); but those who repeat (the offence) are Companions of the Fire; they will abide therein (forever.) helpers. (Al-Baqarah 2:267–70, Koran)

Allah will deprive usury of all blessing but will give increase for deeds of charity; for He loves not creatures ungrateful and wicked. (Al-Baqarah 2:274–76, Koran)

Economic Principles of the Covenant of Allah

The covenant of Allah in the Koran has laid down principles and guidelines for the well-being of the economic life of the believers. Obeying the principles will bring peace, harmony, spiritual enlightenment, and economic prosperity. Disobeying means misery, ruin, and Allah's wrath.

First Principle:

Land and resources of production are not the personal property of individuals.

Land is given to individuals in trust for the welfare of their kith and kin, their community, and the rest of Allah's creation. *Ardh* is the source of sustenance of life and production of food and other resources. The yield of the land, therefore, must remain available to the community of Islam, the *ummah*.

Allah created *ardh* and *sama* and has power over everything in and between them. To Allah belong the heaven and the earth and what is in between them. *Sama* in the Koran signifies the universe and *ardh* man's domain on the earth pertaining to his social and economic world. Allah is the Lord of the heavens and the earth. The divine laws under which the universe functions so meticulously and smoothly should also apply to the economic life of man so that he might achieve a balanced, predictable, equitable, and just financial life. *Sama* is the source of Allah's benevolence to mankind and of His universal laws that govern the human subsistence and sustenance on the earth, controlling man's economic life. Allah's kingdom over the heavens and the earth sustains man's economic life and directly affects man's conduct and his obedience to Allah's covenant.

Ayahs in Sura An-Nahl are explicit. Allah created the heavens and the earth for just ends—to bring peace, harmony, equilibrium, and justice to the universe. He is Allah, the One, Lord of creation. He sends water from the heavens for the sustenance of life on the earth—humans, plants, and animals. Allah sends sunshine to the earth to provide warmth and light to sustain human, plant, and animal life. Allah created the moon and the stars to create equilibrium in the universe, with every object in its intended place revolving in its fixed orbit in perfect harmony and balance.

In other *ayahs* of Sura An-Nahl, Allah clearly mentions all the comforts He has provided man for the sustenance of life and for his economic well-being. Allah created cattle for humans for warmth, food, and transport and horses, mules, and donkeys for riding and to show. With the moisture from the skies, He produces for man corn, olives, date palms, grapes, and every type of fruit. Allah made good things for humans in different colors and quantities so that man can celebrate and praise Allah in gratitude. Allah made the sea subject to humans so that they may eat fresh and tender seafood, obtain beautiful ornaments from the ocean, sail their ships, and plow the oceans around the world. From the cattle, Allah produces milk, pure and wholesome to drink; and from the fruit of the date palm and vine, you get food and drink. And from the bees, there is honey of varying colors that heals ailments.

In the fifth and fourth millennia before the Common Era, Mesopotamia in the north of Arabia had been marshland created by the silt and floods of the Euphrates. The channels of the delta were teeming with fish and wild game, and the soil of alluvial earth yielded hundredfold if tilled. Early Sumerians began to settle down in small communities that grew from mud villages into towns. During the thousand-year Sumerian ascendancy, it developed a dozen such cities, each the heart of a state. The total Sumerian population never exceeded half a million when the total world population was only fifteen million, only large enough to fit the core of a large modern city.

During the earlier Sumerian period, land was owned communally. The people took their surplus produce to the city center to be traded and shared with the community. As the cities grew in size and wealth, they grew upward, layer upon layer, into man-made hills crowned with a step pyramid, the ziggurat, the sacred mountain.

The priesthood had been a committee of wise men who looked after human and divine affairs. They had helped design irrigation canals, gazed at stars, and predicted seasons for sowing and harvesting. The priesthood had initially started as a village cooperative and grew with increasing population and prosperity. From village cooperative, the priesthood grew vertically to become the first corporation with officials and employees to manage and administer the gods' estates. The gods at this time began to own the land, and the Mesopotamians became the serfs of their gods, the landowners. The priests became the managers of their gods' worldly estates. From this priesthood sprung the ruling class, which gradually began to control the land and the wealth of the community through a feudal system.

Historically, land was there for man and beasts to roam around freely and spread through the world. Later, tribes and communities laid claims on pieces of land they needed for their needs with some extra surrounding area for their security. At the beginning of the Islamic era, productive land and water resources were owned by tribes for the use of their clan members. After the message of the Koran was established, the clans, the tribes, the former kingdoms, and the nations amalgamated to form the community of Islam, the *ummah*, which in principle owned the title to the land and resources with theoretical tenancy. The ownership of land by the *ummah* began to change with the downfall of the Abbasid caliphate.

Land, therefore, belongs to Allah, who bestowed it to man and woman, His regents on the earth. The covenant expects man to take care of the land for all of Allah's creatures—men and beasts— as well as conserve its resources for future generations. Whatever is left over after his own needs are met goes to the necessities of the rest of humanity, starting with his *qurba* (near and dear) and then his community, followed by the surrounding communities. The land does not belong to the states, governments, tribal chiefs, military, aristocracy, timars, or *iqtas*. Land cannot be owned by individuals or families nor inherited by them.

Men and women live in small communities. These form a fellowship and a brotherhood that looks after its own who are in need, and such a need may be of sustenance, clothing, shelter, knowledge, well-being, spirituality, understanding, protection, justice, or simple reassurance. And such assistance is extended to the surrounding communities till it reaches the far-flung communities of the *ummah*. Each basic community owns the land in its surrounds, tilled and administered by the community as a whole for its well-being in justice and harmony according to the covenant of Allah. The Islamic economic system is based on capitalism in the production of wealth and communism in its expenditure, with the difference being that individuals are free and able to make wealth but are responsible for the needs of kith and kin and their neighbor. The state has little role in the welfare system. The land owned by the community may be assigned to individuals or may be tilled communally for the mutual benefit of the whole community, producing food and paying for schools, hospitals, roadways, municipal services, and so on. The community is meant to be self-sufficient economically and responsible for each and every individual's welfare, health, schooling, and old-age pensions.

Second Principle:

All surplus money and resources should not remain with individuals.

How much is enough for one's needs? A hundred? A thousand? A hundred thousand? A million? A billion? How much is enough?

A person requires sufficient wealth for food, apparel, housing, travel, education, health services, certain comforts, security, and the similar needs of his extended family. After accumulation of wealth for such needs, any further amassing of wealth becomes an act of obscenity and evil. Passion for such hoarding and ostentation brings out the worse and the foul in man. All surplus money and resources in a Muslim community shall be used for the benefit and uplift of the community.

> They ask thee how much they are to spend (in charity); say: "What is beyond your needs." Thus doth Allah make clear to you His Signs: in order that ye may consider. (Al-Baqarah 2:222, Koran)

Third Principle:

Wealth and commodities should not be hoarded.

Surplus wealth is to be spent for the needs of the community as prescribed by Allah and used as capital for the creation of further wealth and security for the benefit of the community.

> O you who believe! There are indeed many among the priests and clerics, who in falsehood devour the substance of men and hinder them from the Way of Allah. And there are those who bury gold and silver and spend it not in the Way of Allah: announce unto them a most grievous penalty. (At-Tawbah 9:34, Koran)

Fourth Principle:

Wealth should be spread through the community, the ummah.

Wealth should not be impounded, stolen, and looted by conquerors, tribes, rulers, governments, feudal classes, and the *Mutaffifeen* (dealers in fraud) as practiced in the un-Koranic societies, both Muslim and non-Muslim.

> What Allah has bestowed on His Rasool from the people of the townships, belongs to Allah, to His Rasool and to the near of kin and orphans, the poor and the homeless; in order that it may not merely make a circuit between the wealthy among you. So take what the Rasool assigns to you and deny yourselves that which he withholds from you. And fear Allah; for Allah is strict in Punishment. (Al-Hashr 59:7, Koran)

Fifth Principle:

No one shall subsist on the earnings of another, except for those who are incapacitated and disabled.

Everyone shall work. Everyone—man and woman—shall also contribute their labor and sweat toward their own needs and those of their kin, their neighbors, and their community.

The Koran calls the people who stint *Mutaffifeen*, those who get the full measure from others but stint when measuring for others. They lead an easy life from the earnings of others. The Koran mentions three such groups. One group consists of people who "take with an even balance and give less than what is due."

> Woe to those that deal in fraud, those who, from others exact full measure, But when measuring or weighing for others, give less than due. Do they not think that they will be called to account on a Mighty Day, A Day when all mankind will stand before the Lord of the Worlds? (Mutaffifeen 83:1–6, Koran)

Another group comprises those who inherit money, land, and property, and they use that wealth to accumulate more and more without ever giving back to the needy. The third group gobbles up the earnings of others:

> O you who believe! There are indeed many among the priests and anchorites, (or the leaders) who in falsehood devour the substance of men and hinder them from the Way of Allah. And there are those who bury gold and silver and spend it not in the Way of Allah: announce unto them a most grievous penalty. (Al-A'raf 9:34, Koran)

How to Transform the Historic Tenure of Land to the Ownership of the Community

The Islamic system is based on justice and truth. Islamic justice is not revolutionary. Changes in the system are meant to be gradual to mitigate any hardships. The changes in the tenure and ownership of land should be gradual, spanning over three generations. The owners will be justly compensated by the community.

1. During the first generation, 25 percent of the resources from the land will revert to the community to be used at its discretion. Additionally, the landowner should hand over the surplus resources of the land to the community after generously taking produce for the needs of himself and his kith and kin.

2. After the demise of the original owner, his successors will lose the title and the resource of 50 percent of the land and passed on to the community. The community, however, will be responsible for the well-being of the owner's family and dependents.

3. At the end of the third generation, total land ownership will revert to the community.

The community will be economically self-sufficient for all its needs and responsible for the welfare of each and every individual for their food, health, schooling, welfare, and old-age pensions. Every man and woman over the age of fourteen years, until he or she is prevented by old age, provides the community with free service of a minimum of eight hours per week or a total of four hundred hours annually. This work will involve community projects, building housing, agricultural work, teaching in adult literacy and Koranic classes, beautifying the community, care of the elderly, and other needs of the community.

Commerce and Trade

Blessed *Nabi* Muhammad's early life was spent as a trader and a merchant traveling between Mecca and the eastern provinces of the Byzantine Empire that now comprise Sinai, Syria, Palestine, Israel, and Jordan. Mecca lay on the ancient trade route between southern Arabia, Egypt, and the Roman province of Syria. In the eleventh century BC, the land routes through Arabia were greatly improved by the use of camel as a beast of burden. Frankincense and myrrh were carried from its production center in Cana to Gaza. The camel caravans also carried gold and other precious goods, which arrived in Cana by ship from India. Aromatics as frankincense and myrrh were greatly prized in the civilized ancient world and were used as part of rituals in Egypt, Rome, and Greece. Trade was carried out with the barter of goods; however, gold and silver coins were also used to exchange goods.

Trade and commerce is an important aspect of human activity and therefore has formed a part of Allah's revelation and the covenant. Commerce and trade is regulated by the covenant of the Koran:

1. Usury is forbidden.
2. All transactions are to be documented and witnessed.

3. Theft, misappropriation, forgery, deception, bribery, dishonesty, and covetousness are forbidden.

> O you who believe! Fear Allah and give up what remains of
> your demand for usury, if ye are indeed believers.

> If ye do it not, take notice of war from Allah and His Messenger:
> but if ye turn back, ye shall have your capital sums; deal not
> unjustly and ye shall not be dealt with unjustly.

> If the debtor is in a difficulty, grant him time till it is easy
> for him to repay. But if ye remit it by way of charity, that is
> best for you if ye only knew. (Koran 2:278–80)

Those who devour usury will not stand except as stands one whom the Satan by his touch hath driven to madness. That is because they say: "Trade is like usury," but Allah hath permitted trade and forbidden usury. Those who after receiving direction from their Lord, desist, shall be pardoned for the past; their case is for Allah (to judge); but those who repeat (the offence) are Companions of the Fire; they will abide therein (forever).

Allah will deprive usury of all blessing but will give increase for deeds of charity; for He loves not creatures ungrateful and wicked. (Koran 2:275–76)

O you who believe! When you deal with each other, in transactions involving future obligations in a fixed period of time, reduce them to writing let a scribe write down faithfully as between the parties; let not the scribe refuse to write: as Allah has taught him, so let him write. Let him who incurs the liability dictate, but let him fear his Lord Allah and not diminish aught of what he owes. If the party liable is mentally deficient, or weak or unable himself to dictate, let his guardian dictate faithfully. And get two witnesses, out of your own men and if there are not two men, then a man and two women, such as ye choose, for witnesses, so that if one of them errs, the other can remind the other. The witnesses should not refuse when they are called on (for evidence). Disdain not to reduce to writing (your contract) for a future period, whether it be small or big: it is more just in the sight of Allah, more suitable as evidence and more convenient to prevent doubts among yourselves but if it be a transaction which you carry out on the spot among yourselves there is no blame on you if ye reduce it not to writing. But take witnesses whenever ye make a commercial contract; and let neither scribe nor witness suffer harm. If you do (such harm), it would be wickedness in you. So fear Allah; for it is Allah that teaches you. And Allah is well acquainted with all things. (Koran 2:282)

O you who believe! Eat not up your property among yourselves in vanities: but let there be amongst you traffic and trade by mutual good-will: nor kill (or destroy) yourselves: for verily Allah hath been to you Most Merciful!

And in no wise covet those things in which Allah hath bestowed His gifts more freely on some of you than on others: to men is allotted what they earn and to women what they earn: but ask Allah of His bounty. For Allah hath full knowledge of all things. (Koran 4:29, 32)

O you who believe! Betray not the trust of Allah and the Messenger, nor misappropriate knowingly things entrusted to you. (Al-Anfal 2:27, Koran)

Fourteen centuries ago, the covenant of Allah set rules governing the role of money and commerce that formed the basis of trade in the Muslim world till the European powers, with their battleships, began to control the sea-lanes around the world. From that time onward, the control of trade and credit has fallen into the hands of the major countries of the West. The present trading system, as will be discussed in this chapter later, is designed for these countries to maintain their supremacy internationally, economically, and politically. Additionally, the Koranic percepts of justice, equity, and honesty have been denied to the believers and the world of Islam. The Koran forbids the charging of *riba* (excessive interest) on the money lent. Historically, any interest over 3 to 4 percent was regarded as usurious; but during the second half of the twentieth century, interest rates of 12 to 20 percent came to be regarded as a norm. It is quite understandable that when the Koran prohibits *riba*, it involves all interest on money borrowed as, in today's world, all interest is excessive and punitive.

Review of Recent History of Money and International Banking

Before the widespread use of money, trading involved the simplest use of commercial transaction—barter, which is the exchange of two or more products of roughly equal value. Gold and silver became accepted as money nearly five thousand years ago in most cultures. The earliest gold coins were found in the ruins of Sumer, minted nearly five thousand years ago. Coins of measured value have been routinely minted from precious metals in most cultures. The value of such coins was equal to the labor required to produce any other item that this treasure could buy. Over thousands of years, gold has been regarded as money, but it is commodity money.

In the Islamic world, Umar ibn al-Khattab established the known standard relationship between the weight of the dinar and the weight of the dirham. The dinar weighed 4.3 grams of gold and the dirham 3.0 grams of silver. The first dated coins assigned to the Islamic era were the copies of the silver dirham of the Sassanian Yazdegerd struck during the caliphate of Uthman with an Arabic inscription, "In the name of Allah." In the year 75 (695 CE), Caliph 'Abd al-Malik ordered the minting of all dirham according to the standard set by Umar ibn al-Khattab. Gold and silver coins remained the official currency of the Moguls, Safavids, and Ottoman Empire till their disintegration.

Fraudulent use of money was perpetrated by both kings and criminals. When the rulers became strapped for cash, they resorted to debasing their currency by lowering the gold or silver content. The use of gold as money was handicapped by its weight and bulk and the need of protection against debasement. In the nineteenth century, the problems of bulk and debasement were eliminated by printing paper money that could be redeemed for a stated amount of gold and silver. As the paper money was backed by gold, there remained the complication of accumulating and storing this valuable commodity.

The next step in the evolution of money was the use of pure paper money. The First and Second World Wars greatly weakened the old imperial countries' economies as almost all their gold had been traded for war material, purchased from the United States. Having lost their gold reserves, the imperial European powers kept on printing money to continue their wars of acquisition. Their colonial populations were drained of their resources with a systematic pillage of their wealth through subtle trading maneuvers. Colonial produce from India, Africa, and the Middle East was first bought with printed paper money. A million pound sterling notes—which cost less than twenty pounds to print, money created out of nothing—was used to purchase cotton, rubber, oil, and metal ore among other items and exported directly to Britain, for instance, or to the USA. The US goods purchased from the proceeds were then sent to Britain either for the war effort or for rebuilding the shattered cities. The colonial people were left to use the counterfeit state notes to buy their daily needs from whatever was left in the country. Because of the excessive amount of paper money in the colonies, inflation became rampant.

During the second half of the nineteenth century and the twentieth century, there was a systematic transfer of wealth from the third world countries to the West. The Western countries—through their monopolies in shipping, insurance, banking, and manufacturing industries—further multiplied their acquired wealth a hundredfold. The British used Indian paper rupees to bribe and arm the Bedouins of Sharif Hussein to fuel the war against the Ottomans after Britain's Arab Bureau exhausted all its gold stock in the Egyptian treasury[81]. The British used Indian rupees, created out of nothing, to bribe the sheikhs of the Persian Gulf and Emir 'Abd al-'Aziz (Ibn Sa'ud).

---

[81] The Arab Bureau.

The combined interest paying debt of the world of Islam to the *Mutaffifeen* bankers today stands in excess of a trillion dollars. With 10 percent return on principal annually along with the interest compounded daily for the default in payments, the annual repayment to the lenders collected from the Muslim citizens, the taxpayers, amounts to whopping *$122 billion annually*, an indebtedness of the sum of one hundred US dollars for every living Muslim man, woman, and child for the rest of their lives. An estimated 40 percent of the money borrowed by the Muslim countries never reached the people, whose standard of living it was supposed to raise. Out of this sum of $250 billion, half went into commissions, bribery, and the pockets of politicians, ministers, presidents, and kings. The other half, $120 billion, was rolled over into the debt for the interest, compounded daily, which had remained delinquent because of budget shortfalls.

Of the remaining $750 billion borrowed, an estimated $380 billion were put into state-owned and state-operated industries that are constipated by bureaucracy, corruption, and graft. Doomed to economic failure from the start, they consumed the loans with no possibility of repayment. These industries served as a rotating employment exchange for the friends, families, and supporters of the politicians and green pastures for the retired generals of the military governments. The rest, the sum of $180 billion, is consumed for the upkeep of the military, police, and intelligence agencies that keep the politicians, generals, and kings in power.

The Western loans can only be paid in hard currency. Therefore the Muslim countries have to raise $222 billion every year in hard currency in dollars, Euros, pound sterling, or yen just to service the debt. Most Muslim countries do not have a surplus trade balance and thus have fallen into the perpetual debt trap from which they will never ever be able to escape in the present global system.

To accumulate hard currency reserves, the governments encourage the farmers to grow cash crops that are needed by the Western industries to manufacture expensive products. As a result of production of nonfood items such as cotton and tobacco, domestic agriculture is unable to feed the countries' population, necessitating cereal imports, perpetuating the cycle of debt. Muslim countries import seventy-five million tons of cereals per annum from Europe and America. Historically, Muslim nations have been self-sufficient in food and cereals. The pressure to grow cash crops, inefficient agricultural practices, poor seed, high cost of fuel and fertilizer, absentee owners of land, poor technology, and poor irrigation practices are responsible for the food shortages and therefore trade deficits. Cereals are bought from the European common market and the United States, where the farmers are subsidized to grow cereal and other agriculture products in surplus. These two areas of the world produce 140 million tons of surpluses in grains stimulated by subsidies to their farmers. The export of all the surplus grain to the third world countries, plus the freight, shipping, handling, and commissions, nets the producers—the European common market and the USA—$50 billion annually, of which half is spent by Muslim countries. That figure amounts to import of cereals by Muslim countries of $250 billion over a period of ten years, which accounts for a third of the external debt of the Muslim world. Such food shortage is astonishing as the landmass of the Islamic world covers an area of 30,605,212 square kilometers of some of the richest land in the world that, since prehistoric times, has been the breadbasket of the world.

A glance at the major borrowers of the Muslim world tells a story of unstable, corrupt regimes with human rights abuses, poor democratic record, warfare, and subservience to the command of the Western powers. There is a strange correlation among unstable, repressive, undemocratic regimes; human right abuses; civil unrest; arms imports;

food shortage; foreign debt; and collusion with Western governments against Islamic interests.

These countries, no doubt, have larger proportion of the population, but they also have some of the world's greatest resources and a fertile landmass and plenty human resources. These countries have a record of 80 percent of the Muslim world's external debt, and they import an estimated 50 percent of the grain brought into the Islamic world. Their economies are in shambles. They all have a history of human rights abuses and have all been saddled with corrupt robber leadership subservient to outside political and monetary forces.

The rules of the covenant of Allah regarding the Islamic finance are simple:

1. *Any predetermined payment over and above the actual amount of principal is prohibited.* Islam only allows one kind of loan, that is, *qard al-hasan* (good loan), whereby the lender does not charge any interest or any additional amount over the money lent. Any interest on associated benefit is prohibited.

2. *The lender must share the profits or losses arising out of the enterprise for which the money has been lent. Islam encourages Muslims to invest their money and to become partners in business instead of becoming creditors.* The provider of the capital and the user of the capital should equally share the risk of business ventures, be it in industries, farms, service companies, or simply financing of trade deals. In banking terms, the depositor, the bank, and the borrower all should share in the risks and rewards of financing business ventures. In the interest-based banking system, all the pressure is on the borrower. The borrower must pay back his loan and the agreed interest regardless of the success or failure of his venture.

3. *Making money from money is not acceptable in Islam.* Money, in its present form, is only a medium of exchange, a way of defining the value of an item, but in itself has no value and therefore should not give rise to more money by earning interest through deposit in a bank or loaning it to someone else. The human endeavor, initiative, and risk involved in a productive venture are much more important than the money used to finance it. Money deposited in a bank or hoarded is potential capital rather than capital. Money becomes capital only when it is invested in a venture. Accordingly, money loaned to a business is regarded as a debt and is not capital; and as such, it is not entitled to any return, such as interest. Muslims are encouraged to spend (purchase necessities or spend in the way of Allah) or invest their money and are discouraged from keeping their money idle. Hoarding money is unacceptable. Allah's commandments in His covenant with the believers in the following three *ayahs* exhort Muslims to spend in charity after their needs are met, devour not in usury, and hoard not gold and silver.

They ask thee how much they are to spend (in charity); say:
"What is beyond your needs." Thus doth Allah make clear to you
His Signs: in order that ye may consider. (Koran 2:222)

Allah will deprive usury of all blessing but will give increase for deeds of
charity; for He loves not creatures ungrateful and wicked. (Koran 2:275–76)

And there are those who hoard gold and silver and spend it not in the Way of
Allah: announce unto them a most grievous penalty. (Al-A'raf 9:34, Koran)

For the believers, money represents purchasing power; that is the only proper use of money. The purchasing power cannot be used to generate more purchasing power without undertaking the intermediate step of it being used to purchase goods and services.

4. Ghrar *(uncertainty, risk, or speculation) is forbidden.* Any transaction entered into should be free from uncertainty, risk, and speculation. Contracting parties should have full knowledge of the countervalues to be exchanged as a result of their transaction. The parties cannot predetermine a granted profit, and this does not allow an undertaking from the borrower or the customer to repay the borrowed principal, plus an amount to consider inflation. The rationale behind the prohibition is to protect the weak from exploitation. Therefore, options and futures are regarded as un-Islamic; so are foreign exchange transactions because rates are determined by interest differentials.

5. *Investments should not support goods forbidden or discouraged by Islam.* Trade in alcohol or financing a gambling establishment is forbidden. An Islamic bank cannot lend money to another bank at interest. An Islamic government is forbidden to lend or borrow money from institutions such as international banks, the World Bank, or the International Monetary Fund on interest as both usury and interest are expressly forbidden:

> Those who devour usury will not stand except as stands one whom the Satan by his touch has driven to madness.

Currency

The international banking system is based on the system developed in Europe over the last two hundred years and then grafted into the American economy. At the end of the Second World War, the economies of both the victors and the defeated in Europe and Japan were devastated and depleted of all gold reserves. The plans for a new international economic system were worked out by delegates from forty-four countries at the White Mountain Resort of Bretton Woods, New Hampshire, in 1944.

Instead of an international economy where each nation's economy was backed by its stock of gold, the new system made the US dollar the centerpiece of the new structure. The dollar was supported by 75 percent of the world's stock of monetary gold. As a result of arming its allies and acquisition of the gold of the conquered enemies, most of the world's monetary gold was transferred to the United States through arms sales and as rewards of the conqueror.

The Bretton Woods arrangements provided that the United States would be the only nation with a currency freely convertible into gold at a fixed value. All other countries were obligated to make their currencies convertible to dollars, but they were not required to maintain convertibility into gold. The conversion rate between dollars and gold was set at $35 per ounce, and the rest of the world defined their currencies in terms of dollars rather than gold. The Bretton Woods arrangements sought to recapture the advantage of gold standard while minimizing the pain imposed by the gold standard on countries that were buying too much, selling too little, and losing gold. The method by which it was to be accomplished was the same as the method devised in Jekyll Island to allow American banks to create money out of nothing without paying the penalty of devaluation of currency. It was the establishment of a world central bank that would create common fiat money based on the dollar for all nations and then require them to inflate together at the same rate.

When a country spends more than it earns in international trade, a trade deficit exists. This is similar to the situation of a person who spends more than he earns. In both cases, the process cannot be sustained; most governments have chosen the option of increasing money supply by borrowing or by printing more money. This counterfeit option is available to a country in a unique position of having its currency accepted as the medium of international trade. Such countries include the United States, Great Britain, France, Italy, Japan, Germany, Canada, and the Netherlands, the G8 countries. In that event, it is possible to create money out of nothing, and other nations have no choice but to accept it. Thus, for years, a country such as the United States has been able to spend more money than it earned in trade by having the Federal Reserve, a privately owned organization, create as much money whenever it needed.

The United States is one of the safest places in the world to invest one's money. But to do so, one had to convert his native currency into dollars. This gave the dollar greater value in the international markets than it otherwise would have merited. In spite of the fact that the Federal Reserve was creating huge amounts of money, the demand for it by foreigners was seemingly limitless. Thus, America has been able to finance its trade deficit with fiat money, in real terms fraudulent and counterfeit money, a feat no other nation in the world has been able to achieve.

Every government in the world today is printing stacks of money with little regard to its real worth. They determine their spending needs and then offer to sell bonds in the open market to raise the money. The International Monetary Fund/World Bank, acting as the United Nations central bank, is the primary buyer of these bonds. The World Bank decides how much money to allow each regional government and then "purchases" that amount of bonds. This is accomplished by making an electronic transfer of "credits" to one of its correspondent banks. The involved government then can draw on those credits to pay its bills. The IMF/World Bank simply creates money electronically, its correspondent banks charge interest, and the governments spend that money. No tax dollars are involved in that transaction.

This system has a built-in inflation pattern. Instead of the previous world experience of sudden, unexpected periods of disruptive inflations, inflation has now been institutionalized at a fairly constant 5 percent per year. This figure has been determined to be the optimum level for generating most revenue without causing public alarm. A 5 percent devaluation of one's earnings applies to the money earned this year but also to all the money saved during the previous years. At the end of one year, the wage earner's money has depreciated by 5 percent; and by the end of the second year, it is worth 90 percent. At the end of twenty years, the governments will have confiscated 64 percent of all the money we have earned at the beginning of our careers. After working forty-five years, the hidden tax or confiscation amounts to 90 percent of all money earned over a lifetime.

The paper money currency system, without gold standard backing, is a fraudulent scheme perpetrated by the international bankers to indebt all nations and peoples of the world to gain total control of the world's resources. To unfold such a conspiracy will require a whole book. From the Koranic point of view, the Bretton Woods agreement is haram, forbidden, as it introduces usury into our daily life and robs us deceitfully of our annual income by an estimated 5 to 10 percent and causes a loss of 90 percent of purchasing power of our savings over forty-five years.

Allah has removed all blessing from money touched by usury. The governments of all Muslim countries devour fruits of *riba* (usury) whenever they create money out of nothing by printing billions of notes in accordance with a monetary system invented by pagans for their own benefit. The governments of these Muslim countries have knowingly indebted their populations to the tune of one trillion dollars, whereby every man woman and child is paying back $150 in interest and principal every year in perpetuity. It is the responsibility of every Muslim to live within his means and avoid the forbidden (*harramma*), all usury, and fraudulent paper money.

> Allah will deprive usury of all blessing but will give increase for deeds of charity; for He loves not creatures ungrateful and wicked. (Koran 2:275–76)

> O you who believe! Betray not the trust of Allah and the Messenger, nor misappropriate knowingly things entrusted to you. (Al-Anfal 2:27, Koran)

What is appropriate conduct for the individual believer is also incumbent on his government that he has appointed to oversee his affairs. Hence, *riba*, misappropriation, and squandering of money of the public treasury in a pagan monetary system are forbidden. Allah has removed all blessings from such an economy, and the punishment shall be nothing but ruin and disaster. The result is increasing humiliation, poverty, deprivation, and loss of esteem of the nations.

The present world monetary system is haram and forbidden to all believers. Gold has served as the monetary base since the inception of the Islamic state, the economic system was stable, and all the three major Islamic empires—Ottoman, Safavid, and Mogul—were prosperous and the envy of the Western world. The initial rot in the Muslim states came with constant internecine wars among the Muslims—Afghan attacks on the Mogul; Safavid incursions on the borders of the Ottomans; Muhammad Ali's wars against his masters, the Ottomans; and finally the Christian uprisings in the Balkans. The Muslim states lost their grip on science and technology when the madrassa system of the time failed to teach the younger generations advances in humanities, science, and technology. The result was backwardness in industrialization and manufacturing and, consequently, loss of commerce and trade. The Egyptians and the

Ottomans began to borrow heavily from the Western bankers under the satanic, usurious pagan system to finance their extravagances and thus sold their souls to the devil when they were unable to keep up the payments to the bankers. The result was dismemberment and humiliation of the Islamic state.

> Those who devour usury will not stand except as stands one
> whom the Satan by his touch has driven to madness.

The downfall of the Muslim economy and power was brought by the opposite of three factors that had brought them their greatness while Europe was in its dark ages. The greatness of the Islamic civilization arose from the

1. *unity* of the *ummah*,
2. emphasis on acquisition of *knowledge*,
3. mastery of their *commerce* and control of their trade routes.

The end came when the ego of their rulers became greater than their faith, and they set off to acquire greater empires at the expense of the Muslim community and the unity of the *ummah*. The infighting among the ulema and the selfishness of the rulers suffocated their economy and, consequently, their educational system, which until a hundred years previously had been the envy of the world. Finally, the weakness and the ignorance of those ruling the empires let the borders and the oceans to the mercy of the Portuguese, English, Dutch, and French pirates and adventurers to overrun their trade routes and commerce. The rot in the Islamic empires began at the core, and like giant pumpkins, they imploded into their foundations. When the Westerners were done with them, the people of the empires were left disunited, bereft of knowledge, and destitute without the mastery of their commerce. Although individual believers retained their faith, they found themselves to be the saddled by the servitude to their new masters who were, in turn, servants of the West. There is still no unity, enlightenment from knowledge, nor freedom of commerce.

To reconstruct and achieve some semblance of their former glory days, Muslims have to work on the same three factors that are intertwined with their history, fate, and destiny. Allah measures out the good and the evil, the wholesome and the corrupt. Humans have enough freedom to make their own choices; if they make the choice to do beautiful and wholesome deeds motivated by faith and god-wariness, they please Allah and bring harmony and wholesomeness to the world, resulting in peace, justice, mercy, compassion, honor, equity, well-being, freedom, and many other gifts through Allah's grace. In this instance, Allah had taught humans through his prophets and human wisdom

1. unity of the community of Islam,
2. wholesomeness and beauty of acquisition of knowledge and learning,
3. honesty and integrity in trade and commerce and avoidance of usury and deceit.

When Muslims obeyed Allah's commandments, they achieved a great civilization and prosperity for twelve hundred years. When they disobeyed, they faced ruin. During the last two hundred years, Muslims have not heeded Allah's covenant for the unity of the community of Islam, acquisition of knowledge and learning, and gaining control over their commerce and thus shirking pagan practices of usury and deceit in commerce. The result has been subjugation, humiliation, and ruin. Almost every part of the Muslim land had been occupied with the imposition of a pagan economic system on all Muslim lands till today, bringing Allah's wrath on all Muslims.

O ye who believe! Fear Allah as He should be feared and die not except in a state of Islam. And hold fast, all together, by the Rope which Allah (stretches out for you)and be not divided among yourselves; and remember with gratitude Allah's favor on you; for ye were enemies and He joined your hearts in love, so that by His Grace, ye became brethren; and ye were on the brink of the Pit of Fire and He saved you from it. Thus doth Allah make His Signs clear to you: that ye may be guided. Let there arise out of you a band of people inviting to all that is good, enjoining what is right and forbidding what is wrong: they are the ones to attain felicity.

Be not like those who are divided amongst themselves and fall into disputations after receiving Clear Signs: for them is a dreadful Penalty. (Koran 3:102–5)

Say: "Travel through the earth and see how Allah did originate creation; so will Allah produce a later creation: for Allah has power over all things. (Al-'Ankabut 29:20, Koran)

Those who devour usury will not stand except as stands one whom the Evil one by his touch hath driven to madness. That is because they say: "Trade is like usury," but Allah hath permitted trade and forbidden usury. Those who after receiving direction from their Lord, desist, shall be pardoned for the past; their case is for Allah (to judge); but those who repeat (the offence) are Companions of the Fire; they will abide therein (forever).

Allah will deprive usury of all blessing but will give increase for deeds of charity; for He loves not creatures ungrateful and wicked. (Koran 2:275–76)

It is clear from the above *ayahs* of the Koran that Allah is offended by those whose who disobey His covenant and commandments. There is a dreadful penalty for those who divide the *ummah*, and those who deal in usury are the companions of fire.

Be not like those who are divided amongst themselves and fall into disputations after receiving Clear Signs: for them is a dreadful Penalty. (Koran 3:102–5)

But those who repeat (the offence of usury) are Companions of the Fire; they will abide therein (forever). He loves not creatures ungrateful and wicked. (Koran 2:275–76)

The Dar es Salaam therefore cannot continue using an economic system that is unjust, dishonest, and oppressive toward the majority of the world's population, both in the East and the West. The system has been designed to accumulate the world's wealth in a few hands and to maintain dominance of a few Western countries over the economic resources of the Islamic world and other poor countries. The world has enough resources to feed, clothe, house, and otherwise maintain the world population with an adequate standard of living had it not been for several thousand people whose greed and wickedness has continued to perpetuate tyranny, hunger, poverty, and destitution in our time. Therefore, the Muslim world, the *ummah*, the Dar es Salaam, shall separate its affairs from all the iniquitous pagan systems of diplomacy and finance till there is again a rule of justice and truth, all iniquity on the earth has been abolished, and all people on the earth share Allah's bounty. Allah has commanded:

And fight them on until there is no more tumult or oppression there prevails justice and faith in Allah altogether and everywhere; but if they cease, verily Allah doth see all that they do. If they refuse, be sure that Allah is your Protector, the Best to protect and the Best to help. (Koran 8:39–40)

This battle need not lead to violence and bloodshed. It shall come about with the political unity of all Muslims in one unified *ummah* with collective economic, fiscal, military, and diplomatic resources. The doctrine of tawhid calls us to submit to the One, the First, and the Last:

Thus have We made of you an Ummah of the centre, that ye might be witnesses over the nations and the Rasool a witness over yourselves; and we appointed the Qibla to which thou wast used, only to test those who followed the Rasool from those who would turn on their heels (from the Faith). Indeed it was (a change) momentous, except to those guided by Allah. And never would Allah make your faith of no effect. For Allah is to all people most surely full of Kindness, Most Merciful. (Al-Baqarah 2:143, Koran)

Allah's covenant has given the believers regency over the earth with responsibilities to perform works that are beautiful; enjoin truth, equality, and justice; and forbid iniquity and oppression. The root cause of injustice and oppression is greed and covetousness of others' possessions. Such greed has become institutionalized in today's economic and monetary system, which is essentially a pagan system incompatible with the covenant of Allah. For that reason, it is essential that the Dar es Salaam scrupulously divorce itself from such a system and build a firewall between the commerce, trade, and monetary system of the Dar es Salaam and what is controlled by the International Monetary System and the World Bank.

Allah has provided all peoples on the earth sufficient benefits for the need of each person. Those with greed and covetousness, either from among themselves or from the outsiders whom they befriended, cause deprivation and denial of Allah's grace and bounty to the people of the world. The barrier between truth and justice on one side and tyranny and oppression on the other is ordained by Allah. Once the separation between the two monetary systems has occurred, a new world order will emerge based on justice and equality for all trading nations. A common unit of wage factor will be established for the wage earners of the world depending on the complexity of their work. Every man is entitled to the same wage per hour of work performed. Every item of merchandise produced anywhere in the world will then carry a standard value in accordance with this unitary wage factor for all humans.

Until Islamic finance is established on a unified Islamic currency backed by gold and oil; unitary wage factor; interest-free banking; unity of approach to the fundamental principles of shipping, finance, manufacture of raw materials, pricing, and monopolies; and above all honest trading practices, the Dar es Salaam and its constituent parts will lack negotiating strength and will continue to lag in stagnation and poverty from the last two hundred years. Strength in commerce and trade comes from a strong industrial base with production of quality goods in demand, strong currency, control of shipping and transport systems, expertise in negotiation, and dependable and honest trading system. A strong trading system requires the economic, political, diplomatic, and military strength of the country to back its commerce and industry in the international arena.

The purpose of money is to facilitate transfer of value over time and distance, to separate buying from selling, and thus to enable people to trade without having to have recourse to direct barter. Money is an intermediate good used for trading. It helps in the transfer of wealth over time and space; account for individual units of labor, goods, and transport; and keep an account of people's possessions.

Over the last six thousand years, money has been used for trade between people to exchange items of need and to assist in division of labor so that man did not have to produce each and every product needed in his daily existence. He could exchange his surplus grain for money and use the money to purchase clothing during the next season from a different marketplace. He was also able to negotiate the value of exchange and did not have to carry his surplus grain to separate marketplaces for disposal before he could buy his clothes. During the course of history, salt, tobacco, pepper, cowrie shells, gold, and silver have been used as money.

Gold and silver have been accepted as durable currency over the last two thousand years. Both gold and silver possess an intrinsic value and are called commodity money. In today's world, two types of money has been used, *commodity money* and *fiat money*. With the present-day superpower politics, commodity money based on gold has almost been eliminated, and fiat money is now dominant, compounding the world's financial problems.

The believers and other people of the world need to study closely the international monetary system. This system is the basis of injustice and inequality in the share of the world's resources among its people. The following discussion will clarify why the unjust economic system prevails and what the individual believers need to do to rectify it. Where does the money come from? How is *money* defined, and why do people accept money in exchange for their goods?

Commodity Money:

Commodity money as a medium of exchange is the invention of the market. Over the last two thousand years, it has evolved. The market has chosen gold as the most efficient money and then silver. Gold and silver have the lowest transaction costs. Gold is produced in limited quantities and therefore maintains its intrinsic value, which in turn maintains stability in trade. It takes work to create commodity money; therefore, it has an intrinsic value.

Commodity money is defined as "a quantity of a commodity." The second caliph of Islam, Umar ibn al-Khattab, defined the dinar as 4.3 grams of gold and the dirham with a silver equivalent to 3.0 grams. In the year 75 hijra (695 CE), Caliph 'Abd al-Malik ordered the Islamic coins to be struck with the words "Allah is unique, Allah is eternal." He maintained Umar ibn al-Khattab's standard of the commodity content. Gold and silver remained the official currency of the Dar es Salaam till the fall of the caliphate.

The amount of money is limited by the cost of producing it. In the case of gold, it is the cost of prospecting, mining, and refining it. People recognize commodity money as something that has intrinsic value. The concept of money as a medium of exchange is to facilitate trading wealth for wealth, labor for labor, work for work. This has been true all over the world for all times.

Money, in its present form, is only a medium of exchange, a way of defining the value of an item but in itself has no value and therefore should not give rise to more money by earning interest through deposit in a bank or loaning it to someone else. The human endeavor, initiative, and risk involved in a productive venture are much more important than the money used to finance it. Money deposited in a bank or hoarded is potential capital rather than capital. Money becomes capital only when it is invested in a venture. Accordingly, money loaned to a business as a loan is regarded as a debt of the business, and it is not capital; as such, it is not entitled to any return, such as interest.

Muslims are encouraged to spend (purchase necessities or spend in the way of Allah) or invest their money and are discouraged from keeping their money idle. Hoarding money is unacceptable. Allah's commandments in His covenant with the believers in the following three *ayahs* exhort Muslims to

1. give in charity after their needs have been met,
2. not devour gains of usury, and
3. not hoard gold and silver.

For the believers, money represents purchasing power, and that is the only proper use of money. Purchasing power cannot be used to generate more purchasing power without undertaking the intermediate step of it being used to purchase goods and services. Commodity money based on gold and silver is in conformity with the covenant of the Koran. Gold and silver currency was used in the Dar es Salaam from the time of Umar ibn al-Khattab till the end of the caliphate.

Fiat Money: Fiat money violates the following Koranic injunctions. Allah commands that one should not tamper with weights and measures and that dealers of fraud will stand in judgment and will enter hellfire. Fiat money is generated by the printing press, and no more work is required to produce a one-hundred-dollar bill as opposed to a one-dollar bill. It dilutes people's savings. Production of fiat money by bankers and governments is tantamount to institutionalized and legalized theft of massive amounts of money from the people.

> Give full measure when you measure and weigh with a balance that is straight; that is the most fitting and the most advantageous in the final determination. (Al-Isra 17:35, Koran)

> Woe to those that deal in fraud, those who, when they have to receive by measure, from men, exact full measure, but when they have to give by measure or weight to men, give less than due. Do they not think that they will be called to account? On a Mighty Day, a Day when (all) mankind will stand before the Lord of the Worlds? Nay! Surely the Record of the Wicked is (preserved) in Sijjin and what will explain to thee what Sijjin is? (There is) a Register (fully) inscribed. (Al-Mutaffifin 83:1–9, Koran)

Commodity money is created through honest trade, honest work, and labor. The governments can obtain money from people through taxation, and the people with a fair government can resist high taxation. The politicians cannot act unilaterally; else, they will be thrown out of office by the people. It is impossible to create commodity money out of nothing. Commodity money protects private property, and it itself is protected by private ownership. Governments cannot spend more than what they have and sustain deficit budgets as commodity money supply cannot arbitrarily be expanded. Governments can increase spending by increased borrowing that will increase interest rates. Usury is forbidden, and an Islamic government cannot and shall not indulge in a forbidden practice, or its ministers and bureaucrats will be of the *Mutaffifeen* and, as promised by Allah, companions of hellfire. The governments are therefore forced to spend within their means and avoid waste.

With commodity money, the taxes are generally lower since the citizens are more vigilant of their government's functioning. As the people have greater confidence in the stability of the media of exchange, there is greater long-term investment, greater profit, increased capital, lower prices, and improved standard of living. Commodity money is very savable, its value stays constant, and purchasing power does not decrease. The money belongs to the saver, not to a bank or the government. The value does not change from generation to generation. There is no inflation.

With fiat money, the politicians do not have to consult citizens or tax them directly to fund government programs, and they do implement whatever programs they wish. Thus, fiat money is a necessary ingredient of tyranny. Pogroms and wars can be funded by money created through a banking system. George Bush created almost one trillion dollars in printed fiat money to finance his Iraq War. Had he been required to raise one trillion dollars from the taxpayers before the war, Americans would have risen and revolted. Politicians and bankers embezzle the savings of people. With fiat money, the value of money is diluted by the creation of new money out of nothing; the property rights of savers and those who have been promised future payments, such as pensioners, are violated. This is stealing. The trappings of the money system and banking have been compared to that of a cult; only those who profit from it understand its inner workings, and they work hard to keep it that way.

The central banks print notes adorned with signatures, seals, and pictures of presidents and sovereigns; counterfeiters are severely punished; governments pay their expenses with them; and populations are forced to accept them. The notes are printed in vast quantities that represent a wealth equal to all the treasures of this world, all the resources above- and belowground, all the assets of populations, their work and labor to fabricate every item that has ever been manufactured. Yet these notes cost nothing to produce. In truth, this is the greatest hoax, the worst crime against humanity, a swindle of proportions never seen by humanity before. Such counterfeiting of wealth is a crime and a sin.

The fiat money system has a built-in inflation pattern. Instead of the previous world experience of sudden, unexpected periods of disruptive inflations, inflation has now been institutionalized at a fairly constant 5 percent per year. This figure has been determined to be the optimum level for generating most revenue without causing public alarm. A 5 percent annual devaluation of one's earnings applies to the money earned this year but also to all the money saved during the previous years. At the end of one year, the wage earner's money has depreciated by 5 percent; and by the end of the second year, it is worth 90 percent. At the end of twenty years, the governments will have confiscated 64 percent of all the money we have earned at the beginning of our careers. After working forty-five years, the hidden tax or confiscation amounts to 90 percent of all money earned over a lifetime. Fiat money results in a higher interest rate structure and shorter investment time; long-term investments are decreased, causing uncertainty and instability of the economic structure.

Role of Money in Generating Wars

Wars cost money. The only sources of revenues with commodity money are

a) taxes, which people tend to resist, and
b) borrowing, which involves high interest rates.

Therefore, there tend to be fewer wars and wars of shorter duration. With fiat money, the governments of today create money out of ink and paper and continue to fight prolonged wars. Such wars are limited only by defeat of one party, by total devastation of a country, or when money has debased to the extent that other trading nations refuse to accept it.

Summary

Most people of the world do not understand the workings of fiat money and the role of international bankers. The international bankers make money by extending credit to governments. The greater the debt of a political state, the larger the interest returned to the lenders. The national banks of Europe and America are owned by private interests that own or control the Federal Reserve System of America and the banks of England, France, and Germany. These private interests, dominated by a few determined families, control the world's financial system by creating money through debt.

Money is a function of faith, like faith in religion. It requires an implicit and universal social consent that is mysterious and cultlike. To create money and use it, each person, community, and country must believe in it. Only then that worthless pieces of paper take on value. The religion of debt is couched in an ancient and mystical jargon, a conspiratorial connection of a hierarchy of lenders, with greedy politicians dominating government decisions. This cult encourages increased debt by creating situations requiring increased borrowing and therefore more profit for those who create money to lend out of nothing.

The amount of money put into circulation by printing is not enough to cover all the debt, including the interest. This leads to the necessity of borrowing more money to pay the interest, which leads to still more interest. The result is the more we borrow, the more we have to borrow, and the debt based on fiat money is a never-ending spiral leading to more and more debt.

Unfortunately, the leaders of the Muslim countries are oblivious to the facts of debt. They do not understand that debt is a never-ending trap, that usury is forbidden by Allah, and that the circulation of fiat money is tantamount to theft and leads to the slavery of nations, both Islamic and others.

Before the use of fiat money in Western societies, the standard of living was modest, and the wages were relatively low but sufficient enough for the family to pay for their home, car, food, and clothing on the wages of one person in the family, generally the husband. The social structure was intact, the family was the foundation of the society, and juvenile crime was low. Now at the turn of the twenty-first century, to make a reasonable income for a modest lifestyle, both the husband and the wife have to find work outside their home, and children have to work after school hours to pay their bills, bank loans, and taxes. The income tax, property tax, car tax, fuel tax, sales tax, goods and services tax, and numerous other taxes amount to about 65 percent of the family income. Citizens and their governments spend a large part of their income paying their debts. This has caused cracks in the social fabric with the breakdown of society and family structure. Divorce rates are increasing, and over 48 percent of children are born to single mothers. Bank profits are at an all-time high.

In 1997 in North America, after paying bloated salaries and bonuses to their CEOs and directors, the banks declared a profit of more than $110 billion. During the third quarter of 2006, most Canadian banks doubled their profits. The Toronto-Dominion Bank declared a profit of $796 million over a three-month period. This was a profit from creating money out of nothing. In a normal knowledgeable society, this activity would be called theft. Unfortunately, the same theft occurs in the Muslim states; and in dictatorial systems, the citizens have no way of finding out.

The total debt of the people of the United States, the corporations, and the government is $33 trillion that generates an income in usury, brokerage, legal costs, taxes, and processing fees of more than $2 trillion. The beneficiaries of such income are unlikely to relinquish their pot of gold. The holders of such wealth use their money to influence their government's policies to manufacture arms and create wars.

Gold

To study commodity money and its workings in the Dar es Salaam, one needs to understand the history and facts of gold. In the seventh and eighth centuries, the Arabs spread across the known world to spread the name of Allah. Along with the spread of Islam came the Muslim mastery of trade that opened up the source of wealth—gold. At the time of the Muslim conquests of Persia, Syria, Egypt, Palestine, North Africa, and Spain, the Arabs amassed vast quantities of gold. They opened old gold mines in Egypt, Nubia, and Ethiopia. With the acquisition of new territories, Muslims became masters of trade that previously had been dominated by the Byzantines. Muslim ships began to ply up and down the Mediterranean, the Red Sea, the Persian Gulf, and the oceans on the eastern coast of Africa, India, and China. They sailed northward through the waterways of Russia, trading with Scandinavian countries. Trade requires money. Money conveys power. Gold serves as universally convertible money.

Less than fifty years after the death of the blessed *nabi*, Caliph 'Abd al-Malik in Damascus issued a gold coin, the dinar, that was 97 percent pure gold and minted in great quantities, which replaced the bezant, the international currency of that time that had circulated in the Arab domains and everywhere in Christian Europe. The dinar carried a verse proclaiming the oneness of Allah. After the conquest of

North Africa, the Muslims made contact with the West African states that had rich gold mines. For several hundred years, the Muslims had the monopoly of all the gold that the Africans produced.

During the fifteenth century, Europeans developed the name Guinea for the gold-producing area of West Africa. The English spelt it as Ginney. In 1662, the English began to use gold imported from West Africa to mint a coin that they called guinea.

During the first thousand years after the fall of Rome, gold had very little importance in Europe since they had no choice because they did not have any gold. Europe has no gold mines. The Europeans had an insatiable desire for spices and silks and, in the absence of central heating, furs and rugs that the Muslims were only too happy to supply. As the Europeans did not have any gold, European human slaves became one of Europe's primary exports, especially to Muslims.

From 1095 to 1450, thousands of men and women from Europe sailed or walked to Constantinople and Palestine professing to regain the Holy Land for Christendom. During the twelfth and thirteenth centuries, massacring Muslims became less compelling than trade and commerce with the Muslims in the Holy Land. Education, scientific knowledge, and new discoveries flourished among the Arabs. There was a flood of medical, scientific, mathematical, and philosophical innovations among the Muslims. All this attracted Europeans to the Middle East. Arab shipping and transportation routes opened up access to silks, damasks, spices, citrus fruits, and finely woven tapestries of the countries to the East. The Crusaders had accumulated plenty of gold and treasure in the plunder of the Christian Byzantine, Constantinople, and the Muslim lands. European princes and churchmen whose predecessors had been content with bare walls and floors covered with filthy rushes now insisted on having palaces with gilded vaults and furnishings such as curtains, cushions, embroideries, and floors covered with oriental carpets[82].

The Crusades imposed massive financial requirements on an unsophisticated and primitive financial structure. The armies required supplies and equipment; soldiers had to be fed, clothed, housed, and paid in coin acceptable in occupied countries where gold was the basis of all currencies. Much of the gold used by the Crusaders came from the Holy Land, which relieved the need to import gold from Europe. Gold was obtained from a variety of local sources. Subsidies were paid by the Byzantine emperor of Constantinople to the Franks, and tribute was exacted from Arab potentates; booty such as twenty golden lamps weighing twenty thousand mithkals (seventy-two kilograms of gold) was removed by Tancred from the temples and churches of Jerusalem, and taxes raised in conquered areas where the basis of currency was gold. The gold obtained by the Crusaders was truly enormous, but it was soon spent. The Templars bought the island of Cyprus for the amount of 100,000 bezants; Raymond of Tripoli was ransomed from Arabs for 150,000 dinars, and the entire army of the French emperor Saint Louis had to be redeemed from captivity in Egypt for 800,000 dinars.

In the fifteenth century, European sailors incorporated lateen sails to their ships, an innovation of the Arabs that had allowed them to sail all oceans. The European square sail positioned horizontally limited the movement of the ship to running ahead of the wind. The triangular lateen sail positioned vertically to the length of the ship made tacking by the large European ships possible for the first time. Tacking enabled the Europeans to extend the range of their sailing ships. Moorish sailors and lateen sails enabled Columbus and Vasco da Gama to discover new lands and sources of gold and wealth.

---

[82] Arthur Bryant, *Makers of England* (Garden City: Doubleday and Company, 1962), 309.

During the sixteenth century, a monumental amount of gold and silver sailed across the Atlantic from the New World to Spain. The amount of treasure and wealth transported was so enormous that convoys of sixty to one hundred ships, each carrying two to four hundred tons of merchandise, arrived at Seville to disembark their cargo of treasure. At the end of sixteenth century, precious metals formed the bulk of the value shipped from America to Spain. Piracy and plunder was elevated to a patriotic duty act by the monarchs of England, France, and Holland. Pirates were given special commissions to raid Spanish and Portuguese fleets. The pirates who returned with gold were ennobled with knighthoods and estates by the English queen. In March 1569, twenty-two Spanish and Portuguese ships were forced to sail into Plymouth, where they were relieved of their gold, silver, and jewels by the English Crown. In 1586, Francis Drake—the chief pirate in the court of Queen Elizabeth of England—returned from Cuba with thirty-eight ships laden with stolen gold and treasure for the queen. In gratitude for his services, the queen ennobled him with an earldom.

One might think that, by the middle of the sixteenth century, Spain would be the richest country of Europe with the sudden and immense addition to its monetary wealth. It was not. Once the gold started arriving in quantity, the Spanish went on a spending spree and lost all incentive to produce. Spain had committed a costly economic blunder in 1492 by expelling Muslims and Jews. Most Christian Spaniards at that time were peasants or soldiers, illiterate, and without the knowledge of the simplest kind of arithmetic. The Muslims, in contrast, were highly educated, leaders in science and mathematics; they were government administrators and men of business. The Muslims had a long heritage of trading, importing, and exporting. With the departure of Muslims, Spain lost all the native merchant class that was essential to economic development.

After all the convoys of piracy and plunder that brought gold and silver from the New World to Europe, almost none of those precious metals ended up in Europe. The entire flow lingered only briefly in Europe and then continued eastward to Asia. There is evidence that outflow of gold and silver to Asia far exceeded the total imports from America between 1600 and 1730.[83] During the first twenty-five years after the establishment of the East India Company in 1600, bullion accounted for 75 percent of all the cargo shipped eastward. In Asia, Islamic, Hindu, and Confucian cultures turned out to be sponges for gold and silver. Only a tiny quantity ever came back to Europe. The Europeans regarded gold as a source of power and wealth—power to be used for the sake of it and wealth to be spent for the gratification and glory of the monarch and the empire. Charles, the Spanish king, engaged in twenty-seven years of warfare against Francis I of France. Charles also started war against the Netherlands, which was to last another eighty years. These adventures had to be financed. The external debt of thirty-seven million ducats accumulated by Charles during forty years he was king of Spain was far more than the total value of precious metals received by the Crown from America during those years.

Muslims, Hindus, and Chinese did not perceive gold as money in the same way as the Westerners viewed it. The Muslims viewed gold as a commodity to be exchanged for necessities and, in times of turmoil, hoarded gold coins and ornaments. Because of ongoing turmoil, gold was never spent by the common man and was passed on from generation to generation. The social structure of the tribe or village did not change and continued to be democratic for all intents and purposes. The trade was by barter or through the use of the currency of the realm. The farmers and the peasants sold their services to the

---

[83] Charles Kindleberger, *Spenders and Hoarders: The World Distribution of Spanish American Silver, 1550–1750* (Singapore Institute of South East Asian Studies, 1989), 15–18.

rulers in return for gold and silver coins. This money was generally hoarded after paying for the tithe. The relationship of the village unit or the tribe internally was that of cohesion, dealing with the ruling sovereign and his agents as the necessary external evil that collected taxes as a benign protector or as a menacing tyrant. Gold, silver, and coins were hoarded and buried in case of turmoil caused by marauders passing through their territories, which occurred frequently and cyclically.

Unlike all the other elements ever mined on the earth, gold is still around, much of it in museums and dark cellars of banks, lots of it molded into coins and ornaments to adorn necks and shoulders, hands, teeth, and ankles. Tons lie on the ocean bottom in shipwrecks and buried in hoards in the bowels of the earth. If all this gold is gathered into a cube, it will weigh about 145,000 tons, three and a half billion troy ounces valued at about two and a quarter trillion dollars today.

If one were to estimate the amount of gold hoarded and accumulated in state and private collections in the Islamic world, we would find that, during the last few hundred years, an average Muslim couple has inherited or purchased around 120 grams of gold in the form of jewelry. Very poor couples do not own any. Rich couples may be weighed down by tens of kilograms of gold jewelry, the average amounting to more than 120 grams per couple or about ten tolas. This total of gold estimates to 52,800 tons in Muslim lands, accumulated wealth lying idly, while millions of Muslims starve and go without essentials. At today's prices, this wealth totals more than $750 billion. In addition, there is a hoard of precious stones worth another one hundred billion dollars. The zakat levy on the bullion, and the precious stones will amount to fifteen billion dollars annually.

Annual Production of Gold in Muslim States, 2005

Country	Gold Production in Kilogram	Country	Gold Production in Kilogram
Burkina Faso	1,637	Oman	575
Cameroon	1,000	Pakistan	13,000[84]
Eritrea	350	Saudi Arabia	11,000
Guinea	14,000	Sierra Leone	125
Indonesia	168,000	Sudan	5,000
Iran	822	Tanzania	2861
Ivory Coast	2,419	Tajikistan	4700
Kazakhstan	30,000	Turkey	1200
Kyrgyzstan	26,000	Uzbekistan	85,000
Malaysia	4,488	**Total**	**507,309 kg**
Mauritania	1,738	**Dar es Salaam**	**558.03 tons**
Morocco	580	World	2,520 tons
Mozambique	6,804	Percentage of world	22.144%
Niger	2,000	USA	375.1 tons
Nigeria	10	European Union	16.5 tons

Dar es Salaam annual gold production: 558.03 tons

According to estimates, Muslim countries imported more than 350 tons of gold in 2001 in bricks and jewelry. In addition, Muslim countries mined annually another 558.03 tons of gold (22.10% of the world production), which could be increased to a thousand tons with increased demand. The official gold holding of the Islamic states is low and amounts to only 1,133 tons.

Love of gold is evil and brings misfortune to the hoarders and to those who do not spend their wealth in the cause of Allah. Allah's covenant reminds the believers of their duty to their Creator and to their fellow man, only those who *"have faith and do righteous acts"* will have success in their earthly lives and in the hereafter. *Alladhina aaminu wa 'amilu*

---

[84] Projected amount from the Pakistan Ministry of Petroleum and Natural Resources.

al saalihaat. The phrase *amilu al saalihaaat* (to do good and to perform wholesome deeds) refers to those who persist in striving to set things right, who restore harmony, peace and balance. The other acts of good works recognized in the Koran are to show compassion, to be merciful and forgive others, to be just, to protect the weak, to defend the oppressed, to be generous and charitable, to be truthful, to seek knowledge and wisdom, to be kind, to be peaceful, and to love others.

On those who believe and who do good, will (Allah) Most Gracious bestow love.

People who strive to set things right and who are generous and charitable and defend the oppressed have Allah's blessing (*rahma*). Therefore, people who use gold in the service of Allah without greed, do good, give in charity, and defend the oppressed receive Allah's *rahma*. Forbidden is the practice of usury to the Muslims. Forbidden also is making money from money.

They ask thee how much they are to spend (in charity); say:
"What is beyond your needs". Thus doth Allah make clear to you
His Signs: in order that ye may consider. (Koran 2:222)

Allah will deprive usury of all blessing but will give increase for deeds of
charity, for He loves not creatures ungrateful and wicked. (Koran 2:275-76)

And there are those who hoard gold and silver and spend it not in the Way
of Allah: announce unto them a most grievous penalty. (Al-A'raf 9:34)

An Islamic government is forbidden to lend or borrow money from institutions such as international banks, the World Bank, or the International Monetary Fund on interest as both usury and interest are expressly forbidden. Banking based on fiat money is also forbidden. The value of money is diluted by the creation of new money out of nothing; the property rights of savers and those who have been promised future payments, such as the pensioners, are violated.

As we have found, the Koran forbids usury, gambling, speculation, and hoarding of gold and silver. The Koran does advocate trade; spending on good things of life, kith, and kin; and giving wealth in the cause of Allah. The modern economic system is entirely alien to the teachings of the Koran, full of pitfalls and trappings laid down by Satan. The Dar es Salaam has slid downhill, submerged into the quicksand of a make-believe economy. Every successful businessman and trader is forced to operate in the sinful pagan system of economy. Here is the solution for a successful economic system in accordance with the principles of the covenant of the Koran:

1. Elimination of usury and interest in the Dar es Salaam.

2. Elimination of fiat money and of banking based on money created out of nothing with a printing press. There will be no more creation and lending of capital nine times that of the bank deposits. It is dishonest and forbidden because it is based on institutionalized theft, supported by the state and international institutions.

3. Creation of a single currency for the united Islamic state, such as gold dinars and silver dirhams based on the measures established by Umar ibn al-Khattab, the second caliph. A currency bureau, an arm of the state of the Dar es Salaam, will supervise the minting and circulation of the currency.

4. Drastic changes to the Dar es Salaam's trading relations with the rest of the world. All products needed and utilized within the state—whether industrial, agricultural, manufactured, or raw—will be produced within the country so that the *ummah* is self-sufficient and independent of foreign trading systems. All basic consumer goods will be produced within the country to provide employment to the citizens equitably and to develop the industrial base of the Dar es Salaam.

5. Establishment of all highway, rail, and airline connections all across the land of the Dar es Salaam. New harbors will be built, and all financing, banking, shipping, transport, and insurance of goods will be performed by the companies owned by the Dar es Salaam. Ships, airplanes, railway equipment, automobiles, agriculture machinery, and trucks will be manufactured in the Dar es Salaam by its own industries. There will be a ten-year crash program to make the Dar es Salaam industrially self-sufficient in all types of communication on land water, air, and space.

6. Rapid mechanization of farming with improved environmental practices to make the Dar es Salaam self-sufficient in food and agriculture. Water will be conserved by the basic communities with the improvement of irrigation techniques and by building more dams and water reservoirs.

7. Utilization of environmentally clean solar, wind, and tidal energy with research and scientific innovation to produce cheap electrical power for domestic and industrial use in all communities.

The Dar es Salaam has been gifted by Allah with all minerals; regrettably, the self-appointed rulers have let large alien corporations exploit these resources, to the detriment of citizens of the Dar es Salaam, thus impoverishing the nation. The following chart clearly displays that even though the resources have not been fully exploited, they constitute a large fraction of the world production.

Commodity	World Percentage	Quantity
Crude oil	45%	10,260,950,000 42-gallon barrels
Petroleum refined products		3,021,250,000 barrels
Natural gas		7,827,540,000,000 cubic meters
Natural gas (dry)	22%	305,951,000,000 cubic meters
Natural gas (liquid)	84%	1,792,339,000 barrels

Nitrogen content ammonia	17%	18,488,100 metric tons
Salt	19%	10,794,287 metric tons
Uranium	25%	8,971 metric tons
Potash	6%	1,517,000 metric tons
Bauxite	30%	37,568,923 metric tons
Aluminum metal	74%	16,289,024 metric tons
Cement	12.8%	196,079,300 metric tons
Chromite	34%	4,242,388 metric tons
Anthracite	66%	194,128,325 metric tons
Copper content	13%	1,382,695 metric tons
Refined copper	7%	876,232 metric tons
Gold	20%	558.03 tons
Diamonds		1,274,000 carats
Gems		156,880 kilograms
Iron ore	10%	52,367,192 metric tons
Steel	15%	112,384,000 metric tons
Lead refined	10%	280,559 metric tons
Manganese	10%	1,535,176 metric tons
Mercury	60%	1,087,060 metric tons
Refined nickel	44%	459,921 metric tons
Tin mine content	33%	64,482 metric tons
Tin refined	39%	94,491 metric tons
Titanium and rutile	11%	663,642 metric tons
Phosphates	29%	39,761,600 metric tons
Granite		54,065,817 cubic meters
Pozzolana		250,000 metric tons
Asbestos		148,500 metric tons
Antimony		21,892 metric tons
Zirconium		10,311 metric tons
Bentonite		208,161 metric tons
Strontium		106,500 metric tons
Vanadium		350,000 metric tons
Marble		1,704,000 cubic meters

The Dar es Salaam produces commodities that are in great demand in the rest of the world; therefore, the prices of the commodities should be regulated by the market forces of supply and demand rather than by political factors where dynasties seek protection through payment with blood money of their subjects' wealth. In spite of depleted petroleum exports from Iraq, the Dar es Salaam exports

- 10,260,950,000 42-gallon barrels of crude oil;
- 3,021,250,000 barrels of refined petroleum products such as aviation fuel, automobile petrol, lubrication products, and heating oil;
- 7,827,540,000,000 cubic meters of natural gas;
- 305,951,000,000 cubic meters of dry products of natural gas;
- 1,792,339,000 42-gallon barrels of natural liquid gas such as propane, in addition to plastics and other by-products of the oil industry.

The producing countries are paid at the producing oil wells at prices manipulated by major oil companies. These oil companies also control the economies of the Western world and are also responsible for all the turmoil and conflicts around the Middle East, which include the ongoing Iraq conflict. The reason for the conflicts is to keep the flow of cheap Middle Eastern oil by keeping the Gulf oil sheikhs and the Saudis on edge constantly, worrying about their thrones, while stealing their money. The Western economy depends on cheap Arab oil that the quarrelsome, ignorant, and greedy Arab sheikhs willingly subsidize.

For instance, at $30 a barrel (2005), the oil companies buy 10,260,950,000 barrels of crude oil at $300,260,950,000 from the Middle East. They ship it in their own tankers, insure it with their own companies, and refine it in their own refineries. The refined by-products of crude oil, petrol, diesel, jet fuel heating oil, propane, asphalt, and chemical products are sold to the motorists, airlines, transport companies, and textile, plastic, sports goods, nylon, pharmaceutical, highway, pesticide, fertilizer, and tire industries in Europe and North America and the Far East for $3.2 trillion, with $1.2 trillion going to the Western governments of G8 in taxes and over $2.0 trillion to the oil companies before paying for the shipping and refining costs to their own companies. That is a profit of over $1.7 trillion, unimaginable in any other industry. No wonder the president of the United States is a functionary of the oil companies, with the CIA as their security force and the American marines their storm troopers.

Overall, if the Dar es Salaam refined and processed its own petroleum products and developed its own chemical and by-products industry, the total gain to its population will be full employment, with everyone owning a home in a land with fully developed infrastructure on transport, health care, education, human development, and resource sectors. The petroleum and energy sector alone will provide the Dar es Salaam with over $150 trillion worth of economic benefits in jobs, industrial growth, shipping, insurance, and banking, whereas today only the oil-producing sheikhs receive less than two to three hundred billion dollars. With the world's current economic situation, the realistic value of a barrel of unrefined crude oil is $150. The revenue to the Dar es Salaam for selling only the unrefined crude oil should be $1,539,142,500,000. The world's economic structure is based on Islamic oil exports with systematic transfer of wealth to a handful of industrialized countries.

The Dar es Salaam will need to start the drawing board with the mineral, commodity, and oil industries. The oil companies will need to understand the new realities of doing business with the Dar es Salaam.

1. The Dar es Salaam will refine all its oil for the world.
2. It will also ship oil products in its own ships to the importing ports.

3. It will set up a chemical industry providing raw products to the transport, textile, plastic, sports goods, nylon, pharmaceutical, highway, pesticide, fertilizer, and tire manufacturing industries in the Dar es Salaam and around the world at cheap and competitive rates.

4. The Dar es Salaam oil industry will finance and own 50 to 75 percent share of all distribution to the retail pumps in the consuming countries around the globe. With this understanding, the foreign oil companies will be permitted up to 25 percent share in the refining industry in their own countries and in the Dar es Salaam.

5. As part of the petroleum sales agreement, the consuming countries will be obliged to buy petroleum by-products such as plastics, chemicals, fertilizers, textile, sports goods, nylons, asphalt, pesticide, and tires manufactured by industries in the Dar es Salaam.

6. All payments will be in gold and gold coins and the Islamic dinar. No fiat money will be traded in the Dar es Salaam. Goods, however, may be traded with barter and balance of payments adjusted with gold between the countries quarterly. Gold and oil prices will naturally rise to the natural market value as the artificial stimulation of economies through political action, fallacies of stock market, and domino effect of interest rates will disappear from the Dar es Salaam. The price of gold will hit its intrinsic value of $3,000 per troy ounce.

For business trade and commerce, three new types of institutions will be regulated and supervised by an independent judicial-commercial body free of any political interference.

Deposit Banks. These banks will receive money and gold coins for safe deposit at a fixed fee. They will have well-guarded safety-deposit boxes and vaults. The banks will be bonded and responsible for the funds stolen or lost. They will also provide security and transfer services for money between businesses and banks. They will not use or loan the funds deposited. They will be allowed to provide transferable paper notes to the depositor for the amount of gold or silver deposited with the bank. The only purpose of the banks is the security and safety of the money and gold for a fee.

Business Planning House. These businesses owned privately or cooperatively by the communities will be staffed by experts in accounting, planning, commerce, construction, transport, mining, and so on. For an appropriate fee, these houses will advise individuals or communities about the feasibility of investment and planning in various ventures in industry, construction, infrastructure, civil engineering, or merely a small business by using the best expertise available. These planners will approach any project without any personal interest in a hands-off manner. They will plan a project on behalf of venture planning groups and match them to venture investing groups that are being advised by the investment houses.

Investment Houses. These houses will have independent experts who will evaluate the plans of the business planning house and advise their clients about the practicality and feasibility of the plans. The investment houses will introduce and match their clients, a group of clients, or a cooperative body to a business venture planned by the business planning house for a different set of individuals.

Thus, these three types of institutions will perform their functions independent of one another so that there is no conflict of interest, and the general public, whether enlightened in matters of commerce or not, receives an objective advice without the mumbo jumbo of the modern Western commerce. The man in the street does not require anything more complicated than a simple handheld calculator or the old-fashioned abacus to arrive at a complex business decision.

The deposit bank safeguards one's savings at a fee and helps with tedious transfer of funds. The business planning house, with its expertise, helps plan projects, and the investment house expertly scrutinizes plans of venture planners and advises the venture capitalists about the feasibility of the venture. There will be a fee for service. There will be no interest. The venture planners will team up with the venture capitalists to start and run an industry or business and share the risks and profits, working with the advice of two independent groups of experts. During the process, there will be no inflation or unpredictable interest and market fluctuations because of the currency instability of a remote country.

There are four types of dormant wealth owned by citizens of the Dar es Salaam but not available to the country because of political and economic factors.

And give the women (on marriage) their dower as a free gift; but if they, of their own good pleasure, remit any part of it to you, take it and enjoy it with right good cheer. (An-Nisa 4:4, Koran)

1. Gold, silver, and gems: Women, in the covenant of the Koran, were specially blessed with an obligatory dower at the time of their marriage. Traditionally, women have tended to safeguard their dower for use in times of adversity and, when the time came, passed it on to their children. In the old days, most of the dower was in forms of jewelry. During the last few hundred years, an average Muslim couple has inherited or purchased about 120 grams of gold in the form of jewelry. Very poor couples do not own any. Rich couples may be weighed down by tens of kilograms of gold jewelry, the average amounting to more than 120 grams or about ten tolas per couple. This total estimates to *52,800 tons of gold* in Muslim lands, an accumulated wealth lying idly not to hoard

the gold but to keep from ostentation through the traditions of culture and custom. Possession of gold gives the new bride a status in her in-laws' home. Women also inherit from their parents properties in land and buildings. These properties remain their personal possessions, separate from the husband's belongings. The mandate of the covenant is not to hoard; the wealth should be allowed to grow through investment. The Dar es Salaam will require new infrastructure of railroads, airports, harbors, aircraft industries, shipyards, chemical industries, agriculture innovations, space stations, refineries, ship and mining equipment, and so on. Every woman has the opportunity to become an entrepreneur with the expertise of the houses of planning and investment. A two-month crash course in finance, accounting, and business administration, refreshed annually, will place the disadvantaged women at the helm of private enterprise in the Dar es Salaam just as Khadija bint Muhammad—the international trader and entrepreneur, mother of Fatimah and grandmother of Imam Hasan and Imam Husayn—was in her time.

2. The Dar es Salaam does not have a standard world currency and monetary system. The savings and the entrepreneurial funds leave the lands of Islam to be banked and invested in Western lands where they earn an interest of 5 percent with a concurrent devaluation of 7 percent annually. With the introduction of gold dinar currency, there will be an opportunity for honest investment mixed with patriotism. Islamic funds in haram, usurious investments in foreign lands will return home. Such funds are estimated at five trillion dollars. Every day another two billion dollars are transferred to the haram, usurious Western economy to purchase Islamic crude oil.

3. The Dar es Salaam citizens, experts, and specialists in medicine, engineering, education, various sciences, humanities, business, and every other field will one day return home with their expertise and capital to set up high-technology industries and educational institutions.

4. The Dar es Salaam's wealth continues to shift to other countries because of unequal trading practices and advantages of major trading groups. Western monopoly in shipping, transport, insurance, brokerage, and banking has controlled the pricing and evaluation of goods and services to their own advantage. The remedy to this anomaly lies in planning and implementation of a trading system in which

   a) the Dar es Salaam will retain its fair share of the world market with the establishment of an international uniform wage unit for human effort, and appraisal and evaluation of every commodity produced anywhere in the world, as well as shipping transportation, brokerage, insurance, and financing, will be based on this wage unit of human effort (WUOHE);

   b) a strong gold currency, control over pricing of export commodities, and a superior negotiating position over imports will provide the edge the Muslims have lost over the last two centuries.

5. Oil and mineral wealth has been in the hands of foreigners with the connivance of ruling bandit sheikhs and presidents. In unity and with knowledge and proper management of the oil industry, the current gross income of $250 billion can be enhanced to $100 trillion, the wealth needed to rebuild the shattered economy of the Dar es Salaam and the whole third

world in peace and justice. This has to be achieved before the oil tap is sucked dry by the oil-hungry world.

6. The Muslim world is poor and hungry today because on the throne in every Muslim land sits a tyrant, the slave of the Western capitalism and its haram economic system. The tyrant sits on the throne of Islam because the Muslims let him occupy it, and they all together eat the fruits of usury, oblivious to Allah's covenant:

Those who devour usury will not stand except as stands one whom the Satan by his touch hath driven to madness. That is because they say: Trade is like usury, But Allah hath permitted trade and forbidden usury. Those who after receiving direction from their Lord, Desist, shall be pardoned for the past: their case is for Allah to judge;

But those who repeat the offence are the companions of fire. They will abide therein forever. Allah deprives usury of all blessing, and increases reward for the deeds of charity: For He does not love those who are ungrateful and wicked. (Al-Baqarah 2:275–76, Koran)

The Great Mosque, Djenné, Mali.

Chapter Eleven

The Defense of the Dar es Salaam

Islam is a *din* of peace, truth, justice, and harmony. Conflict and war are permitted by the covenant of Allah strictly in self-defense and to fight the evil of tyranny, oppression, and injustice. And in war for self-defense and against oppression, Muslims are prohibited from harming the elderly, women, and children. They are prohibited from destroying trees, crops, water, and natural resources.

The Covenant of Muhammad, written in Medina, has been described as the first constitution of the Dar es Salaam. The Covenant of Muhammad is the brief summary of the covenant of Allah underlining the fundamental obligations of individual believers to their community in times of conflict.

- In the name of Allah the Compassionate and the Merciful.

- This is a covenant given by Muhammad to the Believers.

- The Muslims constitute one Ummah to the exclusion of all other men.

- All believers shall rise as one man against anyone who seeks to commit injustice, aggression, crime, or spread mutual enmity amongst the Muslims even if such a person is their kin.

- Just as the bond to Allah is indivisible, all the believers shall stand behind the commitment of the least of them. All believers are bonded one to another to the exclusion of other men.

- The believers shall leave none of their members in destitution without giving him in kindness that he needs by the way of his liberty.

540

- This Pax Islamica is one and indivisible. No believer shall enter a separate peace without all other believers whenever there is fighting in the cause of God, but will do so only on the basis of equality and justice to all others.

- In every expedition for the cause of God we undertake, the Believers shall fight shoulder to shoulder as one man.

- All believers shall avenge the blood of one another when any one falls fighting in the cause of God. No believer shall slay a believer in retaliation for an unbeliever, nor shall he assist an unbeliever against a believer. Whoever is convicted of killing a believer deliberately but without righteous cause shall be liable to the relatives of the killed. Until the latter are satisfied, the killer shall be subject to retaliation by each believer.

This covenant, in very clear terms, has defined the obligation of each believer to Allah and to every other believer. During the last two hundred years, Muslims have lost in the battlefield in every conflict against the West; and in doing so, they have been subjected to humiliation and colonization lasting more than a century. Why did that happen? The Muslims broke every article of the Covenant of Muhammad the covenant of Allah.

Disunity: The covenant of Allah stresses on the importance of the unity of the believers. Upon submission to the will of Allah, the believer undertakes to adhere to truth, honesty, peace, justice, kindness, and good deeds in Allah's service and to give to the needy. The believers' actions and dealings are in humility because men and women serve Allah and His creation. The believer sheds all ego and pride. All believers have the same rights and obligations. No one is higher than the other except, as the blessed *nabi* said, by the way of virtue. Such a distinction cannot be assumed by a person but is bestowed on him by others because of his virtue. Under such circumstances, there cannot be discord or disunity among the believers.

Yet in the past, disunity repeatedly occurred among the Muslims. It was caused by endless internecine fighting among them as every disagreement had to be settled by sword. Losing an argument in a minor dispute was a major cause of loss of face and honor that needed to be avenged by sword. These needless disputes required allies; the mercenary armies of the West were always at hand to dig in a deep wedge to divide and rule. Greed, acquisition, and desire to control others' wealth caused wars and feuds among individuals, tribes, and nations. The wedge among the Muslims is their craving, ego, and pride.

Awliya: The Muslim rulers took as their *awliya* (friends and protectors) from among the pagan the Jews and Christians, which is forbidden by the Koran. Then they provided hospitality to the pagan invading armies against their own brethren. Those who deliberately disobeyed Allah's covenant fragmented the *ummah* for their own greed and ego.

Greed and covetousness: Wars in the Islamic lands were battles for supremacy among the ruling dynasties for the succession to the throne and for the grabbing of territory and wealth by the robber princes. Once the ruling families had acquired their treasure, the wealth did not satiate their thirst and lust for more. They did not know when enough was enough. Greed called for more treasure till acquisition became an obsession. The evil of acquisition has companions in the circle of evil. The circle of evil has affinity with the people who call themselves "Muslims" and cling to treasures and pleasures of this world. They are the *Munafiqeen*. In covetousness and greed, they have sold the interests of the *ummah* to the devil.

Succession: The Arab and Turko-Mongol dynasties and their modern successors did not succeed in finding a peaceful solution to their succession. They brought their primitive custom of fratricide into the modern world. The common man, the believer, has continued to be excluded from the process of search, selection, and appointment of people in the administration of their affairs.

Polygamy: Polygamy and profusion of princes from numerous antagonistic mothers has remained a perennial problem that has always divided the ruling classes. Families that inherited the primitive, dynastic customs of the desert and the steppes have, through their greed and covetousness, deprived their people of the share of their country. Until a hundred years ago, such families existed, pillaging and plundering their neighbors' animals and wealth. After fourteen hundred years of immersion in the Koran, the Arab kings and their religious advisers have a dismal understanding of their obligations to their covenant with Allah. The covenant of Allah reminds the believers of their duty to their Creator and to their fellow man. Allah says that only those who *"have faith and perform righteous acts"* will have success in their earthly lives and in the hereafter. *Alladhina aaminu wa 'amilu al saalihaat.*[85]

The phrase *amilu al saalihaaat* (to do good, to perform wholesome deeds) refers to those who persist in striving to set things right, who restore harmony, peace, and balance. The other acts of good works recognized in the Koran are to show compassion, to be merciful and forgive others, to be just, to protect the weak, to defend the oppressed, to be generous and charitable, to be truthful, to seek knowledge and wisdom, to be kind, to be peaceful, and to love others.

On those who believe and who do good, will (Allah) Most Gracious bestow love.

---

[85] Koran 2:25; 2:82, 277; 4:57, 122; 5:5; 7:42; 10:9; 11:23; 13:29; 14:23; 18:2, 88, 107; 19:60, 96; 20:75, 82, 112; 21:94; 22:14; 23:50, 56; 24:55; 25:70–71; 26:67; 28:80; 29:7, 9, 58; 30:15, 45; 31:8; 32:19; 34:4, 37; 38:24; 41:8; 42:22–23, 26; 45:21, 30; 47:2, 12; 48:29; 64:9; 65:11; 84:25; 85:11; 95:6; 98:7; 103:3.

Therefore, people who use gold in the service of Allah without greed, do good, give in charity, and defend the oppressed receive Allah's *rahma*.

Hereditary rule: Hereditary rule and the use of sword to grab power and wealth is decidedly against the commands of Allah and His covenant. No individual or tribe has the authority to impose themselves on the *ummah*. Every believer is the inheritor of the Koran, the *din*, and the land of Islam and its institutions. Every believer is equal in rank except by virtue of piety. Allah is the Judge and the Sovereign. No man, family, or tribe has the right of sovereignty over the *ummah*.

Each believer pledges to fulfill his covenant with Allah. Together in unity, the believers form a living force that exercises an ongoing and long-term executive sovereignty over the Dar es Salaam. When each believer fulfills his covenant with Allah, collectively, the believers exercise their executive sovereignty to appoint their *wakils* to administer the affairs of the *ummah* and the *din*. This authority to administer can be bestowed on a person or people, but it cannot be stolen and usurped by kings, dictators, and conquerors. Those who seek and exercise such authority are accountable to the believers and to Allah.

> And pursue not that of which you have no knowledge, for every act of hearing, or of seeing, or of feeling in the heart will be enquired into (on the Day of Reckoning). Nor walk on the earth with insolence: for you cannot rend the earth asunder, nor reach the mountains in height. (Al-Isra 17:36–37, Koran)

Muslim communities are beset with rulers who are traitors and *Munafiqeen*. They look like, dress like, and pray like Muslims. They frequently go for *umrah* and hajj, yet for a price, they disobey every article of the Covenant of Muhammad and the covenant of Allah. For the price of a kingdom and a fiefdom, they betray their *din* and the *ummah*.

During the last three centuries, the Muslim states had many external enemies whose motives were varied. All of them used disgruntled Muslim princes, noblemen, and tribes with the temptation of wealth and territory in fostering their aim. Once the conquering armies managed to gain a stranglehold on the Muslim territory, the traitors were discarded like rags once their usefulness was over. Yet in Muslim history, there has never been shortage of such traitors.

In recent history, those who invited and aided the infidels in the occupation of the lands of Islam are the generals of the Pakistani army, Northern Alliance of Afghanistan, Kurds and Shia of Iraq, the Saudi royal family, Jordanian royals, and the sheikhs of Qatar, Kuwait, Bahrain, United Arab Emirates, and Oman. The result is the occupation of Afghanistan and Iraq, with the resulting loss of life of over 660,000 believers in those countries in the years 2002–2006. The loss of life of over one million Iraqis caused by United Nations sanctions was also aided and abetted by the rulers of the Arabian Peninsula, Turkey, Jordan, and Iran. In fact, all the Islamic states combined are in no better position now to solve their problems of defense, disunity, infighting, poverty, illiteracy, and poor world image than in 1909, when Caliph Abdulhamid was deposed by their ilk. When the Koran says the following, it might as well have been addressed to the present rulers of Islam:

When the Hypocrites come to thee, they say, "We bear witness that thou art indeed the Messenger of Allah". Yes, Allah knows that you are indeed His Messenger and Allah bears witness that the Hypocrites are indeed liars.

They have made their oaths a screen (for their hypocrisy), thus they obstruct (men) from the Path of Allah: truly evil are their deeds.

That is because they believed, then they disbelieved: so their
hearts are sealed, therefore they understand not.

When you look at them, their figures please you and when they
speak and you listen to their words, they are as worthless as decayed
piece of wood propped up. They panic at every shout is against them.
They are the enemies, beware of them. Let the curse of Allah be
on them! How they are perverted! (Al-Munafiqun 63:1–8)

How apt and fitting are Allah's words with regard to rulers of Islam.
You see them sitting on their grandiose gold-covered chairs with thick
velvet cushions dressed in silken robes with gold embroidery, attending
meetings of the Arab League and the Organization of Islamic
Cooperation. We say, "Wow, these are our princes of Islam, all of them
meeting to seek ways and means for our deliverance from tyranny and
oppression." After their hard and difficult deliberations, they speak
out gently in soft tones of their anguish and concern about the state
of the *ummah*. Their words are as worthless as a rotten, hollow, and
a crumbling log unable to support the truth. Their hypocrisy and lies
have dogged the *ummah* year after year for the last three hundred
years. They are insecure and panic stricken in case the believers seek
justice and retribution. The Koran says that these hypocrites are the
enemies and to beware of them.

When you look at them, their figures please you and when they speak and
you listen to their words, they are as (worthless as decayed) piece of wood
propped up. They panic that every shout is against them. They are the enemies,
beware of them. Let the curse of Allah be on them! How they are perverted!

**Murder, theft, robbery, forcible acquisition of land, and possession
of the believers:** Wars and killing among the believers are forbidden.
It is the work of Satan and the *Munafiqeen*. We have seen in this
chapter that there is a distinct circle of evil that does Satan's bidding.
A circle of smart financiers, usually Jews, spins the web of the devil or

sets the trap using Christian armies to snare the Muslims (e.g., Iraq War). Among the Muslims, there are traitors (the *Munafiqeen*) who finally snap the trapdoor shut. Throughout the history of Islam, this story has been repeated over and over again. The trap can be set only with deception and guile.

On the eve of the Iraq War, while the Jews in the Pentagon were planning and the Pentagon and the White House were carrying on with troop deployment, the whole world knew what was happening. The Arab kings, the third dimension of evil, were doing the bidding of the *kafireen*; the only people being fooled were the Arab and Muslim people. Yet the people who drove the fuel tankers to the air bases, the Saudi and Jordanian armies, the diplomats, and the news reporters— all of them knew the game plan. If anyone was deceived by Bandar and Abdullah and their royal kin, they wanted to be deceived.

In this day and age of paper and pen and electronic communication, every believer has access to the guidance of Allah and to the believers' covenant with Him. In Islam, there are no professional kings or rulers, nor are there professional politicians. Today the whole world knows of the *fitnah* (corruption), dishonesty, *Fahasha*, treachery, and disobedience to the covenant of Allah by the Muslim ruling classes and politicians. The kings and rulers of Islam cannot rule unless believers want to be ruled by them. The *Munafiqeen* and the *Fahishah* cannot be guardians of *Beit el Allah* and of the rites of hajj unless the Muslims allow them. If "Muslims" follow the lead of the *Munafiqeen*, disobey the covenant, and do evil, they themselves become colored by the same evil. Every believer is reminded by his covenant to invite others to do all that is good and right and forbid what is wrong.

The oft-repeated phrase in the Koran to proclaim jihad is to fight tyranny and oppression. Yet most of the wars in the Muslim world were civil wars, with Muslims killing other Muslims for the sake of territory, wealth, and power.

Imagine a country with the largest land base, with coasts rimmed by thousands of miles of blue oceans, and with a vast number of rivers flowing from hundreds of snowcapped mountains through its deserts, grasslands, fertile valleys, and plains into rich deltas, lakes, and oceans bursting with marine life and other resources—a land blessed by Allah with resources never equaled in history, peopled with a devout, hardworking population with the knowledge of how to utilize such resources in the service of Allah and His creatures. Again, see in your mind's eye an army, the largest in history of mankind, keeping this land, its borders and resources, its oceans and skies, and its people and wealth secure from marauders who have traditionally raided other lands for their resources. These defense forces compose of an army of six million men in about 300 infantry and mechanized divisions equipped with 30,000 tanks and armored vehicles, an air force of 3,600 aircraft of varying vintages, and a naval force equipped with 230 coastal and oceangoing ships equipped with armaments bought from the West and Russia. There are also 60 submarines in the armada. These armed forces are also equipped with short- and medium-range missiles tipped with about 100 nuclear bombs.

The country has a budding arms-manufacturing industry producing low- and medium-technology arms. The annual budget of the combined forces is eighty-five billion dollars, of which thirty billion dollars annually goes to the Western countries to purchase their discarded, obsolete weaponry. The West then uses these funds to refurbish its own arsenal with the latest high-tech weapons.

You might have guessed that we are talking about the combined might of the Islamic world at the onset of the twenty-first century. This army has never won any battle of significance since the war for the Gallipoli

Peninsula about a century ago. These armed forces have not defended in any significant manner the Islamic world since the disintegration of the Ottoman Empire. The wars of independence of Islamic lands from the colonial rule in India, Iran, Iraq, Syria, Egypt, Morocco, and Algeria were fought by the masses with civil disobedience and guerrilla warfare. The state-organized armies of Islam have failed to safeguard the freedom of the people of Palestine, Iraq, Kashmir, Sinkiang, Iraq, Kosovo, Bosnia, Mindanao, Chechnya, and Russia.

What went wrong? The Muslim army of the twentieth and the twenty-first centuries has its guns pointed toward its own people, whereas the external borders of Islam are guarded and patrolled by the naval fleets of America and Europe. The Muslim state armies should be fighting the treachery and oppression by enemies of Allah and Islam—the *kafaru*, *mushrikun*, *Munafiqeen*, and *zalimun*, who have usurped and plundered resources of the believers for the last two hundred years. Instead, the Muslim armies and security services are themselves the source of oppression and treachery to the *momineen*, resisting tyranny of the circle of evil of the *Munafiqeen* and the *Mutaffifeen*. Clear examples are the armed and security forces of Reza Shah Pahlavi, the mullahs of Iran, Saddam Hussein, the Taliban, Pakistani generals, the Saudi royal family, Suharto, the Assads of Syria, Anwar Sadat, Hosni Mubarak, Gaddhafi, Algeria's dictatorship, and the royal family of Morocco.

This is a clear testimony that the believers of the covenant of Allah and those who control the so-called armies of Islam have not surrendered to the will of Allah and do not strive in His path. The rulers of Islam disobey all the commandments of the covenant of Allah. Their *din*, therefore, is rotten as the decayed piece of wood described in the Koran.

The concept of the covenant symbolizes the relationship between man and Allah's creatures and the rest of His creation. They all share one God, one set of guidance and commandments, the same submission and obedience to Him, and the same set of expectations in accordance to His promises. They all can all, therefore, trust one another since they all have similar obligations and expectations. In view of the Koran, humans, communities, nations, and civilizations will continue in harmony and peace so long as they continue to fulfill Allah's covenant.

The believers prosper when they follow Allah's laws and are the subject of scarcity and subjugation when they turn to human systems. The Koran promises peace and plenty for those who obey their covenant with Allah, and for those who turn away from His covenant, the Koran portends a life of need, scarcity, and restraint.

"But whosoever turns away from My Message, verily for him is a life narrowed down and We shall raise him up blind on the Day of Judgment."

Thus do We recompense him who transgresses beyond bounds and believes not in the Signs of his Lord: and the Penalty of the Hereafter is far more grievous and more enduring.

It is not a warning to such men (to call to mind) how many generations before them We destroyed, in whose haunts they (now) move? Verily, in this are Signs for men endued with understanding. (Taha 20:124, 127–28, Koran)

The obligations assigned to the individual believer in the covenant of Allah are the same for the community of Islam, the *ummah*, and for the leaders whom the believers have appointed to look after and protect their individual and communal interests. The covenant is specific in pointing out the responsibilities of the individual, the community, and its appointed leaders.

Jihad is the internal struggle of the believer to cleanse oneself of the temptations of the evil that surrounds him or her. It is also a constant external struggle to rid the community of the treachery and oppression by the enemy of the covenant and *din*. The oppressor may be obvious, visible, and easily overpowered. The web of intrigues and conspiracies of the *kafirun*, the *mushrikun*, the *Munafiqeen*, and the *zalimun* are hard to detect and overcome. They may be familiar people working from within the community for the circle of evil whose motive is to tempt you away from Allah's path. Their aim is to take control of your land and wealth and enslave you. The following five principles are a guidance for the believers in their striving for the cause of Allah. Defense of the Dar es Salaam is based on the same five principles as at the beginning of Islam.

1. *Faith in the Covenant of Allah and in His Promise.* Join not anything in worship with Him. Allah is the *Waliy* (Friend and Defender) of the believers who obey His covenant. Allah promises His strength and power (*al qawiyy al Aziz*) to aid the believer and victory in their striving for the cause for Allah's *din*. Hence, the believer must maintain his faith in Allah's promise in times of peace and of difficulty. Trust in Allah's promise endows the believer with strength from His might in his determination, struggle, and fight in the cause of Allah. The ultimate strength and power belongs to Allah. All worldly, physical, political, and cosmic strength is nothing before the infinite strength of Allah.

Allah is the All-powerful the Almighty, Al-qawiyy al-Aziz. (Hud 11:66, Koran)

There is no Power except in Allah. (Al-Kahf 18:39, Koran)

Men get drunk in their power, wealth, and military weaponry. All such power is an illusion. Use of human power is through deceit, subterfuge, oppression, tyranny, and destruction. Use of such power is against the laws of Allah, which proclaim justice; compassion; sanctity of human life, property, and intellect; deliverance of the oppressed; equality; mutual respect; and peace for all the people of the world. Allah has promised to the believers:

> Verily it is I and My Messengers who will be victorious Verily Allah is All-powerful, All mighty. (Al-Mujadila 58:21, Koran)

Allah is the *Waliy*, Protector of those who have faith. He leads the believer from misery to felicity and from destitution to fulfillment of His grace. From the depths of darkness, He will lead them forth into light. For those who reject faith, their *waliye* (protectors) are the false deities; from light, they will lead them forth into the depths of darkness. They will be companions of the fire, dwelling therein forever. Allah has promised the believers that His strength is with them when they defend His faith.

Weapons of war are weapons of terror. They are meant to produce terror in the heart of the enemy, to frighten them so that they capitulate and flee. The earliest weapon, a rock and a stick, caused injury, pain, terror, and occasional fatality. With further technological developments, there was the invention of bows, arrows, spears, and swords of different designs to cause offense, terror, and death. These were reinforced with platforms of horses, chariots, elephants, and ships. Countermeasures were found in shields, trenches, fortresses, and battle maneuvers. The purpose of weapons has remained the same—to cause injury, terror, and death and in the end a rout and victory.

In the Islamic world, pagans shelled the sultan's castle with cannonballs. The sultan, his harem, and the courtiers were terrorized into fright and panic by the destruction of their living quarters by the twenty-pound cast-iron balls. The sultan capitulated to become the surrogate of the invading power. The sultans of the Muslim world fought for the survival of their own throne and not for Islam or the believers. Those who lost their freedom were the Muslims.

Today's weapons are nuclear bombs, guided missiles, and satellite- and laser-guided bombs fired from land, air, and oceangoing platforms. These weapons cause injury, terror, and death on a massive scale. Still, the enemy's aim and intention is to terrorize, loot, and rob. The enemy's weapons of terror remain the same, the rock and the javelin, which are now propelled by explosives from sophisticated platforms. These vehicles enable the enemy to deliver their punch into the heart of Islam. The enemy continues to have a formidable ally without whose connivance the enemy's weapons cannot reach the heart of the Dar es Salaam. This ally is the traitor to Islam, identified in the Koran as the *Munafiq*, the *zalim*, the shaitan in human form, forming the circle of evil with the *kafireen*. He is driven by greed, avarice, covetousness, ego, and the life of this world. On the surface, he is a Muslim.

Every believer is duty bound to take his *din* back from the *Munafiqeen*, *zalimun*, and the *kafirun*. The believer is bound to fulfill his covenant with Allah and to strive for His cause and for his freedom, liberty, and the integrity of the *ummah* and of the Dar es Salaam. The believer must remember that Allah's strength and might is with those who strive for His cause, which is in truth, righteousness, and justice. The believers have fought hundreds of battles in the name of Islam, which were truly battles, fought on behalf of their *Munafiq* leaders, who in turn aided the cause of the *kafirun*. Some of these battles appeared to them as victories, but in real terms, they were defeats and long-term setbacks for Islam.

The power of your enemy is an illusion. At first, it was a hurled rock that caused injury and terror and then a hurled javelin, an arrow strung from the bow, a cast-iron ball from the cannon, a bullet shot from the barrel of a gun, a shell from a bigger barrel of a gun, and then explosives hurled from jet fighters and battleships. All these weapons of destruction are instruments of devastation to injure, maim, kill, and terrorize populations into submission; the purpose and the result of their use are theft, plunder, and enslavement of populations.

Islam of Allah's covenant is a *din* of truth, peace, justice, equality, compassion, and goodwill. Allah forbids murder and killing. He permits violence only in self-defense and protection of populations from tyranny, oppression, and injustice. The protection of the Dar es Salaam against predator nations lies in faith in Allah, obedience to His covenant, and preparedness for war in self-defense and in Allah's cause.

2. *Unity.* The blessed *nabi* wrote:

All Believers constitute one *Ummah* to the exclusion of all other men. All believers shall rise as one man against anyone who seeks to commit injustice, aggression, crime or spread mutual enmity amongst the Muslims even if such a person is their kin. Just as the bond to Allah is indivisible, all the believers shall stand behind the commitment of the least of them. All believers are bonded one to another to the exclusion of other men. The believers shall leave none of their members in destitution without giving to him in kindness that he needs by the way of his liberty.

This **Pax Islamica** is one and indivisible. No believer shall enter a separate peace without all other believers whenever there is fighting in the cause of God, but will do so only on the basis of equality and justice to all others.

In every expedition for the cause of God we undertake, the Believers shall fight shoulder to shoulder as one man. All believers shall avenge the blood of one another when any one falls fighting in the cause of God. No believer shall slay a believer in retaliation for an unbeliever,

554

nor shall he assist an unbeliever against a believer. Whoever is convicted of killing a believer deliberately but without righteous cause shall be liable to the relatives of the killed. Until the latter are satisfied, the killer shall be subject to retaliation by each believer.

This factor of unity entails three important conditions that have to be met before Islam can be free from the threat of aggression. To reiterate the blessed *nabi* Muhammad's words:

a) "All believers shall rise as one man against anyone who seeks to commit injustice, aggression, crime, or spread mutual enmity amongst the Muslims." All believers are bonded to one another to the exclusion of other men. The believers shall leave none of their members in destitution without giving him in kindness and liberty what he needs.

b) "All believers shall avenge the blood of one another when any one falls fighting in the cause of God." Whoever is convicted of killing a believer deliberately but without righteous cause shall be liable to the relatives of the killed. Until the latter are satisfied, the killer shall be subject to retaliation by each believer.

c) "This Pax Islamica is one and indivisible. No believer shall enter a separate peace without all other believers whenever there is fighting in the cause of God, but will do so only on the basis of equality and justice to all others."

Had the Muslim communities stood united as one man to avenge the blood of every fallen Muslim and rejected a separate peace with the pagans without all the Muslims participating in it, there would not have been the massacres of Algeria, Palestine, India, Afghanistan, Iraq, Bosnia, Chechnya, and Kosovo. This unity demands revenge, retribution, and reprisal for every act of murder in Dayr Yasin, Sabra,

Shatila, Srebrenica, Jenin, Sarajevo, Falluja, Kosovo, Chechnya, Gujarat, and Kashmir. Had the Muslims stood up for one another, they would not have been groveling in the dustheap of humanity and history.

4. *Murder.* No believer shall slay a believer in retaliation for an unbeliever, nor shall he assist an unbeliever against a believer. Whoever is convicted of killing a believer deliberately but without righteous cause shall be liable to the relatives of the killed. Until the latter are satisfied, the killer shall be subject to retaliation by each and every believer.

5. *Justice.* Justice (*'adl* is a divine attribute defined as "putting in the right place." The opposite of *'adl* is *zulm*, which in Koranic terms means "wrongdoing." Wrongdoing is a human attribute defined as "putting things in the wrong place." *Zulm* (wrongdoing) is one of the common terms used in the Koran to refer to the negative acts employed by human beings. Wrongdoing is the opposite of justice, putting everything in its right place, and every act of humans as prescribed by Allah. Hence, wrongdoing is to put things where they do not belong. *Zulm* is injustice, for example, associating others with Allah, placing false words instead of the truth, putting someone else's property in place of your own, taking a life against divine commandments, replacing people's liberty with oppression, waging war instead of peace, and usurping people's right to govern themselves.

Allah had prescribed His covenant to the humans for the good of human beings. People, tribes, and nations are being helped since Allah leads them into accord, harmony, and justice. Those who refuse to follow His commandments are therefore ungrateful and wrongdoers (*zalimun*). Thus, they only harm themselves. There can be no jihad unless it is to fight for justice and against wrongdoing.

There is a clear reason for the glaring weakness of the state-run armies of the Muslim nation-states. The Muslim states are governed by self-appointed kings, dictators, and politicians who are divorced from Allah's *din*, the believers, and the *ummah*; they belong to the circle of evil and serve its interest.

Two hundred years ago, the circle of evil began its control of the world's wealth through conspiracy, subterfuge, and secrecy by undermining the stability of countries through war, strife, and discord and through the creation of confusion in the financial markets. The Western armies and intelligence services are the foot soldiers of the circle of evil, and the rulers both of the East and the West are their puppets to be manipulated at will for the purpose of control of the power and wealth of the world.

The Middle East and the Islamic world have been the receptacle of such wealth since historic times. All of the Old World's civilizations sprang from what is now the land of Islam and enriched the whole world. The Babylonian, Sumerian, Persian, Indus valley, Egyptian, and Greek civilizations arose from the riches and the peoples of the lands of the Muslims; and in turn, the Muslims synthesized such a rich heritage into the Islamic civilization and presented it to the rest of the world.

The intent of the circle of evil has always been to corrupt, divide, and control the wealth of the land through the manipulation of its rulers who were initially placed in positions of power by the circle with the help of Western armies, intelligence, and diplomacy. The foundation of the regimes of the imperial families of the Arabian Peninsula, Jordan, Brunei, and Morocco and the governments of Hosni Mubarak of Egypt are supported by the British, American, NATO, and Australian armed forces, intelligence, and diplomatic services in opposition to the aspirations of their own people. In return, these regimes provide services to the circle of evil to subvert, undermine, and weaken the neighboring Islamic and Arab countries of Iran, Afghanistan, Iraq, Syria, Libya, Algeria, Sudan, and Mauritania. Turkey and Pakistan are puppets of the circle of evil; the price tag for the subservience of Turkey is a few billion dollars and for the Pakistani dictator a paltry $750 million annually, tagged to some minor trade concessions and toys for his military.

The weakness of the nation-state mercenary armies of the modern Islamic states clearly arises from the nonfulfillment of the commandments in Allah's covenant, the obedience to which is essential to seek Allah's protection from enemies. When an individual believer reneges in the fulfillment of his covenant with Allah, he only does it to the detriment to his own soul. However, such an action on the part of the community and its appointed leaders leads to the undermining, enslavement, and impoverishment of the whole Islamic community for many generations.

The Defense of Dar es Salaam

The Dar es Salaam has three major ocean coastlines to protect from major maritime nations that have attacked it repeatedly over the previous three hundred years. They are the United States of America, Britain, France, Netherlands, Spain, Portugal, and Russia. They are the crusading successors of Pope Urban II who gathered in Clermont in 1095 CE and answered the pope's call to rise and destroy Islam. These nations, under different disguises and pretexts, have carried out the one-thousand-year Crusade against Islam and are continuing to this day with their plans to contain Islam. Their economies, security, and prosperity continue to depend on cheap oil and other commodities produced in the Dar es Salaam. Subordination of the Muslim rulers of the Dar es Salaam continues to provide them with such vital resources at artificially low prices.

The Mediterranean, the Persian Gulf, the Red Sea, the Indonesian coastlines, and their hinterland continue to be vulnerable to the predatory crusader navies. This Dar es Salaam seaboard and hinterland requires a strong defensive organization of mujahideen forces obedient to Allah's covenant and needs to maintain the unity and integrity of the Dar es Salaam. Required are coastal defenses and seven blue-water fleets to defend all of the Dar es Salaam's waters.

The creation of a Pacific/Indian Ocean fleet based in Indonesia will protect the seaboard of Indonesia, Malaysia, Bangladesh, and Maldives. A second fleet will patrol and protect the Arabian Sea, Persian Gulf, and Red Sea coastlines of Pakistan, Iran, the Arabian Peninsula, Iraq, and eastern Africa. The new map of the Dar es Salaam will make the Persian Gulf and the Red Sea internal waters of the Dar es Salaam. No foreign naval forces will be permitted in the Persian Gulf. A right of way will be permitted to only nonnuclear foreign ships through Suez Canal and Bab el Mandeb. Aircraft carriers and ships bearing missiles and nuclear weapons will not be permitted passage. No harbor or refueling facilities will be permitted to foreign navies in the Islamic ports.

The third fleet will protect the coastlines of North Africa, Syria, Lebanon, Turkey, Albania, and Bosnia in the Mediterranean and the Black Sea. The fourth fleet will protect the West African coastline and the Atlantic Ocean. And the fifth, sixth, and seventh fleets will patrol the remaining oceans and protect the interests of the Dar es Salaam in case of belligerency. They will safeguard Islamic shipping, maritime trade, and fisheries.

Shore-based integrated batteries of supersonic guided missiles on the coastlines of the Arabian Sea, Indian Ocean, Persian Gulf, Red Sea,

Java straits, eastern and southern Mediterranean, and West Africa will make the vast armada of Western navies obsolete in any war against the lands of Islam. The Dar es Salaam will establish several thousand supersonic missile-launching stations to protect the nation from ships, aircraft, and missiles in the range of four to twelve hundred kilometers. Five thousand such missile batteries on the Islamic shores will terminate foreign naval and aerial superiority in the Muslim seas. Intercontinental and long-range mobile missile batteries and aircraft positioned in the deserts of North and West Africa will neutralize the aggressive and military technology of Europe and the United States. Western aircraft carriers will become sitting ducks in the internal Islamic lakes of the Persian Gulf, Red Sea, Black Sea, Mediterranean, and Java Sea.

Hard-bodied surface and submarine platforms and naval ships equipped with multirange satellite-guided missile systems and aircraft with modern technology will supplement the shore- and land-based, multirange guided missile systems positioned all along the coastlines of the Asian, African, and European Dar es Salaam. The navy will operate its own air arm of multirange fighters, bombers, and specialized aircraft. The naval forces will be rapidly equipped with the latest technology acquired from foreign and homegrown sources.

Muslim countries in the year 2000 spent over seventy-five billion dollars on their armed forces and another thirty billion dollars on arms purchases from the West. In the previous fifteen years, both Iran and Iraq spent about $190 billion in their mindless internecine war. Saudi Arabia and Kuwait gave away another $120 billion to the USA to evict Saddam Hussein from Kuwait. The same money, $1.36 trillion, spent wisely in the Dar es Salaam run according to the covenant of Allah over a ten-year period would have established the world's largest military-industrial complex. It would not only have industrialized the Dar es Salaam and provided employment to hundreds of thousands of its citizens but would also have equipped and armed an army of six million well-trained men and women with six thousand modern aircraft, one thousand oceangoing aircraft carriers, surface ships, and submarines along with the installations required, with enough money left over for missile, nuclear, and space research programs.

The Dar es Salaam is in dire need of a modern industrial base. There are hundreds of thousands of its citizens trained in complex industrial and technical fields around the world who will return home to build the foundation of a modern industrial complex in an organized and orderly manner to process all the Dar es Salaam's raw material for export. The military-industrial complex and space research in other countries set off their industrial revolution. The quiet and gradual withdrawal of Islamic capital from the West and the purchase of technology both of military and civilian use will systematically build a functioning military-industrial complex in the Dar es Salaam within ten years. Megaindustrial hubs of automobile manufacturing, aero industry, shipbuilding, agricultural machinery manufacturing, communication industry, agricultural products, metallurgy, petrochemical plants, mining equipment, and so on will be set up in southern Asia, Central Asia, Arabian Sea littoral, Persian Gulf, Red Sea, and eastern, northern, and western Africa.

There is sufficient dormant wealth in the Dar es Salaam safeguarded by the mothers, sisters, daughters, and wives of the *ummah* in gold and land that may be converted into a productive asset. Rearming the forces of the Dar es Salaam into a modern defensive army will cost less than 30 percent of the cost paid to Western manufacturers. Development and production of the most complex supertechnological weapons within the Dar es Salaam will cost only a fraction of the cost of procurement from the West and Russia. The Dar es Salaam's economy will save on the payouts to politicians, profits of defense contractors, interest payments to banks, commission payments to buyers and sellers, and surcharge payments to the manufacturing country's defense forces and training missions. The lower wages of the Dar es Salaam workers will eliminate 60 percent of the cost charged by the Western weapon manufacturers. The additional outcome of the domestic manufacturing of arms will benefit the production of civilian aircraft, ships, industrial plants, ports, railways, locomotives, heavy-duty vehicles, automobiles, and consumer goods. Investment of thirty billion dollars in the Dar es Salaam aerospace and missile technology and combustion engine industry will neutralize the six hundred billion defense budget of the world's top defense spenders.

Air defenses are the most expensive, complex, and effective deterrent to an aggressor. The Western air forces with fewer than four thousand frontline aircraft have kept the world hostage to the world's superpowers. Their superior air forces and the ongoing improvements of their military technology have provided them with a perpetual edge in trade negotiations and diplomatic status and four seats on the United Nations Security Council, while the Islamic nation, comprising 20 percent of the world's population, has none.

The united Dar es Salaam can, by garnering its internal resources of technological skills and wealth with assistance from the world's top freelance aerospace engineers, manufacture six thousand frontline bombers and fighters with their ancillary equipment and installations for less than thirty billion dollars in a short period of six years. The Dar es Salaam, in unity, has the world's best-trained and -led mechanized and infantry divisions of six million men. The air forces have over fifteen thousand well-trained and experienced pilots. What they lack is unity and direction. What they need is technology and equipment. The Dar es Salaam has the technical expertise and wealth to provide its soldiers with latest technology; ten thousand domestically manufactured, fast, light, and heavy tanks; and five thousand transport and combat helicopters within a short period of six years. What is required is intention, political will, and direction to break free of the shackles of subservience. The believers have to claim their *din* and freedom bequeathed by Allah fourteen hundred years ago.

Trust in Allah's promise endows the believer with the greatest degree of strength and courage from Allah's might in his determination to struggle for Allah's cause. All strength belongs to Allah. All physical, worldly, political, and cosmic strength is nothing before the infinite strength of Allah.

Allah is the All-powerful the Almighty, Al-qawiyy al-Aziz. (Hud 11:66, Koran)

There is no Power except in Allah. (Al-Kahf 18:39, Koran)

The End

O mine Allah! I have labored in Thine path of Truth, Justice, Unity and Peace. May this work please Thee. O mine Allah shower thy Blessings on this work and on those who read it and follow Thine Path of Mercy. Amen.

—Munawar Sabir

Glossary

adalah: One capable of adjudication.

'adl: Justice.

ad-deen: Commitment, obligation, responsibility, pledge, promise, oath, contract, compact, covenant, pact, and treaty agreement.

ahd: Commitment, obligation, responsibility, pledge, promise, oath, contract, compact, covenant, pact, and treaty agreement.

ahkam: Legal verdict, judgment, permissible.

ain al-yaqin: Eye of certainty.

ardh: The earth, man's domain.

amanah: Trust.

amilu: Deeds.

aql: Intellect, human reasoning.

awliya: Friends and protectors.

ayah: Verses of the Koran.

ayan: Local notables.

babas: Sufi holy men.

batil: Falsehood, untruth, opposite of *haqq*.

beys: Local notables.

bhakti: Sanskrit: love and attachment to God.

burka: Head-to-foot garment worn by some women in the Middle East and South Asia.

covenant: Commitment, obligation, responsibility, pledge, promise, oath, contract, compact, pact, and treaty agreement.

Dar es Salaam: The abode of peace; the land of Islam.

darar: Hardship.

din: Total belief system based on the practice of total submission to God's will, accompanied by acts of beautiful deeds that endeavor to set things right and restore harmony, peace and balance. A synthesis of *islam, iman,* and *ihsan.*

devsirme class: Ottoman custom of taking young slaves from among the Slavic peoples for use in bureaucracy and as loyal officers in the army.

dhikr: Remembrance of Allah.

dynameis: Greek: divine "powers."

ehad: Hebrew: one. Equivalent of Arabic *ahad.*

Enuma Elish: The Babylonian epic of creation.

Fahasha: Shameful, indecent; sexual misconduct.

fasiq: Impostor.

fasiqun: Rebellious transgressors.

fatwa: A religious edict; decree in matters of religious law.

fay: Income from the captured territories.

fiqh: Science of jurisprudence.

fuqara: Those who ask or beg.

furqan: Criterion to judge between right and wrong.

ghazzu: Tribal raids of pre-Islamic times, practiced by the likes of Ibn Sa'ud.

goyim: Hebrew, Yiddish: a pejorative term for non-Jews, used in Talmud, Jewish literature, and speech Hadith; a story; saying and deeds of the prophet.

Hadith: Collection of stories of the prophet's sayings and actions.

hajj: Pilgrimage to Mecca.

halal: That which is permitted.

Haleem: Magnanimous.

Hanafi: Followers of the school of jurisprudence of Abu Hanifah.

Hanbali: Followers of the school of jurisprudence of Imam Hanbal.

haqq: Absolute truth.

haqq al-yaqin: Knowledge of absolute truth.

haraj: Harm.

haram: Unlawful; illegal.

harramma: Unlawful.

hasana: Beautiful, wholesome, good.

hubb: Love.

hukm: Command; edict.

husn: Good, beautiful, wholesome.

husna: Beautiful, good.

ihram: Precincts of Kaaba; in the state of piety and dress for the *hajj*.

ihsan: Doing good and wholesome deeds.

ijma: Mutual consultation.

ijtihad: Capacity to find answers to the dilemmas of the community.

Ikhwan: Brothers.

ilm al akhlaq: Knowledge of conduct of the faith.

ilm al kalam: Knowledge of dogmatic theology; knowledge of reason or rational investigation.

ilm al-yaqin: Knowledge of certainty.

ilm ladduni: Knowledge from Allah.

iman: Faith of Islam; second dimension of Islam.

imam: A person who leads the congregation prayers. In Shiite Islam, a descendant of the prophet who is looked on as the leader of the community.

imitatio dei: Latin: imitation of God.

insan: Mankind, humankind, humans.

iqtas: Land grants in lieu of services.

Islah: Establishing wholesomeness, reform.

islam: A voluntary submission to the will of Allah.

Isr: A firm covenant, compact, or contract that if one does not fulfill becomes liable for punishment.

Jannat: Paradise. Garden of eternity.

Jannat adn: Gardens of eternity.

Jammaa: Community of Muslims.

jihad: Struggle to the utmost; striving to purify oneself; struggle against oppression and tyranny.

jum'ah: Friday (prayers).

kafir: The nonbelievers; infidel, pagan, ungrateful.

kafirun: The plural of *kafir.*

kafireen: The plural of *kafir.*

Karramiya: a Sufi sect organized around khankahs and religious communities.

kavod: Hebrew: glory of divine presence.

khankahs: Sufi hospices.

Kharijites: Seceders, those who disaffiliate.

kufr: The act of disbelief in Allah; ingratitude.

ma'ashiyyat: Economics.

madrassas: Religious schools.

madhab: Fraternity or school of jurisprudence.

madhahib: Plural of *madhab.*

ma'eeshat: Life of hardship; economic hardship.

masha'ikhs: Leaders of fraternities of jurisprudence.

mawla: Protector and helper.

millet: Autonomous religious communities in the Ottoman Empire.

mihnah: Inquisition.

mithaq: Tie of relationship between two parties.

mitzvoth: Hebrew: commandments.

mufsidun: Worker of corruption.

muhsin: Performer of wholesome deeds.

mufti: A jurist and scholar of Islamic law.

malaika: Angels.

Munafiqeen: Hypocrites, truth concealers.

Munkar: Wrong.

mushrikun: Unbelievers.

mushirs: Advisers, representatives.

Mutaffifeen: Purveyors of fraud.

muttaqeen: One with *taqwa*; a true believer.

nabi: The one who is given the divine revelation. It does not mean "prophet." *Prophet* is a Jewish and Christian terminology that means "clairvoyant or a forecaster of events."

nirvana: Sanskrit: the sense of ecstasy or dread in the presence of a reality.

nur: Allah's blessed light.

padishah: An Iranian and Indian title of a king.

pasha: High-ranking official in the Ottoman Empire.

qutb: An imaginary divine axis representing justice.

Rabb: Lord.

Rahamat: Divine mercy.

Rahim: Most merciful.

Rahman: Most gracious.

rashidun: Righteous.

rasul, rasool: The one who receives a revelation and then communicates it to others. "Messenger" is a mistranslation of *rasul*. The *rasul* knows and understands the revelation and, on the basis of this knowledge, communicates this word of Allah.

reava: Flocks; Turkish subjects.

şabr: Patience, fortitude.

şābir: Patient one.

şabbār: Patience.

şābara: Plural for the ones who are patient.

Sahaba: Companions of the Prophet.

salat: Contact prayers; prayers that require standing, bowing, and kneeling to Allah in submission.

salihat: Wholesome.

sama: The heavens; the sky.

shakan: Hebrew: to set up a tent.

Shakoor: Appreciative

sura: Chapter.

tabi'un: Governors.

Taslim: Last part of the salat prayer asking for blessings on the people on the left and the right.

tapulu: Lands given to the military in lieu of services.

taqwa **of Allah:** Awareness of Allah's presence.

timars: Endowment of estates in lieu of military service.

Tawhid: Unity of Allah.

ulema: Scholars of Islam; those knowledgeable in Islamic law.

ulil amri minkum: A person appointed to administer affairs of a community.

ummah: Islamic community; the nation of the Muslims.

ummah el nuqta: Nuqta is a dot. Thus, the *ummah el nuqta* forms the lowest level or the basic community in a democracy.

ummah wast: The middle nation; the nation given to moderation.

wakil: Representative.

waqf: Endowment.

yashmak: Veil; a head-to-toe garment worn by some Muslim women.

zakat: Mandatory charity; cleansing of oneself.

zalimun: Evildoers.

About the Author

Dr. Munawar Sabir was born in Kenya, then a British colony. He received his education in Kenya, Pakistan, England, and Canada. As a product of Muslim and secular heritages of Africa, Asia, Europe, and North America, he has gone back to delve deep into his original heritage of the *din* and the Koran.

Dr. Munawar Sabir has written four books on contemporary Islam, the covenant of the Koran, and the historical events that have shaped the current state of Islamic societies. These books are the culmination of over thirty years of observation, study, and research on Islam and the sociopolitical development of Islamic societies in relation to their fulfillment of the covenant of Allah.

Munawar Sabir is a fellow of the Royal College of Physicians and Surgeons of Canada. He has practiced medicine in Britain and Canada for over forty years and has published scientific papers on neurological disorders of the musculoskeletal system.

In this book, Dr. Munawar Sabir argues that the Koran is a living, vibrant communion between Allah and His creatures. The lines of thought and the step-by-step guidance laid out by Allah for the individual believer fourteen hundred years ago continue to vitalize the community of believers as it did in the course of early Islam's belief, thought, and history. The sense of the word read, recited, and explained by the scholars of Islam has remained anchored to the meaning given to it by the *masha'ikhs* of the schools of jurisprudence at the time of the Umayyad and the Abbasid caliphates of the Middle

Ages. The religion that passes as Islam today—that is, the Islam of the masses, the scholars, and the ruling classes both of the Shia and the Sunni—is the fossilized version of the Islam of the Middle Ages. Its facade, however dilapidated, is there, but the spirit is essentially un-Koranic. It is not the Islam of the Koran, nor it is the Islam of the blessed *nabi*.

It is in the Koran that the Muslims will find the answers to their search. The remedy to the ills of the modern-day Islamic world lies in the pages of the Holy Book in the step-by-step guidance of Allah.